EVANGELICAL AND AFRICAN PENTECOSTAL UNITY

"Hugh Osgood has done as much as anyone in the UK to build bridges between British Evangelicalism and African Pentecostalism. A real friend-maker and bridge-builder, he has lived the story that is told on these pages. I'm so grateful for this historical account of many of the challenges that continue to inform and impact us today. We must learn from the past as we seek to make Jesus known together in the years ahead."

—GAVIN CALVER,
CEO, Evangelical Alliance

"Hugh Osgood's meticulously researched study of relations between British Evangelicalism and African diaspora churches around the turn of the millennium is an invaluable resource for all interested in social and cultural interaction. His passion has long been furthering cooperation and collaboration to enhance both church and society. This study provides a concrete example of such coming together and is also an object lesson in the methodology of participant observation."

—PAUL GIFFORD,
professor emeritus of religion, SOAS, University of London

"This book, by elucidating the challenges which emerged as a result of the interactions between Evangelicals and African Pentecostals in the UK, presents a robust and inclusive unity process, which I believe will facilitate God's agenda for his church. The depth of the relationships that Hugh Osgood began forming before the millennium, and still deepens today, validates this research and points to a way forward that is neither overly judgmental nor overly sentimental."

—NOEL MCLEAN,
bishop, YCF Network of Churches

"This is my 'burden' and story. Since arriving in Britain from Ghana, unity has been a major theme for me, a key posture for accomplishing Christ's mandate for cities. Hugh Osgood has over the years, served as a genuine bridge-builder. He therefore qualifies and is right to highlight the balancing of principles and practicalities that unity requires. I believe this excellent scholarly work serves as a source of understanding, shaping thinking for engagement and oneness."

—CELIA APEAGYEI-COLLINS,
founder, The Rehoboth Foundation International

"Although mainly developed from within a British context, Hugh Osgood's work provides Evangelicalism in general and African Pentecostalism in particular, with a fascinating historical framework too often left untouched by scholars in both camps. This work speaks of precisely the types of amalgamating inter-ecclesial relationships which will continue to produce global ecclesial expressions that give witness to an ecumenism of the Spirit at work within the church and the academy today. This work will serve the church and the academy for years to come."

—EMILIO ALVAREZ,
associate provost for lifelong learning, Asbury Theological Seminary

"Problems that affect the unity of the body of Christ are of vital importance if we are to take seriously the command of Christ concerning his church. Hugh Osgood has tackled this complex problem in his study of *Evangelical and African Pentecostal Unity*. It is most interesting and will stimulate both your heart and mind."

—JIM CYMBALA,
senior pastor, The Brooklyn Tabernacle

EVANGELICAL AND AFRICAN PENTECOSTAL UNITY

Balancing Principles and Practicalities
in Britain around the Millennium

HUGH OSGOOD

foreword by Israel Oluwole Olofinjana

PICKWICK Publications • Eugene, Oregon

EVANGELICAL AND AFRICAN PENTECOSTAL UNITY
Balancing Principles and Practicalities in Britain around the Millennium

Copyright © 2024 Hugh Osgood. All rights reserved. Except for brief quotations in critical publications or reviews, no part of this book may be reproduced in any manner without prior written permission from the publisher. Write: Permissions, Wipf and Stock Publishers, 199 W. 8th Ave., Suite 3, Eugene, OR 97401.

Pickwick Publications
An Imprint of Wipf and Stock Publishers
199 W. 8th Ave., Suite 3
Eugene, OR 97401

www.wipfandstock.com

PAPERBACK ISBN: 978-1-6667-8311-7
HARDCOVER ISBN: 978-1-6667-8312-4
EBOOK ISBN: 978-1-6667-8313-1

Cataloguing-in-Publication data:

Names: Hugh, Osgood [author]. | Olofinjana, Israel Oluwole [foreword writer]

Title: Evangelical and African pentecostal unity : balancing principles and practicalities in Britain around the Millennium / Hugh Osgood.

Description: Eugene, OR: Pickwick Publications, 2024 | Includes bibliographical references and index.

Identifiers: ISBN 978-1-6667-8311-7 (paperback) | ISBN 978-1-6667-8312-4 (hardcover) | ISBN 978-1-6667-8313-1 (ebook)

Subjects: LCSH: Pentecostalism—Great Britain—History—20th century. | Pentecostalism—Great Britain—History—21st century. | Pentecostals, Black—Great Britain. | Africans—Great Britain. | Africans—Religious life—Great Britain. | African diaspora.

Classification: BR1644.3 O84 2024 (paperback) | BR1644.3 (ebook)

VERSION NUMBER 04/16/24

This publication includes a number of long quotations from *Focus*, the magazine of the African and Caribbean Evangelical Alliance. As the charity closed in 2009, permission has been obtained from the Evangelical Alliance to use this archived material.

Dedicated to the Memory of
Rev. Dr. Joel Edwards, CBE (1951–2021)
General Director of the UK Evangelical Alliance, 1997–2009

"There is a background story that needs to be told."

Contents

Foreword by Israel Oluwole Olofinjana | xi

Preface | xv

Acknowledgements | xvii

Abbreviations | xviii

Introduction: Principles and Practicalities in Evangelical Unity | xxi

CHAPTER 1
The development of British evangelical inclusiveness | 1
 The birth of the Evangelical Alliance | 5
 Evangelicalism and British Pentecostalism | 7
 Evangelicalism and the British Charismatic Movement | 15
 Evangelicalism and the Caribbean Churches | 24
 Conclusion | 30

CHAPTER 2
The development of African neo-Pentecostal distinctiveness | 31
 The effect of initial evangelical input | 31
 The outcome of early Pentecostal missionary endeavor | 35
 The emergence of less culturally adjusted forms of Christianity | 46
 The importing of a globalized neo-Pentecostalism | 52
 Conclusion | 57

CHAPTER 3
The introduction of African neo-Pentecostalism into Britain | 59
Constrained to Plant | 60
Sent to Plant | 65
Transferred to Plant | 81
    Matthew Ashimolowo—a case study | 84
Trained to Plant | 90
    Hampstead Bible School of Faith, Finchley—a case study | 91
"Called" to Plant | 103
Conclusion | 108

CHAPTER 4
Principles and practicalities in the interactions of 1985-99 | 109
The Palau/Graham legacy | 109
Cerullo, miracles and money | 118
Issues of African and Caribbean identity | 124
    British charismatic identificational repentance events | 124
    Joint African and Caribbean conferences | 133
    Changes in British public opinion | 137
    Identity, independence, and the appointment of Edwards | 140
Issues of evangelical and charismatic concern | 144
    Word and Spirit | 145
    The nature of hell | 150
    The Toronto Blessing and the National Alpha Campaign | 153
    Evangelicalism and postmodernism | 160
Secular-sensitive and secular-dismissive approaches to Christian broadcasting | 163
Conclusion | 171

CHAPTER 5
Principles and practicalities in the interactions of 2000-2005 | 172
The focus of electoral attention | 176
Caution and concern over deliverance and abuse | 185

Victoria Climbié | 185
Damilola Taylor | 187
Child B and "Adam" | 189
Caution and confusion over governance and the press | 202
  Victory, debt and litigation | 202
  KICC and the Charity Commission | 210
  KICC, prosperity, and the press | 220
Proximity and unanimity over government legislation | 228
  Section 28 and issues of sexuality | 229
  Incitement to Religious Hatred and freedom of expression | 234
Conclusion | 236

Conclusion: Balancing principles and practicalities | 238
The limitations of applying a theoretical methodology | 239
  The challenge of momentum | 239
  The benefits of flexibility | 240
  A theological complication | 240
    Varying concepts of revelation | 241
    Varying concepts of redemption | 242
    Varying concepts of transformation | 243
  A counter to superficiality | 244
Predicting the future | 245

Appendix: Literature Reviews | 247
A review of the literature on the Caribbean Churches | 247
A review of the literature on African Pentecostalism and globalization | 255

Bibliography | 267

Index | 287

Foreword

GLOBAL PENTECOSTAL STUDIES AND scholarship have developed significantly in the last 70 years, and this is particularly true of black Pentecostal studies in Britain. The foundation was laid by the robust scholarship of early Pentecostal pioneering scholars such as Walter Hollenweger (1927–2016), popularly referred to as the doyen of Pentecostalism for his formative thinking on Pentecostalism while professor of mission at Birmingham University and the Selly Oak Colleges from 1971 to 1989. Another formidable pioneer who helped shape early thoughts on black British theology was Roswith Gerloff (1933–2013).

Evangelical scholarship in Britain had developed earlier than black Pentecostal scholarship through the likes of F. F. Bruce (1910–90), Donald Guthrie (1916–92) and the founding of colleges such as London Bible College (now London School of Theology) in 1943 and Tyndale House in Cambridge in 1944. However, these two church movements and their corresponding scholarship did not interact properly until the West Indian Evangelical Alliance (later renamed the African Caribbean Evangelical Alliance) was founded in 1984 through the pioneering work of Philip Mohabir (1937–2004), a missionary and church planter from Guyana, and Clive Calver, a former general director of the Evangelical Alliance. Its formation began to create spaces and opportunities for evangelical and black Pentecostal engagement. One of the most visible fruits of this early engagement was the subsequent appointment in 1997 of Joel Edwards (1951–2021), an African Caribbean Pentecostal from the New Testament Church of God, as the first black leader of the Evangelical Alliance.

It is in this context of the 1980s that the work of Dr. Osgood on *Evangelical and African Pentecostal Unity* is rooted. It is important firstly because it is a work of church history, tracing how British evangelicals relate with African neo-Pentecostal churches over a twenty-year period. Whilst the history of African Pentecostals in Europe is now well documented and continues as a work in progress, at the time Dr. Osgood was researching there was scarcely any historiography of African Pentecostal churches in Britain. This piece of work, therefore, is pioneering, charting some of the emergent developments in the history of African Pentecostal churches in the British diaspora. One can argue that it has set the stage for the plethora of works that we now have on African Pentecostal churches in Britain.

A second contribution of this volume is that it sheds light on African missiology. Dr. Osgood's fivefold descriptive framework of different approaches to African Pentecostal church planting is particularly helpful when seeking to understand the continuing nature of African mission in Britain. Although Dr. Osgood does not use the term, his framework helps us to understand how "reverse mission" is taking place in different contexts.

Thirdly, through his decision to review the history of African Pentecostal growth in the context of its engagement with British evangelicalism, this book affords a look at ecumenism from an evangelical perspective. As the work explores evangelical unity among evangelicalism's various tribes and networks, it gives us a poignant insight into an unfolding of intercultural unity between white British evangelicals and African Pentecostals. This relational unity has had its challenges, especially in terms of the complex process that Dr. Osgood describes as "balancing principles and practicalities." Prosperity teaching, African cosmology, deliverance and the kind of extensive media profiling that raises some individuals into positions of prominence are all issues that have at different stages impacted, and sometimes ruptured, the relationships between British evangelicals and African Pentecostals. All are sensitively considered in the twenty-year period that is the focus of this research.

With such a historiographical, missiological and ecumenical analysis before us, we can see how important this formative phase of relationship-building from 1985 to 2005 has proved to be in terms of subsequent developments within and between British evangelicals and African Pentecostals.

One notable step has been the formation in 2013 of the One People Commission of the Evangelical Alliance. Although it builds on the work of the African and Caribbean Evangelical Alliance (as ACEA was finally named), there are two major distinctions. Whereas ACEA was operating mainly among the African and Caribbean Pentecostal churches, the One People Commission has a wider reach, also engaging South Asian Christians, South Korean churches, Chinese churches and Latin American churches. A second distinction is that while ACEA was set up as an independent charity in its own right, the One People Commission operates from within the Evangelical Alliance structures.

Foreword

The One People Commission started in one of the Evangelical Alliance council gatherings in 2010 when two senior black church leaders, Pastor Agu Irukwu of Jesus House in north London, then the national overseer of the Redeemed Christian Church of God, and Bishop Wilton Powell, then the national leader of the Church of God of Prophecy, gave a prophetic challenge about the need for the Evangelical Alliance to be more diverse in its structures, governance and staff. The conversation and roundtable discussions between 2010 and 2012 led to the genesis of the One People Commission with its first director being the Rev Canon Yemi Adedeji. This appointment is significant because here again is another Pentecostal, on this occasion an African Pentecostal, leading an Evangelical Alliance network. I became the second director in 2021. As an African Pentecostal working with British Baptists I describe myself as a Bapticostal,[1] and am building on the legacy of pioneers that have gone before me.

A second significant development has been the increase in the language of "reverse flow of mission." Since around 2004 there has been a growing number of African reverse missionaries in the UK. For example, I was sent from my Pentecostal church in Nigeria in 2004, and Dr. Anderson Moyo was sent from Faith Ministries in Zimbabwe, also in 2004. Dr. Moyo now leads Sheffield Community Church and serves on the national team of Salt and Light Ministries that gives apostolic oversight to Salt and Light churches throughout the UK. Again, these relationships capture ongoing relationships between British Evangelicals and African Pentecostals.

A third important development since 2005 has been the founding in 2011 of the National Church Leaders Forum (NCLF). NCLF represents the concerns of Black Majority Churches, advocating for them, resourcing them and providing them with a voice in the public square. NCLF is co-chaired by Pastor Ade Omooba, an African Pentecostal, and Dr. David Muir, a Caribbean Pentecostal. This is especially significant in the realm of socio-political engagement. The development of a political manifesto in 2015 facilitated engagement in the political process, being the first of its kind within the black Pentecostal church context. This manifesto has now been updated in preparation for the 2024 general election.

A final major development to note since 2005 is the rise of African theologians in Britain. I mentioned earlier the development of black British theology by Roswith Gerloff. Later formidable black British theologians would be the likes of Professor Robert Beckford, Professor Anthony Reddie, Dr. Dulcie McKenzie Dixon and Bishop Joe Aldred to mention a few. These

---

1. Bapticostals are Baptist church leaders who have embraced Pentecostal dynamics such as Pentecostal spirituality, theology, and ecclesiology.

voices are very strong on the Caribbean contributions of black Pentecostal churches. To complement these scholars, therefore, are the works of African theologians such as Dr. Harvey Kwiyani, Dr. Sheila Akomiah-Conteh, Dr. Girma Bishaw and Bishop Francis Alao. I would add in connection with these developments, my own scholarship in constructing an African British theology as an intercultural theology and public theology that interrogates the mission of African Christians and their public witness in a contested postmodern multicultural society. A visible recent expression of African scholarship in Britain is the founding of Christ Theological College (CTC) with a majority world staff focused on training and developing the next generation of diaspora leaders and theologians.

In concluding this foreword, I want to say that I am very grateful to Dr. Osgood for his diligence in this study, and also for the inclusivity of Churches in Communities (CIC), the mutual accountability body for independent churches, ministries, chaplaincies and networks he founded in 1997. He is one of the leaders who has taken time to build relationships with African Pentecostals over the years and can now view positively the other works that have followed, charting new trajectories and opening up new perspectives for further research.

Rev Dr. Israel Oluwole Olofinjana
Director of the One People Commission of the Evangelical Alliance

Preface

THIS IS A STUDY in inter-church relationships, focusing on the interaction between British evangelicalism and African Pentecostalism around the turn of the millennium. It traces the attempts of evangelicals and African neo-Pentecostals to relate to each other over a twenty-year period. It then uses this information to argue that evangelical unity involves a complex balancing of principles and practicalities.

Initially, the study sets out an overview of British evangelical inclusiveness, noting evangelicalism's particular embrace of classical Pentecostalism, the Charismatic Movement, and the Caribbean churches in the mid-twentieth century. The emergence of a distinct neo-Pentecostalism in Africa is then reviewed, followed by an examination of its introduction into Britain, with minimal cultural adjustment, in the late twentieth century.

The second part of the study examines the interaction between African neo-Pentecostalism and British evangelicalism throughout the twenty-year period from 1985 to 2005. It is the way in which principles and practicalities influenced these interactions that makes this study so relevant now, even to the point of prompting me to publish it for an international readership.

Globalization is causing the church to become increasingly diverse in every nation, and I see in this growing diversity an opportunity for an active engagement that pursues truth in the context of a robust unity. Such unity will bring glory to God, and a Matt 5:13 saltiness to a society that otherwise could become unpalatable and corruptible. This study shows that while principles will always form the backbone of any truth-based unity, it will be practicalities that determine its application. The twenty years of early African Pentecostal growth in Britain selected for this study proved rich in opportunities to consider an extraordinarily wide range of practicalities.

Dr. Olofinjana has been kind enough in his foreword to refer to the encouragement this study has been for British academics seeking to further pioneering work on African Pentecostal histiography and missiology, but the study was always intended to be a guide to further engagement, and it is providential that unforeseen circumstances often set the agenda.

When I started my research in 1999, I was already able, as a participant observer, to write retrospectively about the fourteen years from 1985 onwards. In doing this I selected two distinctly pioneering case studies from that period. The first was Kingsway International Christian Centre (KICC) and the second Hampstead Bible School of Faith, Finchley, and its affiliated church, Victory Christian Centre (VCC). Unexpectedly, as my research progressed into the new millennium, both KICC and VCC faced difficult issues that they and I could not have predicted. As 2005 approached (the end of my pre-determined timespan), it was obvious that these issues were not going to be fully resolved in time for me to describe. Rather than extend my time period, I left things in suspense, content to trust readers to investigate for themselves how the issues would resolve. Practicalities are never constrained by tight timetables.

Overall, the study shows that challenges can arise on every hand: identification with certain large-scale evangelistic events, coming under pressure to resolve historic race issues, coping with the vagaries of public opinion, facing the cross fire of major theological debates, working through differences of approach to media and communication, handling the advances made by political parties, surviving the backlash of unfamiliar spiritual practices and high-profile incidents of racial violence, navigating the minefields of governance requirements, press exposure and debt, dealing with debates around human sexuality, upholding standards in the midst of moral failures (recorded with pseudonyms) and finding ways of handling government legislation that could restrict even when it seeks to liberate.

Nearly twenty years on it all sounds remarkably familiar. I can quite understand why my late colleague and friend, Dr. Joel Edwards, said "There is a back story that needs to be told." Here it is told, and hopefully we can learn from it.

Hugh Osgood
July 31, 2023

Acknowledgements

I AM GRATEFUL TO the incredibly large number of church leaders who have willingly engaged with me, to the academic staff in the Religious Studies Department at SOAS who skillfully critiqued my observations, and to my family and friends who supported me while seeking to produce an accurate account.

Abbreviations

ACEA	The African and Caribbean Evangelical Alliance
ACUTE	The Alliance Commission on Unity and Truth among Evangelicals
AoG	Assemblies of God
AWUCOC	The Afro West-Indian United Council of Churches
BEC	The British Evangelical Council
BEN	Bright Entertainment Network
BET	The Black Entertainment Channel
BMCs	Black Majority Churches
CAACC	The Council of African and Afro-Caribbean Churches
CC	The Charity Commission for England and Wales
CCE	Christian Channel Europe
CCPAS	The Churches Child Protection Advisory Service
CiCInt	Churches in Communities International
CMS	The Church Missionary Society (later Church Mission Society)
COCIN	Church of Christ in Nigeria
CTBI	Churches Together in Britain and Ireland
CTE	Churches Together in England
CU	Christian Union
CUP	Cambridge University Press
EA	The Evangelical Alliance

Abbreviations

ECWA	Evangelical Church of West Africa
FIEC	The Fellowship of Independent Evangelical Churches
GOAL	Governance, Openness, Accountability and Leadership, a conference hosted by the EA and ACEA
GOP	The Grand Old Party, The American Republican Party
HTB	Holy Trinity Church, Brompton, London
IBIOL	The International Bible Institute of London
IDTV	The Identity Television Channel
IMCGB	The International Ministerial Council of Great Britain
IR	Identificational Repentance
KICC	Kingsway International Christian Centre
KPMG	KPMG LLP (UK), British branch of Swiss-based financial services company KPMG International. Appointed as Receiver and Managers to KICC by the CC.
KT	Kensington Temple
LMS	The London Missionary Society
MCWE	Morris Cerullo World Evangelism
MECA	Minority Ethnic Christian Affairs, a department of CTE
MTL	Mission to London (as established by Cerullo in 1992—not the Luis Palau event of 1983–84).
NTA	The New Testament Assembly
OBE	Original Black Entertainment
OFNC	Overseas Fellowship of Nigerian Christians
P/C	Pentecostal/Charismatic (as when the Pentecostal and Charismatic Movements are treated as one).
RCCG	The Redeemed Christian Church of God
SCM	The Student Christian Movement (also the SCM Press).
SLSW	Strategic Level Spiritual Warfare
STL	Send the Light, Christian Book Distributors
TBN	Trinity Broadcasting Network
TREM	The Redeemed Evangelical Mission
TTB	The Toronto Blessing

Abbreviations

UCB	United Christian Broadcasters
UCCF	The Universities and Colleges Christian Fellowship
UPG	United Prayer Groups
VCC	Victory Christian Centre
V2V	From Victory to Victory Church
WIEA	The West-Indian Evangelical Alliance
YWAM	Youth with a Mission

Introduction
Principles and practicalities in evangelical unity

THIS IS AN EXERCISE in modern, almost contemporary, British church history: I have attempted to plot the interaction between those traditionally acknowledged as evangelicals with the burgeoning African neo-Pentecostal churches. The interaction has been complex and I have sought to trace it through all the various issues as they arose. I have also endeavored to relate this narrative to the theoretical debates about evangelical unity as it is my contention that this interaction exemplifies the balancing of principles and practicalities that underlies all attempts at evangelical inclusiveness. Throughout the exercise I have been embedded in the process and my main source of data has been observation of meetings and conversations with participants. I have continually discussed the issues with most of those who have been prominent in the process and have formally interviewed key personnel who have worked alongside them. Central to any study set in the context of evangelical unity must be an appreciation that evangelicals believe that all who are "born again" share a spiritual oneness. Biblical support for this is drawn from verses such as 2 Cor 5:17, "Therefore, if anyone is in Christ, he is a new creation; old things have passed away; behold, all things have become new," and Gal 3:28, "There is neither Jew nor Greek, there is neither slave nor free, there is neither male nor female; for you are all one in Christ Jesus." Added to this is their conviction that breaches in orthodoxy of belief or practice can warrant separation as a disciplinary measure.[2] As not all who claim to be born again share the same beliefs, and this affects their practices, determining orthodoxy is of primary importance. To effect such a determination, evangelicals categorize beliefs into those which are essential and those which are peripheral, agreement on which thus becomes

---

2. Defining evangelicalism from its unity philosophy suggests a breadth that historical definitions would modify. See Bebbington, *Evangelicalism*, 1–2. Lloyd-Jones, *What Is an Evangelical?*, 8–16. Murray, *Evangelicalism Divided*, 1–23.

the prerequisite of evangelical unity. The maxim popularized by the Puritan Richard Baxter (1615-81) is often used to summarize this thinking. It is best expressed as "in essentials unity, in non-essentials liberty, in all things charity."[3]

As the new millennium approached, the leading evangelical John Stott proposed a basis for separating "essential" beliefs and practices from the "non-essential."[4] His framework was "the revealing initiative of God the Father, the redeeming work of God the Son and the transforming ministry of God the Holy Spirit."[5] In effect this summarized the sixfold list proposed by Packer in 1978 and the fourfold list of conversionism, activism, biblicism and crucicentrism proposed by Bebbington in 1989.[6] Stott justified his modification by noting that both list the Bible, the cross, evangelism and conversion, but concluding that Packer's first three points of Scripture, Christ and the Holy Spirit were more important than the conversion, evangelism and fellowship that they led on to. Stott made his case as follows:

> Is it altogether appropriate, I ask myself, that an activity like evangelism, an experience like conversion and an observation like the need for fellowship, even with their theological underpinnings, should be set alongside such towering truths as the authority of Scripture, the majesty of Jesus Christ and the Lordship of the Spirit?[7]

Having created this trinitarian framework, Stott, in effect, went on to deal with biblicism, crucicentrism, conversionism and activism; biblicism under "the revelatory initiative of the Father," crucicentrism under "the redeeming work of God the Son" and conversionism and activism in connection with "the transforming work of God the Holy Spirit."[8] To handle the question of the non-essentials, Stott impressively labelled them "adiaphora," the Greek for "matters indifferent" and listed twelve examples, many of which reflected past tensions between evangelical Anglicans and evangelical

---

3. Quoted in similar format by Stott, *Evangelical Truth*, 143-44. Stott believes Baxter's statement derives from Lutheran theologian Petrus Meuderlin's Latin treatise, ca.1620.

4. See Stott, *Evangelical Truth*.

5. Stott, *Evangelical Truth*, 28.

6. Packer, *Evangelical Anglican Identity*. McGrath expounded Packer's list in *Evangelicalism and the Future of Christianity*. Bebbington, *Evangelicalism*, 2-17. Tidball wrote that Bebbington's "quadrilateral . . . has quickly established itself as near to a consensus as we might expect." Tidball, *Who Are the Evangelicals?*, 14.

7. Stott, *Evangelical Truth*, 28.

8. Stott's categories for the Spirit's transforming work are Christian beginnings, assurance, holiness, community, mission and hope.

Introduction

non-conformists, and between conservative evangelicals and charismatics. Stott's list was baptism, the Lord's Supper, church government, worship, charismata, the position of women, ecumenism, Old Testament prophecy, sanctification, the State, mission, and eschatology.[9] Obviously his list was not absolute since other issues could arise in subsequent intra-evangelical encounters.[10] Nonetheless, Stott's book is important because it implies that evangelical unity has a clear methodology. He does not see evangelical unity as simply a matter of subjective peer assessment where "being in good standing with fellow evangelicals" is the ultimate test.[11] To examine this, I postulate that evangelical unity is also a complex process involving the balancing of participants' principles with contemporary practicalities and will use the interaction between British evangelicalism and African neo-Pentecostalism to demonstrate the point.

Evangelical unity comes under pressure whenever an emerging Christian group claims to be evangelical. Often such groups seek membership of an inter-denominational body to gain acceptance by the wider Christian community and to exercise a measure of influence in society. Those churches that are "evangelically inclined" have more often than not applied for membership of the UK Evangelical Alliance (EA). With the growth of African immigration into Britain throughout the 1990s there was a marked increase in the number of British-based African Pentecostal churches. One strand of these appeared theologically close enough for British evangelicals to consider building a relationship. This strand was helpfully identified by Dr. Jerisdan Jehu-Appiah, Minister of the Ghanaian Musama Disco Christo (Army of the Cross of Christ) Church in London, in his presentation to the "World Council of Churches Consultation with African and African-Caribbean Church Leaders in Britain":

> There are three groups of African churches [in Britain]: branches in the UK of churches originating and operating in countries in Africa; churches started in Africa but which have moved headquarters and operation to Britain, or which were started here

---

9. Stott, *Evangelical Truth*, 142–43.

10. An earlier but similar listing of the main areas of evangelical disagreement cited: church membership, denominations, doctrinal purity, and charismatic experience. Gibson, *Church and Its Unity*, 14–18.

11. For EA membership doctrinal orthodoxy is tested by willingness to sign agreement with its doctrinal statement, and orthopraxis is tested by "being in good standing with fellow evangelicals." The orthopraxis phrase was modified to "in good fellowship with other fellow evangelical churches—particularly in your local area" for the new application form circulated with the membership booklet prepared for the new millennium. *Membership Information for Churches*, 18, and insert.

but have since opened branches in Africa; and churches started in Britain which are completely autonomous and without any formal links with Africa. The churches of the first two groups tend to be more traditional in the sense that they have close roots and links to Africa; the third group tend more towards north-American new-charismatic practice and teaching.[12]

Whilst his analysis needs further clarification, it is his third group that will be the focus of this study. Churches in this group do indeed stand apart from those (such as Musama Disco Christo) that "tend to be more traditional" and they do "tend more towards north-American new-charismatic practice and teaching." However, they are not as "completely autonomous" as Dr. Jehu-Appiah has suggested. Some of them are branches of churches in Africa.[13] Others have opened their own African branches. Indeed, few are "without any formal links with Africa"; there are established congregational connections as well as less formal family and cultural ties. However, in fairness, the congregations that such British churches are linked with in Africa are mostly post-1970 gatherings formed as the "north-American new-charismatic teaching and practice" stimulated new church growth in much of Africa.[14] It is these churches that, for the purposes of this study, will provide the test of British evangelicalism's inclusiveness, as they present British evangelicalism with a logical next step theologically, ecclesiologically and ethnically after its embrace of classical Pentecostalism and the Charismatic Movement in the 1960s and the Caribbean denominations in the 1980s.[15] To distinguish these particular African churches in this study I will label them "African neo-Pentecostal" churches.[16] Frequently I will preface this with "independent" to emphasize that most of them are non-denominational.

As a prelude to examining the interaction between African neo-Pentecostal churches and British evangelicalism, I will outline the historical development of evangelical inclusiveness in Britain and of neo-Pentecostal distinctiveness in Africa. I will then analyze the introduction of African

12. Jehu-Appiah, "Indigenous African Churches."
13. Hunt, "British Black Pentecostal," 104–24; Hunt, *Alternative Religions*, 85–87.
14. Gifford, "Prosperity," 373–88; Anderson, *African Reformation*, 167–90.
15. Randall and Hilborn, *One Body*, 258–67, 288.
16. Anderson used "newer Pentecostal and Charismatic churches" (NPCs). Anderson, *African Reformation*, 167. However, in Britain these churches see themselves as specifically Pentecostal, distinguishing themselves from the British Charismatic Movement.

neo-Pentecostalism into Britain before examining the interaction between African neo-Pentecostal churches and British evangelicalism, first in a chapter covering 1985-99 and second in a chapter covering 2000-2005. In my conclusion I will contrast the balancing of principles and practicalities that occurred throughout this twenty-year period with the more idealistic application of the methodological evangelical unity theory implicit in the work of Stott.[17]

MY ENGAGEMENT WITH THE STUDY

At the time I undertook this study (1995-2005) I had had ample opportunity to experience the breadth of British evangelicalism, having been the minister of an independent evangelical church for twenty years. During the last ten of these, however, I had begun to be closely involved with both the African neo-Pentecostal churches and Caribbean churches, so when I carried out my research, I did so in the role of an observing participant.[18] My London base, and repeated visits to Nigeria between 1993 and 2005, proved relevant. London was home to a significant proportion of Britain's African Christian diaspora and a place of relative evangelical strength. Much of the African Christian diaspora in London was Nigerian.

For the sake of methodological integrity, I will present a summary of my background. Having spent my childhood in the Salvation Army, I offered myself for the Anglican ministry in 1966 whilst set to study medicine and dentistry at St Bartholomew's Hospital and the Royal Dental Hospital. My plans faltered when I was advised by the ordinands' secretary of the Church Pastoral Aid Society to "complete the dentistry." In 1971, after graduation and various hospital appointments, my wife-to-be and I were accepted by the Africa Evangelical Fellowship to work at a hospital in the south of Zambia. When this project was put on hold before our arrival, we actively engaged, bi-vocationally, in a church-planting project in south London within the newly emerging house church movement. At the same time, I began speaking at student events and campus-based missions throughout southern England with the Universities and Colleges Christian Fellowship.

In 1985 I set up a pilot project for the EA designed to bring churches together in southeast London, and on the basis of this was invited to handle much of the London churches element of Billy Graham's Mission '89. In the wake of Mission '89 I was recruited by the EA to help make the southeast

---

17. Stott, *Evangelical Truth*.

18. I prefer this to "participant observer" as it marks a closer degree of engagement. Bernard, *Research Methods*, 138-39.

London project city-wide, and the London Leaders' meetings that resulted from this were ultimately jointly chaired by the EA General Director and me. Whilst working on this London project, I was encouraged to engage with the African and Caribbean communities with a view to increasing mutual understanding and, controversially in the eyes of many evangelicals, served on the council of Morris Cerullo's Mission to London throughout the 1990s. Less contentiously, since 1997 I have served as a Council and Board member of the African and Caribbean Evangelical Alliance (ACEA), and in 1997 was co-opted onto a working group of the Alliance Commission on Unity and Truth among Evangelicals (ACUTE). It was whilst preparing the ACUTE report on prosperity teaching, which again proved to be somewhat controversial, that I was persuaded to undertake this research to close the gaps in the understanding of the relationship between the UK Evangelical Alliance and Britain's independent African neo-Pentecostal churches. During the latter stages of the research I have served as project coordinator for ACEA and the EA's work with the Charity Commission.

My involvement with African neo-Pentecostal churches in Britain began in earnest in 1991 when a church I planted in 1974 re-established its full autonomy after a year of combined worship with an Assemblies of God church of which I had also been appointed pastor. In so doing it acquired an "Independent Pentecostal" label that attracted enquiries from many newly arrived African leaders who were seeking to plant their own independent Pentecostal churches. Their interest was increased yet further when, in 1994, Cornerstone Christian Centre, as the newly formed church was named, took air-time on cable television's Identity Channel before having some church staff go on to establish Britain's first Christian television channel.[19] The network of independent churches and ministries, Churches in Communities International, of which I am the founding president, and which forms part of the Free Churches Group within Churches Together in England, had, in 2005, a majority of independent African neo-Pentecostal churches within it. My visits to Africa up to 2005 were at the invitation of leaders of independent neo-Pentecostal churches who hosted me to speak at their conventions, but since the early 1980s I had been chair of a charity that by 2005 had established relief and educational projects in Uganda, Nigeria, the Caribbean and Pakistan.

---

19. The Identity Channel was owned by America's Black Entertainment Television (BET) Networks and ceased broadcasting in 1996. Britain's first Christian TV Channel was Christian Channel Europe, which was later renamed as GOD TV.

MY CHOICE OF TIMESCALE

The twenty years from 1985 to 2005 may seem an arbitrary period to choose for this study but it covers the time in which African neo-Pentecostalism was being most vigorously introduced into Britain. It therefore provides a window for observing evangelical unity at its most exposed. Every time British evangelicalism has to evaluate its formative relations with yet another new church grouping, the undergirding principles of its unity theory are put to the test.

Obviously, working within any predetermined timeframe means that there is a risk that some stories will be introduced without being completed. In this particular study it has been straightforward enough to set the scene for the specific twenty years in focus by providing background history, but it has proved far too early to write an account that fully traces out every strand of African neo-Pentecostal and British evangelical interaction. The date for producing that document is still somewhere in the future and cannot yet be determined.

I acknowledge that, given some of the issues raised towards the end of my twenty-year period, some might consider that even a slightly longer period would have allowed the study to have ended on a higher note of achievement. Of course, every reader will join me in hoping that discouraging news stories will in time turn into stories of success and, indeed, those considering this study in future years may have the pleasure of knowing positive outcomes to many of the incidents that have their beginnings here. But this exercise stands as a twenty-year test of the interactions between two groups with different histories and different characteristics; one a collection of independent churches and the other an inter-church movement increasingly defined through a specific umbrella agency. If twenty years is too short a period for the principles and practice of evangelical unity to be fully worked through in such a setting, then that tells its own story and is worthy of note.

Chapter 1

The development of British evangelical inclusiveness

IN THIS CHAPTER I will review the history of British evangelical inclusiveness with particular emphasis on evangelicalism's embrace of classical Pentecostalism, the Charismatic Movement and the Caribbean churches. This review begins with a description of evangelicalism's breadth at its inception, but this is no straightforward task.

British evangelicals have usually traced their origins to the Reformation or the period immediately preceding it. E. Poole-Conner, a distinguished evangelical of the first-half of the twentieth century, pinpointed the start of evangelicalism a hundred years before the Reformation with the fifteenth-century pioneers, Colet, Erasmus and Tyndale.[1] Writing at the turn of the millennium, the General Director of the EA, Joel Edwards, connected the use of "Evangelical" with the title "Doctor Evangelicus" given yet a century earlier to another pre-Reformation Oxford reformer, John Wycliffe.[2] By contrast, some of the more recently emerging evangelical groups have seen themselves as the real guardians of authentic first-century Christianity.[3] For them the Reformation was little more than a mid-course correction rather than a starting point.[4] This "back to the beginning" approach is problematic. Patterns of first-century church life varied; the church at Jerusalem, for example, differed from the church at Corinth. Those seeing first-century

---

1. Poole-Conner, *Evangelicalism in England*, 27–41.
2. Edwards, *Lord*, 126.
3. Kay argues a "direct continuity between the church of today and the early church." Kay, "Assemblies of God," 47, 56.
4. For example, Walker, *Restoring the Kingdom*, 143–46.

issues rather than first-century practice as their starting point still face the challenge of demonstrating an evangelical-style commitment to scriptural supremacy in an environment where apostolic teaching largely came by word of mouth. In the midst of the debate, Edwards urged caution:

> An evangelicalism which defines a biblical Christian through the window of the Reformation is likely to draw a narrow circle in which few others may stand. It tends to have a more prescriptive definition and becomes guarded against any definitions which stray too far from a Reformation world view. On the other hand, evangelicals who have come from a post-Reformation and particularly Pentecostal or charismatic position will appeal beyond the Reformation to a definition of an evangelical which includes a wider range of Christians.[5]

Even so, although evangelicals might once have embraced all that was Protestant, it would be a mistake to assume that evangelicalism and Protestantism remained synonymous for long.[6] Indeed, in writing of "an evangelicalism which defines a biblical Christian through the window of the Reformation," Edwards was certainly not referring to an inclusiveness which accepts all that can historically claim to have come via the Reformation window of the past. He was referring rather to an exclusiveness which rejects all that cannot climb through a narrowly defined theological Reformation window now.

Hoping to clarify the position, David Bebbington, a historian of British evangelicalism, leapt forward three centuries from the Reformation for his starting point.[7] Passing over the likes of Latimer, Cranmer, Ridley, Knox, Fox and Bunyan, he linked the birth of British evangelicalism with Wesley and the founding of Methodism. Whilst this distinguishes evangelicalism from Protestantism it can still be confusing. Not all that has flowed from Methodism can ultimately be considered evangelical. Bebbington rightly said of evangelicalism, "The movement has been self-consciously distinctive and unitary."[8] Given such a statement, it could be argued that evangelicals, in practice, are more inclined to recognize each other on the basis of shared beliefs than through shared historical roots. In the strictest sense, therefore, it could be safer to avoid defining evangelicalism as a historical movement with an internal momentum for development and to see it rather as a

---

5. Edwards, *Lord*, 126.
6. Hylson-Smith refers to evangelicals as "archetypal Protestants." Hylson-Smith, "Roots," 137.
7. Bebbington, *Evangelicalism*, 1–2.
8. Bebbington, *Evangelicalism*, ix.

The development of British evangelical inclusiveness

number of connected confessional positions that have to be adhered to. In this framework, development may still occur, but largely through additions and subtractions.

Taking this approach to its logical conclusion, a more accurate view of evangelicalism might be obtained if evangelicals are seen as "owning" or "disowning" famous figures from the past according to how strongly such individuals held to evangelical convictions. The likes of Wycliffe, Colet, Erasmus and Tyndale (and even post-Reformation worthies such as those mentioned above) could all be accepted on the basis of how fully they subscribed to evangelicalism's version of New Testament Christianity (with Fox receiving a question mark because of his tendency to insist on a subjective inner witness in a way that some evangelicals would consider undermined a full reliance on Scripture).[9] This is all part of a recognition of the inappropriateness of finding a starting point in history and accepting as evangelical all that fans out from it.

Clive Calver, the Director General of the EA in the 1980s and 1990s, wrote of the change wrought by the eighteenth-century Evangelical Awakening that birthed Methodism, "Once 'evangelical' had simply meant 'Protestant': now it meant emphasis on the importance of individual conversion."[10] This narrowing down has in many ways been characteristic. Bebbington's generalization that the evangelical movement "has consisted of all those strands in Protestantism that have not been either too high in churchmanship or too broad in theology to qualify for acceptance" needs to be balanced by his subsequent assessment that "evangelicals have not been consistently low-church, dispensationalist or fundamentalist" but "united in the gospel emphases of the Bible, cross, conversion and activism."[11]

To make the same point from a different perspective, it is unusual for evangelicalism to be able to consistently "own" whole denominations. Denominations have a habit of broadening out. They may begin with a commitment to a narrow band of doctrine and practice but as time goes by, they tend to find alternative views expressed (and eventually accepted) in their midst.[12] So evangelicalism is better seen as trans-denominational rather than inter-denominational. Evangelicals in general are happier, say,

---

9. Bebbington cites "The position of the Pentecostalists in relation to Fundamentalism . . . was similar to the position of the Quakers in relation to Puritanism, having similar origins, occupying much common ground and yet totally repudiated by the larger body." Anderson, *Vision*, 6, quoted Bebbington, *Evangelicalism*, 198.

10. Calver, "Rise and Fall," 149. Referring to Griffin-Allwood, "Contemporary Evangelicalism."

11. Bebbington, *Evangelicalism*, 42, 45.

12. Bruce, *Religion in Modern Britain*, 8–13.

to "own" Wesley than to "own" Methodism and more willing to welcome some Methodists than others, depending on doctrinal understanding.

It was the change from an inter-denominational approach to a trans-denominational emphasis that enabled evangelicals in the 1700s to begin to think of defining themselves through alliances. In the early 1740s, the dissenting cleric Philip Doddridge had considered inter-denominational evangelicalism.[13] Ken Hylson-Smith states that at the time "[t]he Church of England . . . found itself in a pluralistic situation in which it was confronted by four fully-fledged denominations—the Presbyterians, the Congregationalists, the Baptists and the Quakers—as well as . . . the recently emergent, ominously energetic and influential Unitarians."[14] However, in 1757, reluctant to add to the divisions, Wesley proposed that there should be an alliance of Methodists and evangelical Anglicans.[15] Wesley was unsuccessful but later attempts fared better. After the formation of a number of denominationally conscious missionary societies in the 1790s, there arose in 1804 what Hylson-Smith described as "[t]he first organization to achieve pan-evangelicalism on a grand scale"—the British and Foreign Bible Society.[16] But unity did not come easily; the division between Church and Dissent in the early 1800s was so strong that evangelicals in both camps found it hard to lay aside their differences.[17] There were divisions within each camp too. The members of the Clapham Sect, noted for their parliamentary reforms, came under fire from their fellow evangelical Anglicans.[18]

To form a lasting alliance, it was clear that evangelicals would have to take each other on trust and be bold enough to assume that none would deviate from the propositions agreed by all as essential. Inevitably, membership being optional, there would be some who would consider themselves evangelicals (or, more relevantly, who would be considered evangelicals by other evangelicals) who would opt out. However, such opting out would not necessarily decrease an alliance's breadth. Those declining membership would more likely do so in protest at the breadth of an alliance rather than at

---

13. Hylson-Smith, "Roots," 140.
14. Hylson-Smith, "Roots," 137.
15. Hylson-Smith, "Roots," 140.

16. The Baptist Missionary Society and Church Missionary Society being prime examples and the London Missionary Society being a pan-Evangelical exception. Hylson-Smith, "Roots," 143.

17. Calver comments "The divisions between church and chapel were a matter of class, culture and politics as well as theology. Anglican leadership largely came from the upper classes who were solidly Tory. Nonconformity was middle-class and decidedly non-Tory in its majority view." Calver, "Rise and Fall," 148.

18. Hylson-Smith, "Roots," 144.

its narrowness. It is in the nature of alliances that those who are inclined to exclusivism are more readily disenchanted than the inclusive. Within evangelicalism there is a constant watchfulness to ensure that its boundaries are not compromised by Catholicism (which is seen as setting church tradition over the authority of Scripture), liberalism (which is seen as setting the human mind over the authority of Scripture) or emotionalism (which is seen as setting experience over the authority of Scripture). Whilst those who fear encroachment most may wish to stand together to hold the ground, they often end up standing apart in order to protect their own integrity. Nevertheless, by the mid-1800s many evangelicals were prepared to consider such an alliance.

THE BIRTH OF THE EVANGELICAL ALLIANCE

In 1846 a conference was held at the Freemasons' Hall, London to launch an international Evangelical Alliance. Delegates representing fifty denominations are said to have come from four continents: "215 Presbyterians, 187 Methodists, 181 Congregationalists, 172 Episcopalians, 80 Baptists. No Roman Catholics or Eastern Orthodox . . . 84% came from Britain, 10% from America and 6% from Continental Europe."[19] In view of the percentages, maybe it is not surprising that the resultant Alliance was British rather than international, but it was not the question of representation that brought this about, rather the issue of slavery. At the conference, J. Howard Hinton, the British General Secretary of the Baptist Union, advised that no slaveholder should be admitted into membership of the proposed alliance. Calver has written,

> As a British evangelical this was perfectly consistent with the stand that had been taken in the successful anti-slavery campaigns earlier in the century. But it presented an enormous problem for the American delegation. At least one of the American churches represented at the conference admitted slave-holders into its membership. It therefore became likely that American opposition to Hinton's motion would destroy the possibility of a worldwide ecumenical alliance. After extensive deliberations it became obvious that it was unacceptable to the Americans for the British to force on them a general measure of exclusion which ignored the involuntary situation in which some slaveholders found themselves. For the British it was intolerable that

19. Calver, "Rise and Fall," 150.

some American evangelicals still attempted to justify slavery on biblical grounds.[20]

This single issue resulted in the abandoning of an international alliance and the acceptance instead of a compromise proposal of "loosely-linked independent national organizations, not accountable for each other's actions."[21] In Britain it was to be the EA. However, despite the specific issue that birthed it, the EA was determined not to become a one-issue organization. It wanted to have a broad and positive agenda. According to Calver this accounts for its early non-strident approach towards Catholicism:

> It has been common to regard EA as purely an anti-Catholic movement. While it is true that some of its early leaders can be readily identified with this emphasis—and EA shared the common anti-Catholic views of evangelicals at that time—such a judgement ignores its failure to launch a crusade on the one issue that would have clearly united the constituency. John Angell James had called for a union of evangelicals to combat, "infidelity, Popery, Puseyism and Plymouth Brethrenism." The Scottish churchman, Dr Candlish, had also seen the wisdom of promoting unity on the grounds of shared antipathy: "The unity of the church is greatly promoted by a resistance to the common enemy." However, these views concentrated on a negative issue, which EA's founders accepted but wanted to keep in check by maintaining the positive merits and gains of their unity.[22]

Frustration with the EA's lack of militancy led to the founding of the vehemently anti-Catholic "Protestant Alliance" late in 1851.[23] This lack of militancy was also evident in that it left campaigning on current evangelical concerns, such as sexual lapses, drunkenness and Sabbath-breaking, to other agencies.[24] Furthermore, the EA did little to support the urban evangelism strategy that had been bringing Anglican and non-conformist evangelicals together since the 1820s and 1830s.[25] It even failed to offer support to the prominent evangelical Charles Haddon Spurgeon in the Down Grade Controversy of 1887–88, when Spurgeon battled in pulpit and press

---

20. Calver, "Rise and Fall," 151.
21. Calver, "Rise and Fall," 151.
22. Calver, "Rise and Fall," 153.
23. Wolffe, "Protestant Societies," 281.
24. Bebbington, *Evangelicalism*, 134–36.
25. Much of this was left to organizations like the London City Mission. Hylson-Smith, "Roots," 145–46.

against what he saw as the scourges of "Modernism."[26] On Calver's admission the key aims of the EA in the first fifty years of its existence were hard to identify: "Shorn of its leadership, devoid of popular issues and deprived of its original vision, EA moved slowly forward—a vehicle for union, yet still searching for a cause that would unite evangelicals under its banner."[27]

In terms of unity, though, there was another sign to consider: evangelicals in the late nineteenth century appeared reluctant to embrace new evangelical groups. Calver has written of Angell James' antipathy to Brethrenism.[28] Spurgeon was similarly negative about the movement:

> Years ago, when a man was converted, he used, as a matter of course, to unite with that church with which he most nearly agreed, and work for the Lord in connection with it; but now, a brother does not like to go to the place where most of the Christians in the town or village assemble, but he prefers to hold a meeting in his own room, in order to show that he dislikes sectarianism, and believes in Christian unity.[29]

An equally dyspeptic tone was adopted by Lord Shaftesbury in his old age when he questioned the Salvation Army, which he had initially supported, referring to it as a "trick of the devil, who was trying to make Christianity ridiculous."[30] The new evangelical movements of the nineteenth century were clearly given a hard time and this presaged challenges for those about to arise in the 1900s. Evangelical inclusiveness was still proving to be a complex concept.

EVANGELICALISM AND BRITISH PENTECOSTALISM

As a new century got underway, the challenge of Pentecostalism came to the fore. According to Baptist academic Ian Randall, the EA was "led . . .

---

26. Bebbington, *Evangelicalism*, 145–46. It later sought to be conciliatory towards Spurgeon and invited him to speak at a series of apologetics lectures. Calver, "Rise and Fall," 158.
27. Calver, "Rise and Fall," 153.
28. Calver, "Rise and Fall," 153.
29. Spurgeon, *All-Round Ministry*, 100–101.
30. Sourcing this quotation has proved difficult. Briggs quotes it in this form. Briggs, "Salvation Army," 522. Other Shaftesbury quotes lend authenticity. See Collier, *General Next to God*, 110, 198.

to distance itself" from the new movement.[31] Part of the reason for such a "leading" could have been the Berlin Declaration of 1909 in which German evangelicals rejected "Pentecostal claims of restoration of charismata, [and] condemn[ed] all pentecostalism as a diabolic manifestation."[32] For Randall, "being 'central' was particularly attractive to the EA in the 1920s when the unity of evangelicalism was strained to breaking point as liberal and conservative theological tendencies diverged."[33] To hold the center ground in the inter-war years the EA sought to distance itself from Roman Catholicism, Liberalism and Anglo-Catholicism by organizing large celebrations of the place of the Bible in Protestant history.[34] It was this inter-war emphasis on the Bible that, according to Randall, eventually led the EA into conflict with Pentecostalism.[35] The Pentecostal churches were consistent in claiming that they had evangelical roots.[36] However, Sir Robert Anderson, an EA apologist, expressed the opinion that "[Pentecostalism] subordinates the great facts and truths of the Christian revelation to the subjective experience of the Christian life."[37] G. Campbell Morgan of Westminster Chapel used emotive language in allegedly calling Pentecostalism "the last vomit of Satan."[38] The mood of the time was accurately summed up in 1922:

> The question as to the possibility of the periodical appearance of miraculous gifts during the course of this dispensation is one which still gives rise to acute differences of opinion. Fortunately, there is no need to come to any definite conclusion on this point in order to see how unscriptural, and, indeed, how utterly subversive of genuine spirituality, are the corybantic exhibitions associated with particular types of present-day "Pentecostalism."[39]

---

31. Randall, "Schism and Unity," 169.
32. Synan, *Century of the Holy Spirit*, 426.
33. Randall, "Schism and Unity," 164.
34. Randall, "Schism and Unity," 169.
35. Randall, "Schism and Unity," 169.
36. Randall quotes Donald Gee saying in 1933 that the AoG was "in agreement with all sections of the Church holding orthodox and evangelical views." Randall, "Old Time Power," 57.
37. Anderson, "Spirit Manifestations," 48.
38. Frequently quoted but never adequately sourced. See Middlemiss, *Interpreting Charismatic Experience*, 32. Morgan was also an EA vice president. Randall and Hilborn, *One Body*, 166.
39. Bebbington, *Evangelicalism*, 198, citing *Life of Faith* (June 14, 1922), 732.

The development of British evangelical inclusiveness 9

A more temperate comment of Campbell Morgan's implied that the age of miracles was over and that the "tongues movement" was evil.[40] In 1939 Bishop Gough affirmed "the commitment of the Alliance to a new evangelicalism that avoided the extremes of either the fundamentalist or liberal wings."[41] Pentecostalism, with its roots in personal experience and an unsophisticated, literalistic biblical hermeneutic would not fit into this new evangelical centrism.[42] Furthermore, to those outside the movement, it appeared to have a disturbing confidence in its eschatological significance. Harvard professor Harvey Cox summarized Pentecostalism's understanding of its prophetic positioning:

> The first Pentecost happened in Jerusalem somewhere around A.D. 34. . . . Centuries passed and Christianity degenerated, but God did not give up. Here and there He sent a sprinkle of blessings, but promised that just before the climax of history He would pour them down in torrents of a "latter rain," foreseen by the prophet Joel, which would surpass even the first Pentecost in its potency. There would be a worldwide resurgence of faith, and the healings and miracles that had been so evident in the first years of Christianity would happen again as a prelude to the second coming of Jesus Christ to establish his visible kingdom.[43]

As the expectation of a climax to history increased in the late 1800s, people again began to look for the signs that accompanied the first-century outpouring of the Holy Spirit, particularly healings and speaking in unknown tongues.[44] In Britain the sense of anticipation was heightened by the 1904 revival in Wales where the principal preacher, Evan Roberts, laid much stress on his personal encounters with the Holy Spirit.[45] Pentecostal historians are agreed, though, that it was the meetings in Azusa Street, Los Angeles, between 1906 and 1909 that played the greatest part in bringing

---

40. Cited by Randall, "Schism and Unity," 169.

41. Quoted by Randall, "Schism and Unity," 165. Separating evangelicalism from fundamentalism was and has been an evangelical preoccupation. Calver, Coffey and Meadows listed eight "vital differences" between evangelicals and fundamentalists. Calver et al., *Who Do Evangelicals Think They Are?*, 6. Stott listed ten. Stott, *Evangelical Truth*, 21–24.

42. To call Pentecostalism fundamentalist at its inception would have been anachronistic. The Fundamentalists (the American anti-modernist, anti-secularization group) was named in the 1920s. Its members soon "rejected pentecostalism and by 1928 had disfellowshiped [sic] all pentecostals from their ranks," Synan, "Introduction," xxi.

43. Cox, *Fire from Heaven*, 47.

44. Acts 2.

45. Evans, *Welsh Revival*, 190, 192.

together all the formative strands of Pentecostalism and in launching the modern worldwide Pentecostal movement.[46] Significantly, it was at Azusa Street that the mainstays of Pentecostal preaching were established: justification by faith (already an established evangelical doctrine), sanctification by the Holy Spirit (a doctrine to the fore in the nineteen-century Holiness Movement), the baptism in the Holy Spirit evidenced by speaking in unknown tongues, divine healing "as in the atonement," and the personal premillennial rapture of the saints at the second coming of Christ (a doctrine propagated in the early days of the mid-nineteenth-century Brethren Movement).[47]

As Pentecostalism spread, the British Pentecostal movement was sustained by an annual convention started in 1908 by the Anglican Vicar of Sunderland, Rev Alexander Boddy, who had been influenced by the 1904 Welsh revival.[48] Further momentum came in 1909 through the setting up of the Pentecostal Missionary Union by Cecil Polhill, a missionary to China.[49] However, by 1911 as the Sunderland Convention continued to grow, Boddy was having to make it clear to all who came to his Whitsun meetings that he had no intention of setting up a Pentecostal denomination. Others were less reticent and by 1924 Britain had at least four Pentecostal denominations. W. O. Hutchinson, a Bournemouth Baptist had established the Apostolic Faith Church in 1911 appointing D. P. Williams, a Welsh Congregationalist, as an overseer and later an apostle. The Apostolic Church of Wales (later, Great Britain) seceded from it in 1916.[50] The Elim Pentecostal Alliance was formed in 1918 by the combining of the Elim Churches and Elim Mission Board with the Elim Evangelistic Band set up in Ulster in 1915 by Welsh evangelist George Jeffreys.[51] The Assemblies of God (AoG), founded in 1924 following an initial meeting in Birmingham that had agreed on a structure to bring Pentecostal churches together without undermining the autonomy of the local assembly.[52]

---

46. Hollenweger, *Pentecostalism*, 18–20. Owens, "Azusa Street Revival," 39–68. For wider antecedents: Anderson, *Introduction to Pentecostalism*, 19–38.

47. Synan, "Introduction," xx. Sometimes these five principles are reduced to four (hence the Pentecostal concept "Foursquare"), points 1 and 2 or 2 and 3 being combined. Synan, *Century of the Holy Spirit*, 425–26.

48. Kay, *Pentecostals in Britain*, 11–15.

49. Kay, *Pentecostals in Britain*, 15, 17. Polhill was one of the Cambridge seven. Pollock, *Cambridge Seven*, 35–50.

50. Hathaway, "Role," 40–57. [Note: Its erratum confirms XV not XVI.] Kay, *Pentecostals in Britain*, 18.

51. Kay, *Pentecostals in Britain*, 20–27.

52. Kay, *Pentecostals in Britain*, 27–31.

The development of British evangelical inclusiveness

Given the influence of the 1904 Welsh revival on British Pentecostalism, it is not surprising that these denominations in their early days were more characterized by revivalism than by theology.[53] Indeed some observers thought that the revivalism of early Pentecostalism was so strong that all Pentecostal meetings were in danger of becoming so celebratory and inward-looking that evangelism would disappear. Jeffreys, however, pitched his "Revivals," as he called his town-wide campaigns, at a wider audience. In February 1913 he wrote to Boddy: "The Lord is giving the answer through this Revival [in Penybont] to the criticism that the Pentecostal people are not interested in Evangelistic work, and only seek to have good times."[54] Not that Jeffreys put "good times" entirely off the agenda. Commenting on Jeffreys' 1930 Birmingham meetings, Elim historian Desmond Cartwright disclosed the flamboyance of the occasions by writing: "The Revival Party, consisting of Robert E. Darragh as song leader, Albert W. Edsor as pianist and James McWhirter as organist, took the city by storm."[55] Indeed there could be an almost theatrical feel to the meetings as Jeffreys was in the habit of asking those who claimed to have been healed to come to the platform to "give their testimonies."[56] His was not the kind of evangelism that offered an intellectual apologetic to those grappling with the secular issues of the day. On the contrary,

> Few early Pentecostal leaders had received a university education and many, such as Smith Wigglesworth, were barely literate. University degrees were even considered a hindrance to Pentecostal ministry and anti-intellectualism was a common early feature. The movement has struggled for most of its life with the mind-Spirit tension. There was a deep suspicion of contemporary theology, with its higher criticism and modernism. Pentecostals were not equipped to engage the academics and were thus content to condemn. They needed no further evidence of the "evils" of such doctrines and of the influences of Darwin, than the decline in the older churches. The answer was not viewed as being located in theological debate, but in a practical demonstration of spiritual power.[57]

Whilst Pentecostalism had established its campaigns prior to the Second World War and borne the brunt of evangelical criticism, within a

---

53. Hathaway, "Elim Pentecostal Church," 31.
54. Cartwright, *Great Evangelists*, 79.
55. Cartwright, *Great Evangelists*, 105.
56. Cartwright, *Great Evangelists*, 76.
57. Hathaway, "Elim Pentecostal Church," 33.

decade of the Second World War ending the EA played its own major role in a large-scale evangelistic event. The EA coordinated much of the Greater London Crusade held at Harringay Arena from March to May 1954 with American evangelist Billy Graham.[58] Here seemingly there was common ground, but the EA and Pentecostalism had yet to resolve their differences. Some recall that Pentecostals were prevented from serving as counsellors at this event.[59] But reconciliation was not far away. Randall stated "[a]fter the Second World War the drawing together of British evangelicals around Billy Graham's crusades in 1954–55 encouraged the identification of Pentecostals with mainstream British evangelicalism."[60] Elsewhere Randall was more specific attributing this progress to the new General Secretary of the EA, Gilbert Kirby, installed in 1956: "Kirby . . . worked successfully at bringing the Pentecostals, previously rejected by the Alliance, into the mainstream of evangelicalism."[61]

The phrase "bringing . . . into the mainstream of evangelicalism" is significant, given Pentecostalism's persistence in by-passing the Reformation to establish its New Testament provenance.[62] A popular evangelical handbook has distinguished Pentecostalism from Protestantism stating "[i]t is important to realize that Pentecostalism is not a denomination or a Protestant sect. In fact, it represents a fourth major strand of Christianity—alongside Orthodoxy, Roman Catholicism and Protestantism."[63] It is a fourth major strand that evangelicalism has become keen to own.

Before moving to evangelicalism's next challenge to inclusiveness, it is worth noting two things. Firstly, the speed at which the EA finally accommodated British Pentecostal denominations on Kirby's appointment in the 1950s had much to do with personal relationships. Kirby had a particularly high regard for Donald Gee, a key figure within British Pentecostalism, referring to him as "one of the great statesmen within the [twentieth-century Pentecostal] movement."[64] Secondly, fifty years on from evangelicalism's protracted acceptance of Pentecostalism, the disputes and mistrust of earlier years received little mention in the official history of the EA. In their determination to be tactful, the authors made a brief mention of interest

58. Randall, "Schism and Unity," 171.
59. Gerald Coates in conversation, 1993.
60. Randall, "Old Time Power," 79.
61. Randall, "Schism and Unity," 172.
62. Kay, "Assemblies of God," 47, 56.
63. Dunn, "Pentecostalism," 646–47.
64. Massey quotes Kirby's reference at Gee's funeral to Gee as a fellow member of Stott's theological study group. Massey, *Another Springtime*, 193.

The development of British evangelical inclusiveness   13

among evangelicals in the 1904 Welsh revival and then covered the expansion of Pentecostalism between 1904 and 1950 in two sentences:

> Evangelists to working class people were, however, emerging in this period. George Jeffreys, the founder of Pentecostalism's Elim Church, together with his brother Stephen, both of whose roots were in the Welsh Revival, led Pentecostal evangelistic and healing campaigns that attracted large audiences in the 1920s.[65]

Such minimalizing is reminiscent of the approach adopted by certain evangelicals towards the Salvation Army's emergence in the 1850s and by detractors of the Methodist movement a century before that. Mary Heimann has sought to explain the approach:

> Methodists, who harangued from the pulpit or met in the open fields to proclaim the Gospel . . ., seemed to be wild unpredictable folk, rabble-rousers and hysterics who, as often as not, were drawn from the most dangerous ranks of society—those who had least to lose by its overthrow. It is therefore not surprising that the "religion of the mob" which they seemed to represent was generally attacked with satire rather than with reasoned debate and treated to loathing rather than to measured criticisms, even by those who prided themselves on their universality, toleration and advocacy of open debate.[66]

To justify the lack of serious debate by suggesting that popular movements are devoid of effective apologists could be seen as condescending. In 2000 the General Director of the EA, when questioned about the many years in which the EA had set Pentecostalism at a distance, sought to offer a more measured explanation: "it just took a while for Pentecostalism to prove itself and for the EA to be satisfied."[67] If the EA in the 1920s had set out its reasoned objections to Pentecostalism, then in the 1950s it could have detailed its grounds for reassessment. In reality, though, it appears that by the 1950s Pentecostals were weary of isolation and had no desire to request even a summary justification of evangelicalism's evident reappraisal lest it reopen wounds caused by past criticisms from senior evangelical leaders.

---

65. Randall and Hilborn, *One Body*, 213. Hastings makes even briefer mention of the Pentecostal denominations setting them amongst unlikely companions: "In the 1920s and 1930s the smaller and new sects undoubtedly prospered—Christian Science, Seventh Day Adventist, Jehovah's Witnesses, Assemblies of God, Elim Foursquare Gospel Alliance." Hastings, *History of English Christianity*, 265.

66. Heimann, "Christianity in Western Europe," 475.

67. Edwards to me in conversation, 2000. He acknowledged it sounded "a little thin."

Pentecostalism's lack of protest and ease of acquiescence, whilst highlighting the levels of attrition involved in over thirty years of stand-off, also signaled a major change in Pentecostal attitudes to inter-church relations. In Pentecostal circles much is made of a "prophetic word" that the Pentecostal evangelist Smith Wigglesworth is recorded as having given to the young South African General Secretary of the Apostolic Faith Mission, David du Plessis, in 1936:

> Through the old-line denominations will come revival that will eclipse anything we have known through history. No such things have happened in times past as will happen when this begins. It will eclipse the present day twentieth century Pentecostal revival that already is a marvel to the world with its strong opposition from the established church. But this same blessing will become acceptable to the churches and they will go on with this message and this experience beyond what the Pentecostal [sic] have achieved. You will live to see this work grow to such dimensions that the Pentecostal movement itself will be a light thing in comparison with what God will do through the old churches. There will be tremendous gatherings of people, unlike anything we have seen, and great leaders will change their attitudes and accept not only the message but also the blessing. Then the Lord said to me that I am to give you warning that he is going to use you in this movement. You will have a prominent part.[68]

Given such a prospect, by the late 1950s Pentecostal leaders in Britain were more than ready for a *rapprochement* with evangelicalism. It appears, however, that the formalities of EA membership took a little longer. The only records that the EA had available in 2006 showed that Elim joined on February 22, 1964 and that the AoG joined on May 25, 1966. The Apostolic Church apparently did not join until January 19, 1989. A limitation of the system, though, is that an EA member organization allowing its membership to lapse loses its record of earlier joining, which might have been the case here.[69]

---

68. Quoted by Hywel-Davies, *Baptised by Fire*, 152–53. The provenance of this prophecy is discussed in detail in Cartwright, *Real Smith Wigglesworth*, 161–67.

69. Information obtained from EA Senior Membership Officer, August 2006.

EVANGELICALISM AND THE BRITISH CHARISMATIC MOVEMENT

As British Pentecostal denominations began to take their place within the EA, further challenges to evangelical inclusiveness hove into view. Historical denominations met with each other during the 1950s and 1960s to consider closer working relationships and evangelicals came to different conclusions as to how the evangelical community should react.[70] When the prominent evangelical leader and then-Minister of Westminster Chapel, Dr. Martyn Lloyd-Jones, offered his advice it came as a call for evangelicals to leave their "mixed" (evangelical/non-evangelical) denominations.[71] However, when he expressed this opinion at the National Assembly of Evangelicals in 1966, John Stott, then Vicar of All Souls' Langham Place, wasted no time in airing an opposing view.[72] Some denominational church leaders did take Lloyd-Jones' advice and joined the British Evangelical Council, set up in 1952 to take a stronger stand against ecumenism.[73] Clearly, Kirby's slogan for the EA in 1962, "Spiritual Unity in Action," was under attack on the "unity" front.[74]

It had been under attack on the issue of "action" too. In the 1950s, Lloyd-Jones had spoken out against American evangelist Billy Graham's style of evangelism.[75] With Graham due to return to London in the mid-1960s, yet more Calvinist voices were raised, protesting that Graham's simple call to people to make a commitment to Christ with a prayer of salvation implied a faulty doctrine of personal regeneration.[76] Under pressure, the EA went through various changes of direction before agreeing to play a central role in Graham's 1966 and 1967 London campaigns.[77]

---

70. Randall and Hilborn, *One Body*, 241–46. This debate continued until February 1990 when EA Council decided against joining the Council of Churches for Britain and Northern Ireland. Lewis, "Renewal," 189.

71. Brencher, *Lloyd-Jones*, 116–41.

72. Brencher, *Lloyd-Jones*, 101–6; Lewis, "Renewal," 179.

73. The Fellowship of Independent Evangelical Churches, an accountability body established in 1922 for churches united in doctrine, ecclesiology, and style, was already in membership with the BEC, but churches could join the BEC without affiliating to the FIEC. For FIEC see Randall and Hilborn, *One Body*, 236. For BEC growth see Lewis, "Renewal," 180.

74. Randall and Hilborn, *One Body*, 261.

75. Brencher, *Lloyd-Jones*, 186–87.

76. Randall, "Schism and Unity," 172.

77. An EA commissioned report, "On the Other Side," published in 1968 criticized crusade evangelism. Randall and Hilborn, *One Body*, 272–74.

Whilst some assert that these challenges of the 1960s had minimal effect on EA membership, most would agree that the EA at this time lost some of the sharpness of its internal debate.[78] Randall and Hilborn have written: "A more avowedly inclusive Alliance would emerge from the crisis of 1966 and would gradually recover to become a powerful force within British Christianity."[79]

One step to the EA's recovery had already been taken. As General Secretary, Kirby had opened the way for local churches to become associate members of the EA.[80] This practical inclusiveness, together with the more theological and ecclesiological inclusiveness referred to by Randall and Hilborn, paved the way for the EA to accommodate the growth resulting in the late 1960s and throughout the 1970s from what became known as the Charismatic Movement. As leaders with a new emphasis on the gifts of the Holy Spirit emerged, both within the historic denominations and outside them, new congregations were birthed.[81] Those outside the historic denominations eventually came together in networks for which the EA increasingly became a point of identity. The Charismatic Movement was partly a reflection of the times, as Nigel Scotland has indicated:

> The 1960s . . . saw the emergence of the hippie culture which was a reaction to the materialism of the "never had it so good" post-war years under Harold Macmillan. . . . The charismatic experience which began to emerge in England in the 1960s was to some extent part of this environment . . . existentialist thinking which emphasized the importance of the present moment prompted people to seek new experiences and the growing popularity of television increased their desire for deeper emotional and spiritual satisfaction.[82]

Scotland's view is reinforced by Doreen Rosman:

> Another reason for the appeal of charismatic Christianity was its congruity with contemporary cultural developments . . . it appeared to be a Christianised version of the new youth culture of the day, encouraging casual dress and uninhibited behaviour.

78. Lewis, "Renewal," 179.
79. Randall and Hilborn, *One Body*, 257.
80. Lewis, "Renewal," 179.
81. "Gifts of the Spirit" listed in 1 Cor 12:7–10.
82. Scotland, *Charismatics*, 36–37.

The development of British evangelical inclusiveness

There was a huge outpouring of charismatic music, much of it folk or rock in style.[83]

These observations are important as it would be wrong to give the impression that the Charismatic Movement of the 1960s and 1970s was a repeat of the earlier Pentecostal movement. British Pentecostalism and the British Charismatic Movement shared a common interest in spiritual gifts (*charismata*) but at their inception differed sociologically and theologically.

The Charismatic Movement itself had two strands, one centering on the gifts of the Spirit within the historic denominations and the other involving the formation of new churches. In the movement's early days, there was a continuity of emphasis and experience.[84] Charismatic historian, Father Peter Hocken, catalogued these as "a changed relationship to God," "a new level of awareness of the persons of the Trinity," "a new capacity to praise God," "a new capacity for hearing God," and "new power in [one's] own life and ministry to others."[85] He also pointed to three common desires: "concern and prayer for revival," "experience of God's power in healing," and "concern for the fullness of the New Testament Church."[86] However, the two strands were inevitable from the outset because of the differences in ecclesiology evident in their various pioneers. Hocken took the views of non-conformist pioneers David Lillie and Arthur Wallis and of Anglican Michael Harper as typical:

> The difference of vision for the future of the church, between the Lillie-Wallis circle (summed up in the term *Restoration*), and those primarily looking to Harper and the Fountain Trust for leadership (finding their vision better expressed by the term *Renewal*), was fundamentally a difference in received ecclesiology. The vision of the church shared by Lillie and Wallis was rooted in the ecclesiology of the Plymouth Brethren, with the new power and life brought by the Holy Spirit and the spiritual gifts being seen as the means by which this vision would be realised. The ecclesiology of Harper and his colleagues was less uniform and less focused than that of Lillie and Wallis, but in the early stages of the movement it represented an evangelical view of the church enriched by a new sense of the church as the body of Christ; yet strongly supported among the Anglican majority by traditional loyalties to the Church of England and its historic

---

83. Rosman, *Evolution*, 292.
84. Hocken, *Streams of Renewal*, 147–58.
85. Hocken, *Streams of Renewal*, 147–50.
86. Hocken, *Streams of Renewal*, 152–54.

role in the life of the nation. It was not easy to see how these two visions could be reconciled.[87]

However, reconciliation between the two strands of "restoration" and "renewal," as Hocken has defined them, was not a pressing issue. Generally there was a mutual respect and a considerable degree of cross-fertilization.[88] Indeed, this has increased as debates about charismatics staying within or withdrawing from the denominations (ironically a near mirroring of the mid-1960s theme of evangelicalism) quickly receded.[89] Each strand had to gain acceptance within its own context and then to find a place in the wider church setting. For evangelical Anglican charismatics, this search for peer understanding came at a time of renewed evangelical Anglican confidence.[90] The 1967 National Evangelical Anglican Conference at Keele had provided a major step forward for evangelicalism as a whole as evangelical Anglicanism seemed to find both a place in the wider Christian world and a new confidence within its own denominational structures.[91] In such a setting, charismatics whose commitment to church growth went hand-in-hand with a commitment to a vibrant Anglicanism retained the respect of their fellow clergy.[92] Adrian Hastings used Harper, together with the then York-based David Watson, as examples: "The Evangelicalism of the 1970s was also increasingly open to Pentecostalism but here too it continued to exercise a certain reserve, though a number of prominent Evangelicals such as Michael Harper and David Watson turned into leading figures in charismatic renewal."[93]

Even so, ten years on from Keele, Watson recorded an "audible gasp" at the Nottingham Evangelical Anglican Congress when he said "in many ways the Reformation was one of the greatest tragedies to have happened to

87. Hocken, *Streams of Renewal*, 172–73.

88. Lewis, "Renewal," 190.

89. In the early 1970s, house church leader John Noble also questioned denominationalism. Noble, *Forgive Us*.

90. Theological differences arose as Harper was Stott's curate at All Souls' Langham Place. Stott countered charismatic teaching on a post-conversion baptism of the Holy Spirit. Stott, *Baptism and Fullness*. Stott's enthusiasm for the Holy Spirit's person and work was respected by charismatics.

91. Hastings called the Keele statement "one of the most important ecclesiastical documents, not only of the sixties but of this century." Hastings, *History of English Christianity*, 554.

92. Watson, *You Are My God*, 74–87.

93. Hastings, *History of English Christianity*, 618.

The development of British evangelical inclusiveness

the Church."[94] For some evangelicals this seemed to be a sell-out to ecumenism.[95] Their concerns were exacerbated by the increasing breadth of the Charismatic Movement with which Watson was so clearly associated. In Hastings' phrase the Charismatic Movement was "fairly successfully domesticated by both the Roman Catholic and Anglican churches."[96] Such Catholic domestication is evident from his further observation with its implicit reference to the internal tensions of Vatican Council II:

> It is true that the charismatic movement at times looked like a refuge for frightened Christians from the intellectual and institutional problems with which the church was failing to cope: it could provide a sort of euphoria of freedom for people in fact deeply enmeshed in legal and theological bonds which they could not, or would not, break. The mechanisms of ecstatic dancing, the making of strange noises and stirring but not intellectually articulated sounds, the lying about in unusual postures, could all be little more than a reassuring psychological get-away for priests and nuns who for the rest of the time were very faithful servants of a system which the reformers of a few years before had wanted to change but had not succeeded in doing.[97]

Watson's statement, however, did find some resonance with those in Hocken's "Restoration" group. The Brethrenism with which Hocken associated them had always preferred to bypass the Reformation in a desire to establish its roots directly in the ecclesiology of the New Testament.[98] For this strand of the Charismatic Movement, developing as it did outside the main denominations, peer acceptance was less of an issue. Adherents simply gathered in homes, seeking a simpler and truer expression of church fellowship, in much the way that the pioneers of the Brethren movement had a century earlier.[99] This time, though, the gatherings were characterized by a belief that "the gifts of the Spirit are for today."

The Charismatic Movement was impacting evangelicalism both denominationally and non-denominationally and the encounter was not always comfortable. In commenting on "the considerable division among

---

94. Hastings, *History of English Christianity*, 102.
95. Hastings, *History of English Christianity*, 102.
96. Hastings, *History of English Christianity*, 619.
97. Hastings, *History of English Christianity*, 619. Vatican Council II (1962–65).
98. For a brethren account of church history, see Broadbent, *Pilgrim Church*; Kennedy, *Torch of the Testimony*.
99. Walker, *Restoring the Kingdom*, 51–86.

evangelicals" occasioned by the Movement in the 1960s, 1970s and 1980s, Lewis observed: "Zeal and antagonism have often been equal and opposite forces in churches and between churches."[100] Even the Pentecostal denominations were at first unsure about charismatic renewal: "some were hostile, others openly supportive, most indifferent."[101] However, throughout British evangelicalism there was a yearning for church growth, especially a desire to reach the "teens and twenties," and here the Charismatic Movement seemed to be having some success. Furthermore, as ecumenical leaders came up with schemes to further ecumenical unity, evangelicals felt the need to demonstrate the unity they believed they already had.[102] With this emphasis on youth and unity the scene was set for a resurgence of evangelical conferences, but this time they were destined to have a strong focus on new worship songs and to use an informality of platform style that fitted well with the casualness of charismatic Christianity.

The holiness movement of the 1850s onwards had spawned the Keswick Convention and it had continued with considerable impact on worldwide evangelicalism.[103] However, in the 1970s its distinctive emphasis on the work of the Holy Spirit was significantly different from that within the Charismatic Movement.[104] So, impressed with the concept of large summer gatherings, the various house church groupings began to hold their own Bible weeks.[105] The success of these prompted British Youth for Christ and *Buzz* magazine to join forces and launch Spring Harvest in 1979. Its Easter timing was tactfully designed to complement rather than compete.

The overall effect of such gatherings was to close the gaps between charismatics, Pentecostals and evangelicals. Malcolm Hathaway commented that "by the early 1980s . . . Pentecostal groups had changed considerably, absorbing many features of the [restoration] movement and the wider renewal. . . . The overall impact can be fairly judged as beneficial to the Pentecostal movement, shaking it out of the traditionalism and insecurities of the post-war period and giving it much greater self-confidence."[106] He has also been quite specific in attributing aspects of this accommodation to the Bible weeks, saying that "[m]any, including Pentecostals, were drawn to the

---

100. Lewis, "Renewal," 190.
101. Hathaway, "Elim Pentecostal Church," 28.
102. Lewis, "Renewal," 187.
103. Established 1875. Price and Randall, *Transforming Keswick*.
104. Price and Randall, *Transforming Keswick*, 250–51.
105. Such as the Lakes, the Dales and the Downs. Walker, *Restoring the Kingdom*, 114–15.
106. Hathaway, "Elim Pentecostal Church," 31.

annual camp meetings established by the leaders of the restoration movement" at which "the ideology of the [restoration] movement was cultivated and propagated."[107] In particular he noted,

> A new, relaxed and exuberant style of worship arose, interpreted through contemporary music and song-writing. The Pentecostals were still largely singing the hymns and songs of the prewar revival. The few new songs they had lacked depth while the restoration songs reflected the new, triumphalistic doctrines of the [restoration] movement and began to influence many Pentecostals.[108]

Furthermore, Bebbington observed that in the ten years between Keele and Nottingham, evangelical Anglicanism had changed to the point where charismatics were on the platform alongside conservative evangelicals and even the worship looked different as hands were being raised.[109] The summary that "earlier antagonisms [to the Charismatic Movement] have gradually given way to a growing degree of mutual respect and recognition" appears to hold for Pentecostals and conservative evangelicals alike.[110]

The long-term impact of the EA joining with Spring Harvest would be hard to overestimate. The link was established when one of its leading lights, Clive Calver, took over as General Secretary of the EA in 1983. Calver's appointment was a unifying move as well as a bold one; he had the credibility of being Kirby's son-in-law.

Calver's fourteen years as General Secretary of the EA largely defused the charismatic debate. Calver developed a way of holding together all the strands of evangelicalism. He liked to speak of the "twelve tribes" of evangelicalism. In a promotional booklet published in the early 1990s these were listed as "Anglican Evangelicals . . . Pentecostals . . . Ethnic Churches . . . Renewal Groupings . . . Separated . . . Reformed Evangelicals . . . Evangelical Majorities [i.e. members of denominations where evangelicals are in the majority] . . . Evangelical Minorities . . . Evangelical Non-Denominational Groups . . . The New Churches . . . Independents . . . [and] Evangelical Denominations."[111] The divisions were contrived and the "tribes" were by no means equal in size (and maybe not even in significance) but it was a clever device for making each feel valued whilst having to acknowledge a greater whole. It was also in many ways a declaration of the breadth of Calver's

---

107. Hathaway, "Elim Pentecostal Church," 29.
108. Hathaway, "Elim Pentecostal Church," 29.
109. Bebbington, *Evangelicalism*, 268.
110. Lewis, "Renewal," 190.
111. Calver et al., *Who Do Evangelicals Think They Are?*, 11.

personal vision. He was determined that the EA should speak for as many evangelicals as possible. He saw increased credibility for evangelical views linked with increased membership of the EA:

> *The Resurgence of the Evangelical Alliance.* Since the early 1980s UK evangelicals have established a corporate vehicle for their united action through the Evangelical Alliance which has maintained a growth rate of 25 per cent per annum. The EA represents evangelical interests to the Government and media and operates Alliances in Scotland, Wales, Northern Ireland and among African-Caribbean churches.[112]

Unity in diversity was becoming the rallying cry of the EA. At times it was more of a dream than a reality but the Charismatic Movement had restored numbers after the confrontation between Stott and Lloyd-Jones, and the EA once again was able to settle down to its more familiar non-confrontational style. Having asked why the EA took so long to accept Pentecostalism, I was eager to know how it was able to accept the Charismatic Movement so quickly. The answer was that many of the leaders of the Charismatic Movement were already operating within the EA when the movement began.[113] This answer is not entirely satisfactory as it implies that evangelical unity is more about who you know than what you believe.

I will add two further insights into evangelicalism and the Charismatic Movement. First, the comment of Peter Masters, the minister of Spurgeon's Metropolitan Tabernacle, London:

> Twenty-five years ago orthodox non-charismatic evangelicals could usually have cordial fellowship with old-fashioned Pentecostalists. In those days, when believers of such differing viewpoints were thrown together as students or during their time of military service, they found that they could often witness and pray together. Many of the old-fashioned Pentecostalists (seemingly rare nowadays) were conservative evangelicals, and whatever our differences on certain points we could respect them as fellow believers who were fully committed to the authority of Scripture as they understood it. But during the 1960s we saw the emergence of an entirely new brand of Pentecostalism—the charismatic renewal movement—and since then we have seen, as it were, a phase a minute! . . . Now is the time to

---

112. Calver et al., *Who Do Evangelicals Think They Are?*, 9.
113. Conversation with Edwards, 2000.

The development of British evangelical inclusiveness 23

sound the alarm and to save countless churches and believers from disaster.[114]

The ease with which the EA accommodated the Charismatic Movement did not impress all who would call themselves "evangelical." Some conservative evangelicals felt the need to set themselves at a distance on this point of principle.

Secondly, there was at least one period in the mid-1980s when all was not well within the EA on the issue of full-scale charismatic inclusion. In 1982, the Jesus Fellowship, a charismatic grouping that arose out of a Baptist church in Bugbrooke, Northamptonshire, joined the EA after a visit by the EA's former General Secretary Gilbert Kirby who seems to have regarded the Fellowship as controversial but doctrinally orthodox.[115] The Pastor, Noel Stanton, opted for a commune lifestyle for his congregational members and adopted a distinctive evangelistic pattern reflected in their frequently used title, "The Jesus Army." However, not all EA members saw things the way Kirby did and in 1986 the Jesus Fellowship was required to resign its EA membership.

This resignation was required at a time when the Jesus Fellowship had asked the EA to help them counter the effects of some externally produced literature that the Fellowship regarded as defamatory. Two leaders of the Jesus Fellowship have written of the incident:

> We had innocently expected the accusations to be dealt with, the vendetta exposed and our integrity upheld, but the matter of the accusations was dealt with quite briefly. However, a different issue of poor relationships with local churches was raised. The EA felt compelled to suggest that we resign on this issue ... the EA prided itself on being an alliance of member churches at local and national level. In their view the word "alliance" hardly described our position.[116]

The perception of poor local relationships seemed to have extended to the local Baptist Association in Northamptonshire and ejection from the Baptist Union followed.[117] Calver, however, asserted in an interview with *Buzz* magazine shortly after he, as then General Secretary of the EA, had presided over the Jesus Fellowship's departure that "[w]e have encouraged

---

114. Masters, *Healing Epidemic*, 11, 20.
115. Cooper and Farrant, *Fire in Our Hearts*, 227.
116. Cooper and Farrant, *Fire in Our Hearts*, 228.
117. Cooper and Farrant, *Fire in Our Hearts*, 230.

the Jesus Fellowship to develop links with other Christians. There were no doctrinal grounds for the EA's decision."[118]

According to the EA it was an accountability issue on which they would have preferred the Baptist Union to take a lead but with the Jesus Fellowship seemingly acting in isolation from its official point of accountability the EA felt obliged to act. The separation proved to be relatively short-lived. The Jesus Army began to build relationships with some leaders of the New Churches Movement and by 1990 was able to assemble a significant number of prominent charismatics and evangelicals to support them at their two Wembley Praise-Days.[119] This paved the way for the Jesus Fellowship's re-entry into the EA.

EVANGELICALISM AND THE CARIBBEAN CHURCHES

An interesting facet of Calver's time as General Secretary of the EA was the establishing of the West Indian Evangelical Alliance. The WIEA was largely the initiative of Philip Mohabir, considered to be a missionary to Britain from Guyana, who was concerned about the twin problems of fragmentation among black-led churches and the polarization between black and white Christian communities.[120] The WIEA began in 1984 with a formal launch a year later, coinciding with the British Labour Party's decision not to form a separate West Indian section. Calver used this fact to speak about the EA being more progressive than the Labour Party.[121] However, if the creation of the WIEA was a progressive act, it marked a significant departure from the way in which the EA had previously signaled inclusion. When the evangelical community eventually accepted the British Pentecostal denominations they were granted direct membership of the EA. When the Charismatic Movement gained its more rapid acceptance by a majority of evangelicals, direct membership of the EA was granted almost as a formality. When the Caribbean churches, which had been in Britain for over thirty years and numbered many Pentecostal congregations in their midst, were to be offered acceptance, a separate charity was formed. This charity

---

118. Cooper and Farrant, *Fire in Our Hearts*, 229, quoting *Buzz* magazine, April 1986.

119. Cooper and Farrant, *Fire in Our Hearts*, 277. Those present included John Noble and Philip Mohabir.

120. Mohabir, *Building Bridges*, 194.

121. Twenty years later "progressive" seemed an unlikely term, despite being relevant at the time as encapsulating a bold response to Caribbean diaspora requests for separate political and spiritual recognition. Edwards noted that supportive links between EA and WIEA initially aroused suspicion. Edwards, *Lord*, 51.

had EA funding, an EA partnership agreement ensuring co-operation and cross-representation and a mechanism whereby its members were granted automatic free EA membership, but it still had rights to self-determination.

The explanation for adopting this level of separation is said to lie in two areas, first in Mohabir's convictions about the right way to resolve black-led church fragmentation and second in his opinions about the way to close the black/white Christian divide.[122] In both cases the EA leadership had to be willing to see things from Mohabir's point of view. It is extraordinary that the EA leadership so readily assented. Taking the black/white Christian divide first, it is hard to believe that they saw the divide between Caribbean Christians and white evangelicals as exceeding anything evangelicalism had experienced in the past. The gap between conservative evangelicals and Pentecostals had been vast in the 1920s, and the divide between conservative evangelicals and the Charismatic Movement could have been even greater, but it had not taken the formation of new alliances to close these gulfs. In reality evangelical leaders realized that they were contending with sensitivities they hardly understood and were determined to respect.

In 1988, Joel Edwards, a former probation officer serving as a New Testament Church of God minister, became the WIEA's first General Secretary. Edwards wrote positively on the setting up of the WIEA from a British Caribbean point of view:

> Some Black Christians were clearly suspicious about a partnership between Black and White Christians which appeared to suggest that there was a dependency on White Evangelicals.... One of our greatest battles in seeking reconciliation was to convince some church leaders that the work we were doing did not amount to a new White evangelical imperialism.... At the outset only a very small part of the Black Church understood the need or wisdom of working closer with White evangelicalism.[123]

Edwards acknowledged that for some "the idea of a separate 'Black Alliance' was a kind of Christian apartheid."[124] However, he was keen not to open old wounds. For him, the situation in the 1950s and 1960s was never simply a failure on the part of white Christians to welcome new Caribbean congregational members on their arrival in Britain. Rather, the Caribbean churches in Britain were not just birthed out of a lack of welcome but out of such churches' actual inability in the 1950s to offer West Indian immigrants

---

122. Edwards, *Lord*, 50.
123. Edwards, *Lord*, 51.
124. Edwards, *Lord*, 52.

the style of church they were used to, the social inclusion they needed, and the spirituality they wanted:

> It is a misrepresentation of Black Church growth to surmise that the inception and development of these groups were due primarily to rejection by "white churches." Many "white churches" made heroic attempts to accommodate others with whom they were totally unfamiliar and which had an identity entirely distinct from their English pentecostal counterparts. Black churches were not brought into being solely as a result of racism. This would make them entirely a community by default.[125]

If much of British church life did seem formal and bland compared with Christian experience in the Caribbean, it could be said that in terms of Pentecostal renewal the Caribbean clock was running ahead of that of the British churches. Separation was not so much being imposed by white Christians on black Christians but there was an acknowledgement by both of differences in belief and practice.

Edwards made no suggestion that the Caribbean churches spent thirty years feeling paralyzed for want of "white" evangelical support prior to 1984 and the founding of the WIEA. By then many Caribbean churches were outstripping their white evangelical counterparts in terms of service in the community. Indeed, theirs had been a story of growing prestige. Edwards characterized the early phases of British Caribbean church development as being the "suitcase church" (1950–65), the "letterhead church" (1960–75) and the "business card church" (1975–88). He saw the 1950s and early 1960s as a time when Caribbean Christians were still very much in "arrival" mode, settling into a new nation. The 1960s and early 1970s were a time when churches were being established and a corporate image determined. The 1970s and early 1980s were a time of increased community involvement when interaction with civic dignitaries was a key factor of Caribbean church life.[126] Such an analysis lends credence to a history of separate Caribbean church development.

Significantly, prior to the establishing of the WIEA, only one Caribbean church had applied for EA membership.[127] Edwards explained that:

---

125. Edwards, "British Afro-Caribbean Community," 103–4.

126. Edwards, "British Afro-Caribbean Community," 107–11. For Edwards, the Caribbean churches had moved since 1988 from inception, consolidation and civic initiation to "dynamic transition" with faith expressions being rethought for a second generation, upwardly mobile Caribbean culture.

127. Randall and Hilborn, *One Body*, 288.

Black Pentecostal faith was unlikely to sit at ease with the pre-renewal ethos of British church life. Pentecostals arriving from the Caribbean between 1950 and 1980 lacked the liturgical polish of their British counterparts. Generally, they were noisier, preached considerably longer and had different expectations of the worship experience.[128]

There is an irony here. Edwards' focus was on a pre-renewal ethos. By 1985 the renewal and restoration movements were well established. Certain areas of British church life were by then noisier with longer sermons and clear expectations of demonstrable ecstatic experiences in worship. There had been a convergence in theory and practice without any outward expression of unity. This irony was not lost on Mohabir and Calver, given their personal involvement with the restoration movement.[129] The Charismatic Movement provided momentum for white evangelicals wishing to bridge the gap with the Caribbean churches.[130]

Turning to the fragmentation factor identified by Mohabir, Mark Sturge, a later occupant of Edwards' post, has also analyzed these early days of Caribbean church integration into British evangelicalism, and saw the establishing of the WIEA as coming at the end of a five-year period of internal Caribbean church integration.[131] For Sturge this period of integration, labelled by him "The integrated church (1980–1985)," follows on from five overlapping periods which he successively defined as: "The scattered church (1948–1955)," "The community church (1952–1960)," "The denominational church (1955–1966)," "The consolidating church (1965–1975)," and "The restless church (1975–1985)."[132] His first three periods correspond roughly with Edwards' "suitcase" phase; his fourth with Edwards' "letterhead" phase; and his fifth and sixth with Edwards' "business card" phase. Whilst the differences are largely a matter of detail, Sturge's highlighting of internal Caribbean church integration prior to the WIEA's creation is significant. It prompts questions about the nature of the fragmentation and the effectiveness of earlier attempts at integration.

On the nature of the fragmentation, Edwards wrote:

> It was not long before the denominational distinctives from the Caribbean replicated themselves in the UK. What began

---

128. Edwards, *Lord*, 50.

129. Mohabir's early links into Britain, whilst based in Guyana, were with Bradford-based restoration movement leader, Bryn Jones. Walker, *Restoring the Kingdom*, 72–82.

130. Forster, "Foreword," 6–8.

131. Sturge, *Look*, 96–98.

132. Sturge, *Look*, 84–98.

as closely knit friendships and fellowships among Caribbean church leaders rapidly re-grouped along old denominational loyalties, with new groups emerging out of personality conflicts and fresh initiatives. Before long, Caribbean Christianity in Britain had become as diverse as our British counterparts with its historic groups and New Church developments of the 1960s and 1970s.[133]

The effectiveness of earlier attempts at integration is harder to assess. Of the three groups highlighted by Sturge, the International Ministerial Council of Great Britain (IMCGB), the Afro West-Indian United Council of Churches (AWUCOC) and the Council of African and Afro-Caribbean Churches (CAACC), he writes most extensively on the AWUCOC. Positively he stated:

> The Afro West Indian United Council of Churches (AWUCOC) was established in 1977, with the aim of uniting church around faith, social, and political issues, and of making representations on their behalf. From its inception, the AWUCOC enjoyed widespread support among the BMCs' [Black Majority Churches'] leadership and could be identified as the most authentic Black Christian voice in the UK. . . . The AWUCOC made a significant impact, working with the Department of Education on the issues of Black pupil underachievement, and with the Departments of Health and Social Security on issues of children in the foster and care system, unemployment and mental health; they also worked with the Home office, and represented the BMCs on CTBI [Churches Together in Britain and Ireland] amongst others.[134]

On the negative side he recorded that by 1985 "the AWUCOC was entering its death throes."[135] He attributed this demise to an "inconsistency in delivery" stemming from the heads of church organizations prioritizing their own organizations over the AWUCOC's agenda.[136] Integration versus fragmentation looked to be a recurrent problem for the Caribbean churches. However, Sturge then credited the WIEA with greater success, citing support from the EA and a consequent re-aligning in Caribbean church identity with evangelicalism as key factors:

---

133. Edwards, *Lord*, 50–51. See also Toulis, *Believing Identity*, 111–20.
134. Sturge, *Look*, 97.
135. Sturge, *Look*, 157.
136. Sturge, *Look*, 97.

The development of British evangelical inclusiveness

> In every sense, this partnership was an historic one, not only for the African Caribbean Christian community but also for the Christian community in Britain as a whole. It acted as a focal point for dialogue with Black Christians. . . . Even at this point, the "Black-led" churches were an unrecognized entity, considered at best to be fundamentalist and at worst to be sects; they were certainly not considered evangelical.[137]

The suggestion by Sturge that the WIEA "evangelicalized" the Caribbean churches is an interesting one. For some of these churches any "evangelicalizing" may have been a change in emphasis, whilst for others it might have been a recognition of an existing reality. There is also the possibility that for some it might have been an unwanted or unwarranted re-labelling. It is sufficient to say that not all Caribbean churches joined the WIEA.

Soon after Edwards' appointment, the WIEA changed its name to the Afro-Caribbean Evangelical Alliance (ACEA). In 1991 it changed again to the African Caribbean Evangelical Alliance, the intention being to reflect the growing African Christian presence in Britain. The assumption was that such a name change would make it a more natural home for African Christianity. It was not entirely a wise choice as African-Caribbean was still understood to indicate a Caribbean background and a further name change to the African and Caribbean Evangelical Alliance proved necessary.[138] However, a name implying the coming together of two communities is one thing; creating the reality is another. Edwards was right to speak of a divide:

> It became evident that the presence of African Christianity in Britain would present WIEA with a new challenge of reconciliation. Before Black consciousness of the 1960s and the growing Afro-centric movements of the late 1970s, most Caribbean Christians were unwilling to be linked to an African identity. In an effort to respond positively to this development WIEA became the African and Caribbean Evangelical Alliance (ACEA) and sought to work across the African and Caribbean divide.[139]

---

137. Sturge, *Look*, 157–58.

138. Changes were: Afro-Caribbean Evangelical Alliance 1989, African-Caribbean Evangelical Alliance 1991, African and Caribbean Evangelical Alliance 1993. Aldred, *Respect*, 105.

139. Edwards, *Lord*, 51.

CONCLUSION

From the above it can be seen that by the mid-1980s when significant African neo-Pentecostal immigration growth began to occur, British evangelicalism had already developed a number of different mechanisms of inclusion. Classical Pentecostalism was accepted after a protracted period of sometimes uneasy observation, the Charismatic Movement found a ready acceptance that left many non-charismatics struggling to come to terms with its assimilation, and the Caribbean churches were included through a form of parallelism that allowed distinctives to be retained whilst closer working relationships were pursued.

In the next chapter I will show how African neo-Pentecostalism developed its distinctiveness prior to being introduced into this diverse British evangelical context.

Chapter 2

The development of African neo-Pentecostal distinctiveness

IN THIS CHAPTER I will argue that Pentecostalism underwent a change within Africa in the final decades of the twentieth century that marked a departure from earlier patterns of transition within African Christianity. Whereas initial evangelical input and early Pentecostal missionary endeavor met with an indigenizing response, from the 1970s onwards there was a reaction against this, with many preferring a less culturally adjusted Christianity. This paved the way for the introduction of a neo-Pentecostalism that considered itself to have modified classical Pentecostalism to a point where it could be adopted in any global situation with minimum local cultural adjustment.[1] Such a perception would also lay the foundation for the manner of African neo-Pentecostalism's subsequent exportation to Britain.

THE EFFECT OF INITIAL EVANGELICAL INPUT

Given the evangelical doctrinal convictions of many of the missionaries initially involved in evangelizing Africa, one might assume that the shaping of an African Pentecostalism capable of integration back into British evangelical church life would be a simple story. However, no matter how confident these missionaries and their home-based missionary societies were that their message, if clearly proclaimed, would be accepted without

---

1. For an assessment of neo-Pentecostalism's globalizing effectiveness see Coleman, *Globalisation of Christianity*. For globalization and identity theory see Meyer and Geschiere, *Globalization and Identity*.

modification, it was no guarantee against the indigenous diversification of it. Three short examples of this thinking will suffice.

In 1841, the London Missionary Society (LMS), just four years short of its fiftieth anniversary, accepted the young Scottish medical doctor, David Livingstone, to join its senior missionary, Robert Moffat, in southern Africa.[2] LMS was an interdenominational society formed to provide overseas opportunities for non-Baptists following the start of Baptist missionary work in India in 1792.[3] By the time of Livingstone's recruitment, it was well established in the South Pacific, India and China. However, despite marrying Moffat's daughter, Livingstone did not settle into the expected role of a Bible-teaching missionary operating from a medical clinic base. On his return to Britain in 1856, LMS committee members were unsettled by reports of his travels, which to their evangelical mindset seemed irrelevant to his missionary calling. In 1858 Livingstone returned to Africa as the leader of a British government expedition instead, still seeking to serve the missionary cause by advocating his "Three Cs" principle of Christianity, commerce and civilization.[4] LMS clearly had fears that Livingstone's explorations might sideline its message.

In 1879 in the East African kingdom of Buganda, the Scottish Presbyterian missionary, Alexander Mackay, was working as part of the Church Missionary Society (CMS) team. When faced with French Catholic Fathers arriving to convert the Buganda alongside him, he was as outspoken against them as he was against the Arab slave traders and Bugandan witch doctors he had previously encountered. In his opinion Catholicism was confusing his message, "sowing tares among [his evangelical] wheat."[5]

By contrast Sierra Leone, established in the 1790s as a refuge for freed slaves, served as a different kind of base for missionary activity into Africa.[6] Some of Sierra Leone's earliest residents were West African slaves rescued from intercepted slave-ships who, having converted to Christianity, served as missionaries on returning to their home countries. So confident were they in their missionary message and methodology that they called on missionary societies in Britain to be more active in their recruitment

2. Nicholls, *David Livingstone*, 5; and Renwick and Harman, *Story of the Church*, 178.

3. Renwick and Harman, *Story of the Church*, 177.

4. Nicholls, *David Livingstone*, 25, 31, 34, 37; Pakenham, *Scramble for Africa*, xxiv; Reader, *Africa*, 531.

5. Quoted by Packenham, *Scramble for Africa*, 301.

6. Sierra Leone was founded partly through the work of the politically active group of Anglican evangelicals known as the "Clapham Sect." Bebbington, *Evangelicalism*, 71–72.

programs. It is a mark of the effectiveness of these emancipated slaves and their ability to present the message in a relevant way that when CMS launched its Yoruba mission in the 1840s a Yoruba church was already in existence.[7] The missionaries from Sierra Leone may not have been aware of the degree of relevance their cultural background brought to the message but, by the same token, Livingstone and Mackay would not have been aware how their own cultural concerns and trappings were obstacles to effective communication.

Early mission churches differed little liturgically from those the missionaries attended in their home countries. The evangelical Anglicans had a prayer book "Morning Prayer" and "Communion Service" and the nonconformists put together their usual "hymn sandwich."[8] In 1861, Henry Venn, then Secretary of the CMS, sought to lessen other areas of missionary dependence by formalizing principles of self-governance, self-support and self-propagation.[9] However, desires to attain these freedoms initially led to frustration which swiftly gave way to some dislocation, with splinter churches re-forming as independent congregations under new leadership.[10]

Other independent churches then came into being more through enthusiasm than frustration. Between 1910 and 1930 there were mass movements towards Christianity through the preaching of African evangelists who often had little or no church status. Of particular note were William Wade Harris in the Ivory Coast, Sampson Oppong in Ghana and Walter Matitta in Lesotho, these latter two having great effect despite being unable to meet the missionary societies' formal requirements for "native ministers."[11] Although such evangelists sought to swell the ranks of the mainline denominations, many who through their ministry rejected witchcraft joined independent churches.[12]

A third, more radical trigger to independent church growth than either frustration or enthusiasm was the reaction against the perceived overriding of traditional customs. Some local believers berated missionaries for

---

7. CMS was set up in 1799 partly though the work of the Clapham sect. Peel covers the entrance of CMS missionaries into Yorubaland in exquisite detail and mentions the role of returning Christian slaves in Peel, *Religious Encounter*, 8, 24, 27.

8. Opening hymn, short prayer, notices, hymn, Bible reading, long prayer, offertory hymn, sermon, closing hymn and benediction.

9. Hiebert, *Anthropological Insights*, 194.

10. One early example of this change is the founding of the Native Baptist Church in West Africa in the 1880s and 1890s. Anderson, *African Reformation*, 61.

11. Harris was clearly initially accepted as a Methodist lay preacher. Anderson, *African Reformation*, 70.

12. Anderson, *African Reformation*, 76.

failing to appreciate certain local marriage customs and aspects of ancestor veneration. Desires to launch new churches in the face of such omissions were sometimes coupled with the citing of supernatural commissionings through dreams and visions. When changes in belief and practice as extensive as these occurred in the process of establishing independent churches, the commentator on African religions, Bengt Sundkler, in using the contemporary term "Zionist" for them, acknowledged their wider objective in seeking, as it were, a utopia or "Zion" of their own. By contrast, in using the contemporary term "Ethiopian" for new churches established without any significant change in belief or practice, he was acknowledging their minimal level of "Africanization."[13] Given the nature of these so-called Zionist churches, some have suggested that "prophet-healing" would be a better term.[14] An alternative approach would be to pursue the concept of the evangelical missionary strategist Hiebert who, having attributed the aforesaid three "selfs" jointly to Rufus Anderson and Venn, went on to propose a fourth "self," that of self-theologizing.[15] It could then be said that the distinction between Sundkler's Zionist and Ethiopian categories lies in the degree of their self-theologizing.

If the Zionist churches were in fact "Pentecostal" before classical Pentecostalism had Africa in its sights (Hollenweger, for example, considered the Kimbanguists to be a Pentecostal-style church not to have emerged from Pentecostal missionary work), questions have to be asked about the impact of the missionaries sent to Africa by Europe's new Pentecostalism in the early decades of the twentieth century.[16] Initial evangelical input, with its tendency to limit the supernatural to biblical history, had already produced a range of churches. There were evangelical mission churches that spoke of self-governing, self-supporting and self-propagating principles but differed little from the Western churches that spawned them. There were independent churches that had barely modified from Western models but no longer had Western ties. Then there were independent churches which had reacted against evangelicalism's strictures and had extensively self-theologized. Such diversity demonstrates the effect that local culture can have on a message regardless of the propagators' expectations to the contrary. When Pentecostal missionaries subsequently arrived in Africa they also had high expectations.

---

13. Sundkler, *Bantu Prophets*, 39–43, 47–50.
14. Turner, *Religious Innovation*, 94–101.
15. Hiebert, *Anthropological Insights*, 195.
16. Hollenweger, *Pentecostalism*, 54. Also Molyneux, *African Christian Theology*.

THE OUTCOME OF EARLY PENTECOSTAL MISSIONARY ENDEAVOR

Classical Pentecostalism usually dates its beginning from what have become known as the 1904 revival in Wales and the 1906 revival in Azusa Street, Los Angeles.[17] The holiness teaching of the Keswick Convention, which began in 1875, played some part in laying a foundation, and the Sunderland Conventions, hosted from 1908–14 by the local Anglican vicar, Rev A. A. Boddy, helped establish the movement. There was some reluctance in the early years to set up Pentecostal groupings of churches, probably as a result of Boddy's influence, but ejection of missionaries with a Pentecostal experience from denominational and inter-denominational missions led Polhill to form the Pentecostal Missionary Union in 1909.[18] This ejection and regrouping is an early indication of the tension between evangelicalism and Pentecostalism in a missionary context.

Initially, many new Pentecostals anticipated that their recently received "gift of tongues" would enable them to communicate fluently on foreign mission fields.[19] Not all thought this way. The work of the Pentecostal Missionary Union proceeded along more conventional lines and training schools were established. The work of the Pentecostal Missionary Union was taken over by the British Assemblies of God in 1925 after the First World War.[20] However, two giants of early African Pentecostal missionary endeavor were already well-established in Africa by then: John G. Lake, an American who went to South Africa in 1908, and William P. F. Burton, a British AoG missionary who went to the Congo in 1915.[21] These men not only made a mark on the nations where they preached but also stirred their constituencies in America and Britain so that a number of Pentecostal individuals rose to take up the overseas challenge supported by their local congregations. Matthew Sinclair who moved to Sierra Leone from his Pentecostal church base in Kilsyth, Scotland, was one.[22]

In 1912, the newly formed Apostolic Church sent James Brooke to South Africa as its first African missionary. At the time the denomination was administered from Bournemouth.[23] By 1928 the Bournemouth con-

17. Kay, *Pentecostals in Britain*, 5–17. For wider antecedents: Anderson, *Introduction*, 19–38; Hollenweger, *Pentecostalism*, 18–388.
18. Kay, *Pentecostals in Britain*, 17.
19. Kay, *Pentecostals in Britain*, 17.
20. Kay, *Pentecostals in Britain*, 17.
21. Lake, *Astounding Diary*; Massey, *Another Springtime*, 56.
22. Personal conversation with Elim's official historian, D. W. Cartwright.
23. Vaughan, *Nigeria*, 2–3.

nection was no longer dominant, following the secession of the Apostolic Church of Wales which then spread to London, the North of England and Northern Ireland and had reorganized with a central administration. This was timely as it put the denomination in a strong position to handle its imminent missionary expansion into Nigeria through ministers such as Turnbull, Williams, Williams and Vaughan.[24]

J. D. Y. Peel's early work examined two Nigerian churches, "Cherubim and Seraphim" and "Christ Apostolic Church." By considering them both as "Aladura" churches he puts them in Sundkler's Zionist category of African Initiated Churches.[25] He drew close parallels between the two, although he did acknowledge that Christ Apostolic Church regarded itself as a Pentecostal church whilst Cherubim and Seraphim regarded itself as a Spiritual Society. The contrast between the two highlights the outcome of early Pentecostal missionary endeavor. Cherubim and Seraphim had no direct missionary input. Christ Apostolic Church was directly linked with the British Pentecostal missionaries of the Apostolic Church after its early phase as Faith Tabernacle Nigeria.

The Eternal Sacred Order of the Cherubim and Seraphim was established as the Cherubim and Seraphim Society in 1925 in Lagos by Moses Orimolade Tunolase.[26] A young woman, Abiodun Akinsowon, had a trance in which she visited the "Celestial region" and saw Orimolade. Orimolade was subsequently venerated as Baba Aladura, while Abiodun was made Archangel Captain. From the outset Cherubim and Seraphim was seen as a healing movement with speaking in tongues, trances, dreams, prophecy, and spirit possession all relatively commonplace.[27]

As the Society developed, regulations concerning buildings were formulated with Old Testament influences much in evidence. An area was designated the Holy of Holies and only appropriately dressed elders were allowed to sit there. Old Testament stereotypes were taken up by the Society's prophets who often grew beards and carried staffs. Liturgical practices were implemented for baptisms, funerals, anniversaries (especially those of the archangels Michael and Gabriel), "Repentant Meeting" days, "Love Feasts," and "Fruitful Revival" services. There were also sacred words, fasting, candles, holy water, sword and staff rituals, taboos, robes, dances, clapping,

---

24. Vaughan, *Nigeria*, 18; Peel, *Aladura*, 166.

25. Ward makes the linkage as follows: "Harris, Shembe and Kimbangu were early, and particularly dynamic and interesting, examples of a movement of 'independency' which became widespread in many parts of Africa. In Nigeria this phenomenon is known as Aladura; the praying churches." Ward, "Africa," 222–23.

26. Omoyajowo, *Cherubim and Seraphim*, 7.

27. Omoyajowo, *Cherubim and Seraphim*, 17.

The development of African neo-Pentecostal distinctiveness 37

stamping and so forth. In one of their hymns the idea is expounded that Jesus pleaded with God for forty years for Orimolade to establish the Cherubim and Seraphim Society.[28]

It is obvious from this that the Cherubim and Seraphim Society has many practices that would be foreign to evangelical believers. Even with prayer, differences are evident. Prayer is at the heart of the Cherubim and Seraphim Society; the term *aladura* is Yoruba for "owners of prayer" and Orimolade's renaming as Baba Aladura loosely translates as "Praying Father." In Aladura, God answers prayer providing correct methodology is employed.[29] This moves beyond liturgical to formulaic. When evangelical Anglicans use liturgical prayers they see no efficacy in the specific words or phrasing. Within the Cherubim and Seraphim Society, as with most other African Initiated Churches, formulaic praying is unquestioningly central.

This Cherubim and Seraphim prayer was proposed by Akindele:

> an elder or superior man is angry with you and wants to do you evil, go to the farm or wayside where you can secludedly pray at 6.30 o'clock am before sunrise. Read Psalm 38 seven times with Psalm 39. Pronounce the following Holy names as you are reading it AHA for 38 and HASI SHA ELIHI-AMATI for 39. Fast through the day, and you will know that there is God.[30]

The wider doctrinal context for this is explained by Amaramiro:

> Professor Omoyajowo in developing the Eternal Sacred Order of Cherubim and Seraphim's concept of Salvation said that since the Africans believe in forces seen and unseen the African concept of Salvation implies solving of these existential problems. There appear [sic] to be a consensus of opinion on this point since Turner writing in *The Life and Faith of the Church of the Lord Aladura* said "The recognition that there are more evils in life than can be traced to human nature and that a demonic domain of principalities and powers stand ranged against both God and man leads to the cosmic conception of evil that serves to reveal the magnitude of the power of victory of God who is still able to deliver man."[31]

It is clear that a doctrinal commitment to a dominant demonology lies at the heart of formulaic praying. The perceived need for protection

---

28. Omoyajowo, *Cherubim and Seraphim*, 107, 143–66.
29. Peel, *Aladura*, 119.
30. Quoted Peel, *Aladura*, 121.
31. Amaramiro, *Doctrinal Ideas*, 10.

leads to a distinctive use of the Psalms. Adamo writing on African cultural hermeneutics comments that in the African context Psalms are categorized into Protection Psalms and Therapeutic Psalms, the latter including a subcategory of Success Psalms.[32] Such categorizations to some extent support a conclusion that formulaic prayers are prayed as much to be heard by the demons that are perceived to need subjugating as by an almighty deity who is expected to effect the subjugation.

By contrast, the origins of the Christ Apostolic Church can be traced to the early 1920s when a Yoruba man, David Ogunleye Odubanjo, obtained from America articles entitled *Seven Principles of Prevailing Prayer*. These were written by Pastor A. Clark of Faith Tabernacle, Philadelphia, and published in his magazine *Sword of the Spirit*. Faith Tabernacle was a fundamentalist, non-Pentecostal church. Odubanjo then set up Faith Tabernacle Nigeria, not only reflecting the insight gained from Clark that "prayer works" but, according to Peel, including Odubanjo's own healing interest and his reliance on visions for guidance. The nine key characteristics set out at Faith Tabernacle Nigeria's foundation were certainly not all in the classical Pentecostal mold. Statement eight took Faith Tabernacle Nigeria in a direction diametrically opposed to classical Pentecostalism:

- Personal holiness,
- Contrast between the wickedness of this world and the godly community of the sect,
- Wrongfulness of litigation,
- Non-participation in national celebrations,
- Persecution as a mark of sanctity,
- Belief in the imminence of the Millennium,
- A distaste for acquiring property because of the imminence of the Second Advent,
- Glossolalic experiences regarded as satanic,
- No use of medicine for healing.[33]

Given this opposition to tongues-speaking, it is remarkable that when Faith Tabernacle Nigeria broke from Clark it sought to align itself with the British Apostolic Church. Indeed, some have argued that it was little more than a marriage of convenience with Odubanjo never fully embracing

---

32. Adamo, "African Cultural Hermeneutics," 69–90.
33. Listed both in Peel, *Aladura*; and Larbi, *Pentecostalism*, 101.

classical Pentecostal views.³⁴ Idris Vaughan, however, one of the Apostolic Church missionaries sent to work alongside Odubanjo, wrote extensively on the relationship between the two churches and saw the connection between Odubanjo's Faith Tabernacle and the British Apostolic Church as something far stronger. With Peel, Vaughan acknowledged that Faith Tabernacle Nigeria received negative publicity after the Babalola revival of 1929, but Vaughan believed that Odubanjo was genuinely distressed over this association which he had come to see as unhelpful and so contacted Clark's organization in Philadelphia for assistance. Whilst awaiting a reply, which eventually confirmed that there would be no American support, Odubanjo received a copy of *Riches of Grace*, a British Apostolic Church publication, with the following result:

> It was in this time of trouble and unrest of mind we were advised to invite our leaders from America to come to our aid. They refused because it was against their practice to go to other countries unless through Christian literature alone. Our American leaders of Faith Tabernacle Congregation refused to come to our aid in our hour of need. We therefore decided to look for missionaries from Great Britain with whom we had connection and who also practice divine healing similar to our own belief.³⁵

How similar the divine healing beliefs were in practice is not at all clear. As noted, Faith Tabernacle Nigeria had for some time adopted a rigorous "no medication" policy and it is possible that the 1931 delegation sent out by the British Apostolic Church did not take full account of this. However, Faith Tabernacle Nigeria got its desired sponsorship and before returning to Britain the three visiting British Apostolic Church ministers, Williams, Williams and Turnbull, ordained the seven Faith Tabernacle Nigeria pastors who had already been accredited from America.³⁶ Faith Tabernacle Nigeria changed its name to "Apostolic Church" and the first resident British Apostolic Church missionaries, Vaughan and Perfect, arrived in 1932 by which time it was reported that some of the African church members had received the "gifts of tongues and prophecy."³⁷ This is significant in the light of Vaughan's later assessment of the Pentecostal inclinations of Faith Tabernacle Nigeria before it sought the sponsorship of the Apostolic Church.

---

34. Opinion expressed in Oshun, "Christ Apostolic Church," quoted in Vaughan, *Nigeria*, 30.
35. Adegboyega, *Short History*, 37, quoted in Vaughan, *Nigeria*, 12.
36. Vaughan, *Nigeria*, 17–18, 23.
37. Vaughan, *Nigeria*, 21, 23, 27.

> It is doubtful in the search for sponsorship whether the Faith Tabernacle leadership would have included pentecostal groups since it seems that they would have had little if any information of the implications of Pentecostalism for a contemporary Christianity. The extraordinary such as dreams, visions, prophesying, exorcisms and the like, would have been familiar to them through their own native culture with its priestcraft, and the practice of ju-juism in its many forms. When such manifestations had appeared to them in relation to their Christian experience, they had understood them to be expressions of the *real* as distinct from the *false*—the *divine* as opposed to the *satanic*.[38]

Faith Tabernacle Nigeria was already quite extensive at the time of its Apostolic Church affiliation and after Vaughan and Perfect had visited its branches, Vaughan moved to the Calabar area. This was in 1933 at a time when, according to Vaughan, many were turning away from Christianity because it was not able to confront the power of witchcraft. In Vaughan's opinion, the view of these disenchanted former converts was being strengthened in the midst of a campaign organized by the non-Pentecostal Protestant missionaries in the Calabar area, a campaign called "Christ or Witchcraft?" During the campaign, the Scottish Institute's principal "gave his conviction after thirty years in the country that there was no real basis for a belief in the power of witchcraft."[39] Vaughan was at one with the crowd in its rejection of this statement and set up his own meetings proclaiming from Mark 16 that Jesus had said, "In my name they shall cast out devils."

In the ensuing weeks, as Vaughan's preaching took hold, the revivalist Joseph Babalola visited the Calabar area. By this time Babalola himself was linked to the Apostolic Church, having become a member of Faith Tabernacle Nigeria in 1931. Vaughan had met him earlier and continued to be impressed by him:

> Although I was happy about the content of Babalola's preaching, after his departure I came to feel some doubts about his approach to the divine healing aspect of his ministry in the Creek Town district. I came to know that in addition to prayers offered for the sick, Scripture-inscribed strips of paper were issued with instructions that they be applied by the sick to the part of the body said to be affected. To my thinking this procedure savoured rather too much of the ju-ju or witchdoctory so prevalent in the land and to which the people had been so long in bondage. The Bible's simple, uncomplicated instruction in James 5:14 for the

---

38. Vaughan, *Nigeria*, 15. Italics as in the original.
39. Recorded by Vaughan as an eyewitness. Vaughan, *Nigeria*, 42.

anointing with oil with the laying on of hands left no place for this or any other sort of deviant. But then, I came to think, might not Joseph the black evangelist, son of the soil and steeped in the customs and lore of his people, himself having been delivered from the bondage and darker implications of these, be, after all, nearer to the heart of the people and more understanding than I, the white newcomer, could hope to be?[40]

Vaughan was clearly accommodating, but to discern from his comments anything that might serve as a standard classical Pentecostal perspective on Nigerian extra-biblical practices is not straightforward. After all, the Apostolic Church was not the only Pentecostal denomination to work in Nigeria, the AoG and the American Foursquare having also by then sent missionaries. Although these denominations differ in some matters of church discipline and government, they basically agree on the traditional Pentecostal message of justification and sanctification of the believer through the "finished work of Christ on the cross" and the "baptism of the Holy Spirit with signs following."[41] Yet it is not clear that they shared Vaughan's commitment to accommodation. An endorsement of the supernatural is not the same as an enthusiasm for all things supernatural. Classical Pentecostalism may have set boundaries around its missionary input into Nigeria but there seems little doubt that some indigenous Nigerian Pentecostal groups with a high level of self-theologizing considered themselves recipients of classical Pentecostal approval. However, if classical Pentecostalism did perhaps unwittingly lend a measure of Western reinforcement to African supernaturalism, it came at a time when indigenization was more valued than externalization. There is no evidence of groups such as Cherubim and Seraphim capitalizing on any synergy.

Regardless of where Vaughan may have been setting the Apostolic Church's external boundaries, the denomination's internal boundaries became open to challenge. In 1940 one hundred assemblies resigned from the Apostolic Church in the Lagos area leaving the area superintendent, a European, with only five congregations. The denomination's subsequent investigations suggested that the likely cause of the exodus was unresolved tensions over Faith Tabernacle Nigeria's original "no medication" rule.[42] Correspondence on the exact requirements for divine healing had been

---

40. Vaughan, *Nigeria*, 59–60.

41. For example, the Apostolic Church's statement of faith, "Things Most Surely Believed." Vaughan, *Nigeria*, 111.

42. Suggestions that polygamy issues played a part are refuted by Hastings in *History of English Christianity*, 83. Christ Apostolic Church was always opposed to polygamy.

passing backwards and forwards between Lagos and the Apostolic Church headquarters in Britain for some months. It was the breakaway churches that formed the Christ Apostolic Church. The Apostolic Church in Nigeria continued separately, receiving around sixty missionaries from 1932 until it gained autonomy.[43]

Given the link with the British Apostolic Church from 1932-40, the Aladura label appended to Christ Apostolic Church by Peel deserves some investigation. Negative reports that arose when Faith Tabernacle Nigeria was associated with aspects of the 1929 revival led by the one-time Anglican layman Evangelist Joseph Babalola may afford a partial explanation. Babalola's revival not only benefited Faith Tabernacle Nigeria numerically but to a much greater degree swelled the ranks of the recently formed Aladura church, the Cherubim and Seraphim Society. Peel's quotes from Odubanjo's post-"Apostolic" diary extracts, however, are more revealing:

> Odubanjo, however, whose influence had been to publicise the need for Bible Study for everyone wrote gnostically of "the science of prayer" and how "we did not yet know in full how to appropriate the power that is in the Name (of Jesus). It heals, saves, protects, provides . . ." [Odubanjo's diary 5 March 1950]. Here Bible knowledge might become to power what a handbook of electrical engineering is to electricity. The "science of prayer" is a craft in which they hope to develop themselves.[44]

There is no doubt that this semi-formulaic approach to prayer would have been grounds for marginalization by the evangelical missionary community, and the expectation would have been that classical Pentecostalism would have taken a similar stand. Even so, such formulizing does seem to fall short of a total commitment to the formulaic praying that is generally considered characteristic of Aladura.[45] It has to be conceded that Vaughan might be right in asserting that Faith Tabernacle Nigeria did go through a phase that produced a genuine alignment with classical Pentecostalism but, even if such a conclusion would be stretching the reality, its hybrid character, as evidenced in Odubanjo's personal spirituality, is nonetheless significantly different from that of Orimolade and the Cherubim and Seraphim.

---

43. Hastings, *History of English Christianity*, 21.

44. Peel, *Aladura*, 141-42.

45. Peel's assertion that Odubanjo's thinking was influenced by religious sources that would have caused concern to evangelicals and classical Pentecostals has not been substantiated by subsequent research. Peel, *Aladura*, 142.

The development of African neo-Pentecostal distinctiveness

If, Vaughan's particular openness notwithstanding, the missionaries of classical Pentecostalism were more open to local practices than their evangelical colleagues, the explanation would lie in cessationist elements within conservative evangelical thinking. Superficially it would seem that the Bible is so full of records of supernatural acts that it would be impossible to communicate the Christian message without an emphasis on supernaturalism. The traditional evangelical opinion, however, is that these acts were specifically required in the past to provide a synchronistic witness to the authenticity of God's primary interventions into human history, namely the incarnation and sacrifice of Christ, the prior raising up of a nation committed to God in covenant and the subsequent establishing of the church. Extrapolating from this position, conservative evangelicals deem that since New Testament times the Bible itself has borne sufficient witness to such authenticity to remove the need for further supernatural testimony. To fully understand the strength of this opinion it has to be kept in mind that this evangelical view of an exclusive dependence on the biblical record was advanced from certain Bible passages at the time of the Protestant Reformation when reforming clergy were reacting against what they saw as the superstition of the Catholic Christianity of the Middle Ages. Miracles and healings were frequently claimed and believed to the point where statues and shrines became the objects of pilgrimage and veneration. Such fascination with the supernatural was seen as detracting from the genuine supernaturalism of Scripture and as trivializing divine power and intervention. It therefore became the norm for Reformers to preach alongside the gospel a form of cessationism.

Any preaching of a message that places miracles more in the past than in the present will be open to misunderstanding in a society that already sets great store by the supernatural. To sustain such a message in these circumstances, efforts would have to be made to distinguish between the supernatural of that society's present and the supernatural of the biblical past. Any such attempt would have to rely heavily upon the proponent's ability to make a distinction between the supposed sources of the supernatural. To do this it is usual to draw on the fact that many societies hold to a concept that the supernatural can emanate both from an ultimate deity and from lesser, more immanent spiritual forces. The ultimate deity is then affirmed and refined whilst the lesser spiritual forces are demonized or dismissed. It is in the demonizing or dismissing of lesser spiritual forces that evangelicals and Pentecostals differ. Most conservative evangelicals, whilst unreservedly accepting the existence of a personal devil, would be reluctant to take all that such societies associate with lesser spiritual forces as directly attributable to the devil or demonic activity. Such evangelicals would see the devil as causing humanity's original fall but would consider the fear and superstition that now dominate the subsequently fallen human condition to be sufficient to account for the negative experiences of daily life.[46] Pentecostals are more open to the concept of direct demonic activity.

As evangelicalism downplays the supernatural in routine living, it is faced with the challenge of how to categorize the responses of those that seek to retain a larger place for the daily experience of the supernatural. To consider them as rebellious reversionists makes little sense when there are angels and demons mentioned in the New Testament and biblical warrant could be claimed for proposing a spiritual worldview where such spiritual forces are still prominent and active. It would take a relatively small local cultural adjustment to rework the identities of traditional local deities into a global evangelical framework that purports to mirror that of the New Testament. Whilst this redefining would not sit comfortably with evangelicals, the greater issue for them would be the recommended handling of these demonized demoted deities. Questions of their reality notwithstanding, Pentecostalism's attempts at rebuking, resisting, and removing would be deemed theologically preferable to any traditional religious placating. Anthropologists Behrend and Luig have documented spirit activity in an African non-Christian setting where trances and whirling dances are attributed to local spirits.[47] Evangelicalism's preference would be to explain these things psychologically but any thought of regarding them positively would be seen as a denial of the gospel. The use of formulaic praying in such circumstances would be seen as calling into question evangelicalism's understanding of the gospel as a triumph of Christ over evil. Those who see themselves as addressing angels would fare little better in evangelical circles; a Christianity that insists on God being approached through Christ in the power of the Spirit, to the absolute exclusion of any other human intermediary, be it Mary or the saints, is not likely to appreciate those who seek mediation and intervention through angels.

Pentecostal missionaries first encountering concepts of greater and lesser deities would have agreed with their evangelical colleagues on much of the above. They would, however, more readily have aligned themselves with a worldview in which demons and angels are currently active and in which miracles are expected. They would not have denied the problems of fallen human nature and would have commanded repentance from sin,

---

46. Correspondence with evangelical Anglican leader Richard Bewes disclosed his antipathy to demonized worldviews. He wrote that his parents' missionary service in East Africa saw much success without recourse to demonic identification and confrontation.

47. Behrend and Luig, *Spirit Possession*, xiii–xx.

seeing sin that had not been repented of as a block to the daily experience of the miraculous. However, they would have been open to the need for deliverance ministry. For Birgit Meyer, writing in the 1990s, this raises the issue of alignment between those who recognize the need for deliverance ministry and the practitioners of traditional religion. In her work on the Ewe in Ghana she sees a clear connection between the two.[48] Although Meyer is at one with many African writers in seeing African society as imbued with traditional religion, unlike many she is not inclined to label the traditional as being particularly "Christian" but rather sees Christianity, especially Pentecostal Christianity, as persisting with traditional thought-forms and practices. John Mbiti was more inclined to see traditional religion and Christianity as compatible.[49] Mbiti's position has been criticized by the likes of Tokunboh Adeyemo.[50] In this ongoing enculturation debate, the fact that traditional religions and Pentecostalism share a common belief in the operation of spiritual forces (be they the operations of the demonic and angelic forces of Pentecostalism or the operations of the "spirits" of African traditional religions), there is no indication of a commonality of response to such operations. Pentecostals seek to enforce spiritual defeat on demons through Christ's triumph within the Christian gospel; those without such a gospel understanding seek to reduce the negative effect of "spirits" through placation. Whilst at times Pentecostals in their treatment of the demonic have welcomed the opportunity to publicly demonstrate the supremacy of God's power, there are indications that early Pentecostal missionaries put a positive interpretation on aspects of pre-Christian engagement with the supernatural, suggesting that societies evangelized by Pentecostals would have had little problem in continuing with such emphases.

As for societies evangelized by evangelicals, the question remains as to whether any form of local cultural adjustment would be acceptable.[51] According to the evangelical Burnett, whose *Clash of Worlds* introduced worldview theory to the general evangelical constituency, evangelicals should be open to cultural adjustment whilst implying that most evangelicals would prefer cultural sensitivity to more extensive accommodation. O'Donovan

---

48. Meyer, *Translating the Devil*, 212.

49. Mbiti, *African Religions*; and Mbiti, *Introduction*. Mbiti's fellow professor at Makerere University, Byaruhanga-Akiiki, gathered useful general material with specifics on Uganda and Botswana. Byaruhanga-Akiiki, *African World Religion*. For Ghana see Ayisi, *Introduction*. For Nigeria see *Traditional Religion*. For East Africa see Spear and Kimambo, *East African Expressions*. Ward cites Okot as one who sees African culture as having "a more radically secular orientation." Ward, "Africa," 232.

50. Adeyemo, *Salvation in African Tradition*.

51. Segun, "Robed in White," 10–11.

and Gehman have both served long periods as evangelical missionaries in Africa. Gehman has written as an evangelical seeking an African understanding of Scripture, working from a conviction that cultural adjustment is essential in governance, finance, gospel propagation, and theology.[52] O'Donovan, on the other hand, has shown no inclination to draw positively on cultural insights but has sought to apply Biblical principles to his areas of concern within African culture.[53] In reality O'Donovan's approach involves no cultural adjustment at all beyond a selecting of topics. This minimizing of local cultural impact is still characteristic of some evangelical missionary endeavor.

THE EMERGENCE OF LESS CULTURALLY ADJUSTED FORMS OF CHRISTIANITY

From the 1930s to the 1970s the Zionist strand of independent churches set the tone for many people's understanding of African Pentecostalism, but changes in the final quarter of the twentieth century worked to undermine that perception. In Nigeria the changes began with the revival of campus Christianity documented by Ojo.[54] I will consider this before making a contrast with the situation in Ghana over the same period.

The 1960s had started well for both Nigerian evangelicalism and Nigerian Pentecostalism in the wake of Nigeria's Independence declaration in 1960. At a church leadership level evangelical mission churches worked to hand over responsibility to local workers, with the consolidation of the Evangelical Church of West Africa (ECWA) and of the Church of Christ in Nigeria (COCIN) in the Hausa speaking areas of central and northern Nigeria being examples. Scripture Union (SU) in Nigeria, a largely campus-based affiliate of the British-based evangelical Bible-reading organization, also began to be Nigerian-led from 1960.

Billy Graham, the American evangelical preacher, held a major campaign in Nigeria in 1960 and T. L. Osborn, the American Pentecostal evangelist, held a similar Nigerian campaign in 1964. For Osborn this was a bold move, given the nature of Nigerian Pentecostalism at the time, with the denominational Pentecostal churches of Foursquare and the AoG standing

---

52. Gehman, *Doing African Christian Theology*; Mugambi, *African Christian Theology*; Parratt, *Reinventing Christianity*; Buthelezi, "Black Theology," 52–59; Setiloane, "Where Are We," 15–26.

53. O'Donovan, *Introduction to Biblical Christianity*; O'Donovan, *Biblical Christianity*.

54. Ojo, "Campus Christianity."

apart from the African Independent Churches. However, such are the attractions of American-led campaigns in Africa that differences between Pentecostals and divisions between evangelicals and Pentecostals became blurred during both events. Not all the independent Pentecostal churches, though, were at such a distance theologically from the denominational Pentecostal churches. As early as 1954 an embryonic neo-Pentecostal strand had begun to develop when Sidney G. Elton, who had arrived in Nigeria in 1937 as a twenty-year-old Apostolic Church missionary, resigned as Apostolic Church superintendent in Ilesha. Elton began a freelance ministry that greatly influenced Pentecostal church life in Ife, Ilesha, and Ibadan in the wake of what became known as the Latter Rain revivals and opened the way for Osborn's earlier visit to Ibadan in 1957.[55]

From 1967 to 1970 the people of Eastern Nigeria, particularly the Igbo, tried to gain independence in what became known as the Biafran War; people were displaced, churches bombed, and mainstream denominations lost adherents. According to Frances Bolton's eye-witness account, people "wanting spiritual reality" went to the "prayer houses" (African Independent Churches such as Cherubim and Seraphim, Brotherhood of the Cross and Star, and the Celestial Church).[56] Even some people who held leadership positions within local SU groups tried to seek spiritual power in this way. Bolton has argued that it was indignation at this compromising behavior, as it was deemed, that led to a fresh assertion of SU's evangelical position. Thus reinvigorated, it quickly gained new recruits and sparked an evangelical revival in Eastern Nigeria in 1970 and 1971, serving as a counter to the prayer houses' work.[57]

Growth in campus-based groups such as SU was timely, as new, impromptu Pentecostal churches with inexperienced lay leadership were filling the spiritual vacuum in the wake of the war.[58] Lecturers and students coming into prominence in Christian circles helped to change the face of an emerging neo-Pentecostalism that coincidentally was becoming known in Britain in the early 1970s through links established between Julius Coker's church in Benin City and a strand of the emerging British house church

---

55. Ojo, "Campus Christianity" gives Elton's age as 70 in 1987 and documents Latter Rain revivals in southern Nigeria, 1952–54. Vaughan, the Apostolic Church missionary and recorder of Nigeria's early Pentecostal history, left the Apostolic Church in 1947 to become a Congregational pastor in Wales.

56. Bolton, *We Beheld*, 1–10.

57. Bolton, *We Beheld*, 11–20. Further work on this topic has been completed by Burgess, "Civil War Revival."

58. Interview with Leonard Amechi on Oct. 3, 2000.

movement.⁵⁹ The mediator was the former Apostolic Church missionary, Edgar Parkyns, and the main inspiration, a young Nigerian evangelist, Benson Idahosa.⁶⁰

Universities and colleges have been effective environments for evangelical Christian expansion in many countries, not least in Britain.⁶¹ In Nigeria there was a considerable campus-based expansion of evangelical Christianity from the 1970s with growth in many of the evangelical Christian Unions, as well as the SCM (Student Christian Movement). Sometimes it was students that were prominent, such as Wilson Badejo, a veterinary medicine student in Ibadan who was an inspiration to many.⁶² On other occasions it was lecturers. Two mathematics lecturers at Lagos University who took slightly divergent paths have both been extremely influential. In 1973 a young Dr Enoch Adejare Adeboye joined the Redeemed Christian Church of God (RCCG), and Dr William Folorunso Kumuyi started a new Bible fellowship for students in his flat on the Lagos campus.⁶³

The founder of RCCG originally had Aladura links. Josiah Akindayomi, baptized by the CMS in 1927 at the age of 18, and a member of the Cherubim and Seraphim Church from 1931, set up a house meeting in 1952 called the Glory of God Fellowship at 9 Willoughby Street, Ebute-Metta, Lagos, with just nine members. Subsequently, according to reports,

> Pa Josiah Akindayomi also had a vision of words that appeared on a blackboard. The words were "The Redeemed Christian Church of God." Amazingly, Pa Akindayomi who could not read or write was supernaturally able to write these words down. In this visitation, God also said to him that this church would go to the ends of the earth and that when the Lord Jesus Christ appeared in glory, He would meet the church. The Lord then established a covenant with Pa Akindayomi, synonymous to [sic] the Abrahamic covenant in the Bible. He said that He would meet all the needs of the church in an awesome way if only the members would serve Him faithfully and be obedient to His

---

59. Parkyns had connections with pioneer house church leader George North. Hocken, *Streams of Renewal*, 9, 14; Walker, *Restoring the Kingdom*, 42–46.

60. Hackett, "Gospel of Prosperity," 199–214.

61. Johnson, *Contending for the Faith*, 149–72; Barclay, *Evangelicalism in Britain*, 64–69.

62. Ojo, *Campus Christianity*, 194–216. Badejo has overseen Foursquare, Nigeria, since 1999.

63. Amechi interview.

Word. It is upon this covenant that the Redeemed Christian Church of God was built.[64]

On joining RCCG, Adeboye was immediately recognized by Akindayomi as his God-ordained successor. Adeboye became an RCCG pastor in 1975 and took over as General Overseer, not without controversy, on Akindayomi's death in 1981.[65]

Kumuyi was a well-established Christian believer with an Apostolic Faith Church background when he started his campus-based Bible-study fellowship. His student group at Lagos University grew rapidly and was soon meeting in a nearby building belonging to the Redeemed Christian Church of God. In the wake of the post-war revival people were keen to learn more and Kumuyi's Deeper Life Campus Fellowship, as it became known, grew rapidly. Catholics, Anglicans, Pentecostals and evangelicals all attended, with many pastors releasing their premises as well as their members.[66] Kumuyi's level of education had its appeal and the large student membership added credibility. A former Deeper Life attendee described the effect as follows:

> When they [the local people] saw graduates coming out of university professing Christ, they started to follow. So it spread like a bush fire. One of the things that really won many people is that they [the students] went right out to the villages. All these university graduates were beginning to teach because they had been taught well by Kumuyi. He was organized, he was educated and he studied the Bible.[67]

For many, Deeper Life offered more than they had previously experienced, including personal holiness:

> Deeper Life had a way to live. They specified how you should dress. They specified [that the] Deeper Life membership shouldn't have a television. You don't wear your wristwatch. You don't wear your wedding bands. In fact, you don't wed with a wedding gown; you just wear whatever you had [sic]. And there was sense in that. People were poor and could not afford some of those things but it became legalistic and even those who could

---

64. "Man Who Saw Heaven," 4.
65. "Man Who Saw Heaven," 4.
66. Amechi interview.
67. Amechi interview.

afford [them] felt that they could not have these things because Deeper Life said they shouldn't.[68]

At one point Kumuyi sought to reduce his own prominence by functioning with a small leadership team but he still remained central. Everywhere people adopted Kumuyi's emphasis on casual clothes and came to meetings in T-shirts and sandals. If Kumuyi was not in town on Sunday, a tape of Kumuyi would be played in place of his preached sermon, endorsing the impression that only one message was allowed. As there was no shortage of finance, Kumuyi's books and tapes were distributed well beyond Deeper Life. In Lagos, at a time when many pastors had no salaries and could not pay their bills, Kumuyi was on television and radio:

> They were very good with evangelism and house groups. They would hire buses and go to remote parts of Kano where... pastors who were not educated and didn't have money couldn't go. Kumuyi had a very large following from university people who had money who could give better offering, better tithing. So... they could send people out to evangelise in the remotest part of the northern state.[69]

The Nigerian system of Youth Service also contributed to Deeper Life's spread in the north. Young people serving for one year in a location of the government's choice founded Deeper Life study groups. However, impact on Islam was minimal and those attracted were mostly Yoruba, Igbos and Bendalites who had once lived in the south and attended African Initiated Churches. Being study groups, Deeper Life services tended to be less noisy than other Pentecostal services, and in the early days hymns with an organ or piano were preferred to songs with keyboards and drums. However, the organization had its night prayer vigils and healing and deliverance sessions and when congregations prayed, they all prayed at once:

> "Let us pray" and everybody (*finger click*) let loose. [And then to stop], like how they do it in Nigeria, someone leading us say[s] "the Lord hear our prayer in Jesus Name," and sometimes somebody will ring the bell, and everybody stops and you move to the next prayer topic. Especially if you have a large crowd, you have to use the bell or, you know, shout it really loud.[70]

---

68. Amechi interview. Kumuyi's attitude to television became more ambivalent once he was appearing on it.

69. Amechi interview.

70. Amechi interview.

In November 1982 Kumuyi surprisingly announced the establishing of Deeper Christian Life Ministry's church arm, Deeper Life Bible Church.[71] Many had been finding it hard to practice Deeper Life's distinctive teachings whilst continuing in their usual congregations.[72] Deeper Life was also extending from simple Bible study and fellowship to an expectation of healing and miracles.[73] Instantly Kumuyi had established a church of thousands, with many existing churches losing members to Deeper Life as it entered this new phase. Clearly there was an expectation on those holding positions in Deeper Christian Life Ministry to be part of Deeper Life Bible Church.

The rise in Nigerian campus Christianity with its early non-denominationalism and reactionary legalism was not paralleled in Ghana. Pentecostalism in Ghana had early links with the British Apostolic Church and, despite splits, some of the resultant churches had retained an essential classical Pentecostalism.[74] The Church of Pentecost even maintained the strong form of Pentecostal legalism that characterized classical Pentecostal churches worldwide until the 1970s.

> It is expected that all women from the age of puberty onwards should, without fail, wear head-kerchief at church service. If perchance a stranger enters with her head uncovered, she is swiftly met with the embarrassing situation of being escorted outside by a deaconess who will immediately provide her with a head covering for that purpose. Women are not to wear trousers (slacks). To wear a lipstick is seen by many as a sign of moral laxity. At church service women and men do not mix.[75]

As for student non-denominationalism, the breaking down of denominational loyalties on Ghanaian campuses was largely circumvented as the various Ghanaian Pentecostal churches each organized its own separate student fellowships in the universities and institutes of higher education. The Ghanaian Pentecostal researcher, Kingsley Larbi, has explained that these groups had retentional value for the denominations, even if a lack of coherent Pentecostal witness reduced the Christian impact on the campuses

---

71. Deeper Life Bible Church also uses the name Deeper Christian Life Ministry.
72. Ojo, *Campus Christianity*, 305.
73. Ojo, *Campus Christianity*, 301, 303.
74. Larbi, *Pentecostalism*, 32–34.
75. Larbi, *Pentecostalism*, 203.

themselves.[76] He concluded that the student groups raised the intellectual level within congregations at a time when academic attainment in the churches was relatively low, and better educated members risked becoming disillusioned through the lack of contact with others of similar or greater intellectual ability. Some Christian students, however, did become disheartened and were lost from the movements that had initially nurtured them. To prevent further loss the Church of Pentecost created three English-speaking assemblies in the mid-1980s, two in Accra and one in Kumasi, with university students in mind. In 1993 the two in Accra merged to form the Accra International Worship Centre (later the Pentecostal International Worship Centre) and here, significantly, the church's behavioral rules were not enforced, which some have seen as a first indication of a traditional Ghanaian Pentecostal church moving towards a neo-Pentecostal style.[77]

THE IMPORTING OF A GLOBALIZED NEO-PENTECOSTALISM

In Nigeria by the early 1980s students began to reject what many of them saw as the legalism of Deeper Life and the lack of charismatic emphasis within SU and to look towards the greater liberty of American neo-Pentecostalism.

> What we used to have was the SU, the Scripture Union, Bible Christianity, which wasn't really charismatic. But then the charismatic influence began to come in. I think most of it was from the States. We started getting Kenneth Copeland, Kenneth Hagin . . . especially in the university campuses and that added a dimension to it. So people wanted more than they were getting from the churches, even the Assemblies of God churches, Elim, the other Pentecostals, Foursquare. They were a bit rigid. Baptist, especially Baptist![78]

Matthew Ashimolowo, the prominent African neo-Pentecostal leader based in Britain since 1985, was at the Foursquare Bible College in Nigeria in 1974 when he first read a book by Oral Roberts on seed faith. He recollects reading his first Hagin book in Nigeria in 1979.[79] Superficially it would seem that for a number of young Nigerians Hagin's appeal came from his lack of emphasis on the previous priorities of Nigerian Pentecostalism,

---

76. Larbi, *Pentecostalism*, 197–201.
77. Larbi, *Pentecostalism*, 201–4.
78. Interview with Bishop Titus David, October 5, 2000.
79. Conversation with Ashimolowo, August 29, 2003.

The development of African neo-Pentecostal distinctiveness 53

such as regulations about jewelry and dress codes for women. It was put to me quite graphically:

> The influence was also there in most churches. [Women] don't wear trousers; that was traditional. Deeper Life went [further] and the ladies weren't expected to wear earrings, and things like that, lipstick and so on. But with American Christianity, there's nothing much to that. I mean, in India that's their costume. They wear trousers and they are not going to hell.[80]

This greater freedom appealed to the educated youth culture that was already looking to the West. The more positive attitude to prosperity in this new American teaching was also attractive. For many of them, Deeper Life and the traditional Pentecostal churches seemed to have something of a "poverty" spirituality. Ruth Marshall-Fratani made a similar point from her research in the early 1990s:

> The wave of conversions to Pentecostalism which has swept across urban Nigeria in the past decade or so has brought a number of changes in doctrine, membership, organisation and transnational affiliation to the already existing Pentecostal churches which expanded or were established in the earlier revival of the 1970s.... The gospel of prosperity offers a doctrine of morally controlled materialism, in which personal wealth and success are interpreted as the evidence of God's blessing on those that lead a "true life in Christ."[81]

A number of people were key in the initial promoting of Hagin's views in Nigeria but among the most frequently mentioned is Tunde Joda who, as a young medical doctor, set up Christ's Chapel in 1983 in Ikeja, Lagos. He was soon in demand around various university campuses:

> I think the first who really blazed the trail was Tunde Joda. Many of the strong independent church leaders now came out of Tunde Joda's church. It was "the Word," "the Word" that was the new emphasis. It started really gaining ground, '84–'85 [particularly in the] University of Ibadan. They would have conferences and things were spreading.[82]

---

80. David interview.
81. Marshall-Fratani, "Mediating the Global," 84, 85.
82. David interview.

His was not the familiar deliverance, holiness, prayer emphasis but an assertion that "the Word will change your life." However, it was the liberty emphasis that appealed to many:

> When he would come to campuses to speak, some of them would go to his church in Lagos because they found they had a liberty; those, now born again, who don't see any need not to wear trousers or to cover our [their] head[s]. Very westernized! And a lot of the younger folks responded to that. They liked that.[83]

Although Joda had contributed greatly to the early Nigerian uptake of Hagin and Copeland's "Word of Faith" prosperity teaching, others quickly absorbed and proclaimed the same gospel. The university theme was again evident with the establishing of The Redeemed Evangelical Mission (TREM) through Mike Okonkwo. Okonkwo presided over it as its bishop, and its proximity to Lagos University resulted in many students finding their way to his services then continuing in the church on graduating. Not least among the new Nigerian "Word of Faith" proclaimers was Archbishop Benson Idahosa of the Church of God Mission.[84] Idahosa had risen to prominence in Nigeria in the 1970s through his bold public confrontation of secret societies, shamanism, and traditional groups in the area around Benin City. Having initially laid hold of the prosperity message when gaining a divinity diploma from Christ for the Nations Institute in Dallas, Texas, his high profile ensured that in the 1980s he was sharing platforms with American Prosperity teachers both in America and in Nigeria.[85] His onetime associate, Ayo Oritsejafor, went on to work closely with the American Pentecostal evangelist Morris Cerullo. For this new generation of Nigerian neo-Pentecostal leaders, the kind of cultural adjustment applied to early Christian endeavor by their predecessors in re-embracing African traditional practices, had no appeal. There was within their emerging African neo-Pentecostalism a conviction that in a rapidly globalizing Africa the less the cultural adjustment, the greater the cultural relevance.

It was not just a transformation of religious life that these African neo-Pentecostals had in their sights. Marshall-Fratani rightly identifies wider considerations:

> Pentecostal discourse on the current economic and political situation in Nigeria entails a fairly bold attack on the Nigerian

---

83. David interview.
84. Formerly evangelist with Julius Coker.
85. "Men Who Obeyed," 33.

state. In its engagement with local forms of knowledge and practice, it develops an ongoing critical debate about government, one which not only indicts the immorality and inequality at the heart of domination, but does this by using a language and imagery that resonates in the imagination of the dominated. ... Pentecostalism is a political force not merely as a result of successful competition with the religious field—providing the spiritual and material benefits that others did not. Its radical success in conversion has as much to do with the fact that it reconceptualises the moral order, claiming a redemptive vision of citizenship in which the moral government of the self is linked to the power to influence the conduct of others.[86]

One Nigerian neo-Pentecostal known for his political outspokenness from the 1980s onwards was Tunde Bakare. Bakare stood for Student Union president at Lagos University while other would-be Pentecostal leaders aspired to the Christian Union presidency. Although not elected to student prominence, his interest in wider affairs characterized his subsequent Christian ministry. He first gained respect as a Lagos lawyer and then offered legal advice first to Deeper Life and then to RCCG. At the beginning of the 1990s he started Latter Rain Assembly on a large plot of land in Ikeja, Lagos. The size of his building enabled him to host Morris Cerullo's African Congress on Evangelism in February 1992.[87] He then spoke regularly for Cerullo in Europe, Africa and America, joining him for a campaign in Uganda in the summer of 1993.

Widely known for his confrontational comments, Bakare is always willing to speak ahead of events. Two months before the June 12, 1993 Nigerian General Election he declared: "SDP will fail; NRC will lose, be cut off and swallowed up; the military will fail: VERDICT '93 OUR GOD REIGNS."[88] One week later Bakare had thousands of "VERDICT '93" stickers printed, such was his confidence in his proclamation, which he later said was confirmed by a vision described a week before the election:

> In that vision we saw two pieces of fried meat with SDP label on one and NRC label on the other and we saw a fat cat dressed in Nigerian Army camouflage uniform eating and swallowing up both pieces of meat and shortly after the cat was struck down by an arrow that appeared from heaven.[89]

---

86. Marshall-Fratani, "Global and Local," 100.
87. See Robinson and Olaleye "African Congress," 8–10.
88. Bakare, "Prophetic Insight," 4.
89. Bakare, "Prophetic Insight," 4.

Subsequently the Nigerian military declared the 1993 elections void. The deaths of the Military Head of State and of Chief Abiola, the alleged winner of the 1993 election, followed just prior to Obasanjo's election as President in 1999.[90] Bakare stood by another 1993 statement that "the tree of liberty shall be watered by the blood of tyrants."[91] Such outspokenness has continued since Obasanjo has been in power and Bakare had his passport confiscated for a period of some months.

Bakare's "prophetic" ministry underscores Nigerian Pentecostalism's long engagement with what is called the "fivefold" ministry. However, when the Apostolic missionaries arrived in the 1930s with their conviction that God wanted to raise up present day apostles and prophets as well as evangelists and teachers, it is unlikely that they ever envisaged a political prophet as confrontational in the public arena as Bakare. Elton's split from the Apostolic Church over the Latter Rain movement in 1954 only intensified the fivefold ministry emphasis, as the Latter Rain teaching focused on a belief that a final end-time outpouring of the Spirit had come on the church to restore to the highest caliber all the five ministries mentioned in Eph 4:11. These latter-day apostles, prophets, evangelists, pastors and teachers were then to equip the church to new levels of spirituality, supernatural power and authority, and enable God's kingdom to be evident on earth in the present age.[92] This theological argument for a virtually utopianized permanence, counters classical Pentecostalism's doctrine of eschatological imminence.[93] Whilst such extended restorationism is often handled with skepticism, even within neo-Pentecostalism, it does have the potential to bond strongly with aspirations of personal prosperity and socio-political transformation.

Throughout the 1980s Elton's wise hand rested on neo-Pentecostal developments in Nigeria. His personal charisma and gift for fatherly encouragement had a major impact on the neo-Pentecostal movement's rising leaders. This was evidenced by Elton's presence as a speaker at a "Unity Conference" in August 1986 alongside the increasingly prominent independent neo-Pentecostal leader David Oyedepo, and the emerging leaders George Adegboye and Francis Wale Oke.[94] Wale Oke is a leader very different in

---

90. Allegedly Abiola was married to Bakare's older half-sister.
91. Emah, "Transition in Nigeria," 14.
92. For a fuller description of the Latter Rain Movement see Barron, *Heaven on Earth*, 74–79.
93. Osgood, "Some Eschatological and Soteriological Aspects."
94. Ojo, "Campus Christianity"; David Oyedepo leads Winners' Chapel, Francis Wale Oke started "Sword of the Spirit" ministry in Ibadan, 1983. George Adegboye started "Rhema" shortly afterwards in Ilorin.

style from Bakare.⁹⁵ In the early years of the twenty-first century Wale Oke, like the late Archbishop Benson Idahosa before him, sought to promote an episcopal structure within Nigerian neo-Pentecostalism. This appealed to many for whom status in the church was a priority. Other neo-Pentecostals yet to succumb to the fashion for self-styled bishoprics have spoken derogatorily of their newly purple-shirted colleagues, referring to some of them as "warehouse bishops" lampooning their non-cathedral-like premises.

The mixture within Nigerian neo-Pentecostalism at the start of the twenty-first century has three elements: the Latter Rain movement's high expectation of ecclesiastical and societal transformation, the worldly-wise sophistication of an American style "Word of Faith" reaction against "holiness through legalism," and a desire for permanence and status to reverse the poverty emphasis of much early missionary endeavor. In all of this African neo-Pentecostalism's focus was very much on the "here and now" and not on the "there and then" of much early classical Pentecostalism.

CONCLUSION

In this chapter the factors contributing to the emergence of a distinct neo-Pentecostalism in Africa have been traced from early evangelical missionary input to the importation of a globalized neo-Pentecostalism from America. The effects of classical Pentecostal missionary input have been considered and some of the results of indigenization observed. The reaction against more culturally adjusted forms of Christianity since the Biafran war have been set out in two stages, firstly the at times rather legalistic holiness response within Kumuyi's Deeper Life and then the more Westernized response within neo-Pentecostalism's subsequent Word of Faith expression. Whilst these changes preceded the significant upsurge in African immigration into Britain that took place from the late 1980s onwards, they did not stop as the immigration into Britain began.

Developments within African neo-Pentecostalism have continued in Africa even as African neo-Pentecostalism has transferred to Britain. Its ability to perpetuate strong links has been a factor, although not the greatest, in determining the patterns of introduction of African neo-Pentecostalism into Britain. Furthermore, the links that African neo-Pentecostalism in Africa has continued to have with neo-Pentecostalism in America, and especially with the African American neo-Pentecostal community there, have been replicated within African neo-Pentecostal churches in Britain.

95. Wale Oke stood successfully for CU president at Lagos University at the same time as Bakare unsuccessfully stood for the Student Union presidency.

The distinctive fervor of African neo-Pentecostalism (the holiness emphasis of Deeper Life, the newer churches' pursuit of prosperity, the prayer style that assaults heaven, and the prophetic word that seeks to provoke society) appears as much in Britain as in Africa. African neo-Pentecostalism had thus made itself into a definable entity.

In the next chapter I will outline the introduction of African neo-Pentecostalism into Britain.

Chapter 3

The introduction of African neo-Pentecostalism into Britain

IN THIS CHAPTER I will show how an increase in immigration from Africa during the last quarter of the twentieth century facilitated the growth of independent African neo-Pentecostalism in Britain.[1] I will trace this growth through five phases of African neo-Pentecostal church-planting. The first phase, which I will call "constrained to plant," began in the 1970s when a few long-term African residents in Britain, professional and businesspeople, felt the need to gather their fellow nationals for prayer, Bible study, and worship. The second phase, which I will call "sent to plant," began in the mid-1980s when neo-Pentecostal churches in Africa sent representatives to establish branch-churches amongst the growing number of their members in Britain.[2] The third phase, which I will call "transferred to plant," occurred in the late 1980s and early 1990s when a few African church leaders who had been sent to plant denominational churches re-planted completely autonomously.[3] The fourth phase, which I will call "trained to plant," also occurred in the late 1980s and early 1990s when some British Bible colleges began to capitalize on the availability of student visas and so filled their

---

1. African immigration has a long history in Britain. Killingray, *Africans in Britain*. Cartwright cites Ghanaian businessman, T. Brem-Wilson (1855–1929), who led a Pentecostal church in London from 1906. Cartwright, "Back Streets."

2. Sending had started a decade earlier for African Indigenous Churches such as Aladura International, Cherubim and Seraphim and Celestial. Sturge and Aldred, *Black Majority Churches*, 139–41.

3. The growing number of independently minded African neo-Pentecostal Christians arriving in Britain was a factor, as was frustration over inflexible structures within sending organizations.

quotas with African students proposing to plant churches on graduation. The fifth phase, which I will call "called to plant," occurred from the mid-1990s onwards as an entrepreneurial church-planting emphasis dominated the independent African neo-Pentecostal church scene and African church members (untrained and unsent) increasingly set up new independent neo-Pentecostal churches.

CONSTRAINED TO PLANT

In this first phase of African neo-Pentecostal church-planting, African residents, particularly Nigerians and Ghanaians, were drawn together within their national groupings to seek refuge from the cultural adjustments demanded by daily life in Britain. Theirs was not a ghettoized existence; being a scattered community, British culture dominated their work, study, and social life and neighborhood relationships. Initially, many early Nigerian and Ghanaian residents sustained themselves in existing British churches with the support of the Ghanaian Christian Fellowship, which met bi-monthly on Sunday afternoons in Tailstock Place, or of the Overseas Fellowship of Nigerian Christians (OFNC), an organization formed in Britain in 1961. OFNC, being the more structured of the two bodies, not only enabled Nigerians to meet and pray but, where appropriate, provided access to immigration advice. Significantly, with its greater pastoral aspirations, OFNC went on to establish a chaplaincy in conjunction with CMS.[4] Ghanaians, who without such pastoral support were seeking more than their bi-monthly meetings could provide, found encouragement through a few Ghanaian businessmen and professionals who were keen to maintain expatriate spiritual fervor. Four particularly deserving of mention are J. M. Odonko, Mark Adu-Gyamfi, Samson Kwaku Boafo, and Prince Hampel.

J. M. Odonko arrived in Britain from Ghana in the 1960s and trained as an architect.[5] He gathered Ghanaians in south London and variously called his group the Ghana Student Fellowship Church or the Universal Prayer Fellowship. Initially he rented a church building in Beechcroft Road, Tooting.[6] In the 1970s he set up offices in the basement of a home in Balham and this soon became the meeting place for the church. As more and

---

4. OFNC secured charity registration in September 1975, establishing the Nigerian Chaplaincy in 1980. Its first chaplain, Canon Okeke, is remembered for his counselling skills and encouragement.

5. Given as "J. H. Odonkor" in Sturge and Aldred, *Black Majority Churches*, 142.

6. This building is now the headquarters of the Caribbean denomination, New Testament Assembly.

The introduction of African neo-Pentecostalism into Britain

more people arrived from Ghana the basement proved too small and meetings were transferred to the Methodist Church in Brixton. This, however, was not the only change. Some of those arriving from Ghana in the 1970s had been influenced by the new Pentecostal move in their country and would no longer accept the practices of the older "spiritual churches." The arrival of one ardent Ghanaian from Faith Church, Ghana, strengthened the determination of members to rid the church of its ceremonies with robes and candles. Odonko, however, still kept his preference for the title "spiritual leader" rather than minister or pastor.[7] By the late 1970s Universal Prayer Fellowship was not only claiming to be the oldest African church in London but was participating in a scheme for providing two years' theological training for key African and Caribbean church members set up by the researcher Roswith Gerloff at Birmingham's Selly Oak Centre for Black and White Christian Partnership. Even so, it is significant that the changes in this particular group are attributable to the influence of those arriving from Ghana rather than from the impact of British culture and church life.

Mark Adu-Gyamfi came to Britain in 1966. Adu-Gyamfi is not a university-educated man but came to Britain to work. He tells a story of his arriving in Britain with £20, a Bible, and a promise to his mother that he would never forget about God.[8] On arrival he seems to have found no church that met his expectations, so eventually started a prayer meeting in his offices in East London where he conducted his business as a shipping agent from 1972. Those who joined him in his Dalston premises were mostly fellow Asante. Out of this prayer meeting Adu-Gyamfi started a church called "New Life International Ministries." Eventually in 1988 he obtained premises at Manor Park, an old church building near Manor Park Station called St Olave's. He also acquired offices at 627 Seven Sisters Road where he opened a bookshop on the ground floor. As Adu-Gyamfi was still working in the shipping business, he used associate pastors to run the church premises, bookshop, and offices. By the late 1980s "New Life International Ministries" was regarded as London's foremost independent Ghanaian church, serving as a "home church" for some of the Ghanaian Bible college students studying outside the capital. Sam Ohene-Apraku, who became the pastor of Edmonton Temple but was then studying at Harvest College in Cornwall, worshipped at New Life outside of term time. The same is true of Kingsley Appiagyei, who later joined the Baptist ministry, and Frank Ofaso, who led Living Springs Church before moving to America. Even some of

---

7. Interview with Isaac Achene, December 3, 2000.

8. Interview with Jacob Adu-Boamah, October 15, 2000. Adu-Boamah's cousin attended Adu-Gyamfi's meetings first, starting ca. 1980.

those who had come to Britain to attend the Bible School at Victory Church, Hampstead, worshipped at New Life. At its strongest the church numbered around seven hundred.

During this time Adu-Gyamfi did much to further Pentecostal Christianity in Ghana as well as amongst Ghanaians in Britain; he used the money from his shipping company to hire a large stadium in Ghana for the Nigerian Archbishop Benson Idahosa to hold a crusade, and subsequently financed some of Idahosa's trips to Britain. He also facilitated the ministry of prominent Ghanaian church leaders into Britain and in so doing earned considerable respect from his fellow Ghanaians. They say admiringly that when he wanted to bring the then-prominent Ghanaian preacher, Amoako, into Britain and Amoako encountered visa difficulties, Adu-Gyamfi flew to Ghana to "change the minds of the embassy officials." Amoako subsequently resided in Britain until his death, setting up Resurrection Power Ministries.[9]

In the 1990s Adu-Gyamfi's church went through difficulties. Adu-Gyamfi, having stood as guarantor when the office premises were bought in Seven Sisters Road, found himself having to unravel complexities with the Charity Commissioners. As a result, the church split. Some members stayed with Laurence Kese, who was originally the associate pastor, and some went with fellow member Alex Gyasi to form Highway to Holiness. Things were complicated still further when Adu-Gyamfi withdrew for a while and New Life International Ministries not only changed its name to "Light of the Word Ministries" but moved to new premises opposite Tottenham police station. Here Kese was replaced by Mensah-Bonsu, originally an elder at New Life. At the end of 1999, Adu-Gyamfi moved back into the premises at Manor Park and restarted New Life International.[10] This rise and fall of fortunes emphasizes an important cultural challenge. Immigrant churches are not exempt from British charity law with its inevitable constraints on leadership decisions. This is one form of cultural adjustment that cannot be avoided.

A third Ghanaian gathering involved Samson Kwaku Boafo who gained a London law degree and was practicing as a solicitor in Hackney before he began drawing together his fellow nationals. In 1984 nine people met with him for prayer at 72 St Paul's Road, Tottenham, near the Tottenham Hotspur football ground.[11] By 1985 the gathering was sufficiently large to warrant a move to St Saviour's Church, Chalk Farm, and by then there

---

9. Interview with Jacob Adu-Boamah, October 15, 2000.

10. Interview with Jacob Adu-Boamah, October 15, 2000.

11. Interview with Hoffman Frimpong-Manso, October 26, 2000. Frimpong-Manso once served as an assistant minister to Samson Kwaku Boafo.

were Nigerians as well as Ghanaians in the congregation, the organization taking the name Universal Prayer Group (UPG). Three years later in 1988 Boafo acquired a church building in Grove Street, Edmonton, and ran this in conjunction with offices and a bookshop at 328 High Road, Tottenham. In the new church building he held three services a Sunday, the church becoming known as Edmonton Temple and the congregation numbering around twelve hundred. The Grove Street building also became home to the Word of Life Bible College, set up with the assistance of Joel Baker, from Rhema College, Tulsa.[12]

A significant addition to the church in 1988 was Dr. E. K. Brown, a Ghanaian Bible teacher, who had been visiting the church to sell his books since its Chalk Farm days. He subsequently became the Bible College principal and joined the church's leadership team. Shortly after this Sam Ohene-Apraku also joined the team, having completed his Bible College training at Harvest College in Cornwall. In 1992, when Boafo returned from a period of time back in Ghana, the team was reorganized with Ohene-Apraku made pastor. This was still the pattern in 1994 when Boafo moved permanently to Ghana to pursue a career in politics and to oversee the churches he was establishing in Kumasi and Accra.[13] The work in Britain stayed very much under the control of Boafo and two elders who were alongside him from the early days in St Paul's Road.

The unusualness of this diverse, semi-delegated leadership structure may have contributed to the frequent changes in the leadership team around Ohene-Apraku throughout the second half of the 1990s. Frimpong-Manso left in 1995 to set up his own church. Dr. Brown retired as Bible College principal and died in 2000. A number of assistant pastors worked as part of the team for a while and then left to set up their own churches. Adewale Olulana, a Nigerian, set up Harmony Christian Ministries under the oversight of George Adegboye, a prominent Nigerian neo-Pentecostal pastor who frequently visits Britain, and George Hargreaves married a Caribbean pastor who, having left the New Testament Church of God, leads Hephzibah Christian Centre, an independent Pentecostal church in Hackney. Shadrach Ofousuware, son-in-law to Boafo who served with Ohene-Apraku as an assistant pastor for a while, set up a south London branch, South London Temple, in 1998. This, along with Edmonton Temple, remains under the oversight of Boafo, together with the Ghanaian churches. There has also been a UPG branch in Birmingham, adding yet further strength to Boafo's

---

12. Frimpong-Manso interview.
13. Frimpong-Manso interview.

network. Celia Apeagyei-Collins was a support to Ohene-Apraku throughout this period of transition.

The American link mentioned in the setting up of this church's Bible College is significant. It shows that there was an openness to expertise from America whilst little was being done to draw on the experience of British church leaders. Taken overall, however, it was the willingness of these three Ghanaian leaders to work with an egalitarian and eclectic structure that has formed part of their legacy to independent African neo-Pentecostalism in Britain. The lack of denominational ties within their groups meant that the patterns of worship and spiritual encouragement that emerged were largely dependent on the background of their conveners and on the past experiences of those that gathered round them. Each group, however, did have a sense of internal loyalty, despite the looseness of their initial structure, and this may explain their relative isolation, each having virtually no contact with the non-African churches around them except for the hiring of premises. Occasionally in the 1970s and 1980s African ministers would arrive in Britain to take meetings for missionary-minded white church leaders, but often they too came and went unknown to these gatherings of African nationals. In time, some of these visiting African leaders were invited onto the staff of non-African British churches in the hope that such churches could transfer their missionary commitment from overseas to the home front and so begin to attract African immigrants.[14] Even in this, though, there was no consultation with these early African prayer groups.

One Ghanaian ordained minister who did to some extent span the divide between these gatherings and the long-established mainstream British churches was Prince Hampel who was invited to preach at St Paul's Anglican Church in York in 1973.[15] His background had intrigued the vicar as Hampel had been a Muslim into his teenage years and had then gone on to be ordained as an evangelist with the Church of Pentecost in Ghana in 1969. In 1971 he had left the Church of Pentecost to set up his own ministry, Bethesda. It was as an independent minister that he first visited Britain and it was in such a capacity that he decided to emigrate to Britain in 1983.[16]

---

14. Some Elim churches adopted this practice. Abraham Lawrence and the late Charles Sarpong, émigrés in London, were recruited by New Court and Rainbow Churches respectively.

15. Not all Ghanaian ministries came to preach. Kwaku Frimpong-Manson, now a community leader in Broadwater Farm, North London, initially visited Croydon in 1985/86 to record singing tracks. He moved to Britain permanently in 1989.

16. The Church of Pentecost itself planted a London branch in 1988 and in 1994 affiliated with Britain's Elim Foursquare Gospel Alliance to become the Elim Church of Pentecost. See p. 77 of this book.

Hampel originally had no intention of planting a church but relates how in September 1984 he was invited to a hairdressing school's graduation party in Brixton and asked to bless the food. He ended up being asked to pray for a Caribbean guest with an injured eye, which he did by blessing some water and washing the eye with it. When a recovery was effected, the woman and her husband started coming to Hampel's then home at 19 St Julian's Farm Road, Norwood, as the nucleus of a church congregation.[17] The fact that his early congregation was predominantly Caribbean Indian rather than Ghanaian provides an example of a cross-cultural gathering but, as with the other early church-planters, Hampel's actions were still more the result of an individual being constrained to meet a need rather than of a highly focused church-planter being determined to break fresh ground.

In overview, this first phase of independent African Pentecostal church-planting was a time of minimal adjustment to local culture, characterized by a considerable degree of isolation from the wider British Christian community and a lack of internal cohesion.

SENT TO PLANT

The leaders sent to Britain as church-planters in the mid-1980s by Africa's independent neo-Pentecostal churches were as varied as those sent by the African Indigenous Churches two decades earlier; some were senior denominational leaders, some were not.[18] The first of the African neo-Pentecostal churches to send a church-planter to Britain was Deeper Life Bible Church who sent Pre Ovia in 1985. Later that year, Foursquare, a Pentecostal denomination with a rather different genesis, followed suit sending Matthew Ashimolowo. New Covenant then sent Titus David in 1986 and RCCG sent David Okunade to start officially in 1990, although it did have an unofficial congregation gathering in London from 1985.[19] I will consider the leadership and development of each of these four initial trans-continental church-plants. Given that all four are Nigerian and that Ghanaian denominational church-planting took a different route, I will conclude with a comparative comment on church-planting by the Ghanaian Church of Pentecost.

With a high proportion of graduates among its Nigerian membership, it is not surprising that by the mid-1980s many Deeper Life adherents were seeking, and finding, employment in Britain. However, as Nigerians did

---

17. Interview with Prince Hampel, October 8, 2002.
18. The African Indigenous Churches are outside the scope of this study.
19. Hunt has given this date variously as 1985 and 1982. Hunt and Lightly, "Growing a Church," 13.

not require visas until 1988, there were also many potential Deeper Life members who, according to the couplet common among Nigerians, "came to shop and decided to stop."[20] It was into this seemingly promising field that Deeper Life sent Pre Ovia to plant its first British branch. When Ovia arrived in 1985, he came expecting his family to follow from Nigeria later and stayed for some months in the home of a long-term Nigerian resident, Mark Olatunji, who taught in the British state school system and had built up good relationships with non-Nigerian churches. This provided an important transition for Ovia who had first joined the Deeper Life Bible study group as a practicing engineer in Kano where he rose to become joint "zonal" leader with a local lawyer. His ordination as pastor had come on moving to Lagos after Kumuyi declared Deeper Life to be a church.[21]

The first meeting place Ovia secured for Deeper Life in London was the Rockingham Estate Community Hall at Elephant and Castle. With Ovia in position, the expectation at Deeper Life headquarters in Nigeria was that many Nigerians in Britain would immediately make their way to the new Deeper Life branch in search of the familiar. A move towards Deeper Life did actually occur but for many it did not happen directly. Many Nigerians had settled in Victory Church, Hampstead, and at Kensington Temple (KT), Notting Hill Gate. Both of these churches were known in Nigeria, not least because they were churches that Benson Idahosa preached at when visiting Britain. Other newly arrived Nigerians were trying more local options. Some in South London, for example, visited local Ichthus congregations. At the time, however, such congregations were so predominantly white that those recently arrived from Africa felt overwhelmed and longed to find people who understood their problems as newcomers to Britain. It was feelings such as these that eventually caused familiarity and friendship to triumph over geographical convenience. Kumuyi, though, did not just leave it to gradual transfer. He held a crusade at Westminster Chapel, August 25-30, 1986, and filled the building with Nigerians.[22] It was clearly an African immigration crusade, reaching those who had come from Nigeria and who, in Kumuyi's eyes, were in danger of spiritual lapse. Underlying his approach was the view expressed in some Deeper Life quarters that Nigerians in Britain would be happier in a totally Nigerian church and safest in Deeper Life.

From the Rockingham Estate Community Hall, the Deeper Life London branch moved to St Botolph's Church in Lombard Street in the City

---

20. EU-wise, "[i]n 1987 a list of 50 countries, whose nationals would require visas to enter the EU, was agreed." Hayter, *Open Borders*, 59.

21. Amechi interview.

22. Ojo, "Campus Christianity," 305–6.

The introduction of African neo-Pentecostalism into Britain 67

and then in 1988 obtained their present headquarters building in Borough Road, London SE1. By 1990, despite considerable growth, there was still only one branch, but the existence of many house fellowships prompted the leadership to follow Deeper Life's Nigerian pattern and decentralize. The decentralization program was implemented in 1991 through the merging of house fellowships on a locality basis to form eight satellite churches. The timing proved appropriate as many who had arrived from Nigeria as singles were now married with children and were beginning to put down roots into local communities. There seems to have been no shortage of finance to facilitate the decentralization project as a high expectation on giving has always been part of Deeper Life's preaching on congregational commitment. In South East London, for example, by the mid-1990s the Deeper Life house fellowships in Ladywell, New Cross, Deptford and Brockley had joined together and bought a large Anglican church on the South Circular Road at Dulwich.[23]

With such developments in Britain, the role of Ovia, who by the late 1990s was in his fifties, was expanding. The new leaders, either rising from the ranks of long-serving members or brought over specifically from Nigeria, all traced their accountability to and through Ovia, acknowledging the trust his loyalty had won from Kumuyi. By the turn of the century, some London boroughs had several Deeper Life congregations and churches had been established in Gravesend, Watford, Leeds, Newcastle, Liverpool, Huddersfield, Nottingham, Birmingham, Manchester and Dublin, though many still used public halls or other churches' buildings. In Europe, Deeper Life branches had been started by members moving on from London and successfully meeting the denomination's expectations of them to start a home Bible study group and then go on to establish a church; all of these, whether in Germany, France, Italy or elsewhere, came to relate to Ovia. Consequently, a hierarchical structure emerged within Deeper Life, a pyramid of command passing through Ovia up to Kumuyi, with Ovia designated European Overseer.[24]

As Deeper Life expanded it also changed its character. "Holiness" regulations proved more difficult to maintain in Europe than in Nigeria. Deeper Life was initially committed to the total opposite of the "prosperity gospel." Deeper Life members would not consider high profile employment because they were not prepared to dress in the way the employers expected. Women were restricted to posts where they could cover their hair and men would not wear ties. The living rooms in Deeper Life members' homes were

23. Amechi interview.
24. Amechi interview.

often furnished with little more than plastic garden chairs and there was no prospect of a television. It was unlikely that they would own a car. For many, such asceticism became a burden and compromise was resorted to. With people choosing to be one thing in their workplace and another on Sundays, the Deeper Life leadership reacted cautiously. Concern was expressed over the possibility of money earned from questionable trade finding its way into the Sunday offerings or being routed back to Nigeria to benefit from the current exchange rate. Kumuyi responded during one of his visits to London by exhorting members not to work if they had no permission and no National Insurance number. In the end a less rigid lifestyle regime was officially accepted, despite the resistance of those who themselves determined to remain unbending. By 2000 Deeper Life was not the Deeper Life of the early 1980s; suits, ties, wedding rings, televisions and cars could all be seen within the membership. It has to be borne in mind, however, that a similar liberalization also occurred within Nigeria. Change was only partly the result of interaction with British social life; there were theological adjustments being made at the heart of the organization.[25]

Turning to Deeper Life's inter-church relationships, for some people progress here was too slow. People left Deeper Life, taking their friends with them to set up new churches. By 2000 most independent African neo-Pentecostal churches in Britain had former Deeper Life members in their congregations. Even so Deeper Life in Britain has not suffered defections as significant as it experienced in northern Nigeria where Ransom Bello, the leader in charge of their whole northern zone of Kano, Kaduna, Sokoto and Maiduguri, left to set up an independent church. In Britain, Deeper Life's losses are balanced by continuing immigration growth as existing Deeper Life members arrive from Nigeria, although this is increasingly challenging with the expansion of Nigerian church options.

Many in Britain's Nigerian diaspora are inclined to see Deeper Life as isolationist. Kumuyi's personality could not be more different from that of the extrovert and outspoken late Archbishop Benson Idahosa of Church of God International and when Idahosa preached at KT and Victory Church it was felt that Deeper Life stood apart, preferring to organize its own large-scale events. However, given that in a little over a decade from its inception in Britain it was able to hold what was essentially an in-house campaign at Millwall Football Stadium, it could be argued that with such support it had no need for such inter-church activity.[26]

25. Amechi interview.
26. Amechi interview.

The introduction of African neo-Pentecostalism into Britain

Over the years, though, there have been isolationist labels. Olatunji was involved in Mission '89 and his death in 1989 in a car accident in France was a great loss to Deeper Life's inter-church relations. Then in the 1990s, Deeper Life appeared in the list of supporting churches for Morris Cerullo's Mission to London (MTL). Knowing that Deeper Life members are taught that they hold truths that others neglect, it is easy to see how, when these truths relate to personal holiness, other churches can seem to them to be in compromise.

As Deeper Life moved on from the Rockingham Estate Community Centre in September 1986, another new African Pentecostal church moved in. The London branch of New Covenant Church was started on the last Sunday of September 1986 by Titus David.[27] There were four people present. The process by which David started this church began in 1984 when he came to Scotland to meet his mother-in-law, his wife being half-Nigerian and half-Scottish. What he encountered church-wise overwhelmed him:

> It was my first time outside of Nigeria. It was cold but I came with all kinds of notions. "Oh! This is where the Gospel came from; let's go and see what's going on there" and I was shocked with what I saw, especially in Scotland, where churches, big nice "cathedrals" . . . you go in . . . 20 people, 25 people! There was one next door to my mother-in-law's place on Bank Street in Glasgow which had been turned into a pub. And I thought "What?" First time outside of Nigeria where if you put two palm fronds together, you can call it church and get people![28]

David, who had been born in Ilesha and raised in Ibadan, wanted to meet the challenge and relocate to Britain. He had been combining business with itinerant preaching since 1982 and the idea of committing to full-time ministry appealed to him. Revisiting Scotland in 1985 for the birth of his first child, he worked temporarily in London to pay for his wife's confinement at the maternity hospital. Christian friends urged him to stay but he returned to Nigeria, a sense of "calling" growing alongside concerns over the low standards of British society. He began preparing for the Baptist ministry.

Whilst his home church in Nigeria, a Baptist church, were delighted at his willingness to give up business for a seminary course, they were less than impressed when he lasted at the college only three days. David accounted

27. David interview.
28. David interview.

for his resignation by labelling his Bible College experience a form of Abrahamic test:

> I was actually in line to register for courses when I knew that I knew [sic] that it was not going to work out for me. It was like a test, like Abraham taking Isaac. I was willing to leave all and shut down the business, which was doing well. We had money. We were travelling and so on. But, you know, later on I realized it was like a test—to leave that and go to the seminary and get going with it. And so when I passed the test, I left.[29]

He not only left the seminary; he also left the Baptist denomination, finding the atmosphere back in his home church less than comfortable. On January 1, 1986, David and his family joined a new church that had started just six months before, the New Covenant Church led by the British-based Paul Jinadu, a Nigerian married to an English woman whom he had met when at the Bible College of Wales in the late 1960s. Although this Ibadan church was Jinadu's first church, Jinadu was already known in Nigeria through his writing and preaching. David had previously hosted him and interpreted for him when David was leading the charismatic fellowship within his Baptist Church. David's opening statement on joining New Covenant was that he saw the move as an interim step as he believed God was sending him to England to minister. Jinadu's rejoinder was that he himself had been trying to start a church in Britain and thought that on his arrival David might be able to work with them. The David family arrived in Britain permanently in July 1986.[30]

The selection of David as New Covenant's British church-planter was very different from Deeper Life's appointment of Ovia. David's time with the organization prior to migration was short and his initial attitude to British church life was negative. He came as a missionary rather than as a gatherer of existing church members. He wanted to see the Christian church in Britain become as vibrant as he perceived the church in Nigeria to be. He had taken time to gather some cultural information in 1984 and 1985 but as a new pastor it would be some time before he could see the positive aspects in British church life alongside its failings. These characteristics made him a different kind of pioneer from those highlighted so far and not being in Britain primarily for his fellow nationals rendered him potentially more open to adjustment to British culture. He was helped in his church-planting by Jinadu's monthly visits and in time it was Jinadu's profile in Nigeria

29. David interview.
30. David interview.

that caused the London church to grow as new immigrants sought out the church from their knowledge of Jinadu's twenty years of Nigerian trips.

Matthew Ashimolowo's initial church-planting experience in Britain was with his sending denomination, the International Church of the Foursquare Gospel. Started in 1922 in America by the Pentecostal evangelist Aimee Semple McPherson, the Foursquare denomination having thrived in America established itself in Africa. Ashimilowo attended the Lighthouse of International Foursquare Evangelism (LIFE) Bible College in Lagos from 1974 to 1976 and then served as the Assistant Pastor of the 2,000-strong Foursquare Church in Shomolu, Lagos, pastored by his now father-in-law. After attempts to enter Canada for further studies, Ashimolowo was sent to Britain by Foursquare in 1985 to found and pastor a London branch of the Foursquare Gospel Church. The church started in Balls Pond Road, Islington with eleven adults and four children and after two moves in search of larger venues settled in Holloway Boys' School.

The prominent American Bible teachers Wilmer and Jean Darnell who were in Britain throughout the 1970s and 1980s also had a background within the Foursquare Pentecostal church network.[31] Their son-in-law was pastor of a Foursquare church in the lower hall of The City Temple, Holborn Viaduct, for a period in the early 1990s. However, this Foursquare church-plant seems to have functioned completely independently from Ashimolowo's Nigerian one. Whilst Ashimolowo's experience of planting a Foursquare branch in Britain is significant in that it represents an introduction into Britain via Africa of a specifically North American Pentecostal denomination, its significance is heightened by the fact that his planting experiment was happening at the same time as others were seeking to accomplish a more direct American plant on behalf of the same original denomination. At the very least this suggests that both sets of pioneers expected there to be something distinctive in what they established.

By the time RCCG in Nigeria prepared the launch of its first official British congregation in 1990 an unofficial congregation had been gathering in London's Baker Street for some years. Although David Okunade oversaw the establishing of the first official parish at the Angel in Islington, North London, it was Ade Okorende who took over responsibility for it when

---

31. The Darnells returned to America in the late 1980s, Jean having exercised a prominent itinerant Bible teaching ministry throughout the 1970s and 1980s and Wilmer, her husband, having run the Christian Life Bible College, firstly at St Mark's Church, Kennington, then at The City Temple, Holborn Viaduct.

Okunade returned to Nigeria and who within seven years had established a number of further "parishes," mostly in north London.

As well as giving himself to church-planting, Okorende began a family-orientated ministry.[32] This involved producing regular pamphlets on topics which he believed to be particularly relevant to Nigerian Christian couples in Britain. His topics were as diverse as "How to ensure your first child is a son" and "What happens if you are being intimate with your spouse at the moment Christ returns and believers are 'caught up to meet the Lord in the air?'"[33] The fact that some non-Nigerian readers were startled by the bluntness of this approach again highlights cultural difference. However, this pattern of a pastor having a personal ministry alongside his or her church responsibility is common practice within RCCG, underscoring the level of ministerial liberty that exists within the denomination from the most junior minister to the most senior. The wife of Adeboye, the General Overseer, runs the vast RCCG conference facility on the Lagos-Ibadan Expressway as her own personal ministry.

If Okorende's focus both in terms of his church leadership and wider personal ministry was exclusively on the Nigerian diaspora, the arrival of another RCCG pastor from Nigeria began to open up other possibilities. In 1993 Tony Rapu, a medical doctor and the pastor of one of the largest RCCG churches in Lagos, followed Okorende in relocating to London. His approach was different from Okorende's from the outset in that he had a vision for a large RCCG congregation to complement the multiplication of parishes that is the standard RCCG approach. He started meetings in the conference room on the top floor of The City Temple, Holborn, and soon saw the congregation, which he named Jesus House, expand to the point where it moved to the Odeon cinema, Leicester Square, and then on to Shepherds Bush. Rapu then handed over the oversight of Jesus House to fellow Nigerian, Agu Irukwu, a lawyer relatively new to full-time Christian ministry. This freed Rapu to start an even more experimental RCCG congregation as a Sunday breakfast meeting in a central London hotel.

International House, Rapu's new church, was distinctive in many ways, not least for the number of young, upwardly mobile white people it attracted. The format of his breakfast services was that a soloist would present worship songs as the food was set aside, then a speaker would bring a gospel message. The whole event was extremely professionally presented with an attractive handout setting out the program for the day with biographical

---

32. Okorende's family ministry was called Chosen Generation Family Ministry. By 1999 it had distributed 105,000 booklets worldwide. "Pioneer Finds New Trail," 13.

33. The "rapture" is part of a dispensationalist interpretation of 1 Thess 4:17.

The introduction of African neo-Pentecostalism into Britain

details of the participants. It was not, however, really typical of RCCG and Rapu's restlessness was evident as he sought more innovative ways to present the Christian message.[34] During the few years of its existence, it achieved cross-cultural appeal through a juxtaposition of the familiar and the unfamiliar. People at ease in a hotel environment were fascinated by a totally unfamiliar packaging of Christian worship and an equally unfamiliar presentation of the Christian message. Rapu made no attempt to completely remove African associations from the event. He realized that far from being a hindrance, any residual African-ness added to the allure. (In reality, in terms of the musical content, the worship was more African American, relying on material borrowed from African-American gospel singers.) Those who found it appealing to have "church" whilst eating a hotel breakfast were obviously more than open to the further novelty of that church being led by highly professional Nigerians. Even when the preaching was by white Christian leaders, the degree of exuberance in the musical presentations ensured the African American ambiance. Despite this experiment it cannot be said that RCCG had by the turn of the millennium secured any lasting success in Britain in terms of reaching beyond its predominantly Nigerian catchment group.[35] Rapu's exercise seems to have been unique. Whilst others who were sent to plant shared his aspirations for impacting British society, his willingness to explore new forms and to focus on the underlying social preferences of his target groups marked him out from his fellow African neo-Pentecostal church leaders.

By way of contrast to Rapu's cross-cultural approach, the RCCG work in London advanced significantly in terms of profile during the mid-1990s when Adeboye, the General Overseer, set up his twice-yearly Holy Ghost Festivals of Life. These all night prayer meetings attracted attention because of the large numbers attending, filling with ease high-capacity venues such as the London Arena in Docklands. They made no concessions to British culture but were a direct import of the events Adeboye had been hosting for some years in the RCCG show-ground on the Lagos-Ibadan expressway in Nigeria. White church leaders began to speak positively of the event and some were invited to be on the platform, but the congregation stayed predominantly Nigerian. This illustrates, as Rapu found, that it takes more than a white speaker to draw a significant white element into the congregation. The prayer nights aided Nigerian diaspora growth in RCCG churches,

---

34. In 1998 Rapu returned to Nigeria and left RCCG to start a work on Victoria Island, bringing his "commitment to excellence" to a worship-oriented church attracting young people.

35. Hunt observed the Nigerian strength of RCCG's British work in his studies of Jesus House. Hunt, "British Black Pentecostal."

and by April 2000 there were sixty RCCG parishes spread over London, Scotland and Manchester, contributing to the standard RCCG growth rate worldwide of three hundred new parishes a year. The global total in 2000 was three thousand.

In evaluating this second phase of independent African neo-Pentecostalism in Britain, it has to be noted that among the leaders sent from Africa to plant branch-churches were some who worked to ensure that the newly planted churches stayed abreast of each other's developments. David of New Covenant in particular sought to maintain links with Ashimolowo and Ovia through the Nigerian Ministers' Fellowship that he set up in the late 1980s. David was joined in this enterprise by a few other Nigerian ministers who had arrived in Britain on their own initiative without having been sent by a parent Nigerian church with branch-planting aspirations. One of these, Abraham Oshuntola, a Nigerian evangelist, was as committed as David to the Nigerian Ministers' Fellowship, seeking to move the project on from its beginnings as, in David's words, a mainly "living room" affair, meeting from home to home in rotation. The member of the fellowship who proved most successful in building relationships outside the Nigerian diaspora, however, was Sunday Fefegha from the University of Science and Technology in Port Harcourt. Unlike most others in the group, he had not been sent to plant a branch-church, although by 1987 he had started one in his home. He had originally come to train and, in contrast to the African ministerial trainees who followed him in the 1990s, he had his focus on an Anglican theological college. Having gained a BA and MA from Oral Roberts University in America and an MPhil from Liverpool, he completed his divinity studies at Ridley Hall, Cambridge, before gaining a PhD in Religious Studies at SOAS, University of London. Whilst church-planting in the capital he formed a friendship with Rev John Stott, Rector Emeritus of All Souls' Church, Langham Place. This illustrates an important point about the possible breadth of relationships formed by African neo-Pentecostal leaders across the British church spectrum. The link between Fefegha and Stott was in many ways a surprising one, given that the convictions evident in Fefegha's church-planting were not those one might expect from his evangelical Anglican training at Ridley Hall. In 1987 Fefegha set up Redemption Ministries. Writing six years later, he disclosed that he had had Pentecostal expectations ("signs following") from the outset:

> The ministry began in Peckham, a highly deprived part of London, as a home fellowship under the supernatural function of the Holy Spirit in March 1987. It has grown to become a

powerful movement, having affected several lives. The ministry is Christ-centred and non-denominational, thus the Lord has always confirmed the Word with signs following. One of our primary objectives is to build up Christian soldiers and disciples beyond denominational barriers.[36]

Fefegha's statement later mentioned "special deliverance meetings for the sick and oppressed, Fridays 7.00 pm."[37] As Stott is not part of the charismatic arm within the Anglican Church, each may have made assumptions about the other's doctrinal stand; certainly Fefegha assumed Stott's support for his deliverance views.[38] Stott may have assumed that Fefegha's training at Ridley Hall had instilled some caution in him about power aspirations and the Holy Spirit's work.[39] Since returning to Nigeria in the 1990s Fefegha has become a Canon in the Anglican Church and serves as Chaplain at Port Harcourt University from this denominational perspective. His time as an independent African neo-Pentecostal church-planter in Britain has proved to be a break in an otherwise straightforward Anglican ministerial career. Despite Fefegha's return to Anglicanism, the Stott and Fefegha relationship stands out as an exceptional example of African neo-Pentecostal and British Anglican collaboration in the London inter-church climate of the 1980s. However, as with Rapu and Adeboye's links with white church leaders, the relationship between Stott and Fefegha was only at a personal leadership level and did not produce ties between the members of the emerging African neo-Pentecostal churches and the existing British church.

By the end of the 1980s David and Oshuntola had closed down the Nigerian Ministers' Fellowship, feeling it to be too exclusive, and had begun looking for other arenas in which to pursue inter-church relationships. The fact that they managed to launch the fellowship in the first place shows that there was a greater degree of corporate thinking among British-based African church leaders in the mid to late 1980s than in the late 1970s and early 1980s. This greater willingness to relate may have stemmed from a greater sense of security in their identity, since as branch-churches they already knew from their African parent churches exactly what shape their church life should take. With such strongly predetermined characteristics,

36. Entry under "Redemption Ministries London" in Vamadeva and Thompson, *Directory*.

37. Vamadeva and Thompson, *Directory*.

38. Fefegha shared this understanding with me in a conversation in 1994.

39. Stott has stated, "I confess to being frightened by the contemporary evangelical hunger for power, even the quest for the power of the Holy Spirit . . . is it a mask for personal ambition . . . to impress, to dominate or to manipulate." Stott, *Calling Christian Leaders*, 41.

it is unlikely that there could be any loss of distinctiveness through interaction. On the surface the group that had most to fear in terms of loss of distinctiveness was Deeper Life, whose anti-materialistic legalism was coming under pressure as members found it difficult to sustain expected dress codes and spartan lifestyles when taking up new posts in Britain. Perhaps it is not surprising that despite David's best endeavors, Ovia was not a regular member of the Nigerian Ministers' Fellowship.

Having observed that relationships between African neo-Pentecostal leaders and their British counterparts were not producing congregational ties, it is important to consider a further aspect of the backdrop against which African neo-Pentecostal church-planting was taking place in the late 1980s. The principle of producing British branches that fully reflected the African parent bodies was providing a sense of identificational security for many, but it was also causing frustration for those prospective congregation members who felt that a different culture required a different response. Despite the efforts of those sent to plant branch-churches, Africans who had arrived in Britain for study or business were at liberty to worship anywhere and some white-led London Pentecostal churches were actively seeking new African immigrant members.

KT, for example, an Elim church in Notting Hill Gate, London, then led by Wynne Lewis, had nurtured a high profile in Africa through regular staff and team visits for participation in missions and conferences. It was not unusual for KT staff members to be on the platform for the Reinhard Bonnke campaigns in his endeavors to hold evangelistic campaigns "from Cape Town to Cairo" throughout the 1980s.[40] By the mid-1980s KT was known in Pentecostal circles in Nigeria, Ghana, Uganda and Kenya and major African leaders from these countries were beginning to be invited to speak at the church in Notting Hill Gate. As one of my interviewees expressed it,

> [In the] early days, the only church we knew back home in Nigeria that was, you know, alive and where you could direct people was KT. KT had gained popularity in Nigeria such that [if] you were going [to the UK] you went to KT. It was the church to go to.[41]

---

40. The minister at KT, Colin Dye, was with Bonnke in Burundi in early 1989, just two years before leaving his post as Principal of KT's Bible College (the International Bible Institute of London) and becoming the Senior Minister.

41. Amechi interview.

This competitiveness could easily have undermined the emerging African neo-Pentecostal branch-churches but from the late 1980s onwards the balance was partly restored by support from senior Nigerian church leaders. Whilst they were often invited to preach at British denominational churches to increase these churches' appeal to prospective African congregation members, some also gave time to their fellow African church-planters. Among such leaders were Tunde Joda of Christ's Chapel, Lagos, George Adegboye of Rhema, Ilorin, Tunde Bakare of Latter Rain, Lagos, and Mike Okonkwo of TREM.

Eventually Okonkwo had a London branch, set up by some members of his Lagos church who moved to Britain. Joda, however, delayed starting his British branch until he had moved his wife and children to Britain so the children could have British schooling. He then travelled several times a month between London and Lagos, leaving the British branch-church in the hands of his wife whilst he ran the churches in Nigeria. Bakare, despite setting up a similar Britain/Lagos arrangement, again for the sake of his children's schooling, never instigated a British church-plant. The comings and goings of such men contributed to the creation of a West African neo-Pentecostal microcosm in Britain that for some strengthened the reasons for staying in the African-led churches. The existence of such a strong itinerant African support base also reduced the need for newly arriving African church leaders to build strong relationships with existing British church ministers. With experience-based advice readily available from familiar sources, the need to form more local mentoring relationships was reduced.

Given these patterns of church-planting and support prevalent within the Nigerian community in the late 1980s, the course of action adopted by the Ghanaian Church of Pentecost is particularly intriguing. In Ghana the Church of Pentecost has a long history tracing back to the input of Apostolic Pentecostal missionaries in the 1930s. The London branch of Church of Pentecost was planted in 1988 under the local leadership of Kwame Blackson. In 1994 it became the Elim Church of Pentecost through affiliating with Britain's Elim Foursquare Gospel Alliance. In his study of the changes that took place in this process, Emmanuel Kwesi Anim looked beyond the decision of the Ghanaian church to link with a British Pentecostal denomination and considered more fundamental changes by comparing salvation as understood by the Church of Pentecost in Ghana with salvation as perceived by its British branch:

> The Church of Pentecost at present is in a situation of struggling to hold in tension, not only the ethos of the old paradigm as experienced in Ghana and the new in Britain but also the entire soteriological motif which underpins both traditions. Whilst mission theology in the Church of Pentecost in Ghana has been characterised by intense experiential pneumatology and expectant eschatology, mission theology in the church in Britain on the other hand has been characterised by the concept of humanisation, as an expression of love and identification with the suffering and marginalised.[42]

What he discovered was that fresh impetus could be added to a longstanding work by a relatively minor change of emphasis, in this case a shift from a mission strategy fronted by personal demonstrations of the Holy Spirit's power and the proclamation of Christ's imminent return, to a community outreach approach expressed through compassion. His concept of tension between Ghana's old paradigm and Britain's new paradigm highlighted the fact that frustrations with old ways of doing things, which began to surface in a country of origin, can become heightened in the face of relocation. A re-presentation of church program is one way of rekindling the motivation of church members. Anim explored seven areas where Ghanaian culture and British culture differ, all of which can contribute to a raised sense of the need for change in church life and ministry: attitudes to time, communalism versus individualism, theocracy versus democracy, absolutism versus relativism, family dynamics under the influence of pervasive television, finance, and immigration and visa issues. In the light of Anim's analysis the challenge for the London branch of Church of Pentecost would lie in the delivering of appropriate, even pragmatic, solutions to the problems he had conceptualized. The experience of other churches that have planted into Europe from Africa indicates that it takes time to move from a concept of compassionate community outreach to the delivery of community action programs.

Gerrie ter Haar has researched one particular Ghanaian "African Initiated Church" in Holland, The True Teachings of Christ's Temple, founded in 1981 in the Bijlmer district of Amsterdam.[43] She sought to analyze the impact that this particular congregation had by way of cross-cultural community-wide social action. Significant was the painful yet unifying effect of a 1992 aircraft crash involving some of the high-rise blocks inhabited

---

42. Anim, "Paradigm Shift," 69.
43. Ter Haar, *Halfway to Paradise*, 30–40.

The introduction of African neo-Pentecostalism into Britain   79

disproportionately by the immigrant communities.⁴⁴ She was also able to cite an example of the church helping a Turkish Muslim family after a house fire.⁴⁵ Most of her findings, however, related to mono-cultural support leading her back into socio-spiritual considerations:

> Some commentators have claimed that the social problems of African communities in Europe receive too little attention from their churches, which prefer instead to concentrate on the spiritual aspects of mission. This observation reflects a conventional sociological perspective which errs in failing to take account of the important fact that, for the believers, their social network includes both the visible and invisible world. Exclusion of the invisible from an academic analysis of religion precludes the possibility that spiritual welfare may have an effect on people's social life in the material world. It is not necessary to be a believer in any sort of religion to appreciate this point, as the connection between psychological and physical or social well-being is well established.⁴⁶

Setting ter Haar's findings against those of Anim suggests that there could be an underlying cycle that moves churches from a spiritual emphasis on mission to a more practical outreach focus and back again. Delivery challenges may play a part in this as programs to meet the needs of the wider community are not only hard to initiate (major tragedies notwithstanding) but hard to sustain. When wearied with outreach, attention returns to the congregation and spiritual needs are re-prioritized.

Anim's conclusion reflects Gerloff's observations on trans-national church-planting:

> Like most African Caribbean churches in Britain, the Church of Pentecost has much to offer: a spirituality of belonging, so relevant in fragmented Europe; the enrichment of community life; theologising at the grass roots, full of vibrancy and meaning to life; a healing ministry which seeks salvation for the whole person; and pastoral care identical with social action and evangelism.⁴⁷

---

44. Ter Haar, *Halfway to Paradise*, 42.
45. Ter Haar, *Halfway to Paradise*, 42.
46. Ter Haar, *Halfway to Paradise*, 45.
47. Anim, "Paradigm Shift," 70. His related footnote states: "Gerloff, R. *Pentecostalism in the African Diaspora* 1996. Cited in Whittaker 1997:12. Emphasis mine." See Whittaker, "Black Spirituality," What emphasis Anim added is unclear. For Gerloff, see bibliography.

There are some weaknesses in this conclusion as it reveals strong presuppositions. Europe is described as fragmented and it is implied that its communities are in some way deficient, its theological input generally hierarchical and lifeless, its soteriology compartmentalized and its pastoral care unlikely to be combined with evangelism and social action. However, disillusioned European Christians and optimistic African Christians do at times use such terms to express a hope that a transformation can be wrought through African and Caribbean input. If the challenges are there to be met and African and Caribbean Christians are the people to meet them, it will take embeddedness in society to achieve these things; a greater embeddedness than would normally have been attained by a church such as the Church of Pentecost that at that time had only been within Britain for a decade. Relevant self-theologizing and truly cross-cultural, community-wide social action agendas take time to evolve.

Overall, Anim's observations notwithstanding, this "sent to plant" phase of African neo-Pentecostal church-planting into Britain in the late 1980s was characterized by a lack of significant cultural adjustment. In some ways this is not surprising as the planting of branch-churches was to the fore and they deliberately bore a strong resemblance to their African parent bodies. Furthermore, for many in the African diaspora there was still a preference for the familiar. However, it is probable that such unmodified introductions would have been much harder to achieve if these churches had clung to a less flexible form of Pentecostalism during their emergence in Africa. By definition, being neo-Pentecostal, most had relatively recently updated their theology and praxis. New Covenant was a relatively young church in Nigeria and still saw itself as a new church for a new era as it moved into Britain. RCCG had undergone considerable change in Nigeria with its leadership passing from Akindayomi to Adeboye in 1981.[48] Deeper Life had its inner stresses, but even so it had seen some changes in Nigeria prior to its planting in Britain, rules had relaxed and it had developed a healing emphasis.[49] Arguably, the churches facing the greatest internal pressure to adjust culturally were those that had undergone least change in their own country in the lead up to trans-continental planting. The challenge seems to have been greatest for Foursquare as a denominational missionary church. As such it provides the closest parallel to the Ghanaian example outlined above. Its development in Britain was to be marked by a departure that has

48. "Man Who Saw Heaven," 4.
49. Ojo, *Campus Christianity*, 303, 305.

proved remarkably significant for British African neo-Pentecostal church growth; it was the subject of a transfer of leadership and this is the category of church-planting I will consider next.

Although the trans-continental planting of branches dominated the introduction of independent African neo-Pentecostalism into Britain in the mid to late 1980s, it did continue beyond this period. The emphasis shifted, though, from the original desire to provide a spiritual home for overseas members to that of adding prestige to the church back home. As one Nigerian pastor explained,

> They actually announce in Nigeria they have got a branch in London; maybe only one person and in somebody's home but they have a branch! They know there will be funds coming from London and with a bad exchange rate they know that if your headquarters is in London then obviously you get your musical equipment, you get you PA systems and things; you have financial advantage and that draws people. In Africa music draws people. If you have all this equipment and all this PA system and your church is above average, instead of benches you have got nice chairs to sit on, people are drawn. And the fact that, you know, you have your headquarters and your pastor will come from abroad, maybe with foreigners, it boosts the image of the church so . . . financial support![50]

The African church leaders who were sent to plant in the mid to late 1980s were subjected to forces that pulled them simultaneously towards integration and isolation. No two leaders responded in a totally identical way and, for some, selecting a point between integration and isolation that fitted their style and convictions became a painful process. By the early 1990s, two of those who were sent to plant in the mid-1980s had moved on from their sending churches.

TRANSFERRED TO PLANT

Titus David and Matthew Ashimolowo both left their original churches to plant independently. New Covenant has grown considerably since David's departure, although from time-to-time other leaders have also transferred out to plant independently. Ashimolowo's departure has minimalized Foursquare's London presence so the denomination in Britain has never reflected its strength in Nigeria.

50. Amechi interview.

For David, his departure from New Covenant in 1988 can be attributed to a minor internal disagreement and some random external prompting. When interviewed, David sought to play down the disagreement aspect, simply saying that there were things that were "just unsatisfactory, so that led to prayer."[51] Whatever these "unsatisfactory" issues were, they certainly had nothing to do with any desire on the part of Jinadu, New Covenant's International Overseer, to take over the London church; in many ways Jinadu seems to have been reticent to take the lead. The "external prompting" dimension centered on a conference in Peterborough led by Colin Urquhart, the former Anglican vicar from Luton who went on to oversee the independent charismatic Kingdom Faith Ministries in Horsham. David went to the Peterborough conference in 1988 in a state of personal uncertainty. It seems that he was not even sure that he should have been attending. His future within New Covenant was weighing on his mind and he was looking for answers. His decision to move on did not come from dispassionate evaluation:

> There, in one of the ministers' sessions . . . he [Urquhart] spoke forth the word and I knew that was for me. So I said, "Lord, if he repeats it within the next 10 minutes, 20 minutes, I will take it as confirmation" and he repeated it. I knew then that I knew [sic] . . . that this was God . . . to leave.[52]

On the basis of this, David returned to London and told Jinadu he would be leaving. Twelve years after the event David still seemed to be regretting the way he had shared his decision: "I overstated some things and overdid some things I shouldn't have done . . . and saw some things I didn't agree with and said so too strongly . . . and repented over and over and apologised to him many times."[53]

Despite these regrets, David was still convinced that God had told him to leave and, moreover, that God had given him the blueprint for a new church. The vision for Christ Family Church came to him on the night of September 5, 1988 and by October 16, he was holding its opening service. He arranged it for 5:00 p.m. so as not to offend New Covenant. That morning New Covenant had held his farewell service and with a sense of nervousness at starting out afresh he felt he needed some sign of divine approval:

---

51. David interview.
52. David interview.
53. David interview.

I had my family with me so we started all over again, you know, started from scratch. And I asked God for a sign. I said "Lord, on the first Sunday let there be twelve there, like you had, twelve disciples; that would be a sign that I'm on the right track" and apart from us there were twelve there, so I said, "OK, good sign!"[54]

Over the years ministers have also transferred from Christ Family Church to plant their own churches, with David's co-pastor leaving him to join RCCG.[55] Whilst it is tempting to trace a trajectory of transferring to plant from Urquhart through David, the more obvious consequence of David's contact with Urquhart was David's growing commitment to integration with non-African churches. It was around the time of his attendance at the Peterborough conference in 1988 that David concluded that his Nigerian Ministers' Fellowship was too exclusive. He briefly considered an African Ministers' Fellowship but then encountered the Afro-Caribbean Evangelical Alliance.[56] Undaunted, five years after the organization's foundation, David was bluntly asking its new General Secretary, Joel Edwards, "What about us Africans?" In David's opinion the recent name change from "West Indian" to "Afro-Caribbean" was insufficiently inclusive and for him the "African Caribbean Evangelical Alliance" would have been better.[57] Edwards listened and David and his colleague, Oshuntola, were warmly welcomed. It still seemed strange to David, though, to be separating out black from white and he reacted when he heard the separation justified: "I think at that meeting they thought I was very naïve.... But still, when I became part of the leadership on the executive of ACEA, somehow I was never really satisfied with it. So I kind of faded away, which some people probably didn't like."[58]

In many ways David seems to have been ahead of many of his fellow African church leaders in being so committed to a unity that crossed all racial barriers. These cross-cultural attachments undoubtedly played a part in his decision to transfer and re-plant. They were also his major preoccupation

---

54. David interview.
55. Andrew Adeleke, the Pastor of House of Praise, Woolwich.
56. The Afro-Caribbean Evangelical Alliance, founded as the West Indian Evangelical Alliance by Philip Mohabir in 1984, changed its name in 1989. Aldred, *Respect*, 105.
57. In 1991 it changed its name to the African Caribbean Evangelical Alliance and in 1993 to the African and Caribbean Evangelical Alliance. Aldred, *Respect*, 105.
58. David interview.

after planting Christ Family Church, even though the church remained predominantly Nigerian.[59]

Matthew Ashimolowo—a case study

Ashimolowo left Foursquare to start Kingsway International Christian Centre (KICC) in September 1992.[60] He believes God gave him the vision for KICC in the early part of that year and is convinced that much of KICC's growth can be attributed to its independence from denominational ties. The church began with three hundred adults, using rented accommodation in Holloway until they purchased a building in Darnley Road, Hackney. Here they eventually accommodated a thousand people, maximizing their capacity by holding four services a Sunday.[61] Within a few years, pressure of numbers and challenges with parking (Darnley Road is in the midst of a residential area) prompted the purchase of a former warehouse property in Waterden Road, Hackney. Here parking problems were minimized by virtue of the area's industrial status but access by public transportation was poor. The new main auditorium could seat four thousand.[62]

Ashimolowo's conviction that such growth was attributable to independence from denominational ties is not entirely straightforward. People who would never join a denominational church do not automatically join an independent one; they might prefer to stay unattached. Furthermore, many congregations within the African Pentecostal denominations differ little in their style of worship from independent neo-Pentecostal churches. Their members may be aware of some denominational requirements concerning, say, courtship and church discipline, but many independent African neo-Pentecostal churches have similar regulations and expectations. The main differences come at a leadership level. The minister in charge of an independent church has much greater freedom when it comes to decision-making and he or she automatically is able to use a stronger and more personalized style of leadership to motivate his or her members, as there is no need to pay heed to an over-arching denominational identity.[63] Ashimolowo was quick

---

59. David was killed in crossfire in Nigeria as police attended a street crime on Feb. 8, 2002. The Memorial service at Ruach Ministries, Brixton, was led by Ashimolowo. I led the committal with Jinadu.

60. KICC, "Birth of KICC," 5.

61. KICC, "Birth of KICC," 5.

62. Rosman records "some six thousand worshippers attended a three-hour service" for the opening of the Waterden Road premises on Aug. 23, 1998. Rosman, *Evolution*, 316.

63. "Automatically" is a key concept here. Some trusted ministers in denominational

to establish a strong identity for KICC through conferences, television and radio and an efficient use of public relations.

Given the need for extensive organization and a level of attendance high enough to be economically viable, large conferences in London have traditionally been planned as inter-church rather than single church events. There is no doubt that as KICC grew in size, Ashimolowo found himself moving into a different position, where he alone could set the agenda. Initially this was not the case. For a brief period in the early 1990s, Ashimolowo, who by nature likes to work alongside others, served on the steering group of the London Leaders' quarterly prayer gatherings initiated after Graham's Mission '89. More importantly, from 1993 he played a key leadership role in Morris Cerullo's MTL; this afforded him some prominence. However, the demands of a large church are such that their leaders have to be selective about time committed to inter-church projects and this does not always make for easy inter-church relationships. There is a correlation between the extent of Ashimolowo's involvement in MTL and the growth of KICC's own conference, the Gathering of Champions, which Ashimolowo began at the birth of KICC.

Cerullo started MTL at Earls Court 2 in the summer of 1992 with a large cast of international speakers. From the outset the event was marked by strong support from London's African churches as well as from members of the Caribbean denominations. One researcher, Nancy Schaefer, described it as embodying "the competing tensions between commonality and diversity, the global and the local at one and the same time . . . tailored to a specific 'niche' in the UK religious market place; that is urban African Caribbean and African migrant churches."[64] Ashimolowo's presence on the platform from 1993 onwards helped to bring some local African leadership to the event. However, his involvement came at some personal cost as the Cerullo mission was never more than a few weeks away from his own event. Despite this dual commitment, by 1994 Cerullo was letting it be known that he intended to hand over the leadership of MTL to key London church leaders and it seemed that Ashimolowo was in mind, along with the leaders of KT and me as the leader of Cornerstone Christian Centre, Bromley. In 1996, however, the chairmanship of MTL passed from Cerullo to Colin Dye of KT, possibly as a result of Dye's concern that a three-person leadership might not work. He had rightly observed that the congregations of KICC and KT were struggling with the growing prominence of their respective

---

churches appear to be given similar freedom in decision-making and exercise an equally personalized leadership style. Independent church leaders are also accountable to the church trustees.

64. Schaefer, "Morris Cerullo's London Revivals," 103–23.

leaders, neither church quite understanding why on occasions the leader of the other church appeared to be given the higher profile. Since this was making even platform etiquette at MTL increasingly challenging, the pressure it would have placed on a joint leadership is easy to imagine. Cerullo sought to explain the decision to Ashimolowo by speaking enigmatically of "a head needing eyes and ears," presumably implying that Ashimolowo would not be redundant under Dye's chairmanship. Lack of leadership role notwithstanding, Ashimolowo did continue to attend MTL for a few years as a guest speaker at Dye's invitation, as did Cerullo. Surprisingly, it was Cerullo who felt the strain of this ahead of Ashimolowo, and by 1998 Cerullo was preferring to preach at Ashimolowo's Gathering of Champions rather than at the event he had founded. This was an early indication that Gathering of Champions was growing at MTL's expense.

1998 proved to be the last large-scale MTL event held at Earls Court under Dye's leadership. For the August 1999 event, Ashimolowo's vacant place on the original three-person team was taken at Dye's request by three other London church leaders: John Francis of Ruach, Agu Irukwu of RCCG and Sam Larbie of Camberwell Elim Church. Dye mandated this new team to organize three "regional meetings" around the capital during the "MTL week" as a lead up to what was to be the largest ever MTL planned for August 2000. However, the August 2000 event never happened and the demise of MTL contributed even more supporters to Ashimolowo's already packed and newly renamed International Gathering of Champions (IGOC). It had grown from The City Temple, Holborn Viaduct, via a marquee in a park in Hackney and The London Arena, Docklands, to a large tent specially erected in KICC's grounds at Waterden Road. People transferring from MTL to IGOC faced few challenges as the format of the events was virtually identical, with guest soloists and speakers coming from Africa and America. Concerning the dynamics of such conferences, Schaefer has written that the MCWE organization "freely admitted that it concentrated its efforts on 'ethnic minorities, immigrants and the less educated working classes'" and concluded that MTL's success had more to do with "savvy business strategies and niche marketing than with divine favor."[65] It could be argued from appearances that Ashimolowo is seeking to reach a niche market of educated Nigerian nationals, all strongly committed to self-improvement, but his publicity suggests that he aims for wider public representation. If IGOC has less of a white presence on the platform and less of a Caribbean presence in the congregation than MTL had, it is partly because Dye's staff

---

65. Schaefer, "Morris Cerullo's London Revivals," 117, 119.

contributed to MTL's white platform presence and Cerullo had a large Caribbean following.⁶⁶

Ashimolowo's use of television and radio has also played a part in building KICC's identity. In 1994, within months of Cornerstone Christian Centre starting to supply the Identity Channel (IDTV) with its regular Sunday service for broadcasting across the capital by cable, Ashimolowo was approaching IDTV prepared to pay for the privilege of airtime. Later, when Cornerstone Christian Centre staff members set up the satellite television station Christian Channel Europe, Ashimolowo was among the first to approach them for airtime.⁶⁷ He was also one of the earliest ministers to make extensive use of the promotional opportunities of Christian radio, working closely with Premier when it was re-formed out of London Christian Radio in March 1997. He had a former Capital FM "DJ" in his congregation, Benny King, and King's transfer to Premier opened the way for Ashimolowo's broadcasts. Premier has come to regard the consequent relationship as a providential synergy. Peter Kerridge the Managing Director of Premier stated when interviewed,

> The radio station had lost its way . . . then Matthew [Ashimolowo] showed an interest. We had been talking to KT and All Souls' but Matthew had sussed that the black churches were tuning in for Benny's late night gospel show and he wanted to sponsor that so we did the deal. . . . The black churches had never been a major revenue driver, far from it, but the black church is media savvy. All the leaders have American role models (Matthew has Eddie Long in Atlanta) and they see media ministry and say "Could we do that?" They find Premier and bang! They want to be involved. The growth is partly spiritual but also Premier has its own audience and so brings in people for their conferences. Churches are growing because of Premier.⁶⁸

Kerridge's enthusiasm for KICC is in many ways surprising as by background Kerridge is an ordained Baptist minister who finds himself personally at odds with any overt emphasis on wealth and a positive confession theology. However, he explains Ashimolowo's approach to both topics as simply motivational and has accepted Ashimolowo's assurances that there is

---

66. Schaefer provided a description of a standard MTL evening rally. "Morris Cerullo's London Revivals," 110–12.

67. Identity Channel became part of the American company Black Entertainment Television and was shut down by the parent company because it was not attracting the levels of "white" viewing being secured by the channel in America.

68. Interview with Peter Kerridge, Mar. 23, 2004. "All Souls" is the evangelical Anglican church in Langham Place next to the BBC.

a substantive difference between the message he preaches and that taught by the American television evangelists that Kerridge has come to assess negatively.[69] In reality all the elements of the prosperity message are present in Ashimolowo's approach but he has to some extent repackaged the message with British sensibilities in mind. He is careful to talk about success rather than wealth and avoids the apparent crassness of "name it and claim it" terminology. His central theme, borrowed from American baseball player Yogi Berra, is "it's not over until it's over" and he uses this to encourage persistence and to help people overcome disappointments and setbacks.[70]

There is a high degree of professionalism about the promotional aspects of Ashimolowo's ministry since he has moved on from Foursquare. As KICC has grown he has employed public relations consultants for his advertising and conferences. Much of the promotion leads on Ashimolowo's personal success in ministry, marketing the exceptional nature of all his accomplishments in preaching and publishing. His photograph is given prominence and no opportunity is missed to give statistics of possible audience reach for his various radio and television programs, these footprint figures being preferred to the lower numbers registered for actual viewers. Even the genuinely unassuming aspects of Ashimolowo's character, such as his preference for being called "Pastor Matthew," are made much of and promoted as symbols of his accessibility and humility. The church's achievements and characteristics are marketed in a similar way in the conviction that success attracts success. Although the Nigerian attendance at KICC is particularly high, Ashimolowo's longing for a truly multi-cultural church comes across in his presentation of attendance patterns. By reporting on a somewhat tokenistic basis, his publicists are able to describe his church by saying that "no fewer than 46 nationalities of the world are represented in his congregation."[71] If the statistics were reported proportionately these publicists might have to admit that those who are not Nigerian, amount to less than 25 percent, with those having a background other than African or Caribbean being less than 5 percent. This reality has been known to surprise those living in central Nigeria who view Ashimolowo's British-recorded television output broadcast from Jos and tune in expecting an African-led church in London to be predominantly white.[72]

69. Kerridge's concerns would focus on Hagin and Copeland who have frequently been written against in the evangelical press; both are writers of whom Ashimolowo has spoken positively.

70. Yogi Berra famously said, "It ain't over till it's over." See https://yogiberramuseum.org/about-yogi/yogisms/.

71. Publicity brochure for 2002 IGOC.

72. Interview with Micha Jaga, parachurch leader from Kano state, Aug. 13, 2003.

The introduction of African neo-Pentecostalism into Britain

In the 1990s Ashimolowo made various attempts to locate himself effectively into British church life. One of the ways in which he sought to do this was by appointing a Council of Reference for KICC that included the "new churches" leader Gerald Coates and the Jamaican-born General Director of the UK Evangelical Alliance, Joel Edwards. Such a council was designed to add a wider credibility to his ministry by setting an indigenous diversity around his exclusively African leadership team. Even so, those preferring a standard British denominational leadership model would have considered KICC at the turn of the millennium to be Ashimolowo-centric. The following points, however, could be set out in mitigation. Ashimolowo was not coming across as arrogant. He had a disarming style and was prepared to relate incidents in a way that was designed to show himself in a modest light. Although he was firmly in control of all that happened in the church he was not a one-man-show in that he was delegating well and had some effective assistant ministers functioning alongside him. Significantly no one assistant minister had an overall brief and male and female were given equal opportunity. He also obviously delighted in honoring his wife in public and appeared to be equally consistent in appreciating her in private. He was also respectful of his two teenage sons, allowing them to find their own level in the church in a way that was neither pressurizing nor nepotistic. He was away from the church on regular overseas trips, often holding high profile campaigns in West Africa with "Winning Ways" being a favorite publicity slogan for stadium-packing events for which he called on the support of his friends in America (mostly African Americans) as guest preachers and vocalists. KICC was always competently led in Ashimolowo's absence and there never seemed to be any financial lack, no matter how daunting the project. The church site alone was of considerable value and, with talk of a future British Olympic bid requiring the land for sports development, the potential worth was being significantly enhanced.

It would be easy to ascribe the greater success of Ashimolowo's independent church-plant over that of David's to something as indefinable as personal drive, but that would be an inadequate analysis. Together they highlight the desire on the part of some African church leaders to adjust more fully to the circumstances in which they find themselves within Britain. It does take boldness to leave a structure that has worked well in Africa and to start afresh in Britain with no existing ground rules. Where they differ is that in some ways David was seeking to be the more radical, laying down much that he had observed in terms of the insularity of African Pentecostal life and wanting to produce something more inclusive. In this he was prepared to be a pioneer rather than a populist and it is therefore not entirely unexpected that the church group he left has prospered more in Britain than the ministry he founded. Despite David's desire to focus on British society at large, his core membership, like Ashimolowo's, was still the African/Nigerian diaspora and people, especially relocated people, do prefer the familiar. Ashimolowo has been astute in that he has managed to promote something as fresh which in reality is familiar. In line with his often stated maxim of setting "obtainable goals," he has not challenged people beyond their willingness to respond comfortably. He sees himself as having left behind the old wineskin of a denominational structure (to use the gospel illustration) and as proffering the "new wine" of personal motivation. His safeguard against creating insecurity is that this "wine" whilst new to many in a church context is familiar to most in a business setting. His members can feel unperturbed as their enthusiasm for personal success is taken to new heights through Ashimolowo's stress on biblical themes of victory, persistence and self-worth to inspire them. Ashimolowo has found that his style of church works in the entrepreneurial culture of London's African diaspora in exactly the same way as his fellow pastors who have broken free of the mold of the older Pentecostal denominations in Nigeria and Ghana have found it does in the midst of the upwardly mobile aspirations evident in Lagos and Accra.

TRAINED TO PLANT

At the time David and Ashimolowo were leaving their denominational churches to plant independently, there was a considerable increase in the African uptake of British Bible college places. The two colleges most affected were KT's International Bible Institute of London (IBIOL) and the Hampstead Bible School of Faith at Victory Church in Finchley. Both of these institutions played a significant role in the introduction of independent African neo-Pentecostalism into Britain. The local cultural adjustment they required was minimal. They believed they had a global calling with a "one-size-fits-all" message for the world. Their African students came to believe that the styles and convictions of neo-Pentecostalism they had adopted in Africa were not just national, regional or continental but had international significance. The churches they planted in Britain carried this confidence.

Hampstead Bible School of Faith, Finchley—a case study

Hampstead Bible School of Faith began in 1983, with Victory Church, Hampstead, starting shortly afterwards. It was founded by Michael Bassett, an Englishman who, having lived in South Africa, moved to America from Britain in the 1970s in order to avoid prosecution for involvement in the pornography trade in Soho. His commitment to Christianity stemmed from watching a program on end-time prophecy shown on an American Christian television channel, then shortly afterwards coming across a person in a bar who invited him to a Bible study where he met his American wife, Denise. Together they became involved in Faith Christian Fellowship in Tulsa, a church led by Buddy Harrison whose father-in-law, Kenneth Hagin, is regarded as the father of the Word of Faith movement.[73]

On his return to Britain in 1978, Bassett, under Harrison's guidance, set up Faith Christian Fellowship, Bath, with a Bible School called Word of Faith Teaching Academy that met two evenings a week. Shortly afterwards, there was some interest in Word of Faith teaching within Full Gospel Business Men's Fellowship circles around Britain, reinforced by a couple distributing tapes and videos from their home in Guildford.[74] After Kenneth Copeland had spoken at a Full Gospel Business Men's Fellowship conference in Blackpool in 1982, Bassett began to sense a need for a London-based Word of Faith church and Bible college.[75]

Hampstead Bible School of Faith and Victory Church, Hampstead, began as white, predominantly English, middle-class establishments: according to one interviewee, "almost upper class."[76] The new work soon had a growing ministry team serving in different capacities.[77] Bassett's connection with Faith Christian Fellowship, Tulsa, and Harrison continued to be important. There was also a link with the International Convention of Faith Ministers, an American Word of Faith ministerial organization. Victory Church, Hampstead acquired property in Finchley Road that became the venue for both Hampstead Bible School of Faith and the church. However, there were aspirations for a larger property and attention soon focused on the nearby Lyndhurst Hall, a large church building in Hampstead. Many

---

73. Interview with Kim Freeborn, former European Director Kenneth Copland Ministries, Oct. 26, 2000.
74. Nicholas Noel-Todd and his wife.
75. Freeborn interview.
76. Interview with Mark van Gundy, November 7, 2000.
77. The team included Norman Dix (an early Hampstead Bible School student), Ed Hornback (the pioneer of the "Word of Faith" church in Kent) and the late Chris Pedley (a Birmingham-based British Bible teacher).

church members donated finance for this relocation and lost out when the deal collapsed. By this time, though, the work was established and the college was seeking to capitalize on its recently discovered connection in name and location with the Hampstead College established much earlier by Howard Carter, the Pentecostal pioneer.[78] Those who left because of the collapsed property deal were soon replaced by others, but not from the white British upper middle class. An African transition was underway; the Howard Carter connection proved less important than the Word of Faith connection.

By the mid-1980s it was already clear that the Word of Faith message was proving more popular in Africa than in Britain. The well-established understanding of personal financial responsibility within British Christianity did not readily pave the way for an uptake of the prosperity gospel message. The history of the Christian church in Britain is replete with examples of wealthy people who have used their personal resources for the furtherance of the Christian gospel and have done so without resorting to a radical theological reappraisal that redefines wealth as a specific blessing of spirituality. For centuries the church in Britain has seen wealth as something of spiritual neutrality that carries with it a responsibility for wise stewardship.[79] Furthermore, in the 1980s there had been a Christian reaction against materialism. In 1982, David Sheppard, the then Bishop of Liverpool, made out a biblical case for favoring the underprivileged in his *Bias to the Poor*. He recognized that for wider society "the dominant philosophy in Britain and the United States is that you will naturally want to 'make it,' to go up in the world to give your children a better chance of success."[80] He also recognized that in the church, attitudes could be more ambivalent, observing that "Christianity seems to be saying that poverty is blessed and at the same time we should try to get rid of it."[81] For Sheppard, personal wealth accumulation was not the theme for the church of the late twentieth century. There were those who shared his critique of the self-centered culture of Britain in the 1970s and were prepared to do something by way of personal protest. The emerging British Charismatic Movement had its radical edge. Even those joining the House Church Movement from a middle-class background were expected to enter in to some form of shared

---

78. Howard Carter's Hampstead Bible School is described in Missed, "Peace Prevails," 27–28.

79. For example, the Salvation Army was grateful for its affluent benefactors. Watson, *Hundred Years' War*, 21.

80. Sheppard, *Bias*, 10.

81. Sheppard, *Bias*, 12.

lifestyle.[82] Britain's Charismatic Movement in the 1980s and 1990s seemed remarkably unimpressed by the prosperity message.[83] The fascination with Word of Faith teaching amongst a few in the British business world marked a departure not only from the stewardship concepts prevalent in British church history but from contemporary British Christian social thinking.

In Africa, by contrast, the teaching of Copeland and his associates was coming across as a tool to break the patterns of poverty, appealing to university students in Nigeria as a liberation from legalism and parochialism. Marshall-Fratani has summarized the Nigerian position well:

> Unlike these older churches, typically denominational, emphasising a doctrine of "holiness" and anti-materialism, expressed in the eschewal of fancy clothes, expensive commodities and modern media such as television, and peopled by relatively disadvantaged social groups, these new organisations place themselves firmly in the "world." Typically young, upwardly mobile, relatively well educated, their leaders privilege international contacts and experiences, incorporating . . . this international image in the operation and symbolism of their organisations.[84]

The African transition in the Hampstead church began, not just with the loss of white upper middle-class members, but also as Bassett, keen to demonstrate the global relevance of his church's core prosperity convictions, decided to broaden the teaching base for his conventions by inviting in African preachers such as Nicholas Duncan-Williams, the Ghanaian neo-Pentecostal church leader, and Benson Idahosa, the Nigerian neo-Pentecostal Archbishop. It also helped that other key African leaders visiting Britain, such as Tunde Bakare, the Nigerian barrister-cum-church-planter, were content to sit in conference congregations and listen to the likes of Ray McCauley from South Africa, and Copeland's associate, Jerry Savelle.[85]

---

82. Walker, *Restoring the Kingdom*, 199–201.

83. Tomlinson, former British "house church" leader, sought to find examples of British Word of Faith up-take in his 1990 foreword to McConnell's book, originally published in the United States in 1988 as *A Different Gospel*. Apart from obliquely referring to "some churches in this country—one in Finchley" he has to content himself with non-specific references. McConnell, *Promise*, ix, x.

84. Marshall-Fratani, "Global and Local," 84–85. This quotation does not disclose the fact that many of the young and upwardly mobile had earlier grasped Deeper Life legalistic holiness teaching with equal enthusiasm.

85. Nicholas Duncan-Williams leads Action Faith Ministries in Ghana. The late Benson Idahosa led the Church of God Mission in Nigeria. Tunde Bakare leads the Latter Rain Assembly in Lagos, Nigeria. Jerry Savelle is an associate of Kenneth Copeland from Dallas-Fort Worth.

The major change in the church's non-conference congregational make-up came, however, when Duncan-Williams encouraged his church members in Ghana to register for the Hampstead Bible College course. Key among the early arrivals was Kofi Banful who was to stay on to serve the Victory Church after graduation, initially as caretaker but eventually as one of its senior pastors. Reports soon spread that Victory Church, with its American-style ministry and Word of Faith message, was a good location for upwardly mobile West African students seeking Bible college training in Britain and the college and church quickly took on an African dimension.

It is at this point in the history of Hampstead Bible School that an element of rivalry with Harvest College in Cornwall emerged. I outline the incident not to emphasize the competitiveness but to underscore the appeal to independent African neo-Pentecostal churches of British-based Word of Faith training institutions (be they only two at the time), even though such attraction could have negative aspects. The Word of Faith emphasis at Harvest College came from its founding Principal, Michael McCann. Initially the students were white British residents. McCann's desire to set up a Word of Faith college in Britain began in the mid-1970s, whilst he was Dean at Christ for the Nations College, Dallas, Texas. McCann encouraged his students to commit to Sunday night prayer groups, each focusing on different nations, with McCann himself committing to England. He followed up his interest by bringing a team of students across the Atlantic each year to hold meetings in various Pentecostal churches and denominational churches experiencing charismatic renewal.[86] In 1978 McCann left Christ for the Nations to set up Harvest Bible College in Cambourne, Cornwall. The selection of Cambourne as the venue was the arbitrary result of a large property becoming available as McCann received a sizeable donation from one of his supporters. McCann brought one of his students from the 1977 trip, Mark van Gundy, to join the staff.[87] After a while, McCann developed African aspirations and flying back after preaching for Duncan-Williams in Ghana he persuaded three young Ghanaians, *en route* to join Kofi Banful as students at Hampstead Bible School of Faith, to switch their allegiance to Cambourne on scholarships he would provide. They accepted but then had a less than positive experience as the Cambourne college, in contrast to Hampstead, was renowned for its unequal lifestyles. Not only was there an inequality between the McCanns and other staff but the African students

---

86. Christ for the Nations was founded in 1948 by Gordon Lindsey, a pioneer in the American healing revival, respected within Pentecostal circles as a man of prayer and vision, who brought many of Revivalists together in the 1940s through the Voice of Healing magazine.

87. Van Gundy interview.

suffered even greater privations having their passports confiscated and held in the college safe.[88] In the mid-1980s, accusations were brought against McCann that caused him to resign from the position of Principal and the college moved to Manchester.[89] The link with African students continued and van Gundy eventually moved to become Dean of the Hampstead Bible School of Faith. The inequalities that arose in Camborne were more the result of the highly entrepreneurial environment that Word of Faith teaching sometimes produces than of racism. The gap between principal and staff was no greater than between Pastor and congregation in some Word of Faith churches in Africa.[90]

By the time van Gundy took over the Hampstead Bible School in 1989 there was a large number of African students. The visa situation in the late eighties had helped the growth of African membership at Victory in two ways. Firstly, through direct application to the Hampstead School, as, throughout the 1980s, it was possible to obtain a visa for Britain by committing to attend full-time Bible college. Most of those obtaining entry to Hampstead in this way were self-financing but in cases of hardship the college offered scholarships. At one time the college had about forty of its two hundred students on scholarships, most of these two hundred students being on a two-year course but some having stayed for a third-year option. The second way in which the late 1980s visa situation helped African growth at both the college and church in Hampstead was by visa transfer, as it was possible to apply for a change of visa without leaving the country. Students who had arrived to study English, say, could subsequently decide to transfer to the Bible college course at Hampstead and having finished at college they could change from a student visa to a work visa and so stay on within the church congregation.

It is these visa considerations that make it hard to discern whether students were coming to Britain to learn how to plant churches back in Africa or to prepare themselves for planting churches in Britain. There is also the possibility that some were seeing the Bible college option as a ticket to the West. This is impossible to substantiate from the Hampstead Bible School records, as the absence of any extensive vetting of students prior to their arrival in Britain meant that any inadequacy in college performance could have been as much the result of a previously undiagnosed lack of aptitude as

---

88. These included Sam Ohene-Apraku of Edmonton Temple.

89. The allegations brought against McCann, though serious, were, to my knowledge never proven and he has been able to continue with ministry, though not so highly profiled.

90. Gifford comments on Idahosa's claims to wealth in Brouwer et al., *Exporting the American Gospel*, 171.

of an absence of interest. The view of those who were responsible for the college is that there were some who secured visas without having any spiritual aspirations but that the majority were keen to train as church-planters.[91] However, those intending to return to church-plant in Africa were far fewer than those intending to stay and church-plant in Britain. The whole package, coming across as "the ideal job in the ideal place" with visions of prestige as a British-trained "Man of God" leading a large and affluent congregation (presumed to be white if staying in Britain and black if returning to Africa) went hand-in-hand with assumptions about a lavish western lifestyle. Discerning motive is further complicated by the fact that the African-recruited students at Hampstead were studying amongst British-recruited students who were coming to the college for reasons other than learning to be church-planters. Some, especially those on the evening class courses, were simply seeking to gain Bible knowledge and ministry support skills. Ethnic backgrounds too differed significantly. In the late 1980s, although most Hampstead students were African, up to a quarter of students were second generation Caribbean British residents. In the early 1990s the overseas numbers began to grow yet further through the arrival of Brazilians who were coming from the neo-Pentecostal revival in South America. They came with much the same expectations as their African counterparts had five years before them; the mixture of motives ranging from church-planting in Britain, through simply being in Britain, to returning home as trained in London.

Victory never seriously kept track of its students or of the churches they planted. Graduating students were expected to fend for themselves and for much of the time there was no alumni association and there certainly has never been a churches network. Even so, the college leadership asserts that there must be well over a hundred such congregations in London alone, given their claim that over a thousand students passed through their hands.[92] Looking at this figure realistically, a proportion of one in ten students succeeding with a London church-plant is high, given both the uncertainty of motivation and the difficulty of the task compared with the ease dreamed of from a distance. There is ample anecdotal evidence too of students staying on in Britain to take up secular work without updating their student visas. Anim, whose work on the Church of Pentecost in London I referred to earlier, makes a similar point, referring to "people who have either overstayed or are still processing their papers for extensions."[93] With Hampstead's former students, some are fulfilling assisting roles in churches in their spare time.

91. Van Gundy interview.
92. Van Gundy interview.
93. Anim, *Paradigm Shift*, 50–51.

The introduction of African neo-Pentecostalism into Britain

In the self-regulating world of independent churches there is no automatic check for immigration irregularities on those who consider themselves capable of ministering. Furthermore, some are leading their own churches, as in such circles the concept of "church" is determined more by intent than by size or program. Some even speak of leading a church when it exists only as a name on a business card or as an idea discussed amongst a few friends who are toying with the thought of renting a venue and purchasing sound equipment. All of this adds up to a rather low return on effort expended but it has to be remembered that the Hampstead Bible School did not set out with a specific strategy to import African neo-Pentecostalism through church-planting. Its initial objective was to promote Word of Faith teaching in Britain out of a conviction that this was more globally relevant than the expressions of Christianity already evident in Britain. The arrival of African students alongside British residents served to confirm this hope.

During this phase, when Hampstead Bible School of Faith was intensely involved in training African students, Victory Church in effect became a white-led, independent African neo-Pentecostal church. Not only did the African students join the church but many other African migrants were attracted to Victory, seeing it as an exciting Word of Faith church with a program of international speakers. People, however, did not always stay. Victory Church was emerging as a membership reservoir for other churches. When interviewed, the former Hampstead Bible School Dean summed up this unintended contribution to the growth of independent African neo-Pentecostal churches in Britain as follows:

> It seemed like a lot of people came through. Then there were other ministries, and unfortunately we still have it today . . . sometimes the back door is bigger than the front door in churches . . . people come for a while and then they go to another church, and then they go to another church. . . . Victory was, some people say, more of a conference center than a church. Thousands would come for conventions and things. [In the] 80's and 90's?—probably thousands![94]

Some of the dispersal occurred as Victory began establishing branch-churches. These were not to be the same as the churches planted by former students but re-localizations of groups of existing Victory members led by Victory church staff. The first to be established, in Tottenham, was placed in the hands of a young single Nigerian Hampstead Bible College graduate, Nims Obunge, who had been leading Victory's Singles' Ministry.[95]

94. Van Gundy interview.
95. Glen Arekion, a Mauritian evangelist and Victory Church member, led his

With Bassett frequently away, Kofi Banful, the first Ghanaian student, also received greater recognition and supervised the Hampstead church. It was Bassett's decision, though, not Banful's, that in 1993 saw the whole Hampstead church move its Sunday morning services to Stonebridge in Wembley. Bassett was seeking to secure growth, but many members who lived in Edmonton, Hackney or East London changed their allegiance; either to the Tottenham branch, to KICC or to Green Pastures Ministries (also known as Glory Bible Church) a new church in Leytonstone started by Nigerian twin brothers Albert and Vincent Odulele, themselves former members of Victory.[96]

By the end of 1993, there were signs of instability throughout the whole work. Banful left Victory Church to set up Praise Chapel and Obunge left to set up Freedom's Ark.[97] On Obunge's departure, van Gundy took over Tottenham and for a brief while leaders were brought in from France to head up Victory, Hampstead. Then in 1995, Bassett telephoned Douglas Goodman, the former Victory bookshop manager who had moved to Florida, to ask him to come back as church administrator.[98] As the church was in debt, soon after arriving Goodman secured the premises in his name. This proved fortuitous when legal action over an unpaid bill brought the ministry into liquidation, preventing the Bassetts from continuing in leadership.[99] Goodman stepped into the breach and declared his intention to do his best as a businessman to enable the church to continue. The Bible College was closed, the church staff members were released and Goodman ran the church himself, assisted by his wife and volunteers.[100] He continued to live in Milton Keynes having easy access to Hampstead via the M1.

Such a simplifying of church affairs was, in Goodman's opinion, bound to release sufficient funds from offerings to enable him to refurbish the Finchley Road premises and to cover the expense of bringing in guest speakers from overseas, as he did not see himself as a pastor or preacher. It

---

homegroup so effectively that it replicated itself. Seeing potential for further growth, he approached Bassett and a Wednesday night meeting was established in Tottenham with Bassett's ministry assistants, Kofi Banful, Mark van Gundy, Jan Owbridge (the wife of Alan Owbridge, Bassett's then media man) and Nims Obunge leading in turn.

96. Around this time, a further Victory branch was opened in Weybridge.

97. These departures were largely due to a tract selling enterprise, "Kingfisher," that Bassett was establishing.

98. Goodman had moved to Florida to work alongside Christian Harfouche, a regular guest speaker at Hampstead who was setting up a church and Bible college.

99. Damage was limited by locating the losses entirely within the company of which the Bassetts were sole directors. They were then declared bankrupt.

100. Owbridge later started a new "Hampstead" Bible College in Camberwell, South London.

The introduction of African neo-Pentecostalism into Britain   99

was reasoned that the increase in attendance resulting from a steady flow of internationally known speakers would then generate further finance for yet more airfares, airport to hotel transport, hotel bills and honorariums. It seemed to be a high-risk strategy out of line with all the models of church life usually practiced throughout Britain but to the faithful core congregation at Hampstead it must have made a kind of sense. The church had for years heard sermons about the place of practical success and the right of Christians to live as "children of the King" and here was a proposal that would create a luxury church with the world's most famed preachers coming in and out of Britain at Hampstead's behest. As Goodman's plans began to be known throughout the independent African neo-Pentecostal community, they found more copiers than critics, although the copying was not done in a way that gave Goodman the credit. Glossy brochures had long been around and hosting international speakers had been the ambition of many. As Victory grew and adopted a style more akin to KICC, a mutually respectful relationship developed between Goodman and Ashimolowo. By the turn of the millennium Victory Christian Centre (VCC), as Goodman had renamed the church, was stronger than it had ever been.

Although it has been appropriate to take Hampstead Bible School of Faith (and of necessity Victory Church) as a primary case study in this section on training to plant, KT and IBIOL also have to be considered.[101] There is a real contrast here. Whilst Victory in the early 1990s was known for its American Word of Faith roots and its predominantly African congregation, KT over the same period was known for its size, location and overseas mission engagement. When the Elim denomination appointed Wynne Lewis as KT's minister in 1980, the church membership stood at about 500. By 1986 it had more than tripled.[102] The Notting Hill area of London where KT has its premises is renowned for its multicultural mix; throughout the 1980s this was increasingly reflected in the composition of the church's congregation. Lewis had a significant overseas ministry and KT under his leadership became known worldwide. When Dye founded the church's Bible college, IBIOL, in 1986, it was this backdrop that guaranteed the college an international student body from the outset. Perhaps surprisingly, with KT being a denominational church and the college assembling a more academically qualified staff, IBIOL taught a syllabus very similar to that of Hampstead

---

101. For a detailed analysis of KT's history and structure see Thompson, *Waiting for Antichrist*, 61–82.

102. Hywel-Davies, *Kensington Temple Story*, 84, 94.

(although without the Word of Faith emphasis) and again the main focus was on equipping church-planters. However, in the late 1980s relations between Victory and KT were strained because of the unease felt by Lewis over both Word of Faith teaching and the flow of members from KT to Victory. The theological gap between KT and Victory began to close after Dye took over from Lewis in 1991 and went on to became a key participant in Cerullo's MTL where some of the speakers that Lewis had been cautious about were accepted on KT's platform.[103]

Unlike Victory Church, KT had a church-planting policy and throughout the 1990s Dye developed this, conceiving the London City Church and articulating his ideas in a book.[104] This was significant as it offered roles within KT, or more correctly in London City Church, for all the would-be church-planters emerging from IBIOL.
Whilst this seemed constructive it had its complications because of the denominational claims it inadvertently placed upon the church-planters because of KT's standing within the Elim denomination. It was particularly difficult for the many who thought they were simply working alongside KT to plant independent African neo-Pentecostal churches. Dye did seek to give clear signals in his writing that independence was not quite what he had in mind but even he was not initially sure how his plans would work out in denominational terms.

One interesting point about Dye's church-planting strategy was his theory of retaining monocultural units within a multicultural whole:

> In recent years church growth analysts have highlighted an important principle of growth. They call it the homogeneous principle. More than 70% of churches that are growing are mono-cultural, that is they have one main culture. This is a good principle of ministry as we are most probably able to reach people like ourselves. Churches function along lines of cultural and social affinity. . . . But homogeneity is not all there is to church life. Though we are different members we are in fact united in one body. We need to have a church that expresses the many cultures present in a city as this ensures that no culture is excluded from the gospel. They can all find valid expression in a city church. At Kensington Temple we uphold a multicultural type of worship, all coming together for big celebrations to express our unity. At the same time those of different nationalities and cultures fellowship in the various ethnic churches and

---

103. These would have included Avanzini, Hinn, Liardon, McCauley, Duncan-Williams and Dollar.

104. Dye, *Building a City Church*.

sub-groups of the church, where they can begin to give fuller expression to their own cultural distinctives.[105]

Dye's deliberate retention of monocultural forms removed the need for IBIOL's would-be church-planters to be cross-culturally trained. With separate congregations for West Africans, Ethiopians, Arabic speakers, people of Caribbean background, Latin Americans and so on, those arriving from Africa could readily grow into leadership roles without rethinking "church" in terms of style, content or context. With neither Hampstead nor KT showing any commitment to bringing cultural modifications to the convictions and practices of their overseas students, the question remains open as to where African students could have gone to gain a cultural understanding of British church life. In fact there were some African neo-Pentecostal students who attended the more traditional non-denominational, non-Pentecostal Bible colleges such as Spurgeon's, London Bible College, All Nations Christian College, Capernwray, Moorlands, Northumbria and Redcliffe, but these were in the minority.[106] All of these colleges, some with a missionary emphasis that might have made them better suited for training those intending to plant back in Africa, are more academic than Hampstead Bible School of Faith was or IBIOL is.[107] Hampstead in particular taught subjects such as the covenant, healing and deliverance, the fivefold ministry, which are not standard fare for non-Pentecostal Bible colleges. The teaching was also quite dogmatic, telling the students what to believe rather than guiding them towards their own conclusions.

I have raised the issue of denominational claims on church-planters encouraged to operate within Dye's London City Church framework. The Elim denomination was quick to require their church-plants to come fully within the Elim fold. The only concern the denomination was prepared to consider was Dye's objection to having his London City Church satellite

---

105. Dye, *Building a City Church*, 71, 72.

106. Though a Baptist ministerial training college, Spurgeon's College has a non-denominational foundation. Kingsley Appiagyei attained a BA there and now leads a largely Ghanaian Pentecostal Baptist church in West Norwood, London. Wale Babatunde, author of *Great Britain Has Fallen!* also attended Spurgeon's but without linking his church to the Baptist denomination. Appiagyei's insights into ethnic church growth are recorded in Appiagyei, "Growth of Ethnic Churches," 60–63.

107. The Centre for International Christian Ministries, Finsbury Park, started in the 1980s and saw itself as a more academic Pentecostal college. It was American-led, linked with the Holiness Pentecostal Church of America, offering American-accredited courses. The original visionary handed on leadership to his son-in-law, Philip Moore. The syllabus emphasized holiness rather than Word of Faith. Few from the twenty or so graduates each year retained any formal link with the college or the denomination. Most stayed in Britain, even those coming from Africa for the course.

congregations treated as congregations within Elim's London region, not accountable to him but answerable directly to Elim's London regional superintendent. The denomination resolved this by agreeing to a separate KT region contiguous with the London region but having its own KT-related superintendent working alongside Dye. This meant that it was possible to have an Elim KT London City Church satellite and a London region Elim church in the same street. It still did not resolve the difficulty for those who thought they were planting independent churches under KT's watchful eye but were in fact planting denominational churches with high levels of accountability back to the center. This unresolved issue would eventually lead to some church-plants splitting from both KT and Elim.[108] However, as the year 2000 approached, Dye set a millennial goal for London City Church of 30,000 members and 2000 satellite churches within the orbit of the M25.[109] In his book *Building a City Church* Dye set these goals in the wider context of British church-planting targets for the year 2000:

> I am sometimes told by pastors, "The last thing we need is more churches." Actually, nothing could be further from the truth. How can we speak of having enough churches when 90% of the population does not attend one? This is extreme "maintenance mentality" and has no place in the kingdom of God. We need 7,000 new churches in London if we are going to see the churchgoing population double within the next ten years. These were the findings of the Challenge 2000 congress held in Birmingham early in 1992. The congress, a British initiative coming from the DAWN 2000 strategy for discipling a whole nation, was attended by over 30 different denominations, many represented at national leadership level.[110]

The era of bringing students from Africa to train to plant, which was so important for independent African neo-Pentecostal churches in the late 1980s and early 1990s, had ceased to become a dominant means of independent African neo-Pentecostal church growth by the turn of the millennium.[111]

---

108. Since 2000, many African churches within London City Church have been granted independence from Elim in order to undo what for some had become a sense of injustice. Some opted to leave London City Church and stay within Elim.

109. Statistics given on the back cover of Dye, *Building a City Church* and in Jack Hywel-Davies, *Kensington Temple Story*, 186. In Hywel-Davies's book, published later than Dye's, "by the end of the decade" is not mentioned.

110. Dye, *Building a City Church*, 52.

111. KT's IBOL has found that since the mid-1990s students coming to train as church-planters have mostly been from Latin America. This reflects the parallel development of neo-Pentecostalism in South America as documented by Martin, *Tongues of*

Bible colleges continued to play a role and indeed a number of the larger African neo-Pentecostal churches had established their own part-time colleges to help their resident members develop their Bible knowledge and acquire ministry skills. However, when these churches wish to start branches, much of the training is given through apprenticeship techniques, potential ministers serving in supervised roles of increasing importance within the main church before being given responsibility for a church-plant. KICC has developed a number of its own church-plants in this way and Glory House (formerly Glory Bible Church) for several years operated a Bible college on the lines described, at times advertising extensively on Premier radio to bring in students from outside its own congregation. With conditions changing, an alternative church-planting strategy was coming to the fore.

"CALLED" TO PLANT

The fifth phase of independent African neo-Pentecostal church-planting in Britain in my categorization has been the most entrepreneurial. It involves people who have "stepped out in faith" in response to the "call of God" without persuasion from fellow nationals, commissioning by a sending denomination or training at a Bible college. They have not come on missionary visas, invited by *bona fide* churches impressed by their ministry experience in their country of origin, but have arrived in Britain with the intention of fulfilling some form of secular employment and then had a change of direction. In some cases the change of direction has been partly prompted by employment frustrations. Christians who have trained as teachers, academics, solicitors or medical doctors in their homeland, when facing revalidation requirements or other employment difficulties in Britain, do consider ministry possibilities rather than take posts as cleaners, caretakers and care assistants. They call on their past experience of church life as a church member, Sunday School teacher or usher to equip them for their newly selected role. They then put themselves through a personal preparation program of reading, praying, seeking advice and assimilating ministry material through conferences, television, videos and tapes before gathering friends and family to help found their ministry, usually in a hired hall with some sacrificially acquired musical instruments and a portable public address system. For others, though, there are no employment frustrations, just a sense that they

---

Fire, and subsequently discussed in Martin, *Pentecostalism*, and Corten and Marshall-Fratani, *Between Babel and Pentecost*. It also reflects the results of relationships built by Dye in Brazil during the early 1990s, following those built by Lewis and Dye in Africa in the 1980s.

should be working in some form of Christian ministry. These people would go through much the same preparatory process but often combine their early days in ministry with a full-time secular post. A few people are driven in this ministerial self-preparation by notions of prestige and finance, as African neo-Pentecostal churches do regard their pastor as a "Man of God" and accord the position a degree of status. Members of congregations who receive a regular diet of motivational preaching, where personal progress is the goal, and who live in a prosperity gospel environment where "blessing the preacher financially" is presented as a key to success, are likely to see full-time ministry as an attractive calling. This, however, has to be balanced against a tendency in such congregations to set the spiritual qualifications of "the Minister" at a level that seems almost unattainable to the average congregation member. This stems from a conviction that the real qualifications for ministry lie in God-given "giftings" and spiritual "anointings" that cannot be acquired by means other than divine intervention or considerable periods of extensive association with those already so gifted and anointed. Those who see themselves as called to church-plant have come to the conclusion that they have come to possess such "giftings" and "anointings" that mark them out from their fellow congregation members, often speaking of divine visitations or significant specific personal contacts.

An added pressure for most Africans in Britain is the need to send money back to their families. Family members who come to Britain are considered to be privileged and, given the nature of corporate family consciousness in Africa, there will often be a sense that, as the whole family contributed in some way to their going, everyone deserves to be blessed as a result. The need for gainful employment, therefore, has increased significance. Proud though families might be of their doctor, lawyer, teacher or accountant son or daughter moving to Britain, there is equal, if not greater, pride in learning that he or she has now been "called" to the ministry. There is a tendency for families to think of success and to look at the ministers around them in Africa that have both status and finance. Indeed, when church-plants with African congregations in Britain are successful they can provide good levels of remuneration, but there is a counterbalance to this in that, during the pioneering phase of church-planting, overheads tend to exceed income. Whilst those who are "called to plant" have to show a high level of entrepreneurial ability, in terms of taking initiatives and assessing risks, they also have to be prepared to make considerable personal sacrifices. The degree of willingness to make personal sacrifice can separate the church-planter with self-seeking motives from the church-planter with altruistic intentions. The same is true of the readiness to endure the time-consuming process of putting in place proper structures of financial accountability, with

The introduction of African neo-Pentecostalism into Britain

its need for trustee appointments, accurate bookkeeping, dependable audits and appropriately drafted documents for charity registration. In the words of one interviewee,

> There is a need to be financially accountable, good stewardship, if you call yourself a "man of God" or a pastor. I would really question the credibility of any pastor, or any so-called "man of God" that set up a church here with the intention to financing any project or his family back home. But what I also know is that there are a lot of people who have set up churches here and they have connections and so they are able to transfer funds to support churches back home because, say, if you came from a church that was poor and needed a roof replaced and you are here, sometimes you transfer money.[112]

Eventually, as their churches grow, all entrepreneurial pastors in Britain have to set up some financial accountability structures. The Charity Commission's registration threshold of a £1,000 per annum turnover for "public benefit" organizations ensures this, although it is usually the attraction of registration with the Inland Revenue for Gift Aid entitlement that drives the process forward.[113] Many, though, continue to manage without any form of ministerial accountability or accreditation. Entrepreneurial church-planters commonly use "Reverend" as a form of "self-styling" and people who know little about independent church accountability assume accreditation accompanies such a title. Whilst being seen to attend conferences and ministers' fellowships adds a degree of public endorsement, which increases when the church-planter begins organizing and hosting his or her own conferences, little may ever have happened to evaluate externally the church-planter's performance as preacher, pastor or administrator. Some self-appointed pastors do seek mentoring from more senior colleagues and some join ministerial associations, though for many linking with a ministerial association has had more to do with gaining certification than securing continuing accountability. The fact that senior ministers approached to provide mentoring are not always resident in Britain also weakens the accountability process. By the turn of the millennium, those approached outside Britain included Ray McCauley in Johannesburg, Eddie Long in Atlanta, T. D. Jakes

---

112. Amechi interview.

113. The Charity Commissioners' threshold has been set at an income of £1,000 per annum since the Charities Act of 1992/1993. It rose to £5,000 when the government passed the Charities Act 2006. Gift Aid is the government scheme whereby charities can claim the income tax paid on a gift from suitably signed-up donors.

in Dallas, Myles Munroe in the Bahamas, Tunde Bakare in Lagos, Francis Wale Oke in Ibadan and George Adegboye in Ilorin.[114]

Until recently the largest ministerial association offering certification to such ministers was the International Ministerial Council of Great Britain (IMCGB).[115] The IMCGB was founded in 1968 by David Douglas, a Jamaican minister resident in Britain who was concerned that the independent Caribbean churches that were forming were being dismissed as sects by those more familiar with the Church of England.[116] When the various ecumenical instruments were set up in the wake of the establishing of the World Council of Churches, Douglas realized that they presented an opportunity for applicant churches to function on a par with the Church of England and the Catholic Church. By bringing independent churches together he established a structure that he felt gave greater validity to independent church leaders and furnished them with a much-needed sense of belonging.

Although when founded IMCGB was more about recognition than accountability, Douglas opted for an episcopal system with all the trimmings of robes, crooks and mitres. However, it was an episcopal system without full episcopal oversight since bishops, as with all other IMCGB church leaders, only oversaw the congregations they had established.[117] After Douglas died in 1998 his Scottish wife was consecrated as a bishop and instituted as Moderator in his place. Though her Watford home continued to be the center for the organization, there were some moves towards a diocesan structure. In the late 1990s Titus David briefly served as an IMCGB bishop with an ambassadorial role, seeking to bring other African neo-Pentecostal church leaders into the organization. Unfortunately, the influence of IMCGB faltered at the turn of the Millennium when a newly appointed General Secretary found himself in conflict with the IMCGB College of Bishops over issues of authority within the organization. The departure of African neo-Pentecostal bishops from IMCGB led them to seek confirmation of their episcopal status elsewhere, often outside Britain. However, by 2000 the number of African neo-Pentecostal bishops in Britain was small.[118]

---

114. This list does not include those who were simply providing oversight for their own branch-churches.

115. Sturge, *Look*, 96, 97. Jubilee Ministerial Association run by Ben Egbujor, a Nigerian pastor resident in Britain since the 1980s, is an example of a smaller accrediting body.

116. David interview. By 2000, David had been involved with IMCGB for three years and was an area Bishop working closely with Sheila Douglas the new Moderator.

117. The same was true for, Malachi Ramsey, the head of Shiloh Ministries and a personal friend of the founder, whom IMCGB consecrated as an Archbishop.

118. Estimates suggest between ten and twenty.

The introduction of African neo-Pentecostalism into Britain 107

This entrepreneurial church-planting phase has been extremely significant for independent African neo-Pentecostal church growth in Britain. Conversations with African church leaders attending the leaders meetings held as part of MTL's daytime training sessions in 1997 and 1998 (and African leaders were always in the majority) revealed that over half had established their churches and ministries in such a way. It was clear they had not chosen an easy route and it had had a definite impact on their lifestyles, as church-planting is demanding in terms of time, patience, energy and finance. To plant a church a full set of core convictions have to be developed at the outset to sustain the preaching and teaching requirement. Changing one's opinions from week to week as one seeks to chart a course through numerous doctrinal possibilities is not an option. Negotiating techniques then have to be perfected to secure premises and to interact with other church and community groups. Pastoral and counselling skills have to be acquired, as those seeking to join new churches often arrive with unresolved problems. Furthermore, the church-planter's family home often has to serve as a store for equipment and a venue for meetings, while the family car becomes a cross between a transit van and a taxi.[119] As such realities take hold, convictions concerning calling can be strongly tested.

One such church-planter I spoke to expressed himself as follows:

> I felt the . . . call of God and I thought, "Well, I will answer." I am in secular work but I am also in ministry. . . . I did not start with . . . a feeder church . . . recruiting for me. . . . We have had to evangelize and be relevant to the community and that's why we are struggling because we haven't poached, we haven't recruited, we haven't had any transfers.[120]

In situations as challenging as this these entrepreneurial church-planters do value each other's affirmation. As the above quotation implies, this affirmation can be jeopardized when a church-planter seems to be growing his or her church by seeking transfer of members from other congregations. Even so, the "honor culture" in African churches would still apply and can at times seem excessive. During conventions the host pastor will expect all visiting ministers to sit in especially reserved seating at the front. Psychologically this may keep alive the positive feelings of mutual respect that most acknowledge accompanied their initial sense of divine calling. A movement, however, where so many leaders function without accreditation and accountability has its weaknesses, especially when seeking to establish

---

119. Ashimolowo has shared his own early challenges of taxiing members. KICC, "London Calling," 5.
120. Amechi interview.

parity with denominations that have long-established programs of training and ongoing supervision. In a British church culture that is keen to increase its multicultural credibility these problems can go largely unaddressed. At times this can leave these particular new churches with issues that are then difficult for both them and the wider church community to handle.

CONCLUSION

In this chapter I have outlined the way in which African neo-Pentecostalism was imported into Britain. Whilst much of this importation took place with a minimum of interaction with British evangelicalism it was not entirely an insular process. In the next chapter I examine the interactions that took place between African neo-Pentecostalism and British evangelicalism in the fifteen-year period from 1985–99.

Chapter 4

Principles and practicalities in the interactions of 1985-99

WITH MOST OF THE EARLY development of African neo-Pentecostalism in Britain contained either within newly formed mono-cultural congregations or within the two large London multi-cultural churches canvassing African students into their Bible Colleges (KT and Victory Church, Hampstead), African neo-Pentecostalism was, for a while, kept from British evangelicalism's view. However, given the African neo-Pentecostal interest in mission and media, it could not remain hidden indefinitely, even during its years of establishment.

THE PALAU/GRAHAM LEGACY

The topic on the mind of many of London's evangelicals between 1985 and 1990 was stadium evangelism. The Argentinean evangelist Luis Palau had held his Mission to London at the Queen's Park Rangers football ground in Loftus Road, Kilburn, in the summer of 1984, having preceded this in 1983 with a series of regional campaigns in various zones of London.[1] For many evangelical church leaders the event was a success, with significant additions to their congregations.[2] Others were disappointed that Mission to London had prevented London's participation in Billy Graham's Mission England, which also took place in 1984.[3] This was particularly true

---

1. Brierley, *Christian England*, 18.

2. Brierley's results for these 1983/1984 campaigns were: "nearly 24,000 people went forward, 56% of them to accept Christ." Brierley, *Christian England*, 18.

3. Brierley, *Christian England*, 18; Reid, *To Reach a Nation*, 53-65; Bebbington,

of the leaders of some of central London's largest churches who were keen to negotiate an early return of Graham to the capital.[4] Graham's visit to Sheffield in 1985 whetted the general appetite for this, as centers were set up around London to receive a satellite link of the campaign.[5] Preparations were soon underway for another London-based Graham mission, Mission '89.[6] Enthusiasm for the large-scale public event was still very much alive post-Palau and the opinion of Gavin Reid, former national Director of Mission England and soon to be Director of Mission '89, carried weight:

> It was my clear conviction that evangelism was best done at either a very small or personal level or on a very large scale. People tended to relate at those two dimensions. They related to family and neighbours (although this could not always be guaranteed). They related to those they worked besides and they related to people who took part in the same leisure pursuits. Apart from that they related, albeit in a different manner, to TV personalities and the people they read about on their newspapers or saw on their television screens.[7]

It was decided early on in the preparations for Mission '89 that there should be a significant role for the Afro-Caribbean churches.[8] Philip Mohabir, who had set up the WIEA in April 1984, was brought onto the Mission '89 Council as Vice-Chairman to co-ordinate this.[9] There was a determination to be better prepared for a response from the African and Caribbean churches this time than had been the case for Palau's mission in 1984. At Loftus Road, significant numbers of people who had responded to appeals for salvation and recommitment had given church details that were unfamiliar to those on the Designation Committee responsible for referring people to appropriate churches.[10] The details were nowhere to be found on the list of participating congregations and many of the church names contained far more words than was then regarded as usual, with "Church of God," "Holy Ghost," "Anointed," "Prophecy," "New Testament," and "Cherubim and Seraphim" variously appearing in the titles. Furthermore,

---

Evangelicalism, 259.

4. Jefferson and Williams, *Mission '89*, 7, 17.

5. Brierley, *Christian England*, 18.

6. Brierley, *Christian England*, 18. This being Graham's fourth London-wide campaign, earlier events being: Harringay in 1954 and Earls Court in 1966 and 1967.

7. Reid, *To Reach a Nation*, 16.

8. Jefferson and Wiiliams, *Mission '89*, 29.

9. Jefferson and Wiiliams, *Mission '89*, 29.

10. I served on this Designation Committee under Kirby's chairmanship.

where church addresses were given for such churches they were often the addresses of familiar denominational churches, clearly just hired meeting places with no contact address. Whilst most non-participating churches could be traced through denominational directories, these churches had no known directories.[11] A telephone call to Mohabir during the Loftus Road mission hoping to uncover such documentation elicited the response, "Be patient! These churches do not even know of each other yet."[12] In fairness, his WIEA was less than four months old. The hope was that five years on, for Mission '89, progress had been made.

Even so, there was a determination to leave nothing to chance. Graham missions depend heavily on mobilizing church members. The numbers that need to be trained as stewards, choir members, house-to-house visitors, counsellors and follow-up workers are such that it is necessary first to select and train trainers.[13] In selecting counselling trainers for Mission '89, efforts were made to include African and Caribbean church leaders. The growth of the WIEA (by 1989 renamed the Afro-Caribbean Evangelical Alliance and led by Joel Edwards), meant that a number of Caribbean church leaders could readily be recruited. However, the involvement of Mark Olatunji of the African neo-Pentecostal denomination, Deeper Life, was entirely due to his own enthusiasm and willingness to serve. The experiences of David and Oshuntola outlined in the previous chapter illustrate the lack of success that the Afro-Caribbean Evangelical Alliance had in engaging African leaders in the first five years of its existence. Limited recruitment success notwithstanding, the system adopted for the training of counsellors was designed to stimulate maximum inter-church co-operation rather than encourage the involvement of a specific group of churches or denominations. The four-week-long training course was held across the capital, one evening a week, in large church buildings chosen to provide central locations for each strategic area within every London borough. Inevitably, with size a consideration, the buildings selected were usually those of the main white denominations. This was not an incentive to African and Caribbean congregations. Beyond the use of one African and various Caribbean trainers, little was done specifically to recruit African and Caribbean counsellors. The fact that a significant number trained is a tribute to their own eagerness. Mohabir's comment when questioned about African and Caribbean involvement in Mission '89 was "until . . . white church leader[s] get involved with the black church

---

11. Help was nearer than we knew; a directory was in preparation: Centre for Caribbean Studies, *Handbook of Afro-Westindian Churches in Britain*.

12. I made the call.

13. "Counsellors" in this context meant, essentially, those trained to share prescribed literature with people responding to the evangelist's appeal.

agenda why should black church leaders be expected to get involved with the white church agenda?"[14]

Graham's meetings took place in June and July 1989, being held at West Ham Football Ground, Crystal Palace Sports Arena, Earls Court Exhibition Centre and Wembley Stadium.[15] These meetings followed the formula used by Graham for Harringay in 1954 and Earls Court in 1966 and 1967.[16] The meetings were relayed to over 220 "Livelink" centers across Britain.[17] In the lead-up to the event, Graham spoke at a church in Brixton to stimulate further Caribbean interest.[18] An effort was made to include Caribbean church leaders on the Designation Committee that oversaw referrals to churches. Edwards was particularly helpful in this regarding West Ham. However, the overall impression of the Designation Committee was that London lacked vibrant churches in its inner-city areas.[19] This opinion was partly attributable to the under-representation of independent African churches and the smaller Caribbean denominations on this designating body, as many more churches existed than was appreciated.

In the wake of the Palau mission, the EA had brought together a few senior church leaders and denominational representatives in the hope of creating a capital-wide evangelical fellowship. For Mission '89 the EA had key people involved ready to rekindle this vision for the 1990s.[20] Initially it was intended to formalize the thirty-two borough groupings (thirty-three with the City) into which the 1,500 participating London churches had been organized, "fostering some of the valuable links established both within and between London Boroughs as a consequence of the Mission."[21] In order to do this, a series of post-Mission consultations was proposed. The first, for London's senior evangelical ministers, took place on September 17, 1991 at Westminster Chapel, partly funded by the Billy Graham Evangelistic Association.[22] Four African leaders were among the seventy-seven attending:

---

14. Mohabir was more direct than this, prefacing his comment to me with "until you as a white church leader."

15. Jefferson and Williams, *Mission '89*, 5.

16. Capon and Williams, *Billy Graham*, 10–17; Harringay now Haringey.

17. Capon and Williams, *Billy Graham*, 10–17; Brierley, *Christian England*, 18.

18. Jefferson and Williams, *Mission '89*, 29.

19. Opinion frequently expressed to me as facilitator of the Committee.

20. London Leaders' Consultation Minutes, March 6, 1990, Evangelical Alliance archive.

21. London Leaders' Consultation Minutes, March 6, 1990, Evangelical Alliance archive.

22. London Leaders' Steering Group Minutes, February 21, 1991, Evangelical Alliance archive.

Matthew Ashimolowo, Charles Buckman, Sunday Fefegha and Henry Kontor. Ashimolowo joined the steering group for the first time as it debriefed at the end of the meeting.[23] Caribbean leaders were represented at the consultation by Les Isaac, Len Anglin, Joel Edwards and Philip Mohabir, Isaac having been brought onto the steering group ahead of the event.[24]

In their debriefing, the steering group concluded that this initial consultation had given the mandate for five area events in 1992, with a sixth for those interested in a London overview.[25] Unfortunately the 1992 consultations made no progress in terms of African and Caribbean attendance (6 percent instead of 10 percent).[26] The decision to use the computer-ready MARC Europe 1989 Church Census mailing list rather than the Mission '89 one, was a factor.[27] Whilst African and Caribbean participation in Mission '89 had been low, it was even lower in the census, as finding postal addresses for questionnaires had proved problematic. Indeed census results were grouped together in an "Afro-Caribbean" category with the larger Caribbean denominations mainly in evidence and no distinction being made for independent Caribbean churches or for African congregations, whether independent or denominational. The results led Peter Brierley, the church statistician, to make a forecast. He based his forecast on three factors relevant in the 1980s: that "black people were more easily able to integrate in white congregations"; that the number of immigrants had fallen "so the natural growth of such churches was curtailed"; and that some "older black people [were] returning to their original country." His forecast was that "a much reduced growth since 1979 . . . might even lead to decline [in 'Afro-Caribbean' churches] in the 1990s."[28] Clearly there was not an overall decline in African and Caribbean church life in Britain from 1990 onwards, even though there was a well-documented decline in the larger Caribbean denominations.[29] The paucity of statistics relating to independent

23. London Leaders' Consultation Delegates List, September 17, 1991, Evangelical Alliance archive. Ashimolowo attended one more steering group meeting on December 10, 1991. London Leaders' Steering Group Minutes, December 10, 1991, Evangelical Alliance archive.

24. Delegates List, September 17, 1991, Evangelical Alliance archive.

25. London Leaders' Steering Group Minutes, September 17, 1991, Evangelical Alliance archive.

26. London Leaders' Regional Consultations Attendance Lists, May–June 1992, Evangelical Alliance archive.

27. London Leaders' Steering Group Minutes, October 17, 1991, Evangelical Alliance archive.

28. Brierley, *Christian England*, 39.

29. For comment on immigrants returning to the Caribbean: Edwards, *Jamaican Diaspora*, 20–22.

churches, both Caribbean and African, and to the African denominations, is the mitigating factor. Outside of the Caribbean denominations there was growth.

The 1992 post-Mission '89 consultations with London church leaders revealed that the borough groupings set up for the mission had been disbanded and enthusiasm for re-forming them was patchy. The initiative was saved by the "London overview" consultation at St Paul's Church, Robert Adam Street on September 24, 1992 where those attending decided to meet regularly to pray for the capital.[30] A pilot prayer breakfast was organized at the same venue for Thursday January 14, 1993.[31] The steering group circulated a questionnaire to all ninety leaders present at the January breakfast hoping to find a way forward. Despite a 68 percent request for regional meetings, the steering group decided to continue with central meetings only.[32] They did, however, accept the 94 percent request that the gatherings be held quarterly and from 8:30–11:30 a.m.[33] They were also largely reassured from the responses that they had the charismatic/non-charismatic balance right, feeling that to be a little less charismatic would be wise.[34] For a second meeting on May 12, 1993 at Westminster Chapel, invitations were sent out on EA notepaper, summarizing the consultations' findings and including the following additional suggestions:

1. **"develop" new relationships** out of which new structures may grow.
2. **encourage borough groupings of leaders** to meet together to tackle, amongst other things, Christian issues at local council level.
3. **pray in a united way** about the activities of the enemy throughout London.
4. **include more black leaders** in our groupings.
5. **take a greater responsibility** for the spiritual state of London.

---

30. London Leaders' Steering Group Minutes, October 1, 1992, Evangelical Alliance archive.

31. London Leaders' Steering Group Minutes, October 1, 1992, Evangelical Alliance archive.

32. London Leaders' Steering Group Minutes, January 26, 1993, Evangelical Alliance archive.

33. London Leaders' Steering Group Minutes, January 26, 1993, Evangelical Alliance archive.

34. London Leaders' Steering Group Minutes, January 26, 1993, Evangelical Alliance archive.

6. **meet together as Leaders to pray** for our respective ministries, communities and London.³⁵

The letter resulted in one hundred and eighty church leaders attending and again questionnaires were circulated.³⁶ Some responders took the opportunity to make more general comments: "Good to have so many African or West Indian participators; more Asians would be welcome. . . . More women to take part would be useful. More young people too."³⁷

This is significant as the African and Caribbean attendance at this and subsequent London Leaders' prayer gatherings never exceeded 7 or 8 percent. The contentment with such low percentages of African and Caribbean attendance may have reflected the limited understanding of the extent of African Christian presence in the capital at the time. Furthermore, there is no evidence in the steering group minutes of consideration being given to the effect on attendance of meetings being held at breakfast time on weekdays. This is surprising given Caribbean leaders' long-expressed protestations of their unavailability for daytime events due to secular work commitments.³⁸ African leaders if approached would have protested their unavailability from 8:30 a.m. to 9:30 a.m. (and 3:00 p.m. to 4:00 p.m.) owing to commitments to school runs to facilitate working spouses.

An ironic response in January 1993 was also revealing: "I would like the interpretation of those languages around where I was seated, so that I would not feel a foreigner among my brothers and sisters in Jesus."³⁹ At that meeting, the African neo-Pentecostal practice of all praying out loudly at once was used briefly.⁴⁰ Subsequent meetings avoided the approach and the favored pattern for prayer was praying in small groups. Furthermore, the steering group recorded: "The importance of people meeting each other and speaking to each other was noted, especially before they pray together, and it was also noted that this can be key to breaking down barriers."⁴¹ Such "socializing" is not part of normal African neo-Pentecostal prayer style. A

---

35. Letter dated March 1993. List based on five-point summary prepared by Dye, Dec. 10, 1992.
36. London Leaders' Steering Group Minutes, May 18, 1993, Evangelical Alliance archive.
37. Summary of Returned Questionnaires, May 12, 1992.
38. Awareness frequently articulated by Mohabir.
39. Results of January 14, 1993 questionnaire.
40. Minutes, January 26, 1993.
41. Minutes, January 26, 1993.

Baptist minister who found herself praying in a small group with the few Africans present commented that they had failed to introduce themselves before praying and that had been a real difficulty.[42]

An entry in the minutes for the London Leaders' Steering Group meeting on November 16, 1994 records:

> We need to be aware that differences may not always be between black and white but also African and Caribbean. Division can also be caused by theological beliefs as well as colour differences, e.g. Africans struggle with attending meetings at HTB [Holy Trinity, Brompton] because its culture is so "white."[43]

Leaving aside the culture of Holy Trinity, Brompton, and the differences between African and Caribbean communities, the "[d]ivision . . . caused by theological beliefs" as it relates to prayer, is also worthy of comment.

When the London Leaders' prayer gatherings began in 1993, the theological concept was that of beseeching an interventionist God in order to see city-wide transformation, summarized as: "[to] pray in a united way about the activities of the enemy throughout London . . . take a greater responsibility for the spiritual state of London . . . meet together as Leaders to pray for our respective ministries, communities and London."[44] Given that African neo-Pentecostals are known for their high expectation of divine intervention in response to their praying, there should have been ample common ground. However, differences in prayer do exist and behind the African neo-Pentecostal stylistic preferences for speaking in tongues, praying aloud simultaneously and rebuking the devil there are some theological distinctives.

Although evangelicals are seen as activists rather than as contemplatives or mystics, they prefer to present their activism in terms of partnership with an active Deity. In Calver's words, "[a]lthough prayer has sometimes been neglected in the face of such intense need for action, at its best evangelical activism includes an activism in prayer."[45] Effective human-divine co-operation for evangelicals sees prayer as a way of conforming human will to the divine, rather than aligning divine will with the human. To quote Hallesby's evangelical classic on prayer, to pray aright is to " . . . give Him the

---

42. Unminuted comment noted at a London Leaders' Steering Group Meeting, November 16, 1994.

43. Steering Group Minutes, November 16, 1994. No African representative was then serving on the steering group. Of the two Caribbean background members, only Edwards was present.

44. Dye's five-point summary.

45. Calver and Warner, *Together We Stand*, 98.

opportunity to exercise His power on our behalf, not only *as* He wills, but also *when* He wills."[46] Although terms such as supplication and intercession are to the fore when evangelicals speak of prayer, they aspire to a greater degree of submission than these petitioning terms imply.[47] The highest level of spiritual partnership for an evangelical involves God's action transcending human endeavor.

African neo-Pentecostalism is one with evangelicalism in wanting to give God all the credit for effective action in the wake of prevailing prayer, but African neo-Pentecostal praying has little of British evangelicalism's sense of patiently waiting on God as a way of producing personal transformation.[48] There is within African neo-Pentecostalism the thought that Scripture makes God's will plain and that it is the Christian's responsibility to insist boldly on its fulfilment.[49] Such insistence then removes the hidden obstacles to God's will being performed.[50] African neo-Pentecostals often believe that such obstacles are demonic.[51] Prayerlessness itself thus becomes a major barrier to God's action. Evangelicals agree with this, confessing that their human frailty constantly frustrates their aspirations to submit more fully to God.[52] Whilst agreement based on a common acknowledgement of prayerlessness is not sufficient to close the gap between submission and insistence, the numbers of Africans present at the London Leaders' prayer gatherings was never high enough for this to impinge stylistically or theologically on the dominant evangelical culture. Nonetheless, it might have accounted for absences.

Interestingly, by 1996 the African neo-Pentecostal denomination RCCG had established its own prayer agenda for London and was holding twice yearly prayer nights at the London Arena and the Excel Centre in Docklands.[53] These events have continued to prove highly popular with London's African neo-Pentecostal diaspora. However, despite the best efforts of RCCG General Overseer, Enoch Adeboye, to have prominent white church leaders on the platform, the white presence has never reached even the 6 or 7 percent minority attendance that would match that achieved by

---

46. Hallesby, *Prayer*, 107. Hallesby's italics.
47. Hallesby, *Prayer*, 13–21. Here Hallesby highlighted submission as "helplessness."
48. Okonkwo, *Breakthrough*, iii.
49. Okonkwo, *Breakthrough*, 86.
50. Don-Dawodu, *War Theatre*, 97–98.
51. Don-Dawodu, *War Theatre*, 14–28.
52. Ravenhill, *Why Revival Tarries*, 59–60.
53. Archives held by RCCG's London Office.

the London Leaders' gatherings.[54] Theological and stylistic differences over prayer, and indeed differences in praying times, may again have played a part.

The London Leaders' prayer gatherings continued through to 1999 but even with both an African and a Caribbean representative on the final eight-member steering group (in addition to Edwards who acted as an absent but supportive co-chair), the African and Caribbean attendance did not rise.[55]

CERULLO, MIRACLES AND MONEY

Whilst the London Leaders' consultations were still in the planning stage, Morris Cerullo, the American Pentecostal evangelist, had his team organize a breakfast meeting at London's Metropole Hotel on Saturday February 22, 1992.[56] Here it was announced that he intended to hold a major London-wide Mission at Earls Court 2 in June 1992. He had been holding annual evangelistic meetings since the 1960s, first under canvas, then at Westminster Central Hall and later in the Royal Albert Hall. He had built up a partnership base mainly from the Caribbean diaspora, capitalizing on his earlier evangelistic campaigns in the Caribbean islands.[57] For the February event, these long-term Cerullo partners were joined by pastors who had participated in Graham's Mission '89 and were looking for a follow-up program. The breakfast meeting constituted one of the most racially mixed gatherings of church leaders the capital had seen, with virtually a 50:50 Caucasian/African-Caribbean mix. For many at the time there was an appropriateness to the event as the 1990s had been declared a "decade of evangelism."[58] By June, however, the London Leaders' consultations were underway and the support base for the Mission had changed. Many who had toyed with the idea of another London-wide mission as the way forward for evangelism settled for a more local church emphasis whilst seeking to maintain some of the inter-church momentum from Palau and Graham through prayer and personal relationships. In the end, Cerullo's first MTL was the preserve of

---

54. Confirmed in June 2004 by the then-organizer Modupe Afolabe.

55. The gatherings restarted in autumn 2003 on a twice-yearly basis within the EA's "Hope for London" initiative. "Hope for London" Steering Group Minutes, April 3, 2003, EA archive.

56. Personal diary archive.

57. Edwards, *Lord*, 102; Cerullo, *Son*, 152–69.

58. The 1988 Lambeth Conference. Nazir-Ali and Pattinson, *Truth Shall Make You Free*.

Principles and practicalities in the interactions of 1985-99   119

London's Caribbean Pentecostal constituency and the newly formed independent African neo-Pentecostal churches.[59]

In her article on MTL, Schaefer stated that "Cerullo's revivals encompassed standard neo-Pentecostal fare but also catered to a specific local context involving black diaspora culture."[60] In reality it was hardly a dual emphasis; neo-Pentecostal fare was little known in London outside black Christian culture. In MTL, London's black-majority neo-Pentecostal congregations could participate without having to change the style or content of their regular evangelistic presentations; only the scale and professionalism differed. Members of the public were expected to appreciate what such churches preferred. Even the involvement of KT, a church within a predominantly white Pentecostal denomination, did nothing to widen the cultural spectrum. As Schaefer affirmed,

> The most important sponsor was Kensington Temple (KT) reportedly the largest church in the UK with 10,000 members. Although technically a white-led Elim church it acts as an independent entity and is known for the exuberant black worship styles preferred by its large African Caribbean congregation.[61]

MTL was as much "unadjusted KT" as it was unadjusted Church of God of Prophecy, New Testament Church of God, RCCG, KICC or Glory Bible Church.[62] For those recently arrived from Africa, MTL was the embodiment of African campaign evangelism. It had the standard publicity, the emphasis on miracles and the evangelistic appeals. The only area of surprise for independent African neo-Pentecostal church leaders would have been the public reaction. Complaints that London was covered in MTL publicity would have seemed strange to a Nigerian neo-Pentecostal pastor. A few posters on official hoardings and on the sides of buses would have seemed as nothing compared with the countless neo-Pentecostal conference banners strung across the main streets of Lagos, all reinforced by handbills pasted on every available wall. However, the temptation to challenge British cultural reserve on this point has so far been resisted and African neo-Pentecostal advertising in Britain has remained far more restrained than it is in West Africa. Participating churches found themselves drawn together year on year in the face of negative secular media reports and a frequently unimpressed

---

59. The Mission was held at Earls Court 2, June 21-28, 1992. The background and churchmanship of participants is evident from the programs, ca. 500 participants listed in both 1993 and 1996.

60. Schaefer, "Morris Cerullo's London Revivals," 119.

61. Schaefer, "Morris Cerullo's London Revivals," 108.

62. Schaefer, "Morris Cerullo's London Revivals," 108.

wider Christian public, each new glossy MTL program listing African and Caribbean churches with names previously unknown during the Palau and Graham campaigns. The addresses of these churches in fact filled the gaps on the London map detected by the leaders of participating churches for Mission '89.[63]

The differences in program content between a Cerullo mission and those led by Palau and Graham were almost as noticeable as the differences in congregational make-up. Schaefer has written of MTL that "a typical healing service consisted of three main parts—the musical 'warm-up,' the sermon and the miracle healing."[64] Palau and Graham's meetings could not be described as healing services. The "third part" of every Palau and Graham meeting was the appeal for people to come forward and receive salvation. From the outset, Cerullo's publicity had a healing emphasis. In the lead-up to the first event in 1992 advertising hoardings around London showed an empty wheelchair with the words "some will be moved by the power of God for the first time" whilst others featured a broken white stick with the caption "some will see miracles for the first time."[65] These claims were subsequently contested in the secular press in a way that left some Cerullo sympathizers indignant. Timothy Pain, a Christian journalist, used his indignation to justify the publishing of his detailed pro-Cerullo report on MTL 1993:

> The press tried to crucify *Mission to London 1992*. Morris Cerullo was universally denounced. Yet—at least to this observer—many of the criticisms were either intellectually flawed or down-right fraudulent. Inevitably, all the fuss created a popular impression of the event which—to me—was far from the truth.[66]

However, it was not just the press that was critical of Cerullo's miracle message at MTL. Some specific complaints were upheld by the Advertising Standards Authority.[67] Furthermore, Joel Edwards, who for the five years that Cerullo ran MTL was the UK Director of the EA, wrote that "[f]or many years, nothing in British evangelicalism has so fired the debate, in public or private, about a God of miracles."[68] Cerullo was the subject of

---

63. Osgood, "Survey."
64. Schaefer, "Morris Cerullo's London Revivals," 110. Note: MTL continued in the 1990s after 1996 but not under the auspices of MCWE.
65. "Mission to London," 6–7.
66. Pain and Manning, *Miracles Are Impossible*, 13.
67. Perriman, *Faith*, 11.
68. Edwards, *Lord,* 103.

Principles and practicalities in the interactions of 1985–99

divisions within Pentecostalism too: "[h]e was from the classical Pentecostal mould, but not all Pentecostals were happy with his approach."[69] Problems over theological content, promotional style and miracle claims were cited.[70]

What made it particularly difficult for the EA was that Cerullo's organization, Morris Cerullo World Evangelism, had its British-based European office established with EA membership.[71] From the outset of MTL, there were those within the EA who wanted this affiliation brought to an end.[72] By 1995, specific pressure was being put on the organization to resign, and more formal discussions were entered into.[73] Edwards was given the responsibility of negotiating a resolution on behalf of the EA and for him the main issue was Cerullo's fund-raising:

> By far the most universally disliked feature of his ministry was his approach to fund-raising which caused a great deal of dissent even from sections of the community who supported his ministry. Appeal letters appeared in rapid succession, and for many individuals they came close to a kind of modern-day "indulgence," offering healing or financial prosperity as a direct result of supporting his work.[74]

It was considered that a "prosperity teaching" emphasis was being used to under-gird Cerullo's appeals. Schaefer cast Cerullo in the "prosperity" mold by saying that "it is clear that Cerullo has espoused themes of health and wealth in his ministry's literature and at his meetings . . . his emphasis on prosperity has been a mainstay almost from the start."[75] The EA was in no doubt about the connection, introducing a subsequent report on prosperity teaching with the sentence: "The identification of prosperity teaching as a cause for concern was prompted to a significant extent by debate within the EA on the exegetical and fundraising methods employed by the evangelist Morris Cerullo and his international organization, Morris Cerullo World Evangelism (MCWE),"[76] Edwards' reference to indulgences, quoted above, seemed in the minds of the EA Council to be amply borne out by Cerullo's apparent claim to be specially anointed to mediate spiritual

69. Edwards, *Lord,* 102.
70. Perriman, *Faith*, 11.
71. Perriman, *Faith*, x.
72. Perriman, *Faith*, x.
73. Perriman, *Faith*, 10, 11.
74. Edwards, *Lord,* 103.
75. Schaefer, "Morris Cerullo's London Revivals," 117.
76. Perriman, *Faith*, x.

and material favor to those giving to his ministry.⁷⁷ As more of Cerullo's letters went out, so the critics saw their evidence increasing.⁷⁸ Throughout 1995 attempts to persuade MCWE to withdraw from the EA were met with refusal.⁷⁹ In 1996 one letter in particular caught the attention of the EA. Cerullo, in celebrating his fiftieth year in ministry, declared 1996 a "Jubilee Year" and took up the Old Testament principle of debt release to assure all his supporters willing to send in 50p for each of his fifty years that "God would release them from their debts and bestow on them a literal (and very material) hundredfold blessing."⁸⁰ Evidently, not everyone receiving such letters appreciated "so automatic an equation between material offering and divine favor."⁸¹

At this point, since it is clear that letters designed for ministry partners were being received by those unfamiliar with Cerullo's methods and disapproving of his theology, it is important to explain the connection between the appeal letters and MTL. Schaefer has recorded that, for the "offertory" at MTL, "[d]onation envelopes were handed out upon (free) admission into the auditorium and large plastic buckets were circulated and gathered up by ushers at the appropriate time."⁸² It was these envelopes that facilitated the MCWE mailing lists. All those attending the Mission were encouraged to give financially and to write their details on the offering envelopes. Many British churches did not use envelope systems for their offerings at the time and it was possibly the novelty factor that made even skeptical visitors oblige. Many people who would never have chosen to sign up for financial appeals found themselves on Cerullo's "partnership" list, unwittingly according themselves the privilege of receiving his requests for financial support throughout the year.⁸³

In September 1996 the full EA Council met for its scheduled meeting at the High Leigh Conference Centre in Hertfordshire and was supplied with a dossier of information on prosperity teaching compiled by Dave Cave, who had been coordinating the Alliance Commission on Unity and Truth among Evangelicals (ACUTE) since its inception in 1993. Armed with this information, those present voted 49-0 with one abstention to formally

77. Perriman, *Faith*, x.
78. Cave, "Truth," 27.
79. Perriman, *Faith*, x.
80. Perriman, *Faith*, 10, 11.
81. Perriman, *Faith*, x.
82. Schaefer, "Morris Cerullo's London Revivals," 110.
83. When MTL passed to Dye in 1996, mailing lists remained the property of MCWE. New mailing lists for invitations had to be created. Fax correspondence between MTL and Cornerstone Christian Centre, June,13 1996. Cornerstone archive.

request the resignation of MCWE from the EA.[84] Within days MCWE had resigned. The EA marked the departure in its magazine for January–March 1997:

> One area of tension relates to US evangelist Morris Cerullo's international group, the Morris Cerullo World Evangelism (MCWE) organisation, which has resigned from the Evangelical Alliance. Cerullo holds an annual large-scale Mission to London and is supported by many Christians from both black and white Pentecostal churches. The 49-strong Council of Management overwhelmingly supported a resolution to deal decisively with the situation by dissociating itself from fundraising letters and requesting to meet personally with MCWE, in order to arrive at a final decision over its membership. A letter of resignation from MCWE arrived shortly afterwards.[85]

These long-running difficulties between the EA and the Cerullo organization were a cause of concern to leaders of independent African neo-Pentecostal churches. They had little patience with the EA position and found no fault in Cerullo's doctrinal stand, as Edwards acknowledged:

> For these people, earnest and dedicated in their service of God, Morris's ministry was an acceptable model that infringed neither their understanding of biblical imperatives nor their own cultural grid.... When we spoke about problems with his evangelical credentials they found it very hard to understand.[86]

Not that Edwards was entirely uncritical in his comments about Cerullo's supporters. He observed that "[t]hey were less inclined to ask questions about cultural sensitivities, or frequent and forceful appeals based on tentative handling of Bible texts."[87] Nevertheless, he attributed an openness to the miraculous to a culture of expectation concerning God's imminent intervention:

> African and Caribbean Christians were the main support-base for Morris's ministry. ... These were not necessarily the unthinking end of the evangelical spectrum. They included many professionals and university students ... these Christians found the emphasis on miracles far less difficult than other sections

---

84. Perriman, *Faith*, x. This detail and the debate surrounding it are omitted from Randall and Hilborn, *One Body*.
85. "Struggling for Unity," 3.
86. Edwards, *Lord*, 104.
87. Edwards, *Lord*, 104.

of our membership. Rightly or wrongly, they were far less concerned about the politics of the events and belonged to a theological and experiential culture in which the idea of God's immediate intervention in the context of worship was more readily accepted.[88]

MTL was the principal inter-church initiative supported by the African neo-Pentecostal churches in the period 1990-1996 and it was the one which the EA appeared to turn away from most decisively on grounds of both spirituality and theology. The effect of this on evangelical and African neo-Pentecostal relations was minimized at the time as the public focus was on Cerullo and fundraising, but the seeds were being sown for difficulties later. The main immediate casualty for evangelical-Pentecostal relationships was the resignation of KT from the EA. Dye, who was in the process of taking over the leadership of MTL, felt that the EA had given insufficient attention to the editorial restraint he had been applying to Cerullo's appeal letters in the months leading up to Edwards' negotiations. He had undertaken this editorial task at the request of Cerullo's organization. It was three years before KT was prepared to renew its membership.[89]

ISSUES OF AFRICAN AND CARIBBEAN IDENTITY

Having seen the joint involvement of African neo-Pentecostal churches and Caribbean Pentecostal churches in MTL, some closer examination of the relationship between them is required. Between 1985 and 1999, both church groups faced identity issues in three different contexts: British charismatic identificational repentance events, joint African and Caribbean gatherings, and changes in British public opinion.

British charismatic identificational repentance events

In April 1992, as the EA was still planning its London Leaders' strategy to strengthen unity across London's evangelical churches, Gerald Coates, the leader of the Pioneer network of churches within Britain's new churches' movement, hosted an event at Westminster Chapel.[90] The gathering was designed to introduce the ministry of the New Zealander John Dawson to the

---

88. Edwards, *Lord*, 103-4.

89. Ironically, MTL under Dye's leadership post Cerullo, registered for EA membership in 1998.

90. Saturday April 4, 1992. Personal diary archive.

capital's charismatic constituency.[91] Dawson had for a number of years been working with the international missionary group Youth With A Mission (YWAM) out of Los Angeles, California, and his 1989 book, *Taking Our Cities for God*, was attracting attention from mission strategists.[92] The day was co-hosted by Lynn Green, Director of YWAM for Europe, Middle East and Africa, an American living at the YWAM base in Harpenden. Green was gaining increasing prominence in British evangelicalism, not least through his involvement in Challenge 2000, the British contribution to a millennial global evangelistic program centering on "Discipling a Whole Nation."[93] Whilst the Dawson meeting did not attract many African or Caribbean supporters, its significance for future relations between white charismatic Christians and African and Caribbean Pentecostals was considerable. Four themes emerged from Dawson's presentations during the day, themes that have come to be defined through much discussion as: territorial spirits, strategic level spiritual warfare (SLSW), wounded history and identificational repentance (IR).[94]

Dawson adopted an anecdotal style on the platform, as he has done in his writing, relating incidents from his travels that have convinced him of territorial spirit activity: "I have spent the last eighteen years in extensive travel . . . I have experienced firsthand the influence of territorial spirits while ministering in over thirty countries."[95] The stories told on the day were similar in style to the following:

> Several years ago I was in a Bible school in New Jersey, browsing through some books on the history of missions to Africa. I began to read the story of Uganda. Many of the first missionaries died of tropical diseases, but others followed heroically until a powerful national church was established. What caught my attention was an account of the tribal king who dominated Uganda. He was proud, sexually depraved and extremely cruel. The description was remarkably similar to the newspaper reports of the dictator ruling Uganda at that time. Idi Amin and his regime of death seemed to match his predecessor in every detail. Since that time I have studied the history of Uganda in greater depth. The cycle of blood bath, followed by revival, followed by blood bath is evidence of the ebb and flow of battle, as

91. Event publicity.
92. Dawson, *Taking Our Cities*; Wagner, *Territorial Spirits*, xvii–xviii.
93. Montgomery, *Dawn 2000*.
94. Notes taken at the time.
95. Dawson, *Taking Our Cities*, 153.

the national church has come against the evil spirit that prevails over the nation.[96]

It is clear from this that Dawson believes that a territorial spirit can be an architect of a region's history. He also believes that the church can in some way curb these powers: "There is no reason why we, the church, should concede one square inch of this planet to the government of territorial spirits. This is our planet. 'The heaven, even the heavens, are the Lord's; but the earth He has given to the children of men' (Ps. 115:16)."[97] In London in April 1992, Dawson made much of defeating territorial spirits by adopting an opposite disposition; for example, countering pride with humility and aggression with peace. This was a departure from what many in his audience expected, as other spiritual warfare teaching in circulation at the time was consistently aggressive.[98] In taking such a line, he may have had in mind a project some charismatic leaders in London had assigned themselves:

> All over the world, praying Christians are arriving at a consensus about the nature of the battle for individual cities. For example, the prayer warriors of London believe that they are battling a spirit of unrighteous trade that has influenced the world through that great city for hundreds of years.[99]

Dawson's approach to spiritual warfare may have been at odds with the aggressive emphasis of others but it was at one with his views on wounded history and IR.[100] In his book he opened his argument on wounded history by asserting:

> When you look into the history of your city, you will find clues as to what is oppressing the people today. . . . An obvious example would be the spirit of greed which was let loose during the Californian gold rush and still dominates the culture of Los Angeles and San Francisco to this day.[101]

---

96. Dawson, *Taking Our Cities*, 52.
97. Dawson, *Taking Our Cities*, 160.
98. Lowe, *Territorial*, 23.
99. Dawson, *Taking Our Cities*, 155.
100. "Identificational repentance" was first used in Dawson, *Healing America's Wounds*, 30. Subsequently "representational confession" was suggested. Parker, *Healing Wounded History*, 91–112.
101. Dawson, *Taking Our Cities*, 79, 80.

He then concluded that "through repentance, reconciliation and prayer, the present generation can work to repair the broken down walls of the city."[102] By the time Dawson got to Westminster Central Hall his aspirations had developed beyond cities. He was able to pave the way for Green to announce that the original Crusade routes were to be re-walked as an apology to the descendants of Muslims affronted by violent Christian militancy in the eleventh and twelfth centuries.[103] Here Dawson's concepts of territorial spirits, SLSW, wounded history and IR were beginning to meet.

Within months of Dawson's visit his views on territorial spirits and SLSW had been echoed by Ashimolowo:

> There is a territorial prince over every country, municipality, local government, and housing estate. Some have been there thousands of years gaining access to a particular place because of various things that have taken place there. For example, on a housing estate in South East London, England, a church, witnessing to the residents on a regular basis, found that people's response was usually warm and promising, giving the church the impression that they would be in church on Sunday. Unknown to the church they were being deceived. This was continuous for months until the church made enquiries and found that the land on which the estate was built was acquired by the original owners through deception. Today the people who occupy that area do not know that they are under the influence of the spirit of deception.[104]

Much of the spiritual warfare theory introduced to London by Dawson could be traced to a lecture on "The Power Encounter and World Evangelism" given in 1988 at Fuller Theological Seminary in America by Professor Timothy Warner of Trinity Evangelical Divinity School. In this he said, "I have come to believe that Satan does indeed assign a demon or corps of demons to every political unit in the world, and that they are among the principalities and powers against whom we wrestle."[105] Expounding this point, C. Peter Wagner, Fuller's leading "spiritual warfare" proponent, has explained:

> It is helpful to remind ourselves that Satan does not possess the attributes of God, and therefore he is not omnipresent. Although he may be able to move from one place to another very rapidly,

---

102. Dawson, *Taking Our Cities*, 81.
103. These happened between 1995 and 1999. "Pilgrimage," 1–2.
104. Ashimolowo, *Warriors of Righteousness*, 15.
105. Quoted by Wagner, *Territorial Spirits*, 85.

he can still be in only one place at one time. Therefore, if he is intent on blinding the minds of three billion people who have yet to receive the light of the gospel and the glory of Christ, he must delegate this responsibility to others, namely evil spirits.[106]

Interestingly, Wagner then resorted to the unexpected source of a Nigerian Sunday School teacher for some statistics:

> I do not know how many evil spirits there are around Planet Earth. One interesting set of figures comes from Friday Thomas Ajah, a Sunday School superintendent at the Assemblies of God church in Oribe, Port Harcourt, Nigeria. For years before his conversion he was a high ranking occult leader, given the name of St Thomas the Divine, purportedly by Satan himself. Ajah reports that Satan had assigned him control of 12 spirits and that each spirit controlled 600 demons for a total of 7,212. He says, "I was in touch with all the spirits controlling each town in Nigeria, and I had a shrine in all the major cities."[107]

However, it is of little concern to an African neo-Pentecostal that his fellow-Africans readily accepted spiritual hierarchies before American missions professors articulated the concepts of "higher-ranking" and "lower-ranking" spirits, or that their African ancestors were praying aggressively before it became fashionable to "assault" the "higher-ranking" ones through "SLSW." Who learnt what from whom is of only marginal importance. John Wimber, the American charismatic leader prominent in Britain in the 1990s, argued in his book *Power Evangelism* that missions professors gained their understanding of spiritual hierarchies from the mission fields of Asia and Africa.[108] He cited Fuller professor Paul Hiebert's dilemma on arriving in India. For Hiebert "the confrontation with spirits that appeared so natural a part of Christ's ministry belonged in my mind to a separate world of the miraculous—far from ordinary everyday experience."[109] Hiebert clearly learnt from his own missionary encounters. By contrast Ashimolowo's terminology seems to be that of Warner and Wagner. In reality, African neo-Pentecostals are more likely to draw from the American missions professors than from African (or Asian) anthropology.

Michael Reid, the former Liverpool policeman serving as a bishop with the independent Pentecostal Peniel Church in Brentwood, Essex, has

---

106. Wagner, *Territorial Spirits*, 87. Lewis used demonic hierarchies allegorically. Lewis, *Screwtape Letters*.
107. Wagner, *Territorial Spirits*, 87.
108. Wimber, *Power Evangelism*, 82–88.
109. Hiebert, "Flaw," 35–47.

Principles and practicalities in the interactions of 1985-99   129

taken an opposite stance to many of the African neo-Pentecostal leaders who attend his ministers' meetings. He has argued that SLSW proponents are those who "accept the animistic belief that spirits determine events and therefore teach that a Christian should be concerned properly with self-protection as well as endeavoring to control demonic powers . . . giving credence to the animistic three-tiered world view."[110] Such a reference to animistic beliefs would be considered by most African neo-Pentecostals to be inflammatory, since they see such insights as biblical. Further criticism stating that "Wagner also sees redeemed man as equidistant between God and Satan, and liable to be preyed upon by evil spirits if he fails to invoke warfare prayer" would also cause disquiet as Wagner is respected as being orthodox and not a dualist.[111] However, conservative evangelicalism can be equally critical. American mission theorist Chuck Lowe has written:

> As post-modernity supplants modernity, objectivity gives way to subjectivity, rationalism to emotionalism, scientism to spiritism, and mechanism to shamanism. In concrete terms, just as the Church Growth Movement was a manifestation of modernity's mechanistic worldview, so SLSW is an embodiment of post-modernity's spiritistic worldview.[112]

Although African neo-Pentecostals are largely in agreement with the British charismatic stand on territorial spirits and SLSW, they are less at one with charismatic convictions on wounded history and IR. Whilst African neo-Pentecostals believe that territorial spirits can be effectively paralyzed by naming and rebuking them, they are less convinced about undermining their power base through repenting for historical wrongs perpetrated within their territorial jurisdiction.[113] Some objections are purely practical. Where people believe that historical wrongs are to be righted through repentance, then, since those responsible and those offended are long gone, "proxy repenters" and "proxy responders" are needed to act on their behalf.[114] It is this concept of identification that lies at the heart of IR and gives the practice its name. From a technical standpoint the quality of the identification is all-important. One commentator has written, "[m]y assertion, then, is

---

110. Reid, *Strategic Level*, 123.
111. Reid, *Strategic Level*, 123.
112. Lowe, *Territorial Spirits*, 150-51.
113. Mills and Mitchell, *Sins of the Fathers*, 14. They refer to Suzette Hattingh's comment that "a spirit of murder was over [England]" but it is not made clear if "a spirit . . . over" is synonymous with a territorial spirit or is an attribute of a territorial spirit.
114. "Saying Sorry," 19-21.

identificational repentance is biblical but *vicarious* repentance is not."[115] He followed this with an explanation:

> What I cannot accept is the idea that Christians can symbolically repent on behalf of other people's sins without admitting their own guilt. Such an activity is meaningless and misleading and out of line with biblical teaching that each person is responsible for their own sin and will be judged accordingly.[116]

There is no doubt that the EA initially smiled on both wounded history and IR concepts. It gave the Crusade Reconciliation Walk front page billing in its *Idea* magazine in 1997 as a prominent wounded history and IR project. To quote its report,

> The Reconciliation Walk is an exciting example of contemporary pilgrimage, taking place through Europe over four years from 1995 to 1999. The purpose of the walk is for Christians to publicly express their regret and sorrow for the terrible acts perpetrated against Jews and Muslims, then referred to as "infidels," in the name of Christ during the Crusades of the Middle Ages. . . . Response to the Walk has confirmed the organisers' belief that public repentance on behalf of Christianity is necessary. "The walkers have noted that their message is consistently a source of astonishment to those who hear it," says Lynn Green of YWAM and a Walk leader. "Both Muslims and Jews have wept when they realise that these Western Christian people have come to them, in humility. Western nations, who so often represent Christianity, have traditionally presented a powerful and sometimes oppressive face to Muslim people."[117]

The more specifically African and Caribbean issues have been addressed by two prominent evangelical leaders in the British prayer movement, Roger Mitchell (a former EA Council member) and Brian Mills (a former EA staff member):

> Our forebears rarely showed any sign of Christian principles in the way they dealt with slaves and people of different races. In Africa it is much the same. As the colonial power we were in the ascendancy. Whilst we have handed over the reins of empire to independent States, nevertheless the seeds of empire are still to be seen in racially motivated attitudes that are sometimes

---

115. Green, "Identificational Repentance," 2. Italics the authors.
116. Green, "Identificational Repentance," 3.
117. "Pilgrimage," 2.

expressed. . . . What can we do about it? Within this country, we can take every and any opportunity to apologise and ask forgiveness for our own personal marginalisation of black people, and that of white Christians generally. . . . We need to go to their churches without waiting for an invitation. . . . Turning up, showing interest, fellowship and love is the black way of doing things. Every time one of us has gone to a West Indian congregation, unannounced and uninvited, we have been asked to bring greetings. The first time I did so, I apologised for the wrong attitudes we white Christians had had and for our lack of welcome to them. What healing took place in that meeting and subsequently between Afro-Caribbean and English evangelicals![118]

Such statements made African neo-Pentecostals a focus for pro-active white, British-born charismatics who identify with past colonial masters and need "the sons of empire" (to use a Mitchell phrase) to apologize to. The pattern is the same when such charismatics identify with white slave traders and apologize to Caribbean Pentecostals. Despite early positive responses, by the turn of the millennium, African and Caribbean leaders were saying that they found such apologizing for the past a distraction from building meaningful equal relationships in the present.[119] It is noteworthy that Caribbean and African church leaders have not adopted the "identificational repentance" approach between themselves to resolve the long standing tensions between the Caribbean and Africa over the history of the slave trade.[120] Nonetheless, in 1999 when the Ugandan neo-Pentecostal prayer leader, John Mulinde, presented a prophecy for Europe, British prayer leaders made much of his coming to Britain as a "spiritual son of mission and empire turning his heart towards us his spiritual fathers."[121]

Although the emphasis on identificational repentance for slavery and colonialism was coming to an end in 1999, the whole concept was to receive fresh impetus in the new millennium when in March 2000 the Pope extended an apology for the Crusades and Inquisition to include "minorities" and "native people." From the standpoint of identification, he was in a unique position to represent the Church of the past and to meaningfully take responsibility in the present. In the words of a *Times* reporter,

118. Mills and Mitchell, *Sins of the Fathers*, 77.
119. Repeated comment by Sturge, 1997.
120. Pope-Hennessy, *Sins of the Fathers*, 174–91.
121. Roger Mitchell used this of Mulinde at the War Room prayer leaders' event, Hemel Hempstead, November 1999. Rennie, "War Room." Mitchell also used the expression to describe Babatunde in his commendation for Babatunde's book. Babatunde, *Great Britain Has Fallen!*, 4.

> Brushing aside the misgivings of many Roman Catholics, the Pope made a comprehensive and unprecedented plea yesterday for forgiveness for the "past sins of the Church," including the Crusades and Inquisition, racial and ethnic discrimination and Christian mistreatment of minorities, women and native people.[122]

The EA followed this up with a consultation on June 30, 2001.[123] The event was heralded by a provocative article in its magazine:

> IR can fairly be described as a hot potato in prayer circles. Even the term Identificational Repentance is challenged by those who prefer Representational Confession, or Identificational Confession, or Healing the Land—and back up their preferences with Scripture. Those on the other side of the fence are concerned that there is little justification in Scripture for this type of prayer. IR, they say, is at least a holy timewaster, and at worst, heresy. As one person put it: "It's a theology looking for a Scripture." Theological problems abound. What does taking responsibility for corporate sin actually mean? Is what is taking place confession or repentance? When is IR complete for a given situation?[124]

The final word on the subject from the EA came in the form of a book review in *Idea* written by David Hilborn, the EA Theological advisor. He sympathetically assessed *Healing Wounded History* by Russ Parker, a leading exponent of Christian healing and a member of the British branch of Dawson's International Reconciliation Coalition:

> As is so often the case with evangelically driven projects like these, the enthusiasm and aspirations of the participants tended to run ahead of detailed theological reflection. Dawson, Mills and Mitchell are all passionate and biblically conscious, but none of their books offers the sort of thorough, scholarly apologetic that might at least gain IR a hearing in the mainstream Church. ... The IR debate still needed to be taken to another level. It was crying out for a careful, full-length exposition, which would engage with pertinent academic work in biblical studies, pastoral theology, church history and systematics. Happily, Russ Parker has delivered the book ... it is refreshing in its willingness not only to engage with the main arguments against IR, but in some

---

122. Owen, "Pope," 5L.
123. "No Apologies," 5.
124. "Saying Sorry," 19–21.

cases, to refine and modify identificational paradigms in the light of them.[125]

In their exploration of spiritual warfare and IR, evangelical charismatics were seeking common ground with African neo-Pentecostals. However, results were mixed as their spirituality and theology did not always fit. Ultimately, the EA was able to adopt a benign stance in the debate, thanks partly to the way in which Parker sought to bring some intellectual credibility to some of IR's more controversial aspects.

Joint African and Caribbean conferences

The joint African and Caribbean support enjoyed by MTL from 1992 onwards might suggest a degree of unity and common interest extending to other conferences and events. ACEA, which from the late 1980s had entertained hopes of bringing the emerging African churches within its predominantly Caribbean fold, had held annual conferences each February between 1991 and 1993 under the title of Accord.[126] In 1994 it tried a different approach, picking up on black identity issues with a conference called Highway.[127] From the outset the Highway organizer, Les Isaac, tried to involve the African churches, even appointing a young Nigerian pastor, Paul Ogedengbe, as his vice-chairman for the event.[128]

When the first event took place on October 20–22, 1994 at St Mark's Church, Kennington, there was a real expectation on the part of the organizers that their prepared program would fully engage both constituencies.[129] They had sought to synthesize two themes. A number of prominent African American church leaders at the time had begun to engage with issues concerning a "sons of Ham" theology. This not only sought to counter the victimization of black people argued from the curse of Canaan in Gen 9:25 but promoted the concept of black prominence in the purposes of God by highlighting the role of black people in the Bible, anticipating a more dominant role for black Christianity on into the late twentieth century.[130]

125. Hilborn, "Long Overdue Apology," 13.

126. The Accord conference was held in 1990, 1991, 1992, and 1993.

127. "Black Church," 14,

128. Highway archive held by Ascension Trust. Highway Conferences were October events, 1993–95.

129. Highway archive.

130. Some disapproved of this approach, regarding it as a Black Christian supremacy emphasis. The case for Black theology has since been argued by Beckford. See Beckford, *Jesus Is Dread*, and Beckford, *Dread and Pentecostal*. In 2004 Ashimolowo used

This was generating interest among Caribbean church leaders in Britain.[131] At the same time, among a number of the African church leaders in the UK, there was a growing interest in "Apostolic and Prophetic reformation." This was being spearheaded by Ogedengbe who had held a "Prophetic Prayer" event at the City Temple in May 1994 and a four day "Prophetic and Apostolic Conference," also at the City Temple, in June of the same year.[132] Ogedengbe's mentor in this "apostolic and prophetic reformation" was the Trinidadian, sometime African Studies lecturer at the University of the West Indies, Noel Woodroffe.[133] Woodroffe had left academia to become "founder of the World Breakthrough Network, a relationship network of ministries and churches across the Caribbean and in other parts of the world" and "President of Elijah Ministries International, a ministry dedicated to the teaching, training and developing of prophetic/apostolic ministry and the advancement of God's present truth purposes in the earth."[134] Woodroffe openly acknowledged his early indebtedness to the ideas of American restorationist teacher Bill Hamon of Christian International.[135] Ogedengbe secured Woodroffe's services as a speaker at Highway 1994. Woodroffe's thesis was that "good leadership in the House of God is not just an administrative or an organizational requirement; it is a spiritual necessity for survival."[136] He was committed to raising up strong leaders.[137] Like Hamon, he saw this as part of a prophetic and apostolic restoration in the midst of an extended restorative program currently being undertaken by God.[138] In his understanding the process was designed not only to recreate New Testament order but to bring about a new reformation of the church that would enable it to embrace "new spiritual technologies" and supersede the power and effectiveness of the church in the first century. He saw this as having individual ramifications as well as corporate ones:

---

black prominence arguments to publicize KICC's annual celebrations of Black History month. "Black and Blessed."

131. Conversation with Les Issac, October 1994.

132. Prophetic Prayer Event May 14, 1994, Prophetic and Apostolic Conference June 20–23, 1994. Personal diary archive.

133. For Ogedengbe's link with Woodroffe see biographical note in Seyi-Ogedengbe, *African Story*, back cover.

134. Woodroffe, *Understanding God's Prophetic Move*, back cover.

135. Woodroffe, *Understanding God's Prophetic Move*, vii.

136. Woodroffe and Taylor, *Spiritual Government*, 20.

137. Woodroffe and Taylor, *Spiritual Government*, dedication.

138. Woodroffe, *Understanding God's Prophetic Move*, 7–14; Hamon, *Apostles*, 190–200.

> Cosmic processes are at work in the world today. The earth is marching towards a date with destiny when in the last great and glorious war the powers of the kingdom of darkness will be destroyed forever. God's timetable is set, and nothing can change the final outcome. Jesus is already victorious! As the end-time Church is being prepared by the Holy Spirit to rule and reign with Christ forever, there arises out of complacency and weakness the pattern of the 21st century saint who will be The Ultimate Warrior![139]

The combining of Woodroffe's apostolic and prophetic reformation teaching with the underlying "Sons of Ham" theology of some other speakers gave the conference overall a self-confident and assertive tone.[140] However, from some of the small group workshops held in the afternoons, it was obvious that African and Caribbean delegates were not always seeing things in the same way and that agreement on the wider view could readily be obscured by differences over detail. Some delegates were particularly concerned about the lack of African involvement in those British social issues, such as education and policing, which were constantly demanding the Caribbean diaspora's attention. Other delegates were more personally focused, picking on matrimonial issues where instability and in some cases bigamy had occurred in marriages between Caribbean women resident in Britain and newly arrived African men.[141] Some were even prepared to attribute these relational difficulties to the "Caribbean victim, African victimizer" theories arising from certain analyses of the eighteenth- and nineteenth-century slave trade whereby the blame for selling West African residents into slavery was laid primarily at the door of their compatriots.[142]

ACEA returned to the theme of possible tensions between the African and Caribbean communities at a conference it hosted in the lead up to the 1998 celebrations for the fiftieth anniversary of the arrival of HMS Windrush, the ship that brought the first wave of post-war workers from the West Indies. *Focus* reported the conference as follows:

> In the run up to the Windrush Celebrations ACEA took the bold step of calling on the Black Majority Churches to unite. Billed as *a plea for unity, understanding and reconciliation among African, Caribbean and the wider Black Majority Churches in the UK*, Rosemarie Davidson-Gotabed, Racial Justice Co-ordinator

---

139. Woodroffe, *Ultimate Warrior*, back cover.
140. Observation as a participant.
141. I chaired a seminar where such views were expressed.
142. Martin, *Britain's Slave Trade*, 22; Pope-Hennessey, *Sins of the Fathers*, 174–91.

for the London Baptist Association, says: "sociologically we are divided as Africans, African-Caribbeans and "Black other." We must leave these boxes that have kept us apart and present new models for church and the wider society as we search for a multicultural Britain at ease with itself."[143]

The conference was a highly charged event from the outset. Rev Nezlin Sterling, General Secretary of the New Testament Assembly and a trustee of ACEA, stated in her address that, "although the Caribbean Churches were large and credible organizations and the way they exercise[d] their social responsibility made them the stabilizing force within the community," they could also be insular, mistrusting and disloyal.[144] She referred to the fact that some had a "dated" leadership and "gave a poor public presentation of themselves," sometimes placing church life above family life.[145] By contrast, Dr. Albert Odulele, Senior Pastor of Green Pastures Ministries, concentrated on the strengths of the African churches, citing their youth and dynamism, the high proportion of educated professionals in their memberships and the determination of their leaders. He saw advantage in the fact that they were "free from legalistic and historical baggage," with "less controlling boards that allow for greater freedom and for the decision-making process to be more decisive and prompt."[146] He believed that they were the fastest growing churches and among the largest because of their "zeal in evangelism and strong belief in the final authority of the Bible."[147]

There was also a contribution by Naboth Muchopa, Secretary for Racial Justice for the British Methodist Church, on behalf of Black Christians in "established denominations." He made a strong appeal for a united Black Christian stand in the interests of justice:

> We must recognise the hurt, the pain, the anger, and the brokenness that many black people experience because of division, racism, poverty, unemployment and violence. These divisions have pushed us to the margins and abused us on the grounds of our race and colour and our church affiliation. We do not need any more subdivisions. Our spirituality and faith must enable us to reject unnecessary divisions from the church of Jesus Christ to which we all belong.... Our unity and togetherness is paramount for our future and survival. Many of us see

---

143. "Africans and Caribbeans," 5.
144. "Africans and Caribbeans," 5.
145. "Africans and Caribbeans," 5.
146. "Africans and Caribbeans," 5.
147. "Africans and Caribbeans," 5.

the integration model in its present form as morally bankrupt. Black people today, as well as generations to come, will suffer from its damning effect unless we can make a case for a new moral vision and more just, fair and equitable social, political and economic arrangements towards those things we can realistically achieve.[148]

At the close of the conference, Mark Sturge, then General Director of ACEA, evenly apportioned blame saying that "one of the greatest charges that can be laid at the feet of the BMCs is the neglect in pursuing, with a passion, reconciliation among themselves." He believed that the Caribbean churches had been "guilty of looking after themselves . . . obsessed with holiness to the point of believing that they, each denomination, were the only true church," adding that "they did not even notice African migration taking place." He felt that the error of the African churches was that "there was an arrogance that supported the stereotypes that Caribbean people were unintelligible, they were not doing a good enough job and that they, the African churches, knew better, if not best."[149] Perhaps shared guilt was not the strongest basis for future unity.

Changes in British public opinion

In the spring of 1993, the national press was gripped by the murder of the black teenager Stephen Lawrence which took place in Eltham, South London, on April 22. Six years later, on February 15, 1999, when Sir William Macpherson published the report of his *Inquiry into the matters arising from the death of Stephen Lawrence*, a national debate into the possibilities of "institutional racism" was launched. Macpherson affirmed that "[a] central and vital issue which has permeated our Inquiry has been the issue of racism," adding that "[t]he chilling condemnation, made by and on behalf of Mr and Mrs Lawrence at and after the Inquest in February 1997, of the police and of the system of English justice, has sounded throughout all the months of our consideration of the evidence." The nub of their argument was that "their colour, culture and ethnic origin, and that of their murdered son, have throughout affected the way in which the case has been dealt with and pursued."[150]

Although the issues raised related to the Metropolitan Police Service, fear of even being accused of institutional racism caused all public bodies,

148. "Africans and Caribbeans," 5.
149. "Africans and Caribbeans," 5.
150. Macpherson of Cluny, *Inquiry*, para. 6.1.

including churches and inter-church organizations, to reassess their levels of racial-awareness. Sturge of ACEA was keen to reinforce the message. In an article on racism he offered an interpretation of Num 12: "When Moses pleaded with God to forgive his sister, God implied that her indiscretion should be equated with that of a father spitting in his daughter's face. In other words, by implication, God spat in Miriam's face for being racist and set a precedent for society." He then went on to write,

> Several British institutions, including the (Metropolitan) Police, Army, and Civil Service, have finally owned up to being institutionally racist and biased against ethnic groups. Churches must take seriously the remarks of Clive Efford, MP of Eltham, who says, "Racism exists in our society today. It permeates every section and every institution. It is the responsibility of us all—the decent minded majority—to confront racism in all of its forms, to provide education where there is ignorance and guidance where there is prejudice and to be intolerant of those who place themselves beyond the bounds of human decency."[151]

As the Inquiry got underway, Neville Lawrence, Stephen's father, sought support from the African and Caribbean churches:

> Stephen Lawrence was murdered because of his race; his death has become the "conscience" of the nation. His father, Neville Lawrence, spoke recently to ACEA. He wants to be able to approach churches for help and support when similar tragedies occur to other families. He believes the press exist [sic] just for a season and the quick story. However, in his view the church genuinely loves people and will offer ongoing support and help for as long as necessary.[152]

In 1998 Greenford Baptist Church held a public meeting at which Neville Lawrence spoke. ACEA's magazine, *Focus*, commented "The Lawrence family's commitment to finding Stephen's killers has served as an inspiration to all, and many are reminded of the 'Persistent Widow,' the woman in Christ's parable who was relentless in her pursuit of justice."[153] However, the Lawrence family's appreciation of the churches faltered and the Nation of Islam became involved. Sturge saw this as filling a gap that should never have been created:

---

151. Sturge, "Why Is the Issue?," 6–7.
152. Encinas-Meade, "Campaigning," 1.
153. Reddie, "Christians," 1.

> The absence of the BMCs both in supporting the Lawrence family and at the inquiry was stark. In general, we gave the tragedy little or no priority, even though the Lawrence's [sic] faith commitment was presented to us.... The presence of the Rt. Rev. Dr. John Sentamu, Bishop of Stepney and an ACEA Vice President, on the inquiry team was treated as "a matter of fact" rather than an opportunity for the BMCs to engage in the process. We even withheld our prayers.... The public perception is that there was no leadership from the black community during the Lawrence's [sic] campaign for justice until The Nation of Islam turned up at the inquiry. While I accept that there were many distortions in the press about the "so-called militant group," I was more disheartened to hear that Neville Lawrence had invited them to be there because he needed protection and the church could not offer that. What is most regretful is that ACEA was never approached by the BMCs or its members to register their concern, nor asked about an appropriate response to the Lawrence's [sic] plight. I feel personally ashamed that I placed the need to maintain unity and the goodwill of the BMCs over and above the cries of justice, and yes I failed to exercise leadership and be faithful to my conscience when it really mattered.[154]

However, if there was a failure of BMCs to engage during the inquiry, there was clearly an attempt to make up for this after the report's publication.[155] On Saturday March 20, 1999 the Black Christian Civic Forum organized a conference on the Macpherson Report at KICC. "The conference was chaired by Revd. Dr Friday Nwator and speakers included Trevor Phillips, Pastor Ade Okorende, Dr Richard Stone, Philip Mohabir and Paul Boateng, Minister of State at the Home office."[156] Two months later, on May 27, ACEA led a delegation to meet with Metropolitan Police Commissioner, Sir Paul Condon. Sturge told the Commissioner "that although he [the Commissioner] urged his force to be intolerant of their colleagues who failed to reach the required standard, he may have set it so low that it was impossible for anyone to fail." He also told the Commissioner that "the Macpherson Report had given the nation a new standard which minority ethnic communities can embrace."[157] This meeting was followed by a Home

154. Sturge, "BMCs Response."

155. Sturge recorded the perceived failure in his draft response: "It was not until phase 2 of the inquiry that R. David Muir, Rev. Abraham Lawrence and Rev. Joel Edwards ... made representation, almost out of embarrassment. (During which time I was abroad on holiday.)"

156. "Conferences Respond," 15.

157. "Church Leaders Meet," 12.

Office meeting on July 21 for Sturge and others with Minister Mike O'Brien when issues arising from the Macpherson Inquiry were discussed.[158]

Clearly Sturge saw this whole episode as a lost opportunity for the African and Caribbean churches. For him, it was a time when the churches should have gained a positive reputation by taking a joint stand with the Lawrences on a matter that he believed affected both groups equally. In the end, the African and Caribbean churches gained little; nothing more than the by-products of British evangelicalism's desire to be seen as more inclusive. In an environment pervaded by fear of institutional racism, it is possible for duty and political correctness to prompt attempts at inclusiveness. In church circles an awareness of the Bible's high expectation on receiving others with equanimity can bring an added pressure on being seen to get it right. Genuine inclusiveness is dependent on both parties being committed to developing mutual understanding.

Identity, independence, and the appointment of Edwards

There is no doubt that throughout the 1990s the independent African neo-Pentecostal churches saw themselves as distinct from the Caribbean Pentecostal denominational churches. This was not always recognized by the wider British church community, the Caribbean churches or academia.[159] This sense of separate identity is not surprising given that the African diaspora in general has always seen itself as distinct from the Caribbean diaspora. African neo-Pentecostal leaders did look beyond ethnic considerations, however, to less formality in church style and greater liberty in governance.[160] The evidence indicated that these differences were more due to freedom from denominational restraint than to any deeply seated national culture. Caribbean leaders who left their denominations in the 1980s and 1990s set up churches that were virtually identical to independent African neo-Pentecostal congregations. Ruach, led by Bishop John Francis, and Rhema led by Mark Goodridge are examples of this.[161] Such similarity could indicate an element of emulation but is more accurately understood as indicating a common African American neo-Pentecostal influence.[162]

---

158. "Delegation Meets," 12.

159. Hunt set his RCCG research historically in a British Afro-Caribbean church context. Hunt, "British Black Pentecostal"; Hunt, "'New' Black Pentecostal."

160. "Africans and Caribbeans," 5.

161. Aldred, *Respect*, 98, 99; Beckford, *Dread and Pentecostal*, 51–57.

162. Eddie Long, Carlton Pearson and T. D. Jakes have all had significant input into African neo-Pentecostal church conferences in Britain.

If there is a significant difference between the independent Caribbean neo-Pentecostal churches and the independent African neo-Pentecostal churches, it is in the area of "Black community" social concerns. In the late 1990s African neo-Pentecostal churches were beginning to have social action programs but they were more geographically specific and problem specific than "Black community" specific. For example, Nims Obunge of Freedom's Ark was working towards the founding of the Haringey Peace Alliance, which models methods for confronting crime issues throughout London boroughs, while Clement Adebayo and Ade Omooba of Christian Victory Group, I Care Projects, had established programs of support for the homeless.[163] By contrast, churches with a Caribbean background were still reflecting their denominational heritage in being more acutely aware of the needs within the Caribbean community and in feeling a strong sense of obligation to address these. It is not that they have ever been intentionally exclusive in their provision but have just had a narrower community specificity in their project selection.

Comparative statistics afford some justification for the Caribbean churches' focus. The 1991 census showed forty percent of Caribbean working men in London in social class III(M), representing skilled manual occupations, and few in social class I.[164] It highlighted the fact that full-time employment amongst Caribbean women was customary, whereas part-time employment was more common among white women and that the percentage of families consisting of a lone parent with dependent children was nearly four times higher in the Black community (then predominantly Caribbean) than in the White community.[165] However, other figures simply highlighted the relative newness of the growing British African diaspora. Africans were more likely to be full-time students than those in the same age range from the Caribbean community.[166] In 1991 one in three black Africans was born within Britain, whereas the figure for the Caribbean community was one in two. The African community was more mobile within Britain than the Caribbean community with a quarter of Africans having moved home in 1990–91 and only one in ten of the Caribbean community having moved within that time. Africans were more likely to be in privately rented accommodation, with nearly one in five of such households being in accommodation that lacked or shared basic amenities.[167] If factors such as

---

163. Haringey Peace Alliance, formally launched on July 2001.
164. "Without Prejudice."
165. "Without Prejudice."
166. "Without Prejudice."
167. "Without Prejudice."

a community's population size and depth of establishment are significant when considering its social profile, then it has to be noted that although the Caribbean community was larger and more established than the African community in 1991, the African community was set to grow faster, with an expected doubling in size by 2001.[168] In time both communities could be facing similar challenges. This, however, was not the perception of the African neo-Pentecostal churches in the 1990s. A specifically Black community agenda was not in their sights and they found little to persuade them to join forces with Caribbean churches to meet such community-specific needs. They wanted to be seen as relevant to Britain as a whole.[169]

Given this deliberate breadth of focus, the appointment of Edwards as the General Director of the EA in June 1997 was not seen by the African churches as such an obvious turning-point, despite being presented to the media as a breakthrough in race relations.[170] Two of the three press releases prepared by the EA stressed Edwards' ethnicity.[171] The third, written for the Christian press, assumed that readers would already know Edwards' racial background and referred only to his past role at ACEA.[172] The statement prepared for widest circulation was headed "Black minister to lead Evangelical Alliance UK" and profiled comments on "society's privatisation of morality" and racial tension:

> As the first black leader in the 150-year history of the Alliance, Joel Edwards said he was "deeply worried" that racial tension would become one of the biggest social and political challenges facing Britain in the next decade.... Joel concluded: "The challenges before us, whether they concern race or personal morality, are very real."[173]

The EA appreciated the "generous coverage" the appointment received in the national press.[174] It was particularly pleased with an article

168. "Without Prejudice."
169. Babatunde, *Great Britain Has Fallen!*, 158–60.
170. Edwards' appointment was announced at Church House, June 6, 1997, 10:30 a.m.
171. EA News Release, "Black Minister to Lead Evangelical Alliance UK," press release, June 6, 1997; EA News Release, "Joel Edwards: Black Churches Are the 'Unsung Heroes,'" press release, June 6, 1997.
172. EA News Release, "Black Minister to Lead Evangelical Alliance UK," press release, June 6, 1997.
173. EA News Release, "Black Minister to Lead Evangelical Alliance UK," press release, June 6, 1997.
174. Edwards, *Lord*, 95.

Principles and practicalities in the interactions of 1985–99   143

in the *Guardian* referring to Edwards' "street cred."[175] The culmination of Edwards' three-day media launch was an interview on BBC Radio 4's "Sunday" program where he declared that he saw his appointment as a vote of confidence for evangelical diversity.[176] However, in an interview with ACEA he admitted that in working with other ethnic groups and cultures the EA had a long way to go, adding "the difficulties involved in having black churches relate to wider evangelicalism would be similar to that of other ethnic groups . . . they enjoy the different liturgical cultures . . . [but frequently] are caught in a perpetual pattern of insular activities, which shields them from greater levels of interaction and wider relationships." He then went on to explain that he believed a solution to this would be for the EA to "help" black and other ethnic groups, saying "certainly, more historic churches are stronger organizationally with administrative expertise, which could be made available to growing ethnic groups."[177]

One method of assessing how African and Caribbean churches responded to Edwards' suggestion that they might access the organizational strength and administrative expertise of more historic churches is to look for a new enthusiasm in their signing up to work alongside such churches within the EA. A rise in the membership numbers of a particular constituency in the months following Edwards' appointment could reasonably be taken as an indication of a new sense of constituency endorsement. An analysis of membership announcements in *Idea* magazine is a useful guide here but it has to be borne in mind that there can be several months delay between a ministry's application and its membership announcement.[178]

Taking the year as a whole, there were twenty-two African and eight Caribbean new member churches and ministries out of a total new EA membership over the twelve month period of two hundred and thirty-three. However, only six of these were accorded EA membership directly, the other twenty-four through its partner charity ACEA.[179] This is not surprising since at the time ACEA was implementing a new membership policy after the appointment of its own new General Director in December 1996.[180] In

---

175. "Meet Joel Edwards," 22.

176. Edwards, *Lord*, 95, 96.

177. "Former ACEA General Secretary," 2.

178. Delays when joining through ACEA have averaged 6.4 months but reached 18 months.

179. ACEA Membership List.

180. Those joining EA directly were: the Caribbean Fellowship of KT; Eagle Wing International Church, Kilburn; Fold of Christ Ministry, London; God's Time Ministries, Manor Park; Hephzibah Christian Centre, Hackney, and Precious Stones Christian Centre, Leyton. Hephzibah and the KT congregation mainly served the Caribbean

a similar period for 1998–99 a further twenty-two African and Caribbean churches joined the EA, twenty through ACEA.[181] Overall the number of new members of the EA dropped from two hundred and fifty-nine in the previous year to two hundred and thirty-three in Edwards' first year, and then to one hundred and ninety-two in his second year. Once the churches and ministries that joined through ACEA are discounted, the figures would suggest that Edwards' appointment as the EA's first black General Director had no significant effect on African (or Caribbean) membership of the EA. This probably says more about African neo-Pentecostal attitudes in the 1990s to Black identity issues than it does about Edwards. For many Edwards was impressive. According to Hastings: "Perhaps, all in all, the most significant ecclesiastical figure of the 1990s was Joel Edwards, black General Director of the Evangelical Alliance."[182]

Clearly there were many in the 1990s for whom Black identity was a bigger issue than it was for the majority of African neo-Pentecostal pastors. Theirs was a balance between acknowledging a distinct African identity and being committed to an impact beyond the Black community. Strongly identifying with the Black community was not their primary aim. Whilst this should have eased interaction with the wider evangelical community, it did run the risk of causing confusion by making African neo-Pentecostalism harder to fit into the existing (even if at times stereotypically Caribbean) Black-led, or BMC, understanding.

ISSUES OF EVANGELICAL AND CHARISMATIC CONCERN

Just as there were issues of African and Caribbean identity which had indirect bearing on relations between African neo-Pentecostalism and British evangelicalism in the lead up to the new millennium, so there were indirect effects from issues of evangelical and charismatic concern. However, it has to be said that the effects were largely due to the high levels of evangelical and charismatic introspective preoccupation causing the on-looking African neo-Pentecostal constituency some measure of bemusement. The primary issues of concern were Word and Spirit, the nature of Hell, the Toronto blessing, and postmodernism.

---

diaspora. The Caribbean Fellowship of KT had had as its pastor the newly appointed General Director of ACEA. Randall and Hilborn, *One Body*, 290.

181. ACEA Membership List. Those joining the EA directly were: Shiloh Pentecostal Church, Dalston, and Mountain of Fire and Miracles Ministries, London.

182. Hastings, *History of English Christianity*, xlvi.

Word and Spirit

In October 1992 R. T. Kendall, the Kentucky-raised minister of Westminster Chapel, held his first Word and Spirit Conference at Wembley Conference Centre.[183] It was sponsored by eleven evangelical churches of various denominations that had come together across borough boundaries in north London to form an association called Beulah.[184] A significant contribution to the program was the inclusion of Paul Cain, a controversial Texan charismatic prophet who had been brought to London by fellow American John Wimber.[185] Cain had joined Wimber in October 1990 for meetings at Dockland's London Arena.[186] During the Dockland meetings Kendall had overcome his theological and pastoral reservations about Cain and established a friendship with him that led to Cain becoming a member of Westminster Chapel. According to Kendall,

> Paul began to say he wanted to be under my own ministry. I had lovingly chided him that he was upholding a defective theology. Sitting in a restaurant in Victoria Street I said, "Paul, you need my theology, I need your power." He said, "You have a deal." In that moment there was born—in my mind—the need to bring the Word and Spirit together. He represented the Spirit, as it were, and I the Word. This vision sealed our relationship.[187]

In terms of his conservative evangelical credentials, Kendall had a strong pedigree, despite his controversial Oxford DPhil thesis questioning Calvin's commitment to a major tenet of Calvinism, limited atonement.[188] Nonetheless, Kendall had, since 1977, been preaching from a pulpit renowned in evangelical circles for its high standards of biblical exposition. He had not only won the respect of those that held to his predecessor's separatist ecclesiology but in January 1990, nine years after Lloyd-Jones's death, had steered Westminster Chapel back into membership of the EA.[189]

The concept of bringing Word and Spirit together was not new but Kendall surprised the fourteen hundred church leaders present in Wembley with his application of the Genesis account of the births of Ishmael

---

183. Kendall, *In Pursuit*, 107.
184. Kendall, *In Pursuit*, 107.
185. Kendall, *In Pursuit*, 99–100.
186. Kendall, *In Pursuit*, 100.
187. Kendall, *In Pursuit*, 105.
188. Kendall, *In Pursuit*, 15.
189. Kendall, *In Pursuit*, 165.

(a blessed child but not the son of promise) and Isaac.[190] His recollections provide an accurate summary:

> I suspect that what has been remembered most from that conference was not Paul's ministry but my own address on Ishmael and Isaac. I spent thirty-five minutes unpacking what I briefly referred to above—that much in the twentieth century which has preceded was but "Ishmael"; but Isaac is coming and the impact will be as proportionally greater over the Charismatic Movement as the promise to Isaac was over Ishmael. People were all, generally speaking, stunned. A stony silence followed. Some felt it was an important statement, among these being Colin Dye, the new minister of Kensington Temple. I am grateful to Lynn Green of YWAM who came to the platform and asked the congregation to weigh this matter carefully.[191]

There is no doubt that Kendall delivered his Isaac and Ishmael message in the hope of increasing unity. He believed that the Word and Spirit conference would not only bring himself and Cain together but create common ground between conservative evangelicals and charismatics. However, he clearly regarded Ishmael as typifying the Charismatic Movement.[192] His wish for unity was not fulfilled:

> My address at that conference ended up getting me into more trouble than any talk I have ever given—bar none. It infuriated a number of charismatic leaders. One man called for a conference to "sit in judgment" on what I had said. Evangelical non-charismatics were unhappy with my message because I had, after all, extolled the Charismatic Movement to a great degree. I said that most churches in England worth their salt were charismatic, as were most of the good hymns and choruses being written.[193]

Pentecostals, rightly or wrongly, tended to place themselves on the sidelines of this Isaac and Ishmael debate, feeling that there was sufficient difference between themselves and those within the Charismatic Movement to avoid the charge. Prior to Kendall's Isaac and Ishmael theory there had been an alternative understanding of the coming together of Word and

---

190. Part of the difficulty for conservative evangelicals was that hermeneutically he appeared to read into the text (*eisegesis*) rather than draw from it (*exegesis*). Noakes later used "Isaac and Ishmael" to analyze the "Toronto Blessing." Noakes, "Personal and Biblical," 146–50.

191. Kendall, *In Pursuit*, 107–8.

192. Kendall, *In Pursuit*, 105–6.

193. Kendall, *In Pursuit*, 108.

Spirit in Pentecostal circles. A prophecy attributed to pioneer Pentecostal evangelist Smith Wigglesworth on tour in South Africa in 1936 includes the prediction that

> there will be evidence in the churches of something that has not been seen before: a coming together of those with an emphasis on the Word and those with an emphasis on the Spirit. When the Word and the Spirit come together, there will be the biggest move of the Holy Spirit that the nation and, indeed, the world has ever seen.[194]

In embracing this, Pentecostals have never believed they have a defective emphasis on the "Word." For them the excitement of any coming together would lie in conservative evangelicals adding their strength to the "move of the Spirit" rather than in Pentecostals receiving theological correction. This is a view in which they might claim some support from Peter Masters, minister of London's Metropolitan Tabernacle, who, as a prominent conservative evangelical, has been keen to distinguish between classical Pentecostals and charismatics:

> Many of the old-fashioned Pentecostalists (seemingly rare nowadays) were conservative evangelicals, and whatever our differences on certain points we could respect them as fellow believers who were fully committed to the authority of Scripture as they understood it. But during the 1960s we saw the emergence of an entirely new brand of Pentecostalism—the charismatic renewal movement—and since then ... charismatics have lurched from one excess to another.[195]

Charismatics have been criticized for theological superficiality not only by non-charismatics but from within their own camp. The charismatic leader David Pawson, a Baptist minister with a Methodist background, wrote in 1993 in his book on uniting evangelicals and charismatics: "theology has sometimes been built on experience, rather than vice-versa. There

---

194. Cartwright, *Real Smith Wigglesworth*, 165. This prophecy is referred to in Stormont, *Wigglesworth*, 114; and Hywel-Davies, *Baptised by Fire*, 151–55. Bob Gordon (died 1997) dated the prophecy as 1947. Gordon, *Personally Speaking*, 144. Frodsham made no mention of it in detailing Wigglesworth's 1937 South Africa tour. Frodsham, *Real Smith Wigglesworth*, 94–95. Personally, in 1994 I approached Lester Sumrall, onetime colleague of Wigglesworth, about the prophecy. Sumrall responded, "if Wigglesworth had said it, he never believed it." Cartwright demonstrated that du Plessis, the original source, was inconsistent with his recollections. Cartwright, *Wigglesworth*, 161–67. A form of the prophecy is quoted earlier in this book, see Hywel-Davies, *Baptised by Fire*, 152–53.

195. Masters, *Healing*, 11. Also quoted earlier in this book.

has been a noticeable streak of pragmatism in charismatic thinking: 'if we felt led to do it and it worked, it must be of the Spirit.'"[196] Even so, Kendall, prior to presenting his Isaac and Ishmael message at the Wembley conference, had spoken earlier in the day on Matt 22:29, emphasizing the importance of both "Scripture and the power of God."[197] According to Jesus both elements were missing from the spirituality of the Sadducees and the inference could be drawn that it is not possible to have one without the other. Charismatic evangelicals clearly believe they have the "Word" as well as the "Spirit" and conservative evangelicals similarly believe they have the "Spirit" as well as the "Word." In reality it is the degree to which the parties adequately systematize their theology, emphasize expository Bible preaching, and base their authority on Scripture that constitutes the debate; hence Kendall "lovingly chiding" Cain about a "defective theology."[198] When charismatics decided not to adopt the theology of Pentecostalism, with its doctrines of initial evidence, healing in the atonement, and dispensationalism, they were cast back on the assertion that "the gifts are for today." Such an assertion, when unsupported theologically, can leave the Movement open to criticisms of theological superficiality, such as those voiced with varying degrees of severity by Kendall, Masters and Pawson.[199] On the issue of authority, Pawson wrote critically, as a comment on "post-evangelical" developments within the charismatic stream, that "[t]he Spirit is said to be moving us beyond scripture or at least away from the evangelical view of its inspiration and authority."[200] He also addressed the reworking of content in charismatic preaching:

> In some ways, Word and Spirit have been drifting apart again. A healthy recovery of worship as an end in itself . . . has often affected the priority and proportion in the service formerly given to systematic teaching, much of which is now topical rather than exegetical.[201]

In the light of all this, it has to be stressed that African neo-Pentecostals do not see themselves within the British charismatic camp. There may be a cultural element to this as indicated in the London Leaders' steering group minutes referred to earlier: "Africans struggle with attending meetings

196. Pawson, *Word and Spirit*, 67.
197. Kendall, *In Pursuit*, 107.
198. Pawson, *Word and Spirit*, i.
199. See above.
200. Pawson, *Word and Spirit*, iii.
201. Pawson, *Word and Spirit*, i.

Principles and practicalities in the interactions of 1985–99   149

at HTB [Holy Trinity, Brompton, London's largest charismatic Anglican church] because its culture is so 'white.'"[202] Issues do, however, go beyond culture. African neo-Pentecostal alignment with American Word of Faith teaching convinces them that they have a well-worked theology with a clear "Word" focus.[203] Furthermore, in arguing that their only basis of authority is the Bible, they use their commitment to literalism as an indication that they are more true to Scripture than many who call themselves charismatic evangelicals.[204] Not least, the time allotted to preaching in their church services is considerable and sermons are consistently based on the Bible. The style adopted, though, is illustrative, relying more on exhortation than exposition and the objective is more likely to be motivational than educational.[205] The "Word of Faith linked" African neo-Pentecostal position is clearly expressed by Nigerian church leader Francis Wale Oke:

> The word of God is the key to a successful, victorious and prosperous life. God said that the man who meditates in His word and walks in the light of it shall deal wisely in the affairs of life and have good success. He shall be like a tree planted by the rivers of living water. He will be fruitful, effective and productive. He will succeed in all he lays his hand upon and he will be blessed and happy. . . . Your ultimate success in life depends on your relationship with the word of God. It is important that the word of God enters you. If you build your life on any other thing apart from the word of God, something will be wrong somewhere, sometimes, and things will fall apart. But if you build your life on the eternal, incorruptible word of God, your success is the success of the word. You will only fail if the word of God has failed. And the word of God cannot fail. The Bible says "*Forever, O LORD, thy word is settled in heaven. Thy faithfulness is unto all generations.*" Psalm 119:89–90. It is therefore imperative that the word of God gets into you.[206]

With such "Word"-based convictions of African neo-Pentecostals in mind, I wrote to Kendall asking if he, as a reformed theologian, thought it was necessary to accept a reformed theology to qualify for believing in the Word

---

202. Steering Group Minutes, November 16, 1994. No African was serving on the steering group in November 1994. Of the two Caribbean-background members only Edwards was present.

203. Oke, *Power*, 52.

204. Emmanuel, *Charismatic Agenda*, 28, 30.

205. Sermons last "nearly an hour." Gifford, *Ghana's New Christianity*, 28.

206. Oke, *Power*, 52.

as well as the Spirit. My letter not only received a personal reply at the time but a further response in his 2002 autobiography:

> Probably not. John Wesley was an example of one who combined the Word and the Spirit in his preaching and teaching and he did not believe in predestination as I do. I do believe, however, that Wesley was a greater proponent of the sovereignty of God than many do today who claim to follow in his steps. It seems to me that a robust theology of the sovereignty of God—providing one is open to the Holy Spirit—is a very good corrective to the man-centred gospel that we all know about so well. I do pray that those who are open to the Holy Spirit will be open to the sovereignty of God as well.[207]

Whether such a reply helps the African neo-Pentecostal cause is open to question. The Word of Faith teaching that most African neo-Pentecostals espouse is often accused of being man-centered and of leaving God seemingly open to manipulation.[208] However, for many the Word and Spirit debate was more about ensuring that "those . . . open to the Holy Spirit" were also open to the authority of God's word. Ensuring that they had a strong understanding of God's sovereignty was not everyone's objective.

The nature of hell

In summarizing the tensions of the 1990s, Edwards asserted that "charismatics were up against it from Pentecostal as well as conservative leaders." One of the criticisms he listed as circulating was that charismatics "had weakened the theology of hell, replacing it with an annihilationist position."[209] This rumor was not entirely true. The views on hell causing such concern were "conditionalist" views being put forward by some conservative evangelicals as well as by some charismatics. These proponents differed over whether their interpretation of Scripture affirmed "conditional immortality" (where only the regenerate are believed to live on after death) or "conditional annihilation" (where the unregenerate are believed to be eventually relieved from endless torment).[210] Both views, however, are foreign to traditional Pentecostal thought.[211]

207. Kendall, *In Pursuit*, 201.
208. Hanegraaff, *Crisis*, 107–27; Farah, *From the Pinnacle*, 142–44.
209. Edwards, *Lord*, 115.
210. John Wenham embraced conditional immortality; Stott tended towards conditional annihilationism. ACUTE, *Nature of Hell*, 72–75.
211. See AoG Statement of Faith. Article 5, 15, "The Final Judgment"; Brumback,

Principles and practicalities in the interactions of 1985-99   151

These tensions came to the notice of African neo-Pentecostals only through the reaction of Dye at KT who, along with many Pentecostals, was concerned about the undermining of what he saw as biblical teaching on eternal punishment. As Dye took over the leadership of MTL from Cerullo after the 1996 event, he began to reassert the Mission's evangelistic intentions by emphasizing the desperation of those "eternally damned."[212] The booklet that he wrote, *The Cry of the Lost*, strongly affirmed the traditional position on eternal punishment. By 1998, MTL, then fully separated from MCWE and in membership with the EA in its own right, had its participants operating on the streets enthusiastically "Reaching the Lost."[213] This said, for Dye, "lostness" had immediate consequences as well as eternal ones and the figurative cry he sought to register in his booklet was about desperation in the present as much as in an afterlife.[214] He wrote from a personal conviction that the 1993 murders of Jamie Bulger and Stephen Lawrence raised major issues about society's depraving effects on children and young people.[215] A figurative approach towards eternal issues is common within Pentecostal circles and Word of Faith teachers have added an anecdotal element. Duplantis and Liardon have both written books on personal visits to heaven that are given wide credence.[216] The New Zealand AoG minister, Ian McCormack, has travelled widely speaking of a hell (and heaven) experience following jellyfish bites when diving off Mauritius in 1982: "total darkness. . . . I'm actually there but there's no physical form . . . my body is back in the hospital . . . cold evil presence . . . a man screams to me 'shut up' . . . 'you deserve to be here' . . . 'you're in Hell.'"[217]

The debate within evangelicalism was more theological and in 1998 the EA asked ACUTE to resolve the conflicting views on the matter.[218] Not surprisingly, with many senior evangelicals having brought their weight to bear, on both sides of the debate, the ACUTE report, eventually published in 2000, sought to preserve unity. It cautiously "affirmed the credentials of

---

Like a River, 163.

212. Dye, *Cry of the Lost*, 7, 8, 14, 15.

213. Dye's street evangelism plans, "MTL School," 7. EA membership confirmed, Dye, *Cry of the Lost*, 5.

214. Dye, *Cry of the Lost*, 7.

215. Jamie Bulger was killed on February 12, 1993; Stephen Lawrence on April 22, 1993.

216. Duplantis, *Heaven;* Liardon, *I Saw Heaven*.

217. Faith City Church, "Life after Death," 40:52—42:55.

218. For launch of ACUTE see Edwards, *Lord*, 93.

conditionalism" but also stated that "the weight of historic theological witness and *de facto* evangelical understanding were against it."[219]

> We recognise that the interpretation of hell in terms of conditional immortality is a significant minority evangelical view. Furthermore, we believe that the traditionalist-conditionalist debate on hell should be regarded as a secondary rather than a primary issue for evangelical theology. Although hell is a profoundly serious matter, we view the holding of either one of these two views of it over against the other to be neither essential in respect of Christian doctrine, nor finally definitive of what it means to be an evangelical Christian.[220]

The conservative evangelicals and the charismatic evangelicals who raised the subject of the nature of hell saw it as a "truth" issue rather than a "unity" issue but were nonetheless surprised that it threatened to split the evangelical camp. Although African neo-Pentecostalism, once it became aware of the debate, saw itself firmly in the traditionalist camp, the flexibility of the EA in the aftermath was such that traditionalism seemed no longer to be the only guarantee of evangelical acceptance. From the sidelines of the debate it seemed that conditionalism had become as acceptable as traditionalism. This did little to endear British evangelicalism to African neo-Pentecostals. It seemed incongruous that a body that could be ambivalent about hell could at the same time be so dogmatic about Cerullo. After all, as even Edwards had to admit, Cerullo on most points was a dogged traditionalist:

> He [Cerullo] too believed in the inspiration of the Bible—believed it fundamentally and, more than most, spoke uncompromisingly against liberal Christianity. Morris did not deny the Virgin birth, the deity of Christ or the Trinity. He accepted the ministry and vicarious work of Christ, His true death and resurrection. He spoke with confidence about the ascension and stood firmly in the classical Pentecostal position on the Second Coming of Christ.[221]

However, it was not just theological differences within conservative evangelical and charismatic circles that left African neo-Pentecostals bemused. Some charismatic behavior in the mid-1990s could be perplexing too.

219. Randall and Hilborn, *One Body*, 342.
220. ACUTE, *Hell*, 134.
221. Edwards, *Lord*, 104.

Principles and practicalities in the interactions of 1985-99   153

The Toronto Blessing and the National Alpha Campaign

By May 1994 some prominent churches and networks in membership with the EA had experienced a phenomenon associated with the Vineyard Fellowship at Toronto Airport, Canada, and the South African evangelist Rodney Howard-Browne, that threatened to alienate them from their evangelical colleagues.[222] The phenomenon involved people exhibiting "not only common manifestations of charismatic worship, including praying in tongues, ecstatic ululation, etc., but also shaking, falling down ("being slain in the Spirit"), an imperative need to laugh or cry, or to make unusual noises, especially sounds analogous to animal noises such as 'roaring' or 'barking.'"[223] This "particular development of the 'Pentecostal-charismatic' tradition within worldwide Christianity" became known as the "Toronto Blessing."[224]

In London, the involvement of prominent evangelical churches such as Queen's Road Baptist Church, Wimbledon, Anglicanism's Holy Trinity, Brompton, branches of the New Church Movement's New Frontiers International and the whole of the Ichthus Fellowship with its multiple south London congregations, again within the New Church stream, prompted such a level of curiosity that it was decided to devote the London Leaders' prayer gathering on July 6, 1994 to the "Toronto" theme.[225] One of those present recalled:

> The Spirit came upon the room in a great wave of power. Brethren and Pentecostal, Anglicans, New church and churches of every other stripe of evangelicalism were represented, and upon leader after leader the Spirit brought the awesome presence of God. It is always difficult to estimate such things, but it looked to me as if about two thirds of those present ended up on the floor at some stage.[226]

In the face of growing press interest in the "Toronto blessing," ACUTE was asked by the EA to organize a consultation and produce a position paper.[227] This was done in December 1994 with a two-day conference held at

222. Randall and Hilborn, *One Body*, 316–22.

223. Richards, "Toronto Experience," 1. For a description of the Toronto Blessing in the New Churches see Cotton, *Hallelujah Revolution*, 266–68.

224. Davie, "Real but Limited," 36. The term "Toronto Blessing" was first made public in Gledhill, "Spread of Hysteria," 12.

225. Hilborn, *"Toronto,"* 171.

226. Warner, *Prepare for Revival*, 17.

227. Randall and Hilborn, *One Body*, 323.

the Ibis Hotel near London's Euston Station producing what became known as the "Euston Statement."[228] Its first three points affirmed a commitment to standard evangelical doctrine, its fifth point restated standard evangelical unity practice, the remaining eight points related either to aspects of revival theology and history or to an evaluation of the current experience and the prevailing sociological context.[229] The overall tone neither condemned nor commended. One of the twenty-three leaders present who signed the consultation document was Matthew Ashimolowo.[230] Ashimolowo was asked to attend to bring an African perspective to the debate. However, he was in effect a disinterested party as the "Toronto blessing" bypassed (or was bypassed by) the African neo-Pentecostal churches. Despite the suggestion made in 1997 by Dr. Anne Richards of the Church of England Board of Mission that the "Toronto Blessing" may be a means whereby advocates are "catching up with what the Two-Thirds World has to teach us about holistic worship," the African neo-Pentecostal churches remained unimpressed by what to them often seemed to be excesses.[231] Many agreed with the comment of a Caribbean church leader who is alleged to have remarked to "Toronto" enthusiasts that "you are asking us to approve the very things [emotional excesses] of which you once accused us."[232]

Despite the fact that none of London's African neo-Pentecostal churches was mentioned in the lists of those affected by the Toronto blessing, there was an unexpected link.[233] Howard-Browne, whose preaching had been influential in launching the phenomenon, served for two years as an Associate Pastor at the Word of Faith Rhema Church in Johannesburg.[234] Anglican Vicar Stephen Sizer has written: "It is not hard to infer . . . that the roots of TTB [the Toronto Blessing] lie not in the Bible, but deep within the 'Health and Wealth,' Prosperity or 'Word of Faith' movement."[235] Consequently, those engaged with "Toronto" found themselves accused of having Word of Faith links through Howard-Browne just as those engaged with MTL were

---

228. EA "Euston" Statement in Hilborn, "*Toronto*," 351-55.

229. EA "Euston" Statement in Hilborn, "*Toronto*," 351-55.

230. EA "Euston" Statement in Hilborn, "*Toronto*," 351.

231. Richards, "Toronto Experience," 3.

232. Attributed to Mark Goodridge of Rhema Church, Croydon. Exact words not recorded.

233. The closest African neo-Pentecostal connection was KT. Hilborn, "*Toronto*," 163, 239. Dye attended Howard-Browne's meetings at Olympia, December 1994 and changed KT's program to accommodate the phenomenon.

234. Hilborn, "*Toronto*," 221. Rhema Ministries itself was not supportive of the Toronto Blessing. Anderson, "New," 66-92.

235. Sizer, "Sub-Christian," 45.

Principles and practicalities in the interactions of 1985–99   155

being accused of having Word of Faith links through Cerullo.[236] Some critics even traced the Toronto Blessing's provenance to the Latter Rain movement, which too had a part to play in African neo-Pentecostal history.[237] For a while, African neo-Pentecostals with their Word of Faith convictions found their associates, if not their theology, being regarded more sympathetically by some charismatics than had previously been the case.[238] The overall effect of this was mixed, as evangelicalism itself was in danger of dividing over spirituality and theology as a result of Toronto. The first coordinator of ACUTE observed that "the time and energy which have been expended on the 'Toronto Blessing' appear not only to have put evangelical against evangelical, but also to have diverted us from our two main tasks—to glorify God and to go out into all the world and preach the good news."[239] Edwards, as General Director of the EA, made a less self-flagellating comment about the period in the foreword to ACUTE's theological papers published some seven years after the outbreak of the phenomenon:

> After two decades or so of growth and relative success, it was perhaps inevitable that evangelicals would sooner or later face stern tests of their relationship, identity and theology. As it happened the Toronto Blessing provided all three. Looking back . . . it seems to me that, at the time, the Alliance handled the relationship and identity issues relatively well. On theology, however, there was always more room for more detailed work.[240]

In the end, the theology focused less on the provenance of "Toronto" teaching and more on the nature of revival. There was little serious theological work on the manifestations themselves, although American sociologist, Margaret Poloma, seemed to echo some of the concerns expressed in the earlier Word and Spirit debate in commenting,

> Although no systematic theology has been developed by renewal leaders (systematic theologians they are not), there is much theologizing by inference and metaphor. . . . Spirit drunkenness may have been reported in the book of Acts, God seemed to speak to Balaam through a donkey, there are Scripture passages

236. Hilborn, "Toronto," 221.
237. Forbes, "From North Battleford," 62–102.
238. Footage of Copeland and Howard-Browne "conversing" in tongues circulated to discredit them intrigued Kendall. For Kendall's attitude to "Toronto" see Hilborn, "Toronto," 234, and Kendall, *In Pursuit*, 115–32. For video, see Alan Morrison's sermon in Neil Richardson, "Toronto Blessing."
239. Dave Cave quoted in Randall and Hilborn, *One Body*, 328–29.
240. Edwards, "Foreword," xiii.

about laughter and joy, Jesus is often referred to as the Lion of Judah, and so on.[241]

Such illustrations notwithstanding, Calver, the Director General of the EA at the time, declared that alongside Bebbington's four characteristics it was possible to "identify two further dimensions of evangelical identity that are both central and essential."[242] The first was Christocentrism and the second a longing for revival.[243] He wrote,

> historically evangelicals have set a high value upon revival. ... This shapes our approach to evangelism, ecclesiology, and pneumatology. Longing for revival shapes our evangelism because, while we pour our energy, time and money into creative initiatives in our mission to the world, we pray beyond our own efforts for an outbreak of revival power, in which God's mighty work transcends our efforts.... The history of revival also shapes our theology of the Spirit.... In modern evangelicalism, the key distinction in terms of the Spirit has usually been whether we see ourselves as charismatic or non-charismatic evangelicals. Historically, the centrality of revival points us to a far more pressing and underlying issue. Are we wary, indifferent or even hostile to revival, with all the attendant outpourings of the Holy Spirit and dramatic manifestations of the divine presence? Or are we revival's passionate advocates?[244]

Given such a defining of evangelicalism, it is not surprising that the "Toronto Blessing" attracted so much attention. Calver believed evangelicals could not afford to be "indifferent" to "dramatic manifestations of the divine presence," even though not all such would indicate "full-scale" revival. In the early stages of the "Toronto" phenomenon Calver gave this assessment:

> Just after this move of God started I was in a set of churches and they said, "Is this an awakening?" And I said, "No. An Awakening is what God does in the world when he turns society around as he did in the 18th century." They said, "Is this revival?" I said, "I don't think so. Revival is what God does when he brings the world into the church." They said "is this renewal?" I said, "Yes, definitely. It's as important as this; you have never had an awakening in history that hasn't started in renewal and revival." Now I want to see an awakening. I want to see God touch our nation

---

241. Poloma, "Toronto Blessing," 378.
242. Calver and Warner, *Together We Stand*, 98; Bebbington, *Evangelicalism*, 4.
243. Calver and Warner, *Together We Stand*, 98–99.
244. Calver and Warner, *Together We Stand*, 99.

and to turn our society upside down and inside out. He won't start in society. He'll start with the people of God.²⁴⁵

Contributors to ACUTE's Toronto report differed on these designations of "renewed" and "revived" and added others of their own.²⁴⁶ Poloma settled for "refreshing, revitalisation and rest."²⁴⁷ She then added,

> I expect other renewals will come in the future, once again to revitalise the P/C [Pentecostal/Charismatic] movement. They will most likely and most commonly take the form of mini-renewals and revivals similar to those that occurred between the first, second and third Waves of the P/C movement prior to TTB, and which have taken place in its slipstream.²⁴⁸

Through all this it has been increasingly clear that the Toronto Blessing was a charismatic initiative which had little effect on African neo-Pentecostalism. This says as much about the set nature of African neo-Pentecostalism as it does about charismatic flexibility. In line with its previous cautious adaptability towards charismatic initiatives, the EA developed the skills required to enable a degree of "Toronto" assimilation. However, as the "Toronto" influence waned, some leaders of the British prayer movement began to see African neo-Pentecostal numerical growth as a sign of further renewal in Britain.²⁴⁹

Holy Trinity Brompton was not only central to the Toronto blessing in Britain but is the home of the Alpha course. Alpha was a further area of evangelical interest in the 1990s that failed to engage African neo-Pentecostalism. On Friday February 27, 1998, Rev Sandy Millar of Holy Trinity Brompton hosted a breakfast in his central London church hall for seventy-five senior church leaders from around Britain. His purpose was to explain the proposed National Alpha Initiative.²⁵⁰ Prior to the breakfast a number of articles had appeared in the national press describing Alpha's success

---

245. "Mighty Wind," 10.

246. Davie, "Real but Limited," 42; Sizer, "Sub-Christian," 48; Cartledge, "Spur," 70; Pawson, "Mixed Blessing," 86. See also Dixon, *Signs of Revival*.

247. Poloma, "Reconfiguration," 123.

248. Poloma, "Reconfiguration," 124. Wagner's division of (American) P/C history into "waves" sets classical Pentecostalism first, charismatic renewal second, Wimber's Vineyard-style churches third. Synan, *Century*, 8–9.

249. Mitchell has labelled African immigration into Britain a move of God. Rennie, "War Room." Babatunde holds a similar view. Babatunde, *Great Britain Has Fallen!*, 14.

250. Personal archive, agenda and list of invitees.

and highlighting the course's 20-year history and Holy Trinity's intention of spending £250,000 on a September 1998 national advertising campaign. Most journalists set the sum against the church's annual income of £2.3 million. The following was typical:

> The 10-week course, which outlines basic Christianity with a charismatic flavour, including speaking in tongues and the laying-on of hands, began in Holy Trinity's parish room 20 years ago. The church claims that 500,000 people worldwide attended Alpha courses last year, using videos and books published by Holy Trinity and co-ordinated from its multiplying offices in Knightsbridge. The £250,000 campaign will start in September with posters and billboards showing a cartoon of a young person, in jeans, struggling under the burden of a huge red question mark. Some 4,500 churches will be given a promotional video presented by the vicar of Holy Trinity Brompton, the Rev Sandy Millar, and the present Alpha chaplain, the Rev Nicky Gumbel.[251]

Quotations from the Archbishop of Canterbury, George Carey, were also included. One referred to the course's "Christianity-friendly-but-uninformed" target audience saying "[t]he great success of Alpha groups in England is a statement that people are not so much questioning the intellectual basis of their faith as realising they do not know it."[252]

The only non-white church leaders invited to Millar's breakfast were Joel Edwards and Matthew Ashimolowo, but neither was able to attend. Ashimolowo's absence came from a background of non-involvement with Alpha, whilst for Edwards the EA had been supportive though aware of the controversy surrounding it in some conservative evangelical quarters. In his autobiographical book Edwards referred briefly to Alpha in his chapter *Reasons to be Cheerful*. Having mentioned the 1990 appointment of Carey as Archbishop of Canterbury, he wrote,

> The Archbishop's Decade of Evangelism was inaugurated shortly after he took up office, and since then the Alpha friendship evangelism program has raised the profile of church-based evangelism, having a rapid impact on thousands of churches across the UK, America, Australia and other parts of the world.[253]

---

251. Combe, "Richest Parish." Similarly, Gledhill, "Invitation."

252. Combe, "Richest Parish."

253. Edwards, *Lord*, 81. For Walker's perspective on Carey's role in the "decade of evangelism" see, Walker, "Foreword," vii.

Whilst many of Alpha's detractors lie outside the EA, some do not.[254] The EA's desire to speak for all evangelicals explains its caution. Some criticism of Alpha has focused around evangelicalism's core tenets: the nature of God, the plight of man, the person of Christ, the work of the cross, the ministry of the Holy Spirit, and the essence of conversion.[255] Most detractors, however, focus on the experience-driven emphasis of the course. An article in the American magazine, *Christianity Today*, quoted Anglican theologian Canon Martyn Percy's concerns over such experientialism:[256]

> An infectious enthusiasm, entrepreneurial spirit, and a bold plan for growth are all trademarks among Alpha's top leaders. Not everyone is cheering Alpha onward. Some church leaders have found Alpha teaching too charismatic, too experience-driven, and too negative about traditional churches. Martyn Percy, director of the Lincoln Theological Institute for the Study of Religion and Society of the University of Sheffield, England, has commented about Alpha that it is "a package rather than a pilgrimage." In a recent essay, he said, "It is a confident but narrow expression of Christianity, which stresses the personal experience of the Spirit over the Spirit in the church.... The Alpha approach has been faulted for pushing an experience-driven approach to evangelism that sidesteps intellectual difficulties."[257]

None of these concerns explain African neo-Pentecostalism's lack of engagement with Alpha. Stephen Hunt, a sociologist of religion who has examined Alpha in some depth carried out a limited survey into the background of Alpha participants.[258] He enquired into occupation, qualifications, employment, gender, age, ethnicity and marital status. His ethnicity result indicated that participants sampled were: 97 percent white, 1 percent Asian, 1 percent other and 1 percent not stated. He concluded:

> There is probably little to say about ethnicity. The sample of churches surveyed were [sic] unrepresentative of the population as a whole in that their congregations were white. At the same time, it is my observation (and only mine) that very few

---

254. Hunt regarded the FIEC as a refuge for churches cautious about Alpha and called it an alternative to the EA. Hunt, *Anyone for Alpha?*, 48. In fact, FIEC is neither interdenominational nor trans-denominational. Eighty FIEC churches were EA members in 2004.
255. Hand, "Alpha Course."
256. Morgan, "Alpha-Brits."
257. Percy, "Join-the-Dots."
258. Hunt, *Anyone for Alpha?*, 48.

black churches (which are usually of the Pentecostal persuasion) have endorsed *Alpha*. There may be various reasons for this. The most obvious is that its general orientation (although undoubtedly not intended) is towards the white middle classes.[259]

Hunt may well have been right. There is clearly still a difference between being white middle class and African middle class in Britain. If this breaks down, Alpha may yet find a place in African neo-Pentecostal churches as middle-class Africans reach out to their unchurched middle-class neighbors through something other than large scale motivational rallies and healing campaigns. Alpha appeals to those who want to form new friends, share food, and discuss opinions (in a polite and non-confrontational way).[260] Alpha offers a "process" approach to evangelism whereas African neo-Pentecostalism has always been more comfortable with "crisis" evangelism through an event.

Evangelicalism and postmodernism

Locating Alpha in contemporary culture has been a concern for those committed to maintaining the evangelistic relevance of the course. Gumbel believes that "those from an essentially Enlightenment background feel at home with the parts of the course which appeal to the mind, but often have difficulty in experiencing the Holy Spirit" whilst "[o]thers coming from the New Age movement find that rational and historical explanations leave them cold . . . but they are on more familiar territory in experiencing the Spirit."[261] Theology lecturer Harriet Harris has described Alpha as "a prominent example of 'mainstream' contemporary evangelicalism that is charismatic, conscious of certain postmodern elements in our culture, and residually fundamentalist."[262] At the end of the twentieth-century evangelicalism and postmodernism were forging links, but the bonding was neither instant nor universal.

When the EA decided to celebrate its 150th anniversary in 1996 with a conference at Bournemouth, the issue of contemporary culture became a major focus.[263] As early as 1994, the newly formed ACUTE team was work-

---

259. Hunt, *Anyone for Alpha?*, 84.
260. Hunt, *Anyone for Alpha?*, 44.
261. Gumbel, *Telling Others*, 22.
262. Harris, "Fundamentalism," 18.
263. Edwards, as UK Director, oversaw the preparations. Calver had health problems 1995–96.

ing on the topic of "What is an evangelical?" in readiness.[264] Their task had hardly begun when Dave Tomlinson, a former leader amongst the New Churches, published a book entitled *The Post-Evangelical*.[265] The tone of the book and its significance for evangelicalism is summed up by the evangelical Anglican Bishop of Maidstone, Graham Cray:

> Tomlinson has written a book that should be read by every person disaffected by their experience of evangelicalism and by every leader of the contemporary evangelical movement. He raises pastoral and theological issues which must be faced and outlines key elements of the agenda which faces evangelicalism at the close of the twentieth century. The term "post-evangelical" is controversial but the claim that Western culture is now entering a new postmodern cultural era is, I believe, beyond question.[266]

Tomlinson's book caused sufficient stir in the evangelical world to necessitate an early published response.[267] He had stated that evangelicalism militates against a "grown-up" experience of faith by placing its adherents into a distinctive but restrictive sub-culture approximating to "christianised, middle-class conservatism."[268] The ACUTE team chose to ignore this and sought to respond instead to the early stirrings of the postmodern debate:

> Evangelicals, because of our commitment to the Bible, must be hot on reformation, theological as well as social. At present we are not, so we are vulnerable to a contemporary post-modern philosophy which threatens to control both our interpretation of Scripture and our definition of an evangelical.[269]

Surprisingly, by the time the ACUTE report was published, the postmodern debate had moved center-stage and a more conciliatory note was evident. Audio-visual presentations on postmodernism dominated the first day at the November 1996 National Assembly of Evangelicals in Bournemouth.[270] The program notes set the tone:

> We live, we are told, in a post-modern era . . . it is no longer possible, say the philosophers, to believe in any "grand story," be it Christianity, Communism or even humanism. What is true

264. Randall and Hilborn, *One Body*, 330; ACUTE, *What Is an Evangelical?*, 8.
265. Tomlinson, *Post-Evangelical*.
266. Gray, "Commendation," back cover.
267. Cray et al., *Post-Evangelical Debate*.
268. Tomlinson, *Post-Evangelical*, 5–7.
269. ACUTE, *What Is an Evangelical?*, 2.
270. Evangelical Alliance, *Shaping the Future Together*, 9.

for you, may not be true for me. We don't ask is it right, but is it relevant . . . consumerism has even extended into religion. We are free to pick and mix the beliefs that suit our style. . . . Absolutes are out of fashion. . . . But all these changes in society have their opportunities if only we can find them. The post-modern generation is looking for spiritual answers as never before.[271]

By the turn of the millennium, some evangelicals believed they had found these "opportunities." John Drane argued for evangelicals to develop a fresh understanding of evangelism based on postmodernism's understanding of fragmentation.[272] For him, an increasingly over-systematized church, adopting a "one size fits all" philosophy, could have little relevance in an increasingly diverse world.[273] Agreeing with sociologist Grace Davie's view of "believing without belonging," he wrote of an interest in spirituality within society that lies beyond conventional Christianity.[274] He recommended that the church adopt more creative and flexible approaches in order to engage beyond its existing congregations.[275] Peter Hicks, the philosophy lecturer at London Bible College, saw the postmodernism debate, with its rejection of metanarratives, as an opportunity for evangelicalism to relocate its truth concept in the concept of God.[276] In his book on evangelicalism and culture, David Hilborn, the EA's theological advisor, sought to give evangelicalism a wider base than "enlightenment rationalism" by affirming its links with Romanticism and Pentecostalism. He then went on to find common ground with postmodernism in evangelicalism's pragmatism.[277] He had no doubt that evangelicalism could adjust to postmodernism by being less conservative in the areas of worship and preaching, witness and discipleship, social action and ethics, theology and doctrine, going on to set out an "Agenda for Postmodern Evangelicalism."[278] Here statements such as "postmodern evangelicals will characteristically accept that God can act in a supernatural way today" were set alongside more challenging predictions such as

271. Evangelical Alliance, "Stop the World," 4–5.
272. Drane based his work on Ritzer, *MacDonaldization*.
273. Drane, *MacDonaldization*, 155–57.
274. Davie, *Religion in Britain*.
275. Drane categorized his unchurched target group as: the desperate poor, the hedonists, the traditionalists, the spiritual searchers, the corporate achievers, the secularists and the apathetic. He advocated creative worship, drama, dance and storytelling to reach them.
276. Hicks, *Evangelicals and Truth*.
277. Hilborn, *Picking Up*, 67–73. For Hilborn's response to Tomlinson, see Hicks, *Evangelicals and Truth*, 91–116.
278. Hilborn, *Picking Up*, 283–90.

"postmodern evangelicals will be less concerned with the formal inerrancy of Scripture than with functional authority."[279] African neo-Pentecostals would more readily affirm the former than the latter.

As the twentieth century closed, a significant number of evangelicals, particularly within some New Church strands, were deconstructing church with postmodern society in mind. Their efforts were to birth the "Emerging Church" Movement.[280] Its experimental models of church with their emphasis on flexible informal groupings were completely different from African neo-Pentecostal methodologies.[281] Perhaps, given the underlying postmodern debate, it was significant that the only African neo-Pentecostal to be given prominence at the EA's 150th Anniversary conference was Ashimolowo, who was invited to speak in a seminar on church-planting held in a building some distance from the main center. The fact that he only attended for that specific part of the program might indicate that the program was not particularly designed with African neo-Pentecostal leaders in mind. With so many internal issues engaging evangelicalism, strengthening ties with African neo-Pentecostalism was, for a season, less of a priority.

SECULAR-SENSITIVE AND SECULAR-DISMISSIVE APPROACHES TO CHRISTIAN BROADCASTING

At Spring Harvest in 1990 Gerald Coates, the New Church leader, publicly laid hands on Peter Meadows.[282] Meadows, who had co-founded the annual Spring Harvest Christian festival in 1979 with Calver, was planning to launch London Christian Radio, and Coates wanted to see him empowered.[283] Whilst serving as Communications Secretary at the EA in the late 1980s, Meadows had become increasingly interested in media evangelism.[284] In the five years that it took, following Coates' prayer, to negotiate a license to broadcast, his views on how a Christian station should function took shape.[285] Meadows' opinions were influenced by mid-1990s evangelical thinking on culturally relevant evangelism as summarized by Warner:

279. Hilborn, *Picking Up,* 285, points 10, 11.

280. Warner, *21st Century Church*; Moynagh, *Changing Church*; Ward, *Liquid Church*; Thwaites, *Church beyond the Congregation*.

281. Vanhoozer attempted to survey a wide range of future ecclesiological options: Vanhoozer, "Evangelicalism."

282. Interview with David Heron, March 23, 2004.

283. Randall and Hilborn, *One Body,* 284.

284. Randall and Hilborn, *One Body,* 297.

285. Heron interview.

As we approach the 21st century, in a context of growing pragmatism and breathless cultural change, two crucial questions need to be asked by every local church: In biblical terms, what is church meant to be and do? In practical terms, what changes must we bring about in order to bridge the gap to the modern world?[286]

It was American Rick Warren's response to this, with his "seeker-sensitive" services, who at that point was to prove most influential: "Create a service that is designed for your members to bring their friends to. And make the service so attractive, appealing, and relevant to the unchurched that your members are eager to share it with the lost people they care about."[287] Meadows extrapolated such ideas and began to develop a broadcast concept that was secular-sensitive, designing it to appeal to the unchurched by using popular music and keeping Christian input to a minimum.[288] Meadows' station launched on June 10, 1995 as Premier Radio, though still retaining its registered company name of London Christian Radio Limited. In preparation for the launch, it built up a financial base through its holding charity, Christian Media Trust.[289] In autumn 1995, financial losses were such that the Christian Media trustees had to take over the running of the station, an expert panel advising them to continue with essentially secular programming, "dropping in Christian vignettes," but using less "pop"-oriented music.[290] In January 1996 the search began in earnest for a new managing director with hopes settling on Peter Kerridge, the managing director of Radio Harlow who had developed an enthusiasm for radio whilst serving as a Baptist minister in Southend. Before Kerridge was approached, however, the chairman of the holding company, David Heron, had second thoughts about the panel's advice. With funds rapidly coming to an end, he began to consider the output of Christian radio stations in America, concluding that "those involved in successful Christian radio programming in the US were not fooling people into listening."[291] It seemed to him that "secular stations could do everything else better (sports, etc.); all except Christian programming."[292] So convinced was he that people would listen to Premier if it were Christian, that he approached Premier's funders to see if they

286. Warner, *21st Century Church*, 15.
287. Warren, *Purpose Driven Church*, 253.
288. Heron interview.
289. Heron interview.
290. Heron interview.
291. Heron interview.
292. Heron interview.

Principles and practicalities in the interactions of 1985-99 165

would finance the change. Surprisingly they agreed, committing additional finance for three successive years.[293] Thus stabilized, the station was ready for Kerridge's appointment and the changes began with his arrival on October 1, 1996. Kerridge recalls,

> The radio station had lost its way. It was losing money and had no sales revenue. It was about to lose ministry revenue too. It was playing mainly a diet of non-Christian music. Christians wanted a Christian station that sounded like a Christian station and non-Christians [expecting a secular station] found there was too much God.[294]

With Kerridge's pragmatism added to Heron's conclusions, a strategy for the transition was developed:

> The decision was taken to become overtly Christian and at first even the staff were not told. The song mix was gradually changed so where there had been twelve songs an hour, two Christian and ten non-Christian, it first went four to eight, then six to six and so on. In March 97 we became Premier Christian Radio: reviving, restoring, inspiring Christian lifestyle and by Easter 1997 we were overtly Christian.[295]

One of the most obvious effects of this change was an increase in the station's support from African Christians, both in terms of listeners and program sponsors. According to Kerridge,

> The black churches had never been a major revenue driver, far from it, but the black church is media savvy. All the leaders have American role models. Matthew [Ashimolowo] has Eddie Long in Atlanta. And they see media ministry and say "Could we do that?" They find Premier and . . . bang! They want to be involved.[296]

Heron, who has continued as chairman of Premier Christian Radio, believes that he has "made two major contributions: the appointment of Kerridge and the move to a 'Christian only' emphasis."[297]

---

293. Heron interview.
294. Kerridge interview.
295. Kerridge interview.
296. Kerridge interview. Churches broadcasting on Premier pay a fee.
297. Heron interview.

Whilst Premier Christian Radio was involved in its initial "secular-sensitive" launch, Christian television was developing along a different route. In September 1992, Channel 4 broadcast a program called an "An American Friend," tracking the American minister Linda Patton as she befriended the transsexual and prostitute communities of Earls Court. Patton described the film-making process as "traumatic."[298] In a desire to see similar programs made but without the pain, Cornerstone Christian Centre, an independent church in South East London, decided to set up a television department in early 1993, employing Howard Conder (later of Revelation TV) and a young South African and his wife, Rory and Wendy Alec.[299] Conder soon recommended that Cornerstone members be trained as camera crew by filming the church's main Sunday service and a library of recordings accrued. Alec developed the idea of offering programs to London's black entertainment cable channel, IDTV (the Identity Channel), and Cornerstone began broadcasting a weekly hour-long program on Sunday May 29, 1994, aired and advertised at the channel's expense.[300] Almost immediately the Cornerstone office started receiving calls on behalf of American ministers such as Morris Cerullo, Kenneth Copeland, Frederick K. C. Price and Carlton Pearson, wanting to secure airtime. Independently, Matthew Ashimolowo made contact with IDTV offering to buy time, as did John Francis of Ruach Ministries in Brixton. Alec, still working for Cornerstone, became an unpaid consultant to IDTV as it sold airtime to British and overseas ministries and gave over its Sunday broadcasting to continuous preaching output. However, he also took the opportunity to approach the ministries that had begun broadcasting to canvas interest in the purchase of satellite time for exclusively Christian programming.[301]

Under Alec and Condor's supervision, Cornerstone produced a promotional video to demonstrate the range of content possible on a specifically Christian channel, and Alec secured a 4:00 a.m. to 7:00 a.m. slot on the Astra satellite. In October 1994 the Alecs left Cornerstone's staff to give themselves full-time to the new initiative, obtaining a broadcast license in March 1995.[302] Christian Channel Europe began broadcasting on October 1, 1995 with the declared aim of promoting a Christian alternative culture. The timing was interesting. IDTV had been taken over by the American Black

---

298. Patton's personal assessment.
299. Alec, *Against All Odds*, 51.
300. Alec, *Against All Odds*, 51.
301. Alec, *Against All Odds*, 51.
302. Alec, *Against All Odds*, 59. Press release for Christian Channel Europe's launch, September 27, 1995.

Entertainment Television (BET) and its Christian broadcasting stopped on Sunday April 28, 1996; the station going off air shortly after. Premier was still a secular-sensitive broadcaster but complementary Christian broadcasting was soon to be its theme. Alec wanted his channel to be able to stand alone; to appear in standard programming schedules alongside the regular secular cable channels yet to be something that Christians could watch all day without recourse to other stations. An article in the EA's magazine, which was broadly supportive, stated,

> Asked why Christians would want a purely Christian TV channel, Rory Alec replied, "There is not one television channel for Christians to get edification, for their children to watch programs that are non-violent and not be subject to what's happening in current TV channels."[303]

Such reasoning presupposes that Christians will thrive on a limited media diet and will benefit from drawing a strong line between the "secular" and the "sacred." This was a long way from the thinking of Warner and Warren, but for many African neo-Pentecostal Christians it was exactly the approach with which they would wish to be identified.[304] They may not all send their children to exclusively Christian schools, given that the selection in Britain is limited and they are reluctant to compromise educational standards, but they do see value in having Christian television in their houses.[305] Some argue that, even if it is not being watched or listened to, it is "sanctifying" the home.

The emergence of this "secular-dismissive" approach to Christian broadcasting in the UK coincided with a downturn in religious output from the BBC. This was highlighted at a debate in the General Synod of the Church of England in November 1999 when Nigel Holmes, a former Senior Producer in BBC local radio, circulated a twenty-four page report:

> For those outside the BBC, it is hard to obtain detailed audience figures, but we do know that the earlier placing of *Sunday* on Radio 4 initially resulted in a 25% loss of peak audience from 1.6 million before the changes. It seems certain that moving *The Moral Maze* from 9 a.m. to 8 p.m. lost at least two-thirds.[306]

---

303. "Christian TV Station," 14.

304. Grace Akanle highlights Satanic aspects in secular society. Akanle, *Satan-Proof*, 13–17.

305. Akanle, *Satan-Proof*, 163.

306. Holmes, *Losing Faith*, 1.

As opportunities for Christian programming on the familiar radio and television stations seemed to be decreasing, Christian broadcasting was growing through cable and satellite technology. By the end of 1999 Christian Channel Europe had re-branded as GOD Digital TV and was broadcasting on two channels.[307] It had also been joined by two other Christian channels broadcasting on satellite from within Britain, Channel 7 and Inspiration, the latter being owned by the Nigerian Kunle Omilana.[308]

In preparing to move into the new millennium, however, the situation was far from stable. The revenue required to run these channels was largely drawn from the broadcast fees paid by churches and ministries. There were many African neo-Pentecostal churches keen to film their Sunday services and by the end of 1999 more and more were investing in recording equipment. When broadcast-quality equipment was beyond a church's budget, home-video cameras on lightweight tripods would appear to impress congregations with a declaration of intent. However, those who owned the channels had to sell their prime-time slots at economically viable rates and there were beginning to be more slots than takers. Selling air-time became the prerogative of a small number of Christian Public Relations Consultancies. In a short space of time the Christian television business had become so highly competitive that channels were being forced off air. GOD TV was secure having established a charitable support base and secured investment from significant donors, but both Channel 7, which had already reinvented itself once, and Inspiration, were to suffer.[309]

Nevertheless, the new millennium was not to be an era of Christian media decline. Within less than half a decade there would be an increase on every front, with television stations coming in from overseas by satellite and new channels being raised up within Britain. Christian radio too was to experience an upturn as programming was to become easier to air on satellite and cable networks as well as through the internet. Indeed, the first few years of the new millennium were to be a time for entrepreneurs. Kunle Omilana, having laid down "Inspiration," was to set up "Wonderful" and the team behind Channel 7 was to launch "Life." Howard Condor, instrumental in the lead up to the 1995 creation of Christian Channel Europe, was to found Revelation TV "working hard to redefine British Christian

---

307. It re-branded in 1997 with advertising on hoardings throughout London.

308. Inspiration launched September 1999. Channel 7 was owned by John Hammond, a former employee of Christian Channel Europe.

309. Angel Christian Television Trust provided GOD Digital's charitable support base. In 2002 GOD Digital's relocated its uplink from Gateshead to Jerusalem, heralding it as a prophetic move. Financial benefits came from removing compliance editing costs that resulted from up-linking within EU jurisdiction.

Television" and the faith-based Loveworld was to promote itself as a station "focused on reaching the UK Christian community."[310] This British theme was also to be evident with the arrival of United Christian Broadcasters' UCB TV, an extension of its radio ministry.[311] Others, such as Morris Cerullo (with Inspiration Network International), Trinity Broadcasting Network (with TBN Europe) and Daystar were to launch with less of a British theme. Even Gospel Channel Europe was to arrive from Iceland and the Catholic Global Network was to have its Eternal Word TV. By 2005 there were eleven exclusively Christian channels.

What would have been even harder to predict in 1999 was a renewed Christian interest in mixed programming. "Life," "Vision," "Passion," and "Classics" were all to arrive on the satellite channels with "family-value" aspirations.[312] Broadcasters from an African neo-Pentecostal background were to play a major role in the launching of ethnic minority interest channels such as BEN and OBE. Perhaps of greatest significance, however, was to be the arrival of RCCG's own channel, "Dove," London-based but with programming from America and Africa. For Adeboye, this was to be a cause for praising God "for the in-roads the mission is making in the United Kingdom."[313] So, from four channels in 1999, Christian television in Britain was in effect to expand within five years to eighteen, eleven dedicated channels (essentially "secular-dismissive") and seven "mixed" ones.[314] Many more African neo-Pentecostal churches were about to be in the public eye, but in the eye of how much of the public, was an issue.

Throughout the late 1990s attempts were made to assess Christian broadcasting's audience size and profile but by the turn of the millennium reliable figures had yet to be obtained. When a professional survey was eventually commissioned, those who commissioned it were quick to dismiss its results as anomalous, pointing to the atypical nature of the panel selected (fifteen hundred people "known from previous surveys to regularly or occasionally watch/listen to Christian programmes"—"51% male . . . about 63% under 45 years old . . . 96% white").[315] Findings showed that whilst average viewing time was fairly evenly shared between the Christian channels, with GOD Channel highest at 69 minutes per person per week

310. https://revelationtv.com/ and https://loveworlduk.org/.

311. http://ucb.co.uk.

312. Offering "safe" entertainment viewing for adults and children alongside some preaching and worship.

313. Anjorin, "Convention of Excellence."

314. For all Christian radio and television listings: https://web.archive.org/web/20150211080622/http://www.christiansat.org.uk/channels.html.

315. Heron, Memorandum, September 5, 2003. Premier archive.

and Life lowest at 36 minutes, the declared favorite Christian program was the BBC's Songs of Praise.[316] The whole exercise did little to advance the cause of accurate viewing/listening figures and the impressions of the commissioning broadcasters soon reverted. They had long been convinced that "all the Christian TV stations and most of the Christian Radio stations have large black audiences," adding that "[i]n the case of talkGospel [a Christian radio program] we know the audience to be over 90% black."[317]

As the turn of the millennium approached it could be said that, although the development of Christian radio and television was not initially an African neo-Pentecostal initiative, it quickly won considerable African neo-Pentecostal support, even as some evangelicals expressed concern about the access into Britain it afforded American television evangelists.[318] Ultimately audience make-up has as much influence on program selection as program selection has on audience make-up. In Christian media, separating principles from practicalities can be challenging when the programming preferences of the owners and executive team are subject to available finance and audience support. Arguably, given that African neo-Pentecostals are not slow to make their programming preferences known, this can blur evangelical distinctives.

To conclude with a contrast, African neo-Pentecostal preferences have had negligible influence on the publishing aspects of British evangelical media operations. Traditional British evangelical publishing houses have been keen from the mid-1990s onwards to break into the growing British African neo-Pentecostal market but the characteristics of their product-lines have long been clearly set, both in terms of content and presentation.[319] Consequently, African neo-Pentecostal writers (and there are many) have preferred to self-publish (as in the case of Ashimolowo) or to approach fellow African neo-Pentecostals to publish for them.[320] There has been minimal market cross-over.[321] Perhaps if there had been a strongly developed evan-

---

316. Arbitron Audience Survey commissioned by Premier Summer 2003.

317. Heron, Memorandum, September 5, 2003. Premier archive.

318. Perriman, *Faith, Hope and Prosperity*, 11.

319. SU and Sovereign World approached me in 2000 to discuss African markets.

320. African neo-Pentecostal books published in Britain are often motivational. Some are self-published (authors creating their own publishing houses) others are published by fellow Africans. Tokunbo Emmanuel is one such publisher. Examples are Ashimolowo, *Keeping Your Dreams Alive*; Ashimolowo, *Take a Giant Leap*; Don-Dawodu, *Glorious People*; Emmanuel, *Ultimate Destiny*; Fola-Alade, *Discover Your Hidden Treasures*; Nanjo, *Dynamic of Moral Integrity*; Omole, *Prosperity Unleashed*.

321. Africans using established British Christian publishers include Wale Oke (four books published by Victory Literature Crusade, Tottenham, 1993–95) and Babatunde (New Wine Press, Chichester).

gelical broadcasting network in Britain prior to the growth of African neo-Pentecostalism, two separate broadcasting entities would have emerged alongside the two separate publishing entities.

CONCLUSION

In the fifteen-year period covered by this chapter (1985–99), those within the evangelical constituency took principled stands on issues as diverse as the styles of corporate prayer, IR, SLSW, miracles, fund-raising, the strengths and weaknesses of charismatic theology, the nature of hell, the Toronto blessing, postmodernism and Christian broadcasting. On some of these there were internal tensions when, say, charismatics differed from conservative evangelicals. This was the case with IR, SLSW, charismatic theology and the Toronto blessing. At the same time African neo-Pentecostals felt strongly about principles involved in the debates over corporate prayer, IR, SLSW, miracles, fund-raising, the relevance (or otherwise) of black identity, and Christian broadcasting.

The practicalities evident throughout the period have not always led to harmonious results. There were practical reasons behind the London Leaders' morning prayer gatherings staying predominantly white and the Holy Ghost Prayer Nights staying predominantly black. The only practical way to avert the tensions over Cerullo's ministry was for his organization to resign its membership of the EA. Practical resolutions were not found to increase African neo-Pentecostal participation in ACEA. However, ACUTE reports, with their irenic approach to principles causing disagreement, did bring a measure of reconciliation in the debates on the nature of hell and the Toronto blessing. Also, differing approaches to Christian media managed to exist side-by-side. Obviously the multiple outlet approach helped here. Differing channels with differing schedules could cater for the breadths of opinions and preferences.

During the period 1985–99 the African neo-Pentecostal churches found little common ground with the Caribbean denominations and found little to relate to in terms of either charismatic or conservative evangelical praxis or theology. They also found little of inspiration in Christian initiatives to affirm black identity. In essence, throughout this period they were entirely self-sufficient, keen to cross racial divides but largely preoccupied with becoming established and securing numerical growth.

In the next chapter I will analyze the principles and practicalities involved in the interactions between British evangelicals and African neo-Pentecostals from 2000 to 2005.

Chapter 5

Principles and practicalities in the interactions of 2000–2005

As THE EA APPROACHED the new millennium, its team of departmental directors, by then settled under Edwards' leadership, were in confident mood. Edwards was receiving positive media coverage and opportunities were opening up for him to speak on Radio 4's "Sunday" program, the "Daily Service," the "Moral Maze" and "Any Questions?"[1] By the end of 2001 he had not only been included in the team presenting Radio 4's "Thought for the Day" but had appeared on BBC television's "Question Time."[2] All of this was in line with the EA's strategy to increase the profile of evangelicals and to be a representative "voice in the public arena."[3] By 2002 it was to claim that it comprised "thousands of individual members," "over three thousand churches," "seven hundred Christian organisations and groups," "thirty entire denominations," plus a further "three thousand affiliated member churches," thus making "one million Christians" the focus of its threefold commitment to network, resource and represent.[4] Its members' appetite for such representation was to be emphasized in its magazine:

> In response to Joel's appearance on "Any Questions." . . . Well done! It was good to feel that in some way you represented us

---

1. "Any Questions?," 5.
2. "Summertime," 4.
3. "Summertime," 4.
4. Evangelical Alliance, *Membership Information*, 7–9, 14. Analysis of 3,183 member churches on EA website mid-2003 showed five main groups: Baptist (847), Anglican (543), Independent (525), denominational Pentecostal (276, including only 8 from Caribbean denominations), New Church networks (212).

members. When so much of religion in general and evangelicals in particular are portrayed in a few stereotypes, it was excellent to have an example of a Christian thinking and speaking so clearly and logically about important issues.[5]

However, speaking reactively on topical issues was not exactly what the directors of the EA had in mind. They were seeking to develop a wider unifying agenda that would move the organization on from its long-established coordinating role into something far more pro-active. For years the EA had been described as "the table on which the jigsaw pieces [of a disparate British evangelicalism] could be assembled."[6] This image was to be dismissed as too static; the EA was to be a "Movement for Change." In Hilborn's words,

> In 1999, the Directors of the Alliance undertook to address the social transformation agenda which may lie ahead for British Evangelicals in the New Millennium. Aware of the significant changes wrought over the previous three decades or so by secularization, multiculturalism and pluralism, and conscious of the major civic and ecclesiastical realignments which had ensued, the Directors resolved to focus the Alliance on the task of encouraging Evangelicals to become a "Movement for Change" in the public life of the United Kingdom.[7]

At the launch of this re-branding in September 2000, Edwards boldly described the new vision, taking the opportunity to set the recently published report of the 1998 English Church Attendance Survey in a positive light.[8]

> The Church in Britain began the new millennium with fresh statistics that confirmed the downward trend in church attendance. Projections were made about the virtual extinction of the church by 2070. But many of us know the other side of the story, which seldom makes the front page. It is the story of ordinary Christians seeking to make a difference in their faithful witness to God. On the whole, evangelicalism, with all its shortfalls, continues to be an area of growth—not just in terms of numbers, but also as it makes its contribution within local and regional ecumenical settings. But our challenge is not to be

5. "Any Questions?"
6. Description of EA (origin unknown) referred to throughout 1990s, mentioned to me in 2005 by EA UK Director and Vice-Chair of Council.
7. Hilborn, *Movement for Change*, xii. For secularization: Bruce, *Religion*; for multiculturalism: Hesse, *Un/settled Multiculturalisms*; for pluralism: Newbigin, *Gospel*.
8. Brierley, *Tide*.

overtaken by notions of revival, nor overwhelmed by a struggle for survival. It is to keep our eyes firmly on God's enduring agenda: the transformation of our society.[9]

It was a timely message. There were certainly evangelicals who were still buoyed up by the revivalism of the mid-1990s and others in danger of succumbing to fears of decline. Focusing both parties on an alternative agenda was astute, but to declare the preferred route as "God's enduring agenda" did have risks. Evangelicalism has throughout its history espoused more than one agenda. Alongside its record of seeking society's transformation, is a strong tradition of seeking to rescue people from the effects of this world in readiness for a new one. At times these approaches have seemed mutually exclusive. American evangelical author Dave Hunt, writing in the 1980s, expressed concern that a church too focused on society's transformation could lose sight of the gospel's eternal dimension. For him heaven and hell had to remain central to Christian thinking. He acknowledged the wisdom of limiting godlessness but did not see transforming society as the church's primary agenda:

> Christians ought to stand against such evils as homosexuality, abortion, pornography, and the abuse of drugs, and do all they can to limit godless influence in society. At the same time the Christian must not forget that his primary responsibility to the world is to present it with the gospel. Too often social and political activism becomes a substitute for saving souls. Moreover Christians must take their stand against moral and social evil as those who are redeemed by the blood of Christ and not join with the ungodly in promoting moralism, a system which is no better than humanism.[10]

For Hunt changing the world would not change people. People needed to be presented with a choice that could provide them with an ultimate escape from the world's corruption.

From the outset of its new campaign, the EA was aware of such thinking and in 2002 ACUTE held an academic consultation resulting in a publication that sought to lend the campaign historical, ethical, theological and missiological integrity.[11] Leicester University's John Coffey made his contribution to the debate and outlined the practical possibilities that could be available to an increasingly politically aware evangelical constituency:

---

9. Edwards' speech to EA Council, September 2002, abridged as "All Change," 15.
10. Hunt, *Whatever Happened*, 216.
11. Hilborn, *Movement for Change*.

[I]t would be naïve to suppose that liberal democratic states cannot act in ways that are offensive or even oppressive to the Christian conscience. Indeed there are signs that some liberals want to exercise a kind of "homogenising pressure on ways of life that do not embrace autonomy" by mandating compliance with a liberal sexual ethic or restricting religious "proselytism." Fortunately, parliamentary democracy permits peaceful resistance to state policy through public protests and political lobbying.[12]

For Edwards, clear moral values in the face of an homogenizing tolerance was to be the campaign's focus for action:

Our society is experiencing a wind-down of a moral consensus and the build-up of its problems. A culture with tolerance as its great absolute must eventually come apart at the seams. Our chat-show morality, customised values, broken relationships and growing crime rate are all prophetic statements of our unhappy future.[13]

In predicting an unhappy future, little did Edwards realize that events outside his control would lead to his new program being outworked in a climate where fear of fundamentalism would produce negative reaction and where all religious zeal was to be eschewed. Hastings, reflecting on evangelical Anglicanism in the mid-1980s, had set up a speculative scenario whereby evangelicalism would have to make a choice:

It may, however, be the case that in England there remains no real alternative for Evangelicalism between an intellectually archaic and fundamentalist sectarianism on the one hand and absorption as a Conservative and biblically conscious wing within an ecumenical Catholicism on the other. Such may seem to have been the message of our story throughout.[14]

After five years of changes within society's thinking, many commentators within the British media would be concluding that evangelicalism had in fact opted for the first of Hastings' two propositions, despite the fact that its socially conservative agenda would be running in line with the policy statements of the Catholic Church. Such would be the strength of public

---

12. Coffey, "State and Societal Transformation," 102.
13. Edwards, "All Change," 16.
14. Hastings, *History of English Christianity*, 618. His context was a dismissive view of (Anglican) evangelical growth: "Evangelicalism looks like a tide always claimed to be just about to come in, yet never quite reaching the shore with the force proclaimed." Hastings, *History of English Christianity*, xlv.

opinion that by 2003, Anglican vicar Giles Fraser would be writing in a newspaper article entitled "Evangelicals have become this century's witch burners" that "the word evangelical is now firmly linked in the public imagination with intolerance and bigotry."[15] For African neo-Pentecostals such comments would prove to be perplexing. To them evangelicalism in the early years of the twenty-first century seemed hindered in its challenge to society's [over-]tolerance by having to tolerate the diverse opinions within its own ranks. However, at the opening of the new millennium British political parties found evangelicalism's activism to be sufficiently restrained to enable them to engage with evangelicals and to reach out to African neo-Pentecostals.

THE FOCUS OF ELECTORAL ATTENTION

Although the first general election of the new millennium was widely expected to take place in spring 2001, the size of the Conservative defeat in 1997 meant that their campaigning would not be left to the few weeks available after an official announcement.[16] William Hague, having been appointed Conservative party leader on John Major's resignation, was tireless in his attempts to raise his party's ratings in the polls.[17] As early as April 2000 he was being accused of courting the evangelical vote by arriving at a Butlin's camp to speak at Spring Harvest.[18] Other party leaders had received invitations but, in the words of one journalist, "Hague was the first to understand that evangelicals cannot be ignored for much longer."[19] Hague also believed there was synergy between Conservative and evangelical opinions on family values.[20] Hague's Spring Harvest speech prompted one leading evangelical, who had earlier expressed her belief that in 1997 the evangelical vote "went predominantly labour," to comment,

> Hague was very clever. He did not just appeal to traditional values. He picked on issues such as Third World debt, he focused on the churches' involvement in social action and welfare. He applauded it and commended it. He knew what to say. It was clear that he had actually listened.[21]

15. Fraser, "Evangelicals."
16. Election held on June 7, 2001, having been delayed by Foot and Mouth disease.
17. Denver, "Results," 9–10.
18. Gledhill, "Praying for Votes," 3, 4.
19. Gledhill, "Praying for Votes," 4.
20. Gledhill, "Praying for Votes," 4.
21. Gledhill, "Praying for Votes," 4. Quoting Elaine Storkey.

Principles and practicalities in the interactions of 2000-2005   177

In June 2000 Hague was again being cited in the press for his wooing of the Christian electorate.²² He had been impressed by the proposals put forward by George W. Bush, then the American Republican presidential nominee, to give responsibility for social care to Christian charities. It was agreed that the director of the Conservative Christian Fellowship, Tim Montgomerie, should bring to Britain Professor Marvin Olasky, a member of Bush's team who, as a Christian and academic, had promoted the concept of "compassionate conservatism" and endorsed "faith-based welfare."²³ On Olasky's arrival the British press was quick to link Olasky's evangelical views on the Bible to his view on capitalism: "The Bible is, he says, not open to discussion. . . . Olasky has used the Bible to develop a closely argued political ideology which he describes as 'biblical free-market economics.' In his view, God is a capitalist who does not approve of shirkers."²⁴

Not surprisingly, given the competitive nature of party politics, the week that Hague welcomed Olasky was also the week in which Stephen Timms, a committed evangelical Christian and then-Labour's Financial Secretary to the Treasury, announced government plans to extend funding for social work programs run by faith communities.²⁵ Furthermore, the press announced that Ministers were "considering giving religious charities an exemption from public sector equal opportunities policies to allow them to employ believers only," the thinking being that they were "concerned that some effective organizations could be excluded or forced to water down religious teaching to qualify for funding."²⁶ However, in the eyes of the leader writers, it was Hague who was in danger of going too far, having also "delighted Churches by calling for stricter abortion laws, opposing the repeal of Section 28 and proposing to bring back the married couples income tax allowance."²⁷ Editorial comment in the *Telegraph* cautioned, "If William Hague is hoping to import to Britain the politics of America's 'Religious Right,' he is making a big mistake. Most Britons have a healthy suspicion of politicians who claim the endorsement of the Almighty for their policies."²⁸ Such suspicions notwithstanding, with both Conservative and Labour

22. Sylvester, "Hague to Consider," 11.
23. Sylvester, "Hague to Consider," 11; Olasky, *Compassionate Conservatism*.
24. Sylvester, "Hague's Latest Helper."
25. Sylvester and Brogan, "Labour and Tories," 10.
26. Sylvester and Brogan, "Labour and Tories," 10.
27. Sylvester and Brogan, "Labour and Tories," 10.
28. "Tory Party at Prayer," editorial comment.

politicians speaking of faith-based welfare, the directors of the EA could not have wished for a more positive climate in which to launch their new Movement for Change. Ahead of its official launch, though, the African and Caribbean churches took the headlines.

ACEA had been heralding its "Faith in the Future" conference since April 1999 claiming that "'Faith in the Future' is ACEA's response to the dawning of a new millennium . . . [it] will provide a unique opportunity to include over 3,000 churches, more than 30 denominations and around 250,000 African and Caribbean Christians in the Millennium festivities."[29] For Sturge, ACEA's General Director, frustrated at the stereotyping of Caribbean denominations, the event was to give "BMCs the chance to raise their profile and confirm that they have more to offer than just gospel choirs!"[30] By November 1999 ACEA's magazine was carrying a full page advertisement for "Faith in the Future" announcing the venue as the Brighton Centre and giving the dates as Wednesday July 5 to Saturday July 8, 2000. Sturge had been working hard to gather African support for the event and highlighted quotes from senior leaders of independent African neo-Pentecostal churches. Rev Dr. Paul Jinadu, General Overseer, New Covenant Church, contributed,

> The new Millennium should provide for Black Majority Churches a unique opportunity for a fresh start. We are all here in the UK, not by accident, nor by the will of man, but I believe, by divine appointment. I am persuaded that this Celebration 2000 will open our eyes to the wealth of talents and potentials God has deposited among our people. It should be a time of bonding and releasing.[31]

The endorsement from Dr. Albert Odulele, Senior Pastor, Green Pastures Ministries focused on the community: "I believe that this will be an opportunity for the church to position itself for its role in the community. It's most certainly an invaluable opportunity that we should not let pass by."[32] David Akande, the administrator for RCCG in Britain, echoed the theme:

> We have a great opportunity to reach not just our community, but our nation in the year 2000. The major task facing the Black

29. "Millennium Celebration," 13.
30. "Millennium Celebration," 13.
31. "Faith in the Future," 19.
32. "Faith in the Future," 19.

… Majority Churches is this: "What structures are we collectively going to put in place to solve some of the problems we have all talked about throughout the 20th century?" The nation is waiting for an answer and I believe this convention is the place for the meeting of minds.[33]

The problems Akande had in mind were detailed in the advance notice given in the EA magazine:

> Opening with a roof-raising praise-and-worship extravaganza on the 5th, the next three days will feature seminars of particular interest to Black Britons, such as racism, the challenge of Islam, prosperity and education. . . . *Faith in the Future* plans to debate whether Black churches should consider setting up their own schools catering to the needs of Black children.[34]

This debate on education was in the end the event's main focus. Numbers overall at the conference were low, mostly in the hundreds rather than the thousands. Ruth Gledhill, whose newspaper article enthused over the music of the opening night, tactfully noted "[t]he promised crowd of 6,000 had yet to arrive, and a couple of hundred worshippers stood patiently waiting; [a]t last the service began, and what a spectacle those thousands missed."[35] Part of the problem with low attendance might have been the deliberate decision announced by the organizers whereby, "[i]n a significant departure from the usual BMC practice of promoting 'big names,' no overseas speakers [have] been invited." In advocating this, Sturge was hailed as "reflecting a new generation's need to assert a unique Black British perspective" saying, "Speakers from the UK will do a far better job than any overseas ones who do not understand the British context."[36] In reality, however, it was only the "big Name" speakers that attracted any attention, and they were UK politicians not UK preachers. The Prime Minister and William Hague attended the conference to contribute to the "black education" debate triggered by Sturge on 11 November 1999 when *Faith in the Future* was officially launched. On that occasion Sturge had taken the opportunity to attack the British education system for failing Black children, saying that "[m]any within the Black Majority Churches were so concerned by the current situation that serious thought should be given to the need for BMCs

33. "Faith in the Future," 19.
34. "'Faith in the Future' Features," 8.
35. Gledhill, "Sound of Pure Faith."
36. "'Faith in the Future' Features," 8.

to establish church-based schools for Black children."[37] Numbers dramatically increased to hear Blair and Hague respond to these issues, with many African neo-Pentecostal leaders making the journey to Brighton to be present both in the main auditorium and at the private receptions beforehand.[38]

At the heart of Blair's speech was the statement that the Government was going to look seriously at proposals for Black schools.[39] He declared himself to be encouraged that a number of churches had expressed an interest in promoting "City Academies," the new state-funded, independently managed, secondary schools to be established in areas of urban disadvantage. He underlined the importance of local communities taking responsibility for running schools themselves by saying "Faith communities have an important part to play in this."[40] For him education needed to be linked with a stress on family, since although "[b]eing Prime Minister is tough . . . being a parent is tougher; family to me is more important than anything else." Education featured again when he was speaking on the New Deal and "action teams," due to start later in 2000, which he believed would work with employers to overcome discrimination. To an enthusiastic response he explained that he wanted to "make this a country where success in education leads to a good job; where hard work gets its just reward; where what matters is who you are, not where you're from."[41] In concluding he challenged Britain's Black youth to venture into politics:

> You perhaps more than anyone can gain from going into politics. . . . They used to say Britain would never have a woman Prime Minister. It happened. One day there will be a Black Prime Minister too. . . . Yes, you can be top footballers, boxers and actors. You know that already. There is an increasing number of Black business people. But I say this too: you can be top police officers too; top judges; you can be generals; you can be Prime Ministers. You can be anything you set your mind to, all you need to bring to the table is talent. We will help you do the rest. We will take down the barriers that hold you back.[42]

The similarities in Hague's speech the next day were remarkable. Hague had come well prepared saying "I thought ACEA's 'Making the

---

37. "When ACEA Speaks," 13.

38. Mohabir commented in private, "If we'd known all it would take to get these people together was a visit from the Prime Minister, we'd have done it long ago."

39. Mwangi, "Brighton Rocks," 9.

40. Mwangi, "Brighton Rocks," 9.

41. Mwangi, "Brighton Rocks," 9.

42. Mwangi, "Brighton Rocks," 9.

Grade' conference on the schooling of Black children focused on some very important issues. . . . New church schools, close to their communities which provide role models that pupils could identify with, would be one way to raise the culture of expectation and make Black children feel fully involved."[43] He set his opposition to the repeal of Section 28, the clause in the 1988 Local Government Act which had banned the promotion of homosexuality in schools, in its educational context asserting that "I believe parents want to be confident that their children are being taught properly in school." On discrimination, he commented, "Your churches stand as shining lights of hope in communities which feel disadvantaged and discriminated against" adding later that "[t]here is plenty of evidence that inner city children who are involved with their local church have a much greater chance of escaping poverty, crime and drug addiction." In Hague's opinion "[t]he work that churches have been doing on strengthening families, teaching parenting skills, micro-employment projects give us a clear idea of the way we should go."[44] He felt that the BMCs had much to offer in the area of "faith-based welfare" and like Blair concluded with a reference to a future Black Prime Minister.[45]

With so many political offers out in the open by the summer of 2000, it was hard to conceive what else could emerge in 2001 as the General Election approached. However, both Blair and Hague were to continue to make faith-centered speeches, Hague in February to the National Council for Voluntary Organisations, and Blair in March at a meeting organized by the Christian Socialist Movement.[46] The EA concluded in its magazine that both politicians were "also watching events unfolding across the Atlantic, where one of George Bush's first acts as the newly elected President of the United States has been to make £5.5 billion of federal funding available to faith groups to provide social services."[47] The article made it clear that the EA would be watching too as the proposed "White House Office of Faith-Based Community Initiatives" had its American Christian critics. Whilst American secularists were concerned about the blurring of the constitutional line between Church and State, American church groups feared that the funding would remain too much under government control. Similar fears were already being expressed in Britain that once a church's social program had become dependent on Government money, it could slowly

43. Mwangi, "Brighton Rocks," 9.
44. Mwangi, "Brighton Rocks," 9.
45. Mwangi, "Brighton Rocks," 9.
46. "Vote of Confidence," 16–17.
47. "Vote of Confidence," 16–17.

capitulate to Government demands, with "more equal opportunity type policies towards employment" being cited as one such possible form of control. It was reasoned that under such circumstances the church could cease "to be the effective social project that perhaps attracted the funding in the first place."[48] There were growing concerns among evangelicals that the relationship between government and faith groups could become too close.

As it happened, fears of too close a relationship developing between Government and faith groups became a matter of public concern too as fears of religious fundamentalism took hold post-9/11. The fundamentalist debate was not new. By the turn of the millennium Martin Marty and other academics had written extensively on the topic and for 2000 Steve Bruce had prepared his *Fundamentalism*.[49] By 2001, the evangelical Chris Partridge had edited his *Fundamentalisms*.[50] But such was the effect of 9/11 on the fundamentalist debate that Partridge's book, awaiting printing at the time, appeared with an additional page at the front asserting that "[t]his volume was written prior to 11 September 2001, the black day on which the World Trade Centre and the Pentagon were attacked by terrorists."[51] Evangelicals faced a dilemma. For many years they had worked hard to distinguish evangelicalism from fundamentalism, but popular definitions of fundamentalism were changing.[52] Jeff Haynes has stated that "Religious fundamentalist movements aim to reform society by changing laws, morality, social norms and political configurations in accordance with religious tenets, with the goal of creating a more traditional society."[53] Harriet Harris has underscored the significance of this by noting that "[p]olitically active religious groups are frequently termed 'fundamentalist' by the media, and political and social science accounts tend to encourage this usage."[54] It was ironic that this occurred at a time when the EA seemed determined to see evangelicals reconnect with their history of political lobbying.

Evangelicalism's first sortie into societal transformation post 9/11 was, however, to prove quite innocuous. At its November 2001 conference in Cardiff the EA gave profile to its "Facevalues" campaign.[55] The intention behind Facevalues was to present a general message about standards in

---

48. "Window of Opportunity," 20–22.
49. Marty, "What Is Fundamentalism?" and Bruce, *Fundamentalism*.
50. Partridge, *Fundamentalisms*.
51. Partridge, *Fundamentalisms*, pre-title page.
52. Stott, *Evangelical Truth*, 20–24.
53. Haynes, *Religion*, ii.
54. Harris, "How Helpful," 12.
55. Evangelical Alliance, *Assembly of Evangelical Christian Leaders 2001*, 41.

Principles and practicalities in the interactions of 2000–2005   183

society. When announced to the press in October 2001, it was portrayed as a poster campaign with a budget of up to two million pounds "designed to survey the values of the UK."[56] Plans were outlined for six different posters to be widely displayed on hoardings from May to September 2002, each poster presenting a moral dilemma and stating "We're keen to know where you draw the line."[57] A number of posters were considered for the campaign but it proved difficult to find images that could confront public attitudes without offending public taste.[58] In the end, following Advertising Standards Agency's recommendations, the campaign was little more than a low-key challenge about forgiveness. It caused no fuss, yet gained little attention.

The March 2003 invasion of Iraq had a different effect on public attitudes to evangelicals. Many in Britain perceived that British participation in the invasion was a direct result of Bush's influence over Blair.[59] Such perceptions led to questions over the political influences on Bush, particularly about those from the religious right.[60] When a year later reports began to circulate of the strength of Christian support for Bush in the 2004 presidential campaign, many commentators perceived that questions about such influences had become more pressing.[61] There was a concern that British evangelicalism in turn might have a disproportionate effect on British politics. Interestingly, similar concerns were not expressed about African neo-Pentecostal influence despite the significant African American neo-Pentecostal support for Bush in 2004.[62] Stories of the effectiveness of Black Pentecostal power were impressive, with rumors circulating of a "fruitful alliance" being sought between the black churches and the Republican party after years of what has been described as the "Black and Democratic" cliché.[63] Explanations for this seemed to rest more with Bush's social conservatism, particularly his opposition to same-sex marriages, than with his faith-based initiatives in urban communities, although the latter had an

56. Petre, "Church to Spend," 15.
57. Petre, "Church to Spend," 15.
58. Edwards, Letter to EA personal members, August 23, 2002.
59. For an American perspective on this: Wither, "British Bulldog," 67.
60. James, "For God's Sake."
61. Cooperman and Edsall, "Evangelicals," A01.
62. Eddie Long discussed African American Pentecostal influence in the Presidential election with Ashimolowo's guests after a 2005 IGOC meeting.
63. Moore, "Black Republicans."

effect.⁶⁴ As the 2005 British general election came closer, some members of the British public wondered what Blair might say to court religious votes.⁶⁵

Six weeks ahead of the May election, Blair was invited to give the third of three Party leader presentations to the evangelical organization Faithworks. Speaking on March 22, 2005 he emphasized the importance of the role of "the churches and faith communities" in social action saying that he would like to see churches "play a bigger and not a lesser role in the future."⁶⁶ On being asked how church-based community work could win the trust of local councils, he replied "I hope [local councils] don't take the view that because you've got your own faith that somehow you are not providing a decent service to the community."⁶⁷ Pursued specifically on the role of such personal faith in political decision-making he drew some boundaries and made some comparisons.⁶⁸ For many evangelicals, and African neo-Pentecostals, these would have sounded disappointing:

> Politics and religion—it's not that they don't have a lot of things in common and that there aren't core issues that both of us are interested in, but it is just that if it ends up being used in the political process, I think that's a bit unhealthy. I don't want to end up with an American style of politics with us all going out there beating our chests about our faith.⁶⁹

Whilst nothing he said was incompatible with personal faith *per se*, evangelicals and African neo-Pentecostals both believe that personal faith must have a public dimension. Four years of heightened public concern over fundamentalism and several years of anxiety over American-style Christian influence seemed to be making faith's public dimension less palatable to public and politicians alike. The day after Blair had spoken at Faithworks, the headline appeared in the national press, "Keep election religion-free, says Blair."⁷⁰ This was a very different message from the one reported just five years before. Evangelicals and African neo-Pentecostals alike were

64. Moore, "Black Republicans."

65. Some evangelicals believed that for the 2005 General Election the Government sought moderate Muslim votes. According to the Christian Voice, "The Rt Hon Charles Clarke MP, Home Secretary, wrote to every mosque in the country before the election promising to bring in [the Incitement to Religious Hatred] Bill if re-elected." See "Stop," para. 2.

66. From the transcript originally provided by Faithworks.

67. Vann, "Faith," 7.

68. The specific question was, "Could you explain what Alastair Campbell meant by "We don't do God"? See "Politicians Should Have the Courage."

69. Vann, "Faith," 6.

70. Petre and Jones, "'Keep Election Religion-Free,'" 8.

amazed at the transition from 2000 when Hague spoke to the Charismatic constituency at Spring Harvest and Blair and Hague addressed the Caribbean and African Christian constituencies at Faith in the Future.

CAUTION AND CONCERN OVER DELIVERANCE AND ABUSE

Edwards' first appearance on Radio 4's "Any Questions?" coincided with the January 2001 conviction of Marie-Therese Kouao and Carl John Manning for the murder of eight-year old Victoria Climbié, whom they had been systematically abusing, physically and mentally. In answer to a question on the topic Edwards replied, "All of us have to look at this incident and equally look to ourselves as a society, in a situation where one child per week is dying at the hands of adults, and say, this is an indicator that we really do have to combine our efforts—social services, police, communities, churches, homes, schools—to do a better job than we are doing at the present time."[71] He added that "churches must take care in dealing with people believed to be 'possessed'" and urged churches to "work in co-operation with medical services before performing exorcisms cavalierly."[72] There is diplomacy in this answer. It is strong on child protection and cautious on deliverance. It reflects the breadth of the British evangelical opinion that Edwards was seeking to represent. To criticize one group of churches on deliverance issues would be inappropriate when other groups within evangelicalism held similar views, even if yet others question present-day demon possession entirely. The consistency of this style of response is worthy of study and I will consider the thinking behind it after outlining four child abuse incidents that brought African churches to public attention between 2000 and 2005.

Victoria Climbié

The death of eight-year-old Victoria Climbié on February 25, 2000 at the hands of her aunt and her aunt's boyfriend less than two years after Victoria had been sent from the Ivory Coast to join her aunt in London, received vast coverage in the press. An aspect of the story highlighted in the media was that three different African church leaders had failed to register that Victoria was in danger and that a deliverance service had been planned for her on the day that she died. According to the report of the government-commissioned

---

71. "Any Questions?," 5.
72. "Any Questions?," 5.

inquiry chaired by Lord Laming, "Kouao [the aunt] visited church towards the end of August and this helps explain why she began to believe Victoria to be possessed." The report then continued:

> On 29 August 1999, Kouao and Victoria attended the Mission Ensemble pour Christ, a church which meets in a hall close to Borough High Street. The Pastor here . . . had a detailed recollection of Victoria's appearance at this stage. . . . Victoria was dressed in heavy clothing that covered all of her body apart from her head and hands. He noticed wounds on both. . . . Kouao told him about Victoria's incontinence and he formed the view that she was possessed by an evil spirit. He advised that the problem could be solved by prayer.[73]

Another church, the Universal Church of the Kingdom of God based in north London, was also visited by Kouao on the Saturday in the week before she died on the Friday:

> At the end of the service, Pastor Lima spoke to Kouao about the difficulties she said she was having with Victoria, particularly her incontinence. He expressed the view that Victoria's problems were due to possession by an evil spirit and said he would spend the week fasting on Victoria's behalf. . . . Kouao was advised to bring Victoria back to church the following Friday . . . the day on which prayers are said for deliverance from "witchcraft, bad luck and everything bad or evil."[74]

The following Thursday "Kuoao was sufficiently concerned to bring Victoria to the church and ask for help . . . Lima advised them to go to the hospital and a mini-cab was called."[75]

These three brief visits came relatively late in the abuse process. For the three months between May and August Kouao had been attending a Baptist church, where the Ghanaian pastor seems to have made no mention of either deliverance or injuries.[76] According to David Pearson, a former senior social worker who had set up the Churches Child Protection Advisory Service,[77] it was failure to report injuries once observed that constituted the gravest lapse. "The primary failure in relation to child protection would appear to be that church leaders, having observed on Victoria obvious bruising and

---

73. Lamming, *Victoria Climbié Inquiry*, 26.
74. Lamming, *Victoria Climbié Inquiry*, 30.
75. Lamming, *Victoria Climbié Inquiry*, 30.
76. Lamming, *Victoria Climbié Inquiry*, 30.
77. Later renamed Thirtyone:eight.

Principles and practicalities in the interactions of 2000–2005   187

signs of neglect, failed to make a referral to the statutory authorities . . . the churches showed a lamentable lack of awareness that Victoria's disturbed behaviour might be indicative of abuse."[78] It is equally possible that being relatively new to Britain they had no awareness of the referral process. What often went unsaid was that the aunt presented herself as the child's mother, explaining that "her daughter" had recently arrived from Africa with these various difficulties which she, as the "caring parent," was seeking to rectify.[79] Furthermore, she never released Victoria to the care of any of the churches' children's workers where Victoria might have been separately observed.[80] Nevertheless, Pearson made a valid point:

> A significant reason for the lack of alertness to these child protection issues may be that the church bought in, uncritically, to the notion that Victoria was demonised and it blinded them to the abuse. Although it seems that Victoria herself believed that she was evil and possessed this should have been seen as a childish response to sustained emotional and psychological cruelty. By accepting, without question, this interpretation of Victoria's evidence of disturbance, the church effectively colluded with the abusers. To categorise a severely disturbed child as possessed by the devil is an extreme example of blaming the victim.[81]

Leaving aside the important issue of whether the thought of demonic possession came initially from Victoria, her aunt or the pastors (an issue which has been made much of but appears to lack clarity), there remains the churches' attitude to the demonic possession of children.

Damilola Taylor

The death of ten-year-old Damilola Taylor on November 27, 2000 on the stairs of a housing estate in Peckham, South London, brought racial issues to public attention at the start of the new millennium.[82] His death also brought together the Christian community as the Taylor family attended an African neo-Pentecostal church meeting in Peckham Civic Halls, and Edwards

---

78. Pearson's evidence to Laming Inquiry quoted in Hickin, *Uncomfortable Reality*, 80.
79. Interview with Pascal Orome, Pastor of Mission Ensemble pour Christ, Aug. 15, 2002.
80. Orome interview.
81. Hickin, *Uncomfortable*, 80.
82. Sentamu made comparisons with the Lawrence Inquiry in his report to the Metropolitan Police. Sentamu, "Damilola Taylor Murder Investigation," 5.

attended the memorial service along with African church leaders such as Ashimolowo, and the government minister Paul Boateng.[83] Mark Sturge of ACEA addressed some of the issues, sensitive to the fact that "Mountain of Fire and Miracles Ministries, where Dami attended Sunday School, [was] an ACEA member church":

> As with the murder of Stephen Lawrence, the country was appalled to hear of this senseless killing. All the written reports seem to suggest that Dami, as he was affectionately known, was killed by young children. Therefore, it struck the same chords as the murder of toddler Jamie Bulger who was murdered by two children several years ago. . . . If the early reports prove to be true—that black children killed Dami—it means that there is something unique about this situation. It brings a new perspective to the "Black on Black" violence in our community. In the last months there has [sic] been at least four such killings. . . . The question we are left with is, how should the church, and BMCs especially, respond to a community that is freewheeling into lawlessness? . . . Churches should lead the way in challenging the way in which society measures and evaluates itself. . . . One of the main misnomers is when we talk about community. The truth of the matter is there is no such thing as the Black community. What we have are numerous pockets of communities and not the macro version we have come to accept. It has become a label of convenience for everyone, politicians, sociologists and Black people themselves.[84]

Chief Lola Irende, a Lambeth Counsellor, made a similar point about the existence of "Black communities" rather than a "Black community" in a radio interview when she was questioned about the issue of Black-on-Black crime, given speculation about tension between African and Caribbean youth in the wake of Damilola's death.[85]

In the subsequent trial, details of the defendants were never released to the press as all four defendants were juveniles. Their trial was held at the Central Criminal Court, Old Bailey between January 23, 2002 and April 25, 2002. Two defendants were discharged during the course of the trial and the remaining two were found not guilty in respect of all counts on the

---

83. "Mountain of Fire and Miracles Ministries," part of a Nigerian denomination known for its prayers of commination ("Denouncing of God's Anger and Judgements against Sinners"—1662 Prayer Book). The London branch later became independent and changed its name to "Everlasting Arms."

84. Sturge, "Lord, Have Mercy," 10, 11.

85. Radio 4, "Today," Jan. 15, 2001.

Principles and practicalities in the interactions of 2000–2005   189

indictment. The subsequent review chaired by John Sentamu, then Bishop of Birmingham, identified exclusion of evidence as a major factor in the conduct of the trial.[86] Such exclusion makes it difficult to comment on the nature of any abuse that may have occurred. The significance of the incident here rests in its effect on public perceptions.

Child B and "Adam"

In May 2005 two women and a man were sentenced at the Central Criminal Court in London for abusing an eight-year-old girl they believed to be a witch. Throughout the trial, the child, an Angolan orphan, was known as Child B. The case, initially investigated by Hackney Social Services, involved the child being beaten and cut to "beat the devil out of her."[87] She was eventually placed in a laundry bag to be thrown into the canal "to throw her away for good."[88] Richard Hoskins of King's College London who advises the police on religiously motivated crime believed "it was sheer chance that this little girl was rescued in time."[89] Two years before the events took place, the aunt had attended the Dalston branch of the Congolese denomination, *Combat Spirituel*. Despite an investigation exonerating the church, the press turned to Congolese churches to enquire more about the nature of "Ndoki," the evil spirit said to have been affecting Child B.[90] Hoskins had advised, "belief in witchcraft has spread rapidly in some parts of central and southern Africa over the last few years; 'Ndoki' [is] said to target children particularly either when still in the womb or in early childhood through a piece of food infected with the evil spirit."[91]

The BBC carried out its initial investigation into Congolese churches by sending a reporter to the Church of the French Christian Community Bethel near Harlesden. When interviewed, the pastor, Modeste Muluyu confirmed that "he and the one hundred and twenty members of his congregation believe[d] absolutely in the existence of evil spirits and witchcraft."[92] He added, "We know that Ndoki does exist. Back home and everywhere else too there are people who are used by the devil to bring a curse or bad luck

---

86. Sentamu, "Damilola Taylor Murder Investigation," 30.
87. Vallely, "Believers," 34.
88. Westhead, "Abuse Case."
89. Westhead, "Abuse Case."
90. Vallely, "Believers," 34.
91. John, "Exorcisms."
92. John, "Exorcisms."

to other people's lives, even to kill them."[93] Significantly, throughout the interview he stressed that "violence was not needed for deliverance even when witchcraft was involved," explaining that "[s]ometimes we hear that some servants of God have been very violent when they're doing deliverance, but disciples should only do what the Master did. I never read in the Bible about Jesus Christ being violent with anybody to cast out any spirit."[94]

The interviewer subsequently took up this theme of violence with Hoskins and the editor of the Congolese newsletter, *Congo Panorama*, Antoine Lukongo. Lukongo said that "exorcisms in themselves were no bad thing and part of Congolese culture . . . 'part of our identity.'" He believed that "the growing violence in exorcisms is due to western influence."[95] Hoskins confirmed that "instances of extreme violence are very rare," commenting that "[m]y experience of Africa and the Congo where I've lived for years and travelled a lot is that Congolese people love their kids; true they fear sorcery or witchcraft but they don't tend physically to harm a child who may be thought to be a conduit."[96] Later in 2005 the BBC's "Today" reporter Angus Stickler investigated Dr. Tukela, pastor of the Congolese Church of Christ the Mission in north London. According to a former church elder, Tukela had advised that "children should be beaten until they confessed themselves to be witches."[97]

Much of this radio reporting was able to build on the imagery placed in the public mind by television programs such as Robert Beckford's "God is Black," first broadcast in June 2004. Beckford sought to show the challenge facing British Anglicanism in the light of a new tide of evangelicalism evident in Britain and Africa. As well as highlighting KICC he recorded scenes of healing and deliverance at T. B. Joshua's Synagogue Church of All Nations, at Ikotun-Egbe on the outskirts of Lagos, and showed them alongside a commentary from Nigerian Anglican Archbishop Akinola:

> In the full glare of the television camera they do miracles, they do a lot of things, alright! It's a church of materialism, They have no gospel of the incarnation. They have no gospel of the passion and cross of Jesus Christ. They have no gospel of the end times.

---

93. John, "Exorcisms."
94. John, "Exorcisms."
95. John, "Exorcisms."
96. John, "Exorcisms."
97. This report was not broadcast until January 12, 2006. Tukela was arrested hours after it was aired on "Today."

The only gospel they have is of now and money. So . . . people troop to see them.⁹⁸

Edwards issued a written statement on behalf of the EA in which he criticized Beckford's program for "falling back on stereotypes" and for failing to adequately define terms such as "evangelical" and "fundamentalist." According to Edwards, "[h]e too easily looked for the sensational and in so doing gave a distorted picture of what is really happening."⁹⁹ Such a press release would have done little to change the public perception of what Beckford described in the program as "mind boggling."¹⁰⁰

Press coverage of the Child B case and the subsequent Radio 4 investigations into London's Congolese churches also brought back into the public domain information about what police believe to have been the ritualistic killing of a four-to-seven-year-old Nigerian boy, whom they named "Adam," whose torso was found in the Thames by Tower Bridge in September 2001. In the course of this investigation the police had sought to identify the child by checking school attendance records in the London area. During the three month period on which they focused, it was found that schools had lost trace of three hundred African boys whom they had once had on their school registers. Whilst police were prepared to see this in the light of a constantly shifting population, the press in 2005 sought to give these statistics a sinister twist, conflating the figures with stories of Child B and Adam to suggest that children were being sacrificed in London churches.¹⁰¹ To reinforce the story it was stated that information had come from a new report prepared for the Metropolitan Police. One journalist wrote, "African boys are being murdered as human sacrifices in London Churches, according to a shocking Scotland Yard report" and "[t]he leaked report also reveals countless examples of African children being killed after being identified as 'witches' by church pastors."¹⁰² The report referred to was never officially released but subsequently made available for private discussion to a limited number of concerned senior London church leaders.¹⁰³ It was in fact a survey of community opinions conducted with focus groups drawn from two

98. Interview with Akinola in Beckford, "God Is Black"
99. Staff Writers, "Evangelical Alliance Lays," para. 9.
100. Robert Beckford in Quinn, *God Is Black*.
101. Edwards, "Children Sacrificed," 1.
102. Edwards, "Children Sacrificed," 1, 3.
103. Privately researched report commissioned by the Metropolitan Police in conjunction with its abuse-related Operation Violet.

London boroughs, Newham and Hackney.[104] Some focus group members did speak about deliverance and witchcraft in some London-based African churches, with some respondents also expressing opinions about male child sacrifice. Researchers did record, however, that "no specific details were forthcoming."[105]

Anger among African church leaders over the leaked report was considerable and twelve days after the press reports senior police officers met with African church leaders to listen and apologize. The authors of the report were present and were roundly criticized by the church leaders for a lack of balance in the presentation of their findings. However, there was some acknowledgement that it was the limitations of the focus group approach that had led to the difficulties. Such an approach affords no easy way of accurately according appropriate weight to statements made; participants' opinions were left to stand unchallenged.[106]

As the furor over the child sacrifice claims continued, Katei Kirby, Sturge's successor at ACEA, was approached by the *Independent* for a comment on the prevalence of deliverance in London's Black churches.[107] Her approach was to encourage a re-focusing: "there is a big difference between what can look like an emphasis on the practice of exorcism and making the leap to assuming that the atmosphere encourages the abuse of children."[108] There is no change here from the re-focusing approach adopted by Sturge. Throughout the Climbié hearing he sought to shift the emphasis from exorcism and to speak positively of the church as a safe environment. When called as an expert witness, Pearson told the Inquiry that churches could be "extremely dangerous places for children" as "[t]he church is probably unique in working with children, and those who abuse children, within the same four walls."[109] Sturge took issue with him in the press, again seeking to focus on a positive profile for the church:

104. Holloway, "What the Juju?"

105. "Community Partnership Project 2004–2005: Final report," Aditi Consultancy Services for the Metropolitan Police, May 20, 2005, para. 29.14. Cited with Metropolitan Police permission.

106. Notes taken at meeting convened by the Metropolitan Police June 28, 2005.

107. The EA was also drawn into the debate with press references to churches involved as "evangelical black churches." Evangelical Alliance, *Evangelical Alliance Annual Review 2004-2005*, 1.

108. Vallely, "Believers," 36.

109. "Churches Pose Threat."

Church is no more dangerous for children than any other place. ... I would say it is much safer because by all probabilities, people who attend church do so because they love God and they are, by definition, law-abiding people of integrity. ... Victoria's case is unique where the level of deception her aunt went through is something that makes the mind boggle. If someone says to a pastor "This is my child and all I am looking for is some kind of help or assistance" then you would have to take that at face value.[110]

ACEA made submissions to three Laming Inquiry seminars. For Seminar 1 on Discovery and Inclusion, the inquiry set the question: "How can children who are not known to national or local agencies be identified (including those newly arrived in England, recently moved within England, or not living with their birth parents) to ensure that they receive the services they are entitled to?" In response Sturge sounded a confident note:

> ACEA takes the view that if there is to be a dramatic improvement in the services offered to children and young people, then faith communities and places of worship should be encouraged to play a far greater role in finding and delivering the outcomes that best serve children in need.[111]

Some paragraphs later, Sturge extolled the potential effectiveness of faith communities in identifying new communities:

> Places of worship are by far the best place for identifying a large section of new communities. However, they will be reluctant to participate [in an identification process] if their involvement is seen as being "spies" for the authorities. Churches and other places of worship should not be asked to disclose immigration status of their attendees, as is the case with witnesses of crime. Instead, they should be encouraged to seek the welfare of all their adherents. In so doing they should have a responsibility to at least keep a log of all children who use their services. This log should be accessible to relevant agencies.[112]

The only difficulty with this assertion was that identifying new places of worship within new communities (particularly African communities) has long presented a challenge not only to ACEA but also to statisticians and

---

110. "Churches Pose Threat."
111. ACEA, "Response Seminar 1," para. 1.3.
112. ACEA, "Response Seminar 1," para. 4.2.

sociologists.[113] If new places of worship cannot be readily identified, then the effectiveness of using faith communities to identify new communities becomes questionable.

In ACEA's submission to Seminar 3 on Determining Requirements, more general issues of child protection returned to the fore, with Sturge again affirming a commitment to best practice: "ACEA believes that it is absolutely important to determine the requirement for protecting children in need. We take the view that the current Framework is adequate but more must be done to ensure agencies work together."[114] Thus committed, this strong public stand had to be supported by best practice within the constituency. In 2002 ACEA agreed to restrict its membership so that only churches with a satisfactory Child Protection Policy could join, such a policy requiring all children's workers to have been vetted through the Criminal Records Bureau. To help the implementation of this it was announced that

> Our aspirations are to offer as much support and assistance to churches as possible. We have already applied to the Criminal Records Bureau to register as an umbrella body. This means that those organisations that are too small or do not want to handle the detailed administration could do so through ACEA.[115]

From Climbié to Child B the evangelical response was to speak positively of child protection in public and then to work with its constituency in private to ensure best child protection practice. This was clearly a pressing concern for all evangelicals and it could be argued that concerns about African deliverance practices were marginalized as a result. However, the existence of diverse views on deliverance within the evangelical constituency probably contributed to the chosen emphasis.

To evaluate the different evangelical views on deliverance and compare these with the prevailing views within African Pentecostalism, I will first summarize a critical view of charismatic demonology from within evangelicalism. David Middlemiss has produced the standard evangelical work on charismatic practice and has analyzed charismatic demonology. He set it within the wider charismatic assumption that "the supernatural becomes an expected part of life" and described anticipation of divine healing and

---

113. A frequent complaint of Brierley at Christian Research.
114. ACEA, "Response Seminar 3," para. 9.1. Seminar 2's submission was on an unrelated matter.
115. "ACEA to Lead Disclosure Campaign," 13.

anticipation of demonic activity as examples of "supernatural immanence."[116] He believed that for those outside the charismatic movement such an emphasis on the demonic could appear "extreme and obsessive with a paranoid way of looking at the universe."[117] He saw both theological and practical problems with charismatic demonology. Theologically he concluded that

> [t]his supernatural demonic concept can become an all-pervading way of thinking which attributes that which is strange to the direct intervention of God or to Satan. There are no neutral areas, but two kingdoms at war with each other; all events have a moral and spiritual dimension. It is a variation of a "God-of-the-Gaps" thought pattern, which attributes unexplained (and much explicable) phenomena to the supernatural. In this case, however, it is more a "Devil of the Gaps" who is conjured up as an explanation of areas of experience which are not understood.[118]

Given such a charismatic thought-foundation, it comes as no surprise to Middlemiss that, with charismatics seeing demons as the Devil's agents, they detect a wide range of demonic activity within everyday occurrences. Practically he concluded that

> mental states, illness, and all kinds of common events in every area of life are considered to be capable of being influenced by the demonic. If one is tired, it is "the spirit of tiredness" which needs to be cast out; a hard-going service in a church needs "the spirit of heaviness" casting out; a murderer is influenced by the "Spirit [sic] of murder," and so on. Anger, sin and unforgiveness are entry points for "demonization." Both people and every-day inanimate objects can be carriers of demons . . . children's toys . . . have been seen by some as demonic. This appears more like outright superstition than the immanent supernatural.[119]

As Middlemiss developed his argument, he became increasingly convinced that charismatic practitioners prefer "direct revelation" to reason and are content for apparent divine intervention to circumvent theological debate.[120] He observed that a person could, for example, develop "a complex doctrine of demons and their work, beginning with the Bible, but going well beyond this, based on the authority of experience such as putative

---

116. Middlemiss, *Interpreting Charismatic Experience*, 13.
117. Middlemiss, *Interpreting Charismatic Experience*, 14.
118. Middlemiss, *Interpreting Charismatic Experience*, 14.
119. Middlemiss, *Interpreting Charismatic Experience*, 14–15.
120. Middlemiss, *Interpreting Charismatic Experience*, 22.

conversation with demons during exorcism."[121] The uncertainty of such interpretations was further highlighted by his comparison that "if someone thrashes around in a charismatic service, this would be attributed to the demonic, whereas in the time of Wesley . . . it would be as likely to be seen as a sign of deep conviction of sin."[122]

Moving from Middlemiss's conservative evangelical observations to the writing of charismatic deliverance practitioners themselves, I will consider their opinions in three related areas: "entry points," "manifestations" (perceived indicators of demonic presence) and deliverance techniques. However, it must be borne in mind that not all charismatics share their views. Nonetheless, their views are relevant because they have written from within the Charismatic Movement, having gained a degree of personal acceptance from one or more of its strands. All of the opinions expressed below, therefore, can in some measure be found within the charismatic arm of British evangelicalism.

Middlemiss has written of anger, sin and unforgiveness as being seen as demonic "entry points" by charismatics. Charismatic writers on deliverance have usually presented a more extensive list. Writing on deliverance, Peter Horrobin, director of the British-based deliverance ministry "Ellel," mentioned fifteen types of entry point, some of which he then subdivided further. His main categories were: the generation line, personal sin, occult sin, some alternative medical practices, religious sin, ungodly soul ties, sexual sin, "hurts, abuse and rejection," trauma or accident, death (including miscarriage or abortion), curses (including inner vows and pronouncements, and wrong praying), cursed objects and buildings, addictions, fears and phobias, and, finally, fatigue and tiredness.[123] More succinctly, Anglican Bishop Graham Dow listed six: false worship, other religions, cults, occult practices, sin and wrong attitudes, and traumatic events and oppression.[124] Later in his book, however, he added community history, rejection, miscarriage or abortion, dysfunctional families and alternative medicines.[125] Uniquely, the late Derek Prince, who considered there to be seven, included the "laying on of hands."[126] The confidence exhibited by all these charismatic

121. Middlemiss, *Interpreting Charismatic Experience*, 23.
122. Middlemiss, *Interpreting Charismatic Experience*, 169.
123. Horrobin, *Healing through Deliverance*, 35–207.
124. Dow, *Deliverance*, 32–37.
125. Dow, *Deliverance*, 46.
126. Prince, *They Shall Expel Demons*, 112–20. Americans Frank and Ida Mae Hammond listed sin, life circumstances and the "ruse of inheritance." Hammond and Hammond, *Pigs in the Parlour*, 23–26. New Zealander Bill Subritzky listed: hereditary; disobedience on the part of parents; friction between parents; molesting of children

writers in these "entry points" stands in contrast to Middlemiss's skepticism. In each case the writer asserted that these "entry points" gave the demon certain "rights" to residence.[127] Furthermore, all writers appeared to be open to a person having more than one demonic spirit and Dow was at pains to point out that demons may be "of varying strength."[128] A further underlying point here is that it is believed that "evil spirits have no fairness" so their impact may be out of proportion to the appropriateness of "the opportunity" afforded them.[129] Theoretically this means that, in charismatic understanding, sexual sins that repel society, say, carry no guarantee of a greater degree of demonization than a socially acceptable foible that falls within the range of charismatic "entry points." All "entry points" might, it is believed, result in much, little or (possibly) no demonic activity.[130]

"Manifestations" is the second area that merits consideration. Here the signs considered by charismatic deliverance practitioners to indicate possible demonic presence have again prompted the compiling of lists. Dow listed seventeen indications and Horrobin twenty-eight.[131] The ranges were considerable and included depression, reaction against worship, hearing voices, addiction, sexual aberrations, anorexia and suicidal tendencies. However, Horrobin in particular was anxious to point out that people can have such problems without there being any demonic influence.[132] Obviously, therefore, there are other factors that charismatics engaged in deliverance have to rely on in order to reach their conclusions. According to Americans Frank and Ida Mae Hammond, "discernment" could be backed up with "detection."[133] Furthermore, they indicated that if demonic influence was correctly discerned or detected, additional confirmation may come through dramatic mid-deliverance manifestations:

> When demons are confronted and pressurised through spiritual warfare they will sometimes demonstrate their particular

---

by parents; from the womb; through sin; sowing and reaping; giving place to the devil ("Satan is a legalist"); occultic involvement; possessions: general rejection; shock; transference from other people; a dominating personality; through entering buildings; obsessions; and curses. Subritzky, *Demons Defeated*, 67-82.

127. Horrobin, *Healing through Deliverance*, 85; Dow, *Deliverance*, 30; Subritzky, *Demons Defeated*, 73; Hammond and Hammond, *Pigs in the Parlour*, 23.

128. Hammond and Hammond, *Pigs in the Parlour*, 49; Dow, *Deliverance*, 21-22.

129. Hammond and Hammond, *Pigs in the Parlour*, 24.

130. This seems to be the implication of Horrobin's caution. Horrobin, *Healing through Deliverance*, 55.

131. Dow, *Deliverance*, 39-48; Horrobin, *Healing through Deliverance*, 55-82.

132. Horrobin, *Healing through Deliverance*, 55.

133. Hammond and Hammond, *Pigs in the Parlour*, 27, 28.

natures through the person in a variety of ways. These evil spirits are creatures of darkness. They cannot bear to be brought into the light. When their presence and tactics are exposed they may become excited and frenzied. The manifestations which can come forth seem to be endless.[134]

> Among the mid-deliverance manifestations they listed were rapid tongue movements, hissing through the nose, tingling hands, rigidity of the fingers, unnatural eye movements, odors, loud shouting and rhythmic bodily movements.[135] According to Dow "[c]oughing is common and vomiting has occurred on occasions."[136] Horrobin is more comprehensive, listing a possible thirty-one different mid-deliverance manifestations.[137] The physical nature of all these manifestations seems to accord with the equally physical exit charismatic deliverance ministers expect demons to make. The Hammonds wrote: "when demons are cast out they normally leave through the mouth or the nose."[138] Even Dow, whilst playing down the dramatic by stressing that "[d]eliverance does not need noise, it needs faith in God," wrote of physical exit paths:

> Most spirits leave through the mouth, while some leave in the way they came, for example, through the eyes, the sexual orifices or the fingers. They hold on to parts of the body (the person being set free is often aware of this), but this hold can be released in Jesus' name.[139]

For Horrobin there were nine physical exit routes.[140]

The fact that charismatic deliverance ministers appear to agree on so much relating to "entry points" and "manifestations," could appear to give their words weight. Nonetheless, it still has to be borne in mind that for conservative evangelicals Middlemiss's observation that charismatics can construct a "complex doctrine of demons and their work . . . based on the authority of experience" would hold true.[141]

---

134. Hammond and Hammond, *Pigs in the Parlour*, 47.

135. Hammond and Hammond, *Pigs in the Parlour*, 47–51. The Hammonds believed that hand manifestations usually indicated "demons of lust, suicide or murder." Hammond and Hammond, *Pigs in the Parlour*, 48. Horrobin listed thirty-one mid-deliverance manifestations. Horrobin, *Healing through Deliverance*, 247–51.

136. Dow, *Deliverance*, 54. Similarly, Horrobin, *Healing through Deliverance*, 252–53.

137. Horrobin, *Healing through Deliverance*, 55.

138. Hammond and Hammond, *Pigs in the Parlour*, 51.

139. Dow, *Deliverance*, 54.

140. Horrobin, *Healing through Deliverance*, 253.

141. Middlemiss, *Interpreting Charismatic Experience*, 23.

The third area to consider is deliverance techniques. Conservative evangelicals and charismatics agree that deliverance was a significant part of the ministry of Jesus in New Testament times, but they disagree on whether or not such practices should be copied today. As a charismatic, Prince was in no doubt that they should:

> When Jesus cast out demons, He went beyond the precedents of the Old Testament. From the time of Moses onwards, God's prophets had performed many miracles that foreshadowed the ministry of Jesus. . . . But there is no record that any of them had ever cast out a demon. This was reserved for Jesus. . . . This makes it all the more remarkable that this ministry has largely been ignored by the contemporary Church in many parts of the world. Evangelism, especially in the West, has been practised as if demons did not exist. Let me say, as graciously as possible, that evangelism that does not include the casting out of demons is not New Testament evangelism. . . . It is unscriptural to pray for the sick if one is not prepared also to cast out demons. Jesus did not separate one from the other.[142]

Some charismatic deliverance techniques, though, are harder to derive from the biblical record than others. Finding biblical justification for a team approach is straightforward; Jesus sent his disciples out in pairs.[143] However, it would seem that today's teams are expected to carry out forms of diagnostic work which seem absent from the biblical pattern. To aid diagnosis Horrobin recommends a six-point inquiry: "Investigate False Beliefs and Occult Involvements . . . Check Out the Generation Lines . . . Explore the Sexual History . . . Look for Signs of Rejection . . . Investigate Other Ungodly Soul Ties . . . Find Out About Accidents and Traumas."[144] Furthermore, whilst commanding evil spirits to depart is standard New Testament practice, it is common in charismatic circles today for the person receiving ministry to be asked to pray prayers of preparation, confession and consecration in advance of the spirit being commanded to go.[145] Something else taught by charismatic deliverance ministers that is not directly evident in the New Testament record is self-deliverance.[146] There is, however, evidence of Jesus

---

142. Prince, *They Shall Expel Demons*, 2,13.

143. Hammond and Hammond, *Pigs in the Parlour*, 87–98; Horrobin, *Healing through Deliverance*, 211–17.

144. Horrobin. *Healing through Deliverance*, 224–33.

145. Dow, *Deliverance*, 54–57; Horrobin, *Healing through Deliverance*, 235–43.

146. Prince, *They Shall Expel Demons*, 237–40; Hammond and Hammond, *Pigs in the Parlour*, 57–59.

ministering deliverance to children in the gospel record and the Hammonds included a chapter on such deliverance in their book:

> Since it has already been shown that demon spirits are able to gain entrance to a fetus [sic] and to children, it is obvious that there should be deliverance for them. Demons can be called out of children in the same way as they are called out of older persons. There will be manifestations of the spirits leaving through the mouth and nose as in other deliverances. Ordinarily children are quite easily delivered. Since the spirits have not been there very long they are not so deeply embedded in the flesh. There are exceptions to this, as in the case of children who have been exposed to demonic attack through severe circumstances. The manifestations of the demons can be quite dramatic, even in children.[147]

Again there are physical details here that do not occur in the gospel record and one is left wondering whether the Hammonds carried out such ministry publicly. The indications are that they probably did not. Elsewhere in their book one of them wrote that "[u]p to this point in my own ministry, most of the deliverance has been on the basis of a private conference-type ministry."[148] As to wider charismatic deliverance practice, public deliverance ministry has not been a feature of the British Charismatic Movement.[149]

Those who are familiar with African Pentecostal deliverance practice will see much similarity with charismatic practice. However, there are four differences: deliverance at public meetings is more readily accepted in African Pentecostal circles than it is in charismatic circles, although counselling room deliverance also has a prominent place; more reliance tends to be placed on discernment in African Pentecostal deliverance practice than on detection and investigation; preparation of the person receiving ministry through private prayer and counselling is not regarded as so essential within African neo-Pentecostal deliverance, although it does occur; and witchcraft is much more frequently cited as an "entry point" in African Pentecostal deliverance than it is in charismatic deliverance. Before considering these differences it has to be acknowledged that deliverance is not a priority for all African Pentecostal churches, any more than it is for all British charismatic churches. Many of the African neo-Pentecostal churches covered in this study do not have a deliverance emphasis and would not practice deliverance in their public meetings. They frequently offer their

---

147. Hammond and Hammond, *Pigs in the Parlour*, 65.
148. Hammond and Hammond, *Pigs in the Parlour*, 54.
149. Horrobin, *Healing through Deliverance*, 208–24; Dow, *Deliverance*, 52–57.

congregational members who fear personal attacks through witchcraft alternative understandings from Scripture. Indeed, it is a concern of many of the African neo-Pentecostal churches in Britain that they have no simple way of informing the public that not all African Pentecostal churches are the same.[150] Deliverance for them is a point of difference and not a point of unity. This is particularly true on witchcraft issues, which is where I will focus my attention.[151]

Whilst all four differences cited could be attributed to culture, the first three have more to do with a British perceived need for privacy and a preference for a conversational approach to problem solving than to anything of significant depth. It is the fourth, witchcraft, which marks a more important distinction. Interestingly, though, there are numerous references to witchcraft in theoretical British and American charismatic writing on deliverance.[152] However, prior to the turn of the millennium British and American stories of deliverance from witchcraft, though dramatic, were relatively few.[153] This has not been the case in Africa. Abraham Chigbundu, for many years an associate of Idahosa, included in his book numerous accounts of deliverance from disturbances which people attributed to witchcraft.[154] Indeed, in his chapter devoted to witchcraft he paid particular attention to manipulation through dreams; a theme repeated by other African writers on the topic.[155] Those writing on witchcraft from an African perspective clearly see themselves as people with experience and not just theorists. Keith Ferdinando, has argued that "the absence of serious demonological reflection in the West hinders the development of an adequate response to the development of new and exotic theories of the demonic."[156] This being so, a dialogue that brings together the theoretical charismatic deliverance thinking on witchcraft with the more applied African Pentecostal experience, would seem to be appropriate.

150. Frequently expressed comment in interviews. Reaffirmed at ACEA's Senior African Church Leaders' Meeting, Mar. 15, 2006.

151. See my earlier discussion of Onyinah's work on "witchdemonology" in ch. 2.

152. Harper, *Spiritual Warfare*, 43–44; Ungar, *Demons in the World Today*, 101–37; Prince, *They Shall Expel Demons*, 141–54.

153. A British example is Irvine, *From Witchcraft to Christ*. An American example is Brown, *He Came*.

154. Chigbundu, *I Believe in Deliverance*, 78–109.

155. Chigbundu, *I Believe in Deliverance*, 54–60. Akwaboah makes a similar point. Akwahboah, *Bewitched*, 71–88. For those familiar only with British charismatic demonology, "marine" spirits mentioned by Chigbundu are believed to come from the sea and manifest as (or possess) attractive women (p. 86).

156. Ferdinando, "Screwtape Revisited," 132.

Having briefly considered the potential overlap between the demonology of charismatic and African Pentecostal deliverance practitioners, my observation would be that at the end of 2005 both British evangelicals and African neo-Pentecostals would have wished to confront the issue of deliverance attempts on children suspected of exerting witchcraft influences. However, evangelicals have been reluctant to speak out for fear of stepping on charismatic sensitivities or of bringing indirect criticism onto African neo-Pentecostal churches through mistaken association. Likewise, African neo-Pentecostal churches have been reluctant to speak out, realizing that their desire to stand apart from some aspects of a wider African Pentecostalism could be better expressed if others, such as British evangelicals, were to stand alongside them. If the suggested dialogue occurred, maybe a joint British evangelical and African neo-Pentecostal approach on witchcraft and child deliverance could result.

CAUTION AND CONFUSION OVER GOVERNANCE AND THE PRESS

In chapter 3 of this book I presented case studies of the Hampstead Bible School of Faith and Matthew Ashimolowo. In 2002, VCC and KICC, the churches connected with the Finchley-based Bible School and Ashimolowo, both came into public prominence. Although each situation involved the Charity Commissioners, the underlying issues were very different.

Victory, debt and litigation

The strength of VCC at the turn of the millennium was indicated by the size of its income. In 2001 it registered an income of £3,500,000.[157] Its pastor was enjoying a high profile with his personal story appearing in the February 2001 issue of Kenneth Copeland's *Believer's Voice of Victory*. The first half of the article covered Pastor Davidson's[158] conversion experience during his time as a London bus driver and the second half of the article concentrated on his role with VCC.[159] It spoke positively of his early days as a practicing Christian battling against a corrupt system:

> One of the lessons [Pastor Davidson] was learning was that of integrity: integrity with God, integrity to the Word of God,

---

157. Charity Commission, "Report of the Inquiry."
158. A pseudonym used to protect the individual's identity.
159. Hemry, "Heir," 9.

> integrity in finances and in every area of life. As he applied integrity with his faith, he became a very diligent steward . . . they had joined a new young church, Victory Christian Centre, that brought Harrison House books to London. [Pastor Davidson] became the head usher and trained those in the helps ministry. . . . By 1990, he was set in place as an associate pastor. But in 1994, aware that the church money was being mishandled, [Pastor Davidson] resigned and went to work with a ministry in America. While he was gone, the church he'd attended in London experienced the shame of public accountability, the pastor removed from office, a church split and the bank taking control of the finances.[160]

The article then went on to explain Davidson's return and how "the congregation wept . . . too wounded to give." It ended on a high note:

> Today, Victory Christian Centre has grown from a faithful few to 3500 members. Pastor [Davidson] preaches six services on Sunday, two on Wednesday and holds church-wide prayer every Friday night. God breathed such life into the congregation that they recently purchased a building for 4.1 million pounds ($5.6 million) that seats 2200 people per service. [Pastor Davidson] made a commitment to never forget where he came from. That's part of the reason why he helps the poor and faithfully provides marriage counseling [sic] to those in need. . . . In October of 1999, he fulfilled a lifelong goal when Victory Christian Centre financed the Copelands' meeting in England.[161]

By April 2002, however, the Charity Commission had "received a number of complaints alleging that large sums of the Charity's money had been misapplied, and that the Pastor and his wife were receiving significant personal benefit from Charity funds."[162] "Concerns were also raised that, despite resigning as trustees of the Charity in 1999, the pastor and his wife exerted a dominant influence over the trustee body."[163] Having evaluated these complaints, the Commission opened an inquiry on May 31, 2002 and appointed an administrator on October 29, 2002.[164]

---

160. Hemry, "Heir," 9, 10.
161. Hemry, "Heir," 10.
162. Charity Commission, "Report of the Inquiry," para. 5.
163. Charity Commission, "Report of the Inquiry," para. 6.
164. Comment (intended as a point of differentiation) contained in Charity Commission press release on appointment of interim manager at KICC, December 1, 2002.

The church was closed down on December 18, 2002 after "the Receiver and Manager . . . found that the trustees were unaware of the large debts owed by the Charity and the lack of funds to discharge these."[165] The subsequent report stated that

> The Charity Commission investigation revealed evidence of misconduct and mismanagement, including significant unauthorised salary payments and other benefits provided to the Pastor and his wife, as well as a number of the trustees. The trustees were not in control of the Charity and were not aware of the scope and measure of the expenditure of the Charity's money. The Pastor signed the majority of cheques as sole signatory, in breach of the Charity's Constitution. There was a lack of financial controls surrounding cash collections and charitable expenditure was not accounted for.[166]

The problems at Victory were compounded throughout the summer and autumn of 2002 as some female members of the congregation began to bring accusations of a sexual nature against Davidson in his role as church pastor. The initial report was made to the church elders in March 2002.[167] By the time of the administrator's appointment, press reports were referring to "emerging sexual and financial scandal at VCC."[168]

When the church closed in December 2002 the level of accusation had reached the point that an injunction had been taken out against Davidson preventing him from attending the church property. When the congregation members wanted to continue meeting, it was Davidson's wife who assumed the role of senior pastor and set up afresh in rented premises, re-branding the church "From Victory to Victory" (V2V).[169] The accusations of inappropriate sexual behavior came to court in May 2003. The charges involved one case of rape and twelve of indecent assault, as well as perverting the course of justice.[170] The proceedings were widely reported.[171] As it continued into June, the court was told of Davidson's earlier contrition at a church meeting: "The Old Bailey heard how [Davidson] allegedly confessed to unnamed failures at a special church meeting in April 2002. The meeting

---

165. Charity Commission, "Report of the Inquiry," para. 10.
166. Charity Commission, "Report of the Inquiry," paras. 8, 9.
167. Shaw, "Women 'Lured.'"
168. Slater, "It's Easy."
169. "Church Charity Cash Mismanaged."
170. Yaqoob, "Minister 'Groomed' Teenage Girls," 43.
171. "Prey" was used to create a play on words. Hepburn, "Let Us Prey," 11; Aguiar, "Rape Pastor' Praying On," 4.

took place after five women went to the elders of VCC with their complaints against [Davidson]."[172]

The case was retried in May 2004. Davidson's influence on his old congregation was evident as many who had gone on to join V2V stood outside the Old Bailey to sing hymns and show their support.[173] On May 7, 2004 he was sentenced to three and a half years for indecent assault, attempted indecent assault and perverting the course of justice.[174] Newspaper reports used the opportunity to refer to the Charity Commission investigation and his lavish lifestyle:

> An evangelical preacher whose charismatic style drew capacity congregations to his church and brought in millions of pounds of donations was convicted yesterday of preying on young women in his flock. [Davidson], 47, a former bus driver, faces a jail sentence and an enquiry into the finances of his former church in north London, which was closed down by the Charity Commission . . . despite an estimated income that year of £7 million. When he took over the VCC in 1996 it had fewer than 100 members. But soon the church attracted congregations of 3,000, with people queuing outside to get in. . . . Stewards went around with collection buckets and members contributed 10 per cent of their income. [Davidson] who preached in an American evangelical style, earned even more money from videos and books. He spent lavishly, using £21,000 from the church for a family holiday to Hawaii, buying designer clothes and giving expensive presents to a variety of young women, it was claimed at an earlier hearing.[175]

Four months later the Commission posted its report on VCC on its website, stating that "in accordance with section 3(4) of the Charities Act 1993" it had been "removed from the Central Register of Charities."[176]

The fall of a prominent church leader is always painful for the church community. In 2000 the EA magazine carried an article entitled "When Superman slips" addressing the topic in general terms:

172. Aguiar, "Pastor in 'Cinema Assault,'" 6.
173. Clough, "Preacher Preyed," 6.
174. Clough, "Churchgoers Pray."
175. Clough, "Preacher Preyed."
176. Charity Commission, "Report of the Inquiry," para. 12.

> News of the downfall of a Christian leader—be it a nationally known figure or your local vicar—leaves the church in shock. Those close to the one in crisis often say they had no idea that things were going wrong. Why is it that one day a leader is saying and doing the right things, apparently sincerely, and the next has fallen apart? . . . Overload is one of the biggest pressures . . . Leaders, especially those with wider ministries, must have an "accountability group" of close, wise friends and colleagues, says Gerald Coates. He meets regularly with a group of two or three, and says he has "given them permission to ask me the hard questions about money, sex, time away from my family."[177]

Before the verdict, African neo-Pentecostal leaders were as uncertain about Davidson's guilt as were the members of Victory's congregation. Part of the reason for this was Davidson's degree of self-containment resulting from his only point of accountability being Ray McCauley, the pastor of a large "Word of Faith" church in Johannesburg, South Africa. Fellow leaders in Britain wanted to be supportive but were not in a position to know what to do or say.

Another article, published before the facts of the Davidson case had fully unfolded, appeared in ACEA magazine, again looking at the pressures on church leaders. This time, though, it concentrated on an issue that would have surprised many denominational evangelicals on meager stipends, that of materialism.

> I take issue with . . . the blind following of what seems to be the latest craze (or craziness) [whereby] some pastors are negotiating as much as £25,000 for three days of preaching, travel by limousine and fly first class (or in their own jets), with their entourage. Added to that, special offerings are taken up for them, or they negotiate a percentage of the offering as a fee. Some pastors who once saw their roles as vocational, are now avowed careerists. Having witnessed the earning potential of some of their members they believe it is right for them to have an opportunity to excel in their chosen profession. This outlook is correct to some degree as Scripture suggests that we should not "muzzle the ox when it is treading out the grain" (Deut.24:4). However, although Jesus told His disciples that a "worker deserves his wages," he warned them not to "move around from house to house" (Luke 10:7). The underlying message is that the

---

177. "When Superman Slips," 21, 22.

disciples should not be bought, and the Gospel cannot be sold to the highest bidder.[178]

The writer then went on to point out that "the money received by leaders usually comes from tithes and offerings which ought to be to advance the Kingdom rather than inflate egos." He questioned the legality of not retaining a "clear distinction between a charitable purpose and a business venture" adding that "the law demands that there should be no 'benefiting [of] individuals in a way which outweighs any benefit to the public.'" He concluded that "churches . . . will end up losing their charitable status."[179]

With so much written in the Christian press before (and during) the trial, there was a reluctance to be seen to be vindictive once it had finally been ruled on.[180] Sturge was particularly anxious to stifle comments about Davidson's ethnic background and his independent church status: "let us be clear; Pastor [Davidson's] actions were not due to his colour or churchmanship, but, to quote the Prosecution at the trial: 'He acted in a predatory fashion, singling out those who were vulnerable . . . mainly younger members of the congregation [by] posing as a paternal figure, rendering them susceptible to his advances.'"[181]

Sturge's comment about churchmanship was particularly relevant as both he and the secular press had been significantly outspoken about independent churches at various stages of the legal and pre-legal process. In November 2002, a *New Nation* journalist wrote,

> The scandal that has engulfed Victory Christian Centre prompts one immediate question—how easy is it to set up a church? The number of so-called black majority churches has mushroomed over the past 15 years. According to the Black Majority Churches UK Directory for 2000 there are 1,351 of them but experts say the figure could easily be double that. . . . More worryingly, about half of these black churches, like VCC, are totally independent, set up by charismatic individuals who have been "called" by God and left to operate in the ultimate free market where only followers keep a check by voting with their feet.[182]

The same journalist then went on to quote Robert Beckford saying: "It has always been easy to set up a church . . . [i]n terms of checks and balances

178. Reddie, "Stars in Their Eyes," 6, 7.
179. Reddie, "Stars in Their Eyes," 7.
180. Before the first trial Sturge wrote a critical article about accountability in independent churches. Sturge, "Where Are the Apostles?," 10–11.
181. Sturge, "We're So Sorry," 10.
182. Slater, "It's Easy."

there are none, apart from those churches which are part of larger denominations... the independents are a law unto themselves." For Beckford it was pertinent that "[m]any pastors have not actually been to Bible college or taken a degree in theology."[183]

Sturge was also quoted in the same article having been asked to consider Beckford's suggestion that ACEA "could give churches a rubber stamp of good practice":

> It is not fair to say there are no checks and balances. Most register as charities because it makes financial sense and even the independent churches tend to belong to church networks such as local Councils of Churches. ACEA is already involved in validating churches because we are frequently approached by government, local authorities or schools to vouch for particular churches. Now and then we have simply never heard of them.[184]

The journalist then went on to express surprise, given the above, that "ACEA were [sic] not tipped off about the emerging sexual and financial scandal at VCC."[185] Shortly before being interviewed by *New Nation*, Sturge had written an article for *Focus*. It stood as a complete contrast to his positive defense of independent churches in the secular media. It was a long, strong, direct and sustained challenge to the leaders of independent churches to make themselves more accountable. In Sturge's eyes they were a long way from getting it right. I quote in part:

> Most readers will [have heard] the... words: "I'm only accountable to God."... My response to these claims is simple; anyone who is only accountable to God is a deluded maverick who does not know the difference between being at the end of someone else's shoelace and the wisdom or guidance of God and His Spirit. Biblical accountability demands that we are accountable to and for each other. The Apostles and the early church had structures in place to promote the Gospel, clarify doctrine and praxis, guard against heresy, unrighteous living and to deal with matters that would bring the church into disrepute.... In the BMC's brief history of 54 years, we have more than ten times the number of denominations than the UK's historic churches, and an ever-spiralling number of independent churches.... The primary reason for establishing a church should be "the humble submission to the call of God to serve His people and

183. Slater, "It's Easy."
184. Slater, "It's Easy."
185. Slater, "It's Easy."

to be His bold yet compassionate witness to those who have no knowledge of Him." . . . Independent churches, with their "can do, must do" outlook, can at times be a breath of fresh air to barren, inactive or bureaucratic denominations. However, their great asset is often their major weakness as it can breed what I call a "truly independent or free spirit." Accountability is wrongly seen as an obstruction, an interference that delays the programme of God and undermines the authority of leadership. Sadly, accountability is often viewed as a man-made vice, having no basis in Scripture because God's kingdom is not a democracy but a theocracy. . . . Senior leaders often ask me about accountability issues and suggest that the African and Caribbean Evangelical Alliance (ACEA) needs to play a far greater role in this debate. The questions that immediately come to mind are "Where are the apostles and prophets?" Where are the leaders of integrity who are not carried away by personal pride, selfish ambition and contemptuous [sic] of their colleagues? Why is it that the men and women of the appropriate stature disqualify themselves due to their narrowness of vision and poor understanding of the Kingdom? It does not take too much discernment to comprehend that the true value of accountability is only known when you become accountable yourself.[186]

The difference between the two statements is startling. Sturge was obviously keen to create a positive public perception, despite all the negative publicity arising from the Davidson case. However, he was also determined that there should be no repetitions and in private strongly exhorted leaders of independent churches with this in mind. Nevertheless, many African neo-Pentecostal leaders were offended by Sturge's exhortations with their implicit accusations. Furthermore, as they only heard Sturge speak in private on these matters, they assumed that he addressed such issues with similar implicit accusations in public. This misunderstanding led to concerns among African neo-Pentecostal leaders about the ambassadorial role they had hoped ACEA would undertake on their behalf.[187] In the midst of a difficult situation they felt abandoned without any adequate public representation.

186. Sturge, "Where Are the Apostles?"
187. Minutes of ACEA's Senior African Church Leaders' Meeting, February 20, 2003.

KICC and the Charity Commission

On 1 December 2002, African neo-Pentecostal concerns were exacerbated when the Charity Commission issued a press release that caught the attention of the capital's media:

> The Charity Commission announced today the appointment of an interim manager to take control of Hackney-based Kingsway International Christian Centre (King's Ministries), one of the capital's largest black churches and a registered charity. The watchdog has taken this temporary action in order to protect the church's assets as part of an ongoing investigation into concerns about its governance. . . . Head of the Commission's investigation team in London, David Rich, said: "People will naturally be concerned, but the appointment is a temporary and protective measure. The interim manager will take control of the church both to secure its assets and to allow it to continue to function normally. The aim of the investigation is to work with the Senior Pastor and other trustees to enable the church to continue on an improved footing. We are committed to enabling this strong and successful church community to flourish. The appointment of an interim manager is a step to that end."[188]

At the end of the press release were three sentences designed to offer reassurance.[189] However, they had the opposite effect:

> Today's announcement follows the separate appointment of a receiver and manager to the Kilburn-based Victory Christian Centre on 29 October 2002 following evidence of an extensive range of abuse and mismanagement against the church. David Rich said: "We would like to reassure London communities that there is nothing to suggest widespread wrongdoing against [sic] Christian charities in the capital, the overwhelming majority of which are extremely well run by committed volunteers, staff and trustees. There is no evidence to suggest that these two distinct investigations represent any trend of abuse or mismanagement."[190]

---

188. Charity Commission press release, December 1, 2002.
189. The Commission apologized through David Rich and Tessa Denham at an EA meeting on December 12, 2002.
190. Charity Commission press release, December 1, 2002. Rich's "wrongdoing against" was ambiguous: wrongdoer unidentified.

Principles and practicalities in the interactions of 2000–2005   211

The shock among London's African and Caribbean Christian community was considerable. Ashimolowo, as Senior Pastor at KICC, had been given a few days warning of the press release and used the opportunity to inform his Sunday congregation twenty-four hours before the official announcement. He had contacted a number of senior church leaders to find people willing to stand beside him as he told the church, and Edwards made himself available.[191] Special prayer meetings were then held each night of the subsequent week, although by mid-week Ashimolowo himself had had to travel, leaving things in the hands of his wife and an assistant pastor. Whilst many in the congregation were indignant over the Charity Commission action others looked for a higher purpose. The following extracts were given in a prophecy typed out and circulated at the Thursday evening prayer meeting at Waterden Road:

> I am doing a new thing. Where I am taking my servant, this storm is the vehicle. . . . Parliament will turn to you. . . . Hell shall not be able to prevail. The world will see and know that I am God. . . . Get ready for greater glory. Get ready for showers of miracles. This shall become a reference point. People shall say the God of Abraham, Isaac, Jacob and Matthew Ashimolowo. . . . I am the Lord I do not change. Peace to you, My church, saith the Lord of Hosts.[192]

The background to the press release was that the Commission had carried out a review visit in March 2002 because KICC's governing charity (The King's Ministries Trust) had submitted an annual return for the financial year ending September 30, 2000 showing that £76,487 (out of a total income of £4,980,280) had been paid to trustees of the charity.[193] An Inquiry was started on June 20, 2002 and the appointment of the interim manager was part of this process. Because of its incredible growth, KICC had governance structures that in some areas had grown complex and yet in other areas had stayed too simple. The trustee board still consisted of four members of the church's Pastoral Board plus two trustees based in America, and it was the Pastoral Board that made the majority of the decisions.[194] The head of the Pastoral Board was Ashimolowo, who as Senior Pastor also served as a trustee and over time he and the three other trustees on the

---

191. KICC had been EA members since 1995. EA and ACEA press release, January 9, 2004.

192. "Prophecy for KICC," December 4, 2002.

193. Charity Commission, "Report on The King's Ministries," para. 4 and Charity Commission, "Register of Charities."

194. Charity Commission, "Report on The King's Ministries," para. 6.

Pastoral Board (Ashimolowo's wife and two assistant pastors) had all become salaried because of the increase in their ministry workload. Unfortunately the trust documentation had not been modified through the Commission to take account of this, so there were no clear guidelines for the payment of trustees. This aspect of the governance structure was simple but it had broken down. As far as complexity was concerned, as the ministry had developed, Ashimolowo had set up private companies to handle his ministry income and his media work.[195] The church had also set up two subsidiary companies: one to deal with the church bookstore and the other to deal with church conferences.[196] The relation between these entities had never been fully defined and the issue of intellectual property rights for books, videos and tapes had never been clarified.[197] Furthermore, the church wanted to handle part of the Senior Pastor's remuneration through special gifts and "payments in kind" (such as free accommodation), a complex approach requiring careful documentation.[198] By 2002, after a decade of remarkable growth, the combination of complexity and simplicity was beginning to show signs of strain. Even so, the leadership at KICC clearly did not feel that the point had been reached where a solution had to be imposed and it was far from comfortable with the interim manager's appointment. Tensions continued until the interim management team left in March 2005.

Immediately after the announcement of the interim manager's appointment, the EA and ACEA jointly called a meeting between church leaders and members of the Commission's Investigation Team. This took place on December 12, 2002 in the sixty-seat conference room at the EA offices. The meeting was packed and the atmosphere tense. Edwards chaired proceedings with Sturge acting as evaluator. Anger and concern were expressed by African neo-Pentecostal leaders on a number of issues, not least over the Commission's press release that linked the Victory and KICC cases and the fact that the Commission's appointed managers were to be paid not by the Commission but out of the Charity's income. Confidence in the Investigation Team was further undermined when a question about trust deeds permitting salary payments to trustees was wrongly answered and an apology from the Head of the Commission's London Investigation Team had to be circulated to delegates after the meeting:

> There was one point raised at the meeting that needs clarification. . . . An individual asked what would happen if the

195. Charity Commission, "Report on The King's Ministries," para. 13.
196. Charity Commission, "Report on The King's Ministries," para. 8.
197. Charity Commission, "Report on The King's Ministries," paras. 10, 14.
198. Charity Commission, "Report on The King's Ministries," para. 12.

Commission had registered a charity with a governing document which authorised such general trustee payments.... After the meeting I discussed this with Commission lawyers and they have said that my advice was wrong. If a charity already has a governing document authorising such payments, and the Commission at the registration stage accepted this, then it would be taken that these payments had been authorised by us.[199]

This issue cut to the core of the KICC problem. Investigating teams had been sent in by the Commission to check for compliance. Had the KICC trustees renegotiated their governing documents with the Commission and obtained authorization for certain payments to trustees at the time some of their number became salaried, the investigating team would have had their key concerns removed on consultation with Commission lawyers. It was this realization that began to dominate the thinking of key people within the EA and ACEA. As KICC struggled on with their problems a campaign began on these issues. In March 2003 ACEA devoted *Focus* to charity-related topics, saying "there is a discrepancy between the leadership philosophy of many BMCs and the guidelines of the Commission."[200] In his article, the editor referred to fundraising saying that the Commission's guidelines "fail to consider the entrepreneurial spirit of BMCs with their numerous income generating schemes that bolster finance."[201] However, it was the issue of the Commission's perceived side-lining of leadership that drew his strongest comments:

> All God-fearing church leaders would not condone wrongdoing.... However, consider this: After years of blood, sweat and tears in order to promote the work of God, their vision and mission are questioned by Charity Commission guidelines which state every charity must appoint trustees to control the management and administration of the church. The Commission's press officer, Kevin Snow, states " . . . these [responsibilities] include the duty of trustees to avoid conflicts of interest such as taking up any paid role in the organisation that they are responsible for governing." This would rule out pastors from acting as trustees, leaving some to argue "Where was the Charity Commission

---

199. Apology from David Rich circulated by Joel Edwards in a letter dated Dec. 20, 2002. A tense follow-up meeting for African neo-Pentecostal Leaders was held at Royal Connections, Plaistow, December 17, 2002. Sturge controversially sought to defend the Charity Commission's case.

200. Reddie, "Is the Charity Commission Undermining?," 7.

201. Reddie, "Is the Charity Commission Undermining?," 6.

when pastors had to do the work of ten men and women to fulfil the Commission of God?"²⁰²

Sturge indicated that ACEA intended to do something about the "discrepancy":

> The governance of our churches [was] brought into view by the Charity Commission's recent investigation into the affairs of two of the largest churches in London, which resulted in one closing . . . it has also demonstrated that the Charity Commission does not understand the way church works particularly BMCs with their unique culture and context. In the coming months ACEA will be addressing these issues with the authorities that be. It will be pressing for drastic changes to ensure that the essence of our faith and practices are not compromised.²⁰³

The same magazine edition announced the GOAL conference planned for May 20, 2003: "Issues of leadership, accountability and best practice . . . will be further explored at the ACEA and . . . EA organised Governance, Openness, Accountability and Leadership (GOAL) Conference."²⁰⁴ For the organizers the event achieved a significant breakthrough. In the lead-up to the event they had held discussions at the Charity Commission offices. On the day at Ruach Ministries, Brixton, Mary Cridge, Head of Customer Services at the Charity Commission, responded by announcing that the Commission "will be working with ACEA and the Evangelical Alliance (EA) as well as other umbrella groups to produce a model governing document specifically aimed at churches."²⁰⁵ Sturge welcomed the announcement and "the swiftness of the Charity Commission's response to find a solution which could have potentially undermined the function and integrity of churches."²⁰⁶ Cridge told conference delegates that the governing document would, "[c]ontain all the provisions that you and we think are necessary to provide a good and appropriate governance framework for churches."²⁰⁷

Sturge might have been right in welcoming the swift response of the Commission in May 2003 but the production of a new "model governing document specifically aimed at churches" was to prove a painstaking task. A year after the GOAL Conference senior African and Caribbean Church

---

202. Reddie, "Is the Charity Commission Undermining?," 6.
203. Sturge, "Churches under the Spotlight," 10.
204. "Aiming for GOAL," 13.
205. "GOAL Conference," 12.
206. "GOAL Conference," 12.
207. "GOAL Conference," 12.

Principles and practicalities in the interactions of 2000–2005 215

leaders were invited to a meeting at the offices of the EA to consider the form new model governing documents should take.[208] A week later, in a further discussion at the Charity Commission's offices, it was brought to the Commission's attention that the majority of African neo-Pentecostal churches and the churches set up as part of the New Churches Movement had at some point been faced with a dilemma: either they breach their documents, as KICC was alleged to have done, or they decide to run the risk of being accused of having "exerted a dominant influence over the trustee board," from the side-lines as it were, as had been the case with the pastor at Victory.[209] In the eyes of such churches it would be unbiblical to stop the key decision-maker from making the key decisions just because he had become salaried; visionary leadership and remuneration of leaders are both biblical concepts. Whilst historically most have overcome this by negotiating a clause whereby the senior pastor can be a salaried trustee, it was argued that such provision has by no means been standard and churches the size of KICC had gone on to salary a number of key decision-makers.

In the light of this it was agreed that the initial work should focus on creating new model documents for independent churches with non-voting memberships.[210] The aim of the new model document would be threefold: to allow all key decision makers to be named as trustees, to build in adequate safeguards for ensuring that salaried trustees do not breach regulations for trustee benefit, and to ensure that where there are trustees who are not part of the spiritual leadership of the church such trustees do not exercise undue influence over matters of spiritual governance. This went slightly further than Cridge had indicated in her article in the September 2003 issue of *Focus* but the generalities were already in place. She detailed "[t]wo general principles [that] have caused concern when they are applied to pastors who are also church trustees . . . are that trustees should not be paid and that all trustees are equal."[211] On the matter of paying trustees she wrote,

> The general principle is that trustees cannot be paid for any service they provide unless they have permission from the Commission or the Courts. The permission to pay is called a "remuneration clause." If your governing document says you can pay your pastor then you can. If it does not, but the church would like to, then the trustees need to seek an amendment from the Commission. The new model we are developing will

208. Minutes of meeting held May 21, 2004. ACEA archive.
209. Charity Commission, "Report of the Inquiry," para. 6.
210. Minutes of meeting held at the Charity Commission, May 27, 2004.
211. Cridge, "Church and Charity Commission," 15.

include an optional provision to permit the pastor to be a paid trustee. . . . We strongly recommend that all charities disclose payments to trustees in their accounts (this is a legal requirement if accounts are prepared on an accruals basis). It is also important to ensure that there are open methods to determine the level of pay which we would expect to be reasonable in relation to the job undertaken.[212]

Her comments on equality of trustees were also relevant:

> The equality of trustees is a given; in law they share equal responsibility for the care of their charity or church. However, sharing responsibility for good governance does not stop the pastor trustee from taking the lead on spiritual matters. We recognise the crucial leadership role that pastors have in relation to their church, their congregation and the communities they serve. I recognise the inherent tensions here but feel it is possible to reconcile these roles—and the work we are doing will help.[213]

The fact that the work had not been completed by the end of 2005 despite a number of drafts and meetings between charity solicitors, the Commission and interested parties, indicates the complexity of the process. Press reports did not always help either, understating the optional nature of the model governing documents being prepared. The following appeared alongside further reports about Davidson on the day before the Commission posted its report about Victory on its website: "A loophole that has allowed pastors of black majority churches to extort money from vulnerable congregations is to be closed under new rules . . . which will be introduced in the autumn and will cover all independent church charities."[214]

An autumn 2004 launch proved unachievable. A progress report from Cridge published in the January 2005 edition of *Focus* spoke of the "draft documents currently being finalized" and mentioned how the process had

---

212. Cridge, "Church and Charity Commission," 15.
213. Cridge, "Church and Charity Commission," 15.
214. Gledhill, "Charity Law," 3. Two weeks later the Charity Commission announced its investigation into London-based Kenyan Pentecostal pastor Gilbert Deya. Charity Commission press release, September 20, 2004. Despite extensive reporting of alleged baby trafficking, the case did not impinge on the BMCs/CC debate. CC censure of Power Praise and Deliverance Church in November 2005 did provoke comment on BMCs/CC debate. Little, "Pay Scandals," 1.

Principles and practicalities in the interactions of 2000-2005   217

enabled the Commission to develop "an understanding of the unique nature of the relationship between a founder pastor and his congregation."[215] Legal complexities and positive lessons notwithstanding, a process begun in 2003 and still uncompleted in 2005 was little help to KICC. The new documents might ultimately be expected to resolve KICC's problems, reflecting as they would the basic governance principle of decision-makers serving as trustees, but KICC wanted voices to be raised on its behalf in the autumn of 2003 and the spring of 2004. The promise of new model documents in the long-term was too slow and remote. KICC was seeing its income spent on a professional firm carrying out interim management; a firm that in its opinion did not always follow its Pastoral Board's wishes. On January 7, 2004 KICC issued a press release entitled "UK's biggest church contemplates walking away from £25M assets":

> Unless the Charity Commission is prepared to remove KPMG [the city firm appointed as managers] without delay and take account of our church culture, we feel that we have no other course of action than to walk away from the charity so that we can run our church without compromising our beliefs.... KICC has been footing the bill for the interim managers whose daily rates could be as high as £10,000 a day, or £4 million to date. KICC has continued to survive this action.... The church has assets worth over £25 million, including savings, land and property, and is still thriving, with an income of around £7.5 million over the last 14 months ... we feel that the Charity Commission can't see past their racial stereotypes—they are acting as if the church's money is at risk because it's headed by an African. They also have failed to try and understand the black church culture and modify their regulations accordingly. Even Tony Blair has said that Charity law is outdated.[216]

On January 9, 2004, the EA and ACEA issued a joint press release that sought to be supportive of KICC yet cautious on the charges of racism against the Commission. The statement acknowledged KICC's membership of the EA which it had joined directly, by-passing ACEA:

> The Hackney-based Kingsway International Christian Centre (KICC) has been a member church of the Evangelical Alliance UK since 1995 . . . and . . . has grown to be one of the largest and most successful churches in the UK . . . we are saddened

---

215. Cridge, "Church and Charity Commission," 17.

216. KICC press release, January 7, 2004. Total cost of administration proved to be £1.2M.

> that the relationship between KICC, the Charity Commission and the interim management appears to have broken down... The Charity Commission has made a commitment to work with us... to develop new model governing documents specifically for churches.... All institutions need to exercise sensitivity in matters of race... we have been given assurances that black churches are not being treated any differently from anyone else.[217]

Far stronger support for KICC came in a press release from the Association for Charities. I reproduce this in some detail as it presented the most positive interpretation of KICC's position and went well beyond any endorsement given by either the EA or ACEA:

> In a December 2002 broadcast interview, a Commission spokesman alleged that "hundreds of thousands of pounds of charity money may have been put to inappropriate use."... Some 14 months later, it appears that there is a possibility that the "hundreds of thousands of pounds of charity money may have been inappropriately used"—not as a result of any actions or inaction on the part of the trustees, but as a result of the fees and expenses charged by the Receivers and Managers and other professionals appointed to assist them![218]

The Association continued,

> It is our understanding that no evidence of fraud, financial impropriety, or financial irregularity has been found which could have served to justify the appointment of the Receivers. It appears that the major income of the Church charity comes from the sacrificial giving of its 10,000 members; and that the Church charity had a well-managed set of financial procedures and controls to ensure that the funds received were properly accounted for and used—prior to the appointment of the Receivers. It further appears that the major area of activity following the Receivers' appointment related to discussions about the appointment of additional trustees and alternative forms of governance; and that these discussions were the subject of proposals from the Church charity and were agreed between the charity's management and lawyers acting on behalf of the Commission/Receivers by the summer of 2003.[219]

---

217. EA and ACEA press release, January 9, 2004.
218. Association for Charities press release, January 2004.
219. Association for Charities press release, January 2004. Another supportive

Principles and practicalities in the interactions of 2000–2005 219

This additional pressure seemed to help. On January 21, 2004 *The Guardian* published an article declaring "Church victorious in management wrangle":

> Talks between the Kingsway International Christian Centre (KICC) and the interim managers sent in by the Charity Commission 14 months ago have brought agreement over a timetable to settle outstanding issues and complete the transfer of church assets to a reconstituted charity during February. The team of managers from professional advisers KPMG is expected to leave soon afterwards.[220]

Despite this timetable, the administrators were not finally discharged by the Commission until 23 March 2005. Work completed in the final period of their administration included appointment of a new trustee board, recruitment of new senior management staff, and negotiations with regard to KICC's premises.[221] Each of these had its ironies. The new trustee board reflected less effectively than the previous one the preference being considered by the Commission with the EA and ACEA for all key decision-makers to be included on the trustee board. The new senior management team was recruited at annual salaries that appeared to be higher than that paid to the senior minister in the period 1992-2000.[222] The negotiations on the premises were outside the original remit of the administrators yet extended as far as trying to secure the church alternative premises. This final topic is one I will return to before the close of the chapter.

The Commission's "statement of the results of an Inquiry under Section 8 of the Charities Act 1993 into the King's Ministries Trust" was posted on the Charities Commission website on October 6, 2005. The next day the *Times* carried an article headlined "Pastor to repay £200,000 after buying Florida timeshare on church Visa card."[223] Although technically correct the headline conflated the issue of items of trustee benefit, taken alongside salary, with the issue of intellectual property rights, whereby Ashimolowo had agreed to pay the charity for the right to publish and market what he had

---

article was Bowder, "Change of Status."

220. Shifrin, "Church Victorious."

221. Charity Commission, "Report on The King's Ministries," paras. 26, 28, 30.

222. Posts were advertised at £45k–£55k *per annum* (for two) and £55k–£75k p.a. (for one). Recruitment email circulated by Public Sector Practice of Norman Broadbent, June 18, 2004. Ashimolowo and his wife had jointly received an average salary of £48k *per annum* though with some benefits in kind, 1992–2000. Charity Commission, "Report on The King's Ministries," para. 11.

223. Gledhill, "Pastor to Repay," 3.

prepared and preached.²²⁴ As I shall show, it was press interpretations such as this that by 2005 had contributed to a breakdown in relations between KICC and the EA. It is arguable that throughout the whole period the EA believed it was acting appropriately behind the scenes, meeting needs it perceived to be important, even if they were not the ones that KICC and the African neo-Pentecostal constituency considered most pressing.

KICC, prosperity, and the press

The difficulties between British evangelicals and African neo-Pentecostals over prosperity teaching occurred in 2003 and, although exacerbated by the press, were largely the result of evangelical ignorance of African neo-Pentecostal beliefs and practices. To appreciate the roots of the misunderstanding it is necessary to go back to the 1980s and to look again at the British Charismatic Movement in the closing years of the Thatcher government. As Walker has documented, the 1970s had seen divisions in the movement over the "shepherding" emphasis promoted by the so-called "Fort Lauderdale Five."²²⁵ Some charismatic leaders were concerned that a Word of Faith, prosperity teaching emphasis might come in as the new charismatic fascination for the 1990s. Although this never proved to be the case, by the late 1980s David Tomlinson, who worked for the C. S. Lewis Centre, was identifying signs of an "anti-poverty-spirit." He quoted charismatic leaders who had made statements such as "We British are bound by the spirit of poverty," "What's wrong with prosperity, we need some in this country?" and "Why are we Christians afraid of money?"²²⁶ One comment provoked him a little further:

> I recently heard another charismatic preacher telling fellow leaders that, "only certain attitudes and ideas can flourish in Britain right now." He went on to explain that in "Thatcher's Britain, our message had to have an offer of success built in. Anything that had the feel of being a 'loser's gospel' would not stand a chance."²²⁷

With anxieties such as these in mind, and aware of Bassett's ministry in Finchley (then still largely a white "upper-middle-class" phenomenon), Tomlinson decided in 1989 to publish in British format McConnell's critique

---

224. Charity Commission, "Report on The King's Ministries," paras. 34, 35.
225. Walker, *Restoring*, 87–126. On shepherding, Walker, *Restoring*, 157–58.
226. Tomlinson, "Foreword," x.
227. Tomlinson, "Foreword," x.

of the prosperity movement in America.[228] Sales were not good but it stirred the concern of a few, especially those few theological students and Christian academics who had read Jackson's 1989 article in the Religious and Theological Studies Fellowship journal, *Themelios*.[229] The stimulus was sufficient, though, for the EA with Christian Impact (later known as the London Institute for Contemporary Christianity) to convene an investigation. The meeting, in many ways the pre-cursor of ACUTE formed in December 1993, operated on limited resources and insights. Prosperity teaching was clearly not a major British church issue in the early 1990s.

> We looked at this theme at the request of the Evangelical Alliance. Via the Alliance two documents came to us for comment. One was Harry Greenwood, "Light in your darkness" chapter 3, and the other was the booklet by Kenneth Hagin, "How God Taught Me About Prosperity" . . . we also referred during the meeting to an article which appeared in *Themelios* in October 1989 written by Robert Jackson and titled "Prosperity Theology and the faith movement." However Commission (henceforth TC) members doubted if these documents were representative of the Prosperity Gospel (henceforth PG). Although there are extreme churches, such as Rhema South Africa, that effectively deny that God sometimes teaches through suffering, most PG churches accept this. Yet the paradoxes involved here are not brought out in these documents under present consideration. On the other hand, TC members were not agreed on the range of differences in the PG churches.[230]

In the months that followed, occasional papers on different aspects of prosperity continued to be written for the group by Christian academics, and in January 1996 the EA Information Office released a series of quotes on "Prosperity Theology" from people as varied as Benny Hinn, J. I. Packer and the World Evangelical Fellowship.[231] Even so, when the EA requested that Dave Cave, the first coordinator of ACUTE, provide information on the prosperity gospel for its September 1996 full Council meeting, he still only had a handful of papers representing work in progress. It was on this information that the Council made its decision on MCWE's membership. Given the limited scope of the papers they would have done little to

---

228. McConnell, *Promise of Health and Wealth*.

229. Jackson, "Prosperity Theology," 16–24. Sales comment from the head of STL. A further publication attaining limited UK circulation was Hanegraaff, *Christianity in Crisis*.

230. Evangelical Alliance/Christian Impact, "Prosperity Gospel."

231. Evangelical Alliance, "Quotes on . . . Prosperity Theology."

facilitate a discussion on how typical Cerullo's theology was in terms of "Word of Faith" teaching and done nothing to prompt any consideration of the possibility that those from the African and Caribbean communities who attended MTL might themselves subscribe to a Word of Faith theology.

On this second point, it was common throughout the 1990s to hear British evangelicals assert that there was a difference between the motivational messages commonly preached to African and Caribbean congregations and the health and wealth gospel subscribed to by Americans.[232] The assumption was that motivation was legitimate for those in challenging circumstances; this view was reinforced when Caribbean church leaders spoke of the straitened circumstances of their members. Even Edwards writing of his childhood in a Caribbean denominational church referred to how "[o]n Sundays and during the mid-week prayer meetings they experienced the rejuvenation of their spirits and recovered a sense of worth which was so often suffocated during the working week."[233] Such statements enabled British evangelicals to conclude that lack would always provide a check on people from Africa or the Caribbean believing for material prosperity as a part of God's plan. Indeed, up to the turn of the millennium, many British evangelicals, who were in no way attracted to prosperity teaching themselves, thought it obvious that prosperity teaching could never work in the developing world. A quote from the 1980s could still summarize their thinking: "A paramount problem with the gospel of success is that it is a product of the Western mind, oriented to Western ideology and culture. Try to apply it to situations around the world and the success-prosperity pitch becomes glaringly absurd."[234] The increasing numbers of African neo-Pentecostals in Britain, the growing availability of African neo-Pentecostal teaching on Christian broadcast outlets and the expanding quantity of academic research affirming an African neo-Pentecostal prosperity teaching link, seemed to do little to change this mindset.[235]

Surprisingly, Cerullo's resignation from the Alliance did not close the matter. A consultation on prosperity teaching with fifty-four evangelical leaders attending was hosted at the EA offices in June 1998. Given underlying evangelical assumptions at the time, it is unremarkable that no African neo-Pentecostals were included on the speaker list.[236] Doug Williams, who

---

232. Kerridge was of this opinion concerning Ashimolowo.

233. Edwards, *Lord*, 11.

234. Bulle, *God Wants You Rich*, 30.

235. Gifford published in 1998 extensively covering prosperity teaching. Gifford, *African Christianity*, 335–40 and Gifford, *Christianity*.

236. Perriman, *Prosperity*, xii.

presented a paper, though African, was a denominational Pentecostal with the AoG. Bishop Joe Aldred, who chaired the day, was also a denominational Pentecostal but with the predominantly Caribbean Church of God of Prophecy. Throughout the day most arguments were theological but those that focused on practical concerns related to American influences: American preachers holding events in British conference centers, American preachers appearing on British Christian television and American ministries circulating their magazines free to British church members.

To consolidate the points discussed, it was initially intended to publish the papers presented on the day. On further reflection, however, David Hilborn, who had succeeded Cave as ACUTE coordinator, decided that a more balanced document would result if the papers of the day, and those produced earlier, were complemented by a few additional papers from those on the working group and then edited into a logical whole.[237] It did, however, take several years to find an editor and once appointed editorial privilege prevailed and another approach was adopted. In the final publication little remained of the original papers in their presented form and a considerable amount of additional material from already published critiques of the Word of Faith movement was added. In many ways this strengthened the work but it did mean that the first part of the book, on the history and teaching of the Word of Faith movement, was a rehearsal of the arguments against Word of Faith teaching already set out by American writers such as McConnell and Hanegraaff. This set a tone for the book that was considerably less irenic than the working group had envisaged, despite the declaration on the cover:

> This book, produced by the Evangelical Alliance's Theological Commission, aims to give a fair hearing to the Word of Faith movement. Its shortcomings are acknowledged and thoroughly critiqued. But account is also taken of the historical, religious and cultural circumstances that have shaped this distinctive subspecies of Pentecostalism. As such, the report offers grounds for mutual understanding and for a more biblical theology of prosperity.[238]

Furthermore, there were areas where those who had taken over the vetting of the project (Perriman, the editor, had to submit his work to the Chairman of ACUTE as well as to Hilborn) were concerned to strengthen the report's conservative evangelical stance so as not to be seen as too

---

237. I was co-opted onto the working group in June 1998 and wrote three papers in addition to the paper on "Prosperity Teaching and Evangelical Unity" presented at the consultation.

238. Perriman, *Faith, Hope and Prosperity*, back cover.

conciliatory. This affected some of the concluding recommendations on how to create a constructive and progressive dialogue between prosperity teachers and evangelicals.[239] Nevertheless, the second section of the book, an evaluation of Word of Faith teaching, still retained some examples of the balance originally sought between the shortcomings of prosperity teaching and evangelicalism's comparable faults. Three examples will suffice:

> Most of the misreadings of Scripture that have been detected in Word of Faith teaching can be traced to a number of persistent flaws in the movement's hermeneutic—the largely undeclared set of presuppositions and rules that governs interpretation. These flaws are not unique to Word of Faith teaching—they can also be illustrated to a greater or lesser degree from much popular evangelical exposition.[240]
>
> Although there are significant flaws in Word of Faith teaching, we should not overlook the fact that much of the oddness may be attributed to the distinctive rhetoric employed by its proponents. Protestant evangelicals can be at times rather too fastidious and prosaic in their manner of expression and may have difficulty appreciating the more vivid and histrionic language that has always characterised Pentecostalism and its offshoots. . . . The rhetoric is notably populist.[241]
>
> Evangelicalism obviously has no objection to the view that the Word of God is true and should be taken as the authoritative basis for the life of faith. Moreover, many would admit that the evangelical church frequently falls short of the ideals of discipleship and faith that appear in the Bible. We may, then, regard the Word of Faith movement's refusal to settle for mediocrity and compromise in response to the assurances of Scripture with some feelings of inadequacy.[242]

Having mentioned the commitment to expanding the content and strengthening the suppositions contributed to the report's development, it is important to highlight one other area of change. The working group had decided not to focus on African neo-Pentecostal churches, as there was no detailed documentation of their beliefs or practice in a British context.[243] Needing, with the passage of time, to give some reason for publication other

---

239. Perriman, *Faith, Hope and Prosperity*, 230–35 compared with Osgood, "Prosperity Teaching."
240. Perriman, *Faith, Hope and Prosperity*, 81.
241. Perriman, *Faith, Hope and Prosperity*, 100.
242. Perriman, *Faith, Hope and Prosperity*, 195.
243. This led to the suggestion that I write this work.

Principles and practicalities in the interactions of 2000-2005   225

than a seven-year-old encounter with Morris Cerullo, the following were added:

> Increased access to American televangelism through cable and satellite networks such as the God Channel, God Revival and Inspiration channels has meant that the teachings of Hagin, Copeland, and others are readily available for private consumption, whatever the official position of UK churches might be.[244]
> The rapid growth of African churches in recent years, especially in London, has provided a much more receptive audience for prosperity teaching.[245]

This then was the report, somewhat different from that which the working group had originally foreseen but nonetheless in part conciliatory. To those involved in its production it still seemed relatively non-provocative with the potential for promoting mutual understanding, a contribution to a debate that had never generated much British interest. Press comments such as "the report states [there] is enough to provide common ground for bridges to be built" were expected to be the norm.[246]

When Gledhill of the *Times* received her copy, however, she interpreted it as an evangelical correction to African neo-Pentecostal churches. Whilst it is unlikely that the wording Hilborn chose as a summary when circulating initial copies of the book could have triggered the "corrective" interpretation (he wrote of "a scholarly, balanced and fair-minded assessment which concludes that the so-called 'Word of Faith' movement espouses 'a peculiar mix of truth and error'") it seems that Gledhill considered a story on KICC to be due and used the ACUTE report as the opportunity.[247] The juxtaposition of a large picture of Ashimolowo, two articles and some Bible verses were used to establish an EA: KICC confrontation. In her article entitled "Poor Christians Are Deluded by 'Grab it' Gospel" Gledhill wrote,

> Thousands of Christians in Britain are being deluded by a new style of preaching that promises untold wealth to the believer whose faith is strong enough, according to a report. Followers of the so-called prosperity gospel—known by its critics as the "blab it and grab it gospel"—are encouraged to believe that it is acceptable to pray for material wealth. An authoritative report by the Evangelical Alliance, an umbrella organisation for Britain's evangelical Churches, raises concerns about teachings

244. Perriman, *Faith, Hope and Prosperity*, 11.
245. Perriman, *Faith, Hope and Prosperity*, 11.
246. Davies, "EA Examines." See also Dixon, "Gospel of Greed."
247. Letter from Hilborn dated March 12, 2003.

that if the believer gives a sum of money to the preacher, God will multiply it by a hundred times or more in favour of the giver. . . . The prosperity gospel has proved particularly fertile for leaders of black-led churches, among the fastest growing churches in the world. . . . Already, rapidly expanding black Pentecostal Churches in Britain are being strongly influenced by preachers from Nigeria, where believers have proved particularly susceptible to prosperity teaching. In addition preachers often use Christian channels on cable and satellite television to raise money for themselves by preaching that what the believer donates to him and his wife, God will magnify a hundredfold.[248]

The second article, which appeared alongside this and was written by her colleague, profiled KICC:

Greediness is next to godliness, according to worshippers at one of Britain's fastest growing Churches yesterday. More than 8,000 worshippers a week flock to services at the Kingsway International Christian Centre in an old warehouse near Hackney Marshes, East London. . . . Worshippers are encouraged to pray for wealth. Sermons delivered by Mr Ashimolowo, a Nigerian-born convert from Islam, have titles such as "101 Answers to Money Problems" and "Sweatless Wealth." Prayers include sentiments such as: "Ask the Lord to open your eyes to that which shall be profitable." . . . KICC had an income of £7.4 million in 2001, of which £6.5 million came from "tithes" and other offerings from worshippers. . . . The Church is under investigation by the Charity Commission over the possible misapplication of funds and is under the financial control of a receiver and manager. A spokeswoman for KICC declined to comment.[249]

The EA was immediately aware of the damage the Gledhill article would inflict on relationships with KICC and sought to redress the balance in an article by Marcia Dixon in the *Voice* newspaper:

Leaders of Britain's black Christian community are furious about an article in *The Times* which effectively accuses churches of brainwashing poor worshippers into handing over wads of their dosh. Rev Joel Edwards, General Director of the Evangelical Alliance was none too impressed with the article, written by the paper's religious correspondent, Ruth Gledhill. He said: "We are deeply disappointed at Ruth Gledhill's very unbalanced

---

248. Gledhill, "Poor Christians," 4.
249. Peek, "Prosperity," 4.

article. . . . The Evangelical Alliance report opens up an effective dialogue for brothers and sisters within the black church and those within the prosperity movement to engage as equals within the wider Christian community and look at this issue of prosperity."[250]

The *Voice* article also included quotations from Mark Sturge: "Rev Mark Sturge, also of ACEA, claimed *The Times* was guilty of 'highly inaccurate and non-factual reporting.' He said: 'If we read the report in its entirety we would see that there is a balanced approach to the case made for prosperity, but the piece comes down hard on the excesses.'"[251]

Dixon also drew on comments from two leaders of independent churches, one African and one Caribbean:

> Rev Dr. Tayo Adeyemi, pastor of the New Wine Church in Woolwich, south east London, said *The Times* article was a poor reflection of black faith. He fumed: "It is unfair and narrow-minded. I do believe God blesses his people, materially and spiritually. In my own church I have seen the life of members improve materially. It is not because they have embraced the prosperity gospel, but embraced the whole of the gospel, which has transformed their lives." Bishop Wayne Malcolm leader of Christian Life City in Walthamstow, east London said: "I think *The Times* owes the black Christian community a front-page apology for implying they are deluded. Our faith is biblically based, theologically sound and our churches are filled with people whose quality of life has dramatically improved through their association with the church and its teachings. God has always positioned himself as a champion of the poor and the enemy of poverty. Don't condemn us if we have a gospel for the poor that is changing lives."[252]

In conversation five months later, Ashimolowo expressed his puzzlement that the EA could "commission such a report in the midst of African Pentecostal church troubles, knowing that prosperity is what all African churches believe."[253] Furthermore, he thought that the report had been "written by a black Anglican who is anti-'Faith'" (Perriman is white and a

---

250. Dixon, "Cash, Bang, Wallop," 9.
251. Dixon, "Cash, Bang, Wallop," 9.
252. Dixon, "Cash, Bang, Wallop," 9.
253. Conversation with Ashimolowo, August 28, 2003.

member of an independent charismatic church). Confusion about the report's authorship resulted from Gledhill's muddling of Edwards' foreword with Perriman's introduction when she stated "Andrew Perriman, the editor, left Jamaica at the age of eight."[254]

The sense of betrayal felt by many African neo-Pentecostal churches over the prosperity report was considerable.[255] KICC did not renew its EA membership in 2004, even though the press had undoubtedly contributed to the tension.[256] A year later, when *The Times* reported on the Commission Inquiry into KICC, it printed the same picture of Ashimolowo used eighteen months earlier and set out a similar selection of Bible verses expressing contrasting views on prosperity. The article, written primarily to highlight matters of financial administration, included,

> Churches such as Kingsway promote wealth as a reward for hard work and living a godly life. They use the opening text of the third letter of John, in which the apostle prays for his friend's prosperity and health, and other texts espousing the abundance of harvest reaped from the well-sown seed, to support this view. A prosperous pastor is seen as proof that prosperity preaching—known to its detractors as the "blab-it-and-grab-it gospel"—works. Vast sums are generated by the congregations of these churches, where "tithing," or donation of 10 per cent of net income, is common.[257]

Inter-church relations between African neo-Pentecostals and evangelicals went through some difficult phases between 2000 and 2005. The prosperity issue was probably the most serious. There were, however, some areas where working together was a viable option; several of these related to government legislation.

PROXIMITY AND UNANIMITY OVER GOVERNMENT LEGISLATION

As the Labour party was returned to power in 2001 and elected again in 2005, there were items in its legislative agenda that caused concern to both African neo-Pentecostals and evangelicals. However, the discipline of speaking with one voice had its challenges.

---

254. Gledhill, "Poor Christians," 4.
255. I hosted a meeting on the issue at which Perriman was present, May 14, 2003.
256. Response to membership enquiry, February 18, 2005.
257. Gledhill, "Pastor to Repay," 3.

Principles and practicalities in the interactions of 2000-2005   229

Section 28 and issues of sexuality

In January 2000 the abolition of Section 28, the clause in the 1988 Local Government Act which had banned the promotion of homosexuality in schools, became the focus of public attention. However, the British public initially became aware of the strength of African Christian opposition to homosexuality not through British-based African neo-Pentecostal churches protesting about the legislation but through Anglican bishops from West Africa in the summer of 1998. When the bishops of the Anglican Communion met for their ten-yearly Lambeth conference, conflicting opinions on the ordination of homosexuals were expressed by Rev Richard Kirker of the Lesbian and Gay Christian Movement and Rt Rev Emmanuel Chukwuma, Bishop of Enugu, Nigeria. Verbal exchanges quickly gave way to more distinctive action as Rt Rev Chukwuma sought to practice deliverance ministry on the unappreciative Rev Kirker.[258] The national press took the opportunity to give the story maximum publicity. ACEA commented,

> The recent Lambeth Conference saw bishops from Africa deal a decisive blow to the influential "liberal" movement within the Anglican Church... they voted on a resolution which stated that homosexuality is incompatible with Biblical teaching, and that sex should be only permitted within marriage ... controversial US bishop, John Spong ... [p]rior to the start of the conference ... described African Christians as "... moved out of animism into a very superstitious kind of Christianity."... He was subsequently forced to retract many of his opinions on African Christians during the conference ... the Rt Rev Duncan Buchanan suggested that, "Africa was not 'innocent' of homosexuality."[259]

The strongly polarized Lambeth debate took place against the backdrop of ongoing discussions on sexuality within the broader church throughout the 1990s. The January-March 1997 edition of *Idea* contained some reactions to a survey of evangelical attitudes:

> Evangelical Alliance members' views on same-sex relationships made headlines in the run up to the controversial celebrations at Southwark Cathedral of the Gay & Lesbian Christian Movement's 20th anniversary. News that 96 per cent of churches

---

258. For an analysis of this exchange see Carrette and Keller, "Critical Theory," 21–43.
259. "African Bishops," 7.

linked to the Alliance believe homosexual sex to be wrong was reported on main BBC news bulletins.²⁶⁰

Soon after Labour's general election victory in May 1997, legislation was being considered to lower the age of consent and repeal Section 28. Martyn Eden, the EA's Public Affairs Director, wrote of an evangelical response,

> First, we can pray.... Second, we can prepare ourselves to present a Christian view on homosexuality persuasively.... Then we can write to our MPs and to the press.... Finally, we can support Christian projects which seek to minister to people with a homosexual orientation.²⁶¹

The presentation work was placed in the hands of ACUTE. It was aware that it had to tread carefully. Whilst there was to be a public dimension, it also had to address the debate in the main Christian denominations and be sensitive to the discussions spreading into evangelicalism. In 1995 Michael Vasey, a lecturer at the Anglican evangelical college, St John's, Durham, had sought to condone homoerotic intimacy from the Bible.²⁶² In producing its report ACUTE set itself three aims:

> To help Christians who hold the classical view to respond more effectively to the "gay lobby." ... To help Christians relate more pastorally to homosexual people.... To affirm Christians ministering alongside those who seek to move away from lesbian and gay sexual activity.²⁶³

The "classical view" referred to was that "in the witness of the Bible, sexual activity outside marriage is sinful and homosexual practice is presented as a stock example of sexual sin."²⁶⁴ The report's emphasis on homoerotic activity was unequivocal:

> We believe habitual homoerotic sexual activity without repentance to be inconsistent with faithful church membership. Where someone is publicly promoting homoerotic sexual practice within a congregation, there may be a case for more stringent disciplinary action.²⁶⁵

260. "Media Spotlight," 31.
261. Eden, "Challenging," 5.
262. Vasey, *Strangers and Friends*, 124–40.
263. ACUTE, *Faith, Hope and Homosexuality*, ix–x.
264. ACUTE, *Faith, Hope and Homosexuality*, 20.
265. ACUTE, *Faith, Hope and Homosexuality*, 34.

Principles and practicalities in the interactions of 2000–2005

The report, however, did seek to communicate a degree of inclusivity:

> We call upon evangelical congregations to welcome and accept sexually active homosexual people, but to do so in the expectation that they will come in due course to see the need to change their lifestyle in accordance with biblical revelation and orthodox church teaching. We urge gentleness and patience in this process, and ongoing care even after a homosexual person renounces same-sex sexual relationships.[266]

In order to publicize ACUTE's report, the April-May 1998 issue of *Idea* featured an article asking if the church had let homosexual Christians down. Its tone was intentionally pastoral:

> Many evangelicals are unsure how to respond when a Christian they know speaks up about his or her homosexual orientation. They fear that by loving and supporting the homosexual, they may be condoning any sexual sin he or she may be involved in. . . . Recognising this dilemma, the Evangelical Alliance . . . has published a report on homosexuality and the Church, which attempts to examine the issue pastorally from a traditional biblical perspective . . . the document rejects homophobia and expresses deep regret for "the hurt caused to lesbians and gay men by the Church's past and present hatred and rejection of them." It reminds Christians that homoerotic sexual practice is a sin no worse than any other, on a par with any sexual acts performed outside marriage.[267]

The article included contributions from leaders of the evangelical homosexual-help organization, Courage:

> "Homophobia in the Church has declined quite significantly in the past 10 or 20 years, but there is still a long way to go," says Jeremy Marks of Courage. . . . "There are a few evangelical churches which create an environment where people feel it is safe to share."[268]

Not all evangelicals were comfortable with this pastoral approach.[269] Some found the report too conciliatory, particularly given the talk of repealing Section 28. Many evangelicals were already set to take up Eden's lobbying call but they had to wait until January 2000 for the opportunity.

266. ACUTE, *Faith, Hope and Homosexuality*, 34.
267. "Hall of Shame."
268. "Hall of Shame."
269. Hilborn, "Beyond Belief," 12–13.

It was the first evangelical lobbying opportunity of the new millennium. By January 25, the BBC was reporting that "the government has been on the offensive over repealing the ban in the wake of growing opposition from clergy, conservative groups and some peers."[270] The protests persisted from January to July and on July 24 the clause received its second defeat in the House of Lords, the Local Government Bill going on to be passed without it.[271] Baroness Young who led the stand against the clause had received five thousand letters in support.[272] However, after the defeat the Government said it remained committed to repealing Section 28. It was a battle that would have to be fought again.

In the autumn of 2000, with evangelical relief over the initial securing of Section 28 still running high, the EA had to face one of its Council members, Dr. James Ryan,[273] declaring his homosexual orientation. It could discipline, or demonstrate its declared commitment "to balance biblical sexual morality with biblical grace."[274] Ryan had been prominent in evangelical circles for many years and had delivered a keynote address at the 1996 Bournemouth Convention. Even in the months following the publication of the ACUTE report he had been commended in *Idea* for his pioneering views, as he called for a "religionless Christianity" saying "[w]hen we fail to distinguish cultural trappings from truth issues . . . we risk undermining the Gospel itself."[275] He gave no indication then that he saw issues of sexuality as "cultural trappings" but, by the time the EA held its annual Council Meeting at High Leigh conference center in 2000, his resignation was announced on the grounds that he had "a celibate relationship with a younger man." At the time of his resignation Edwards reflected,

> We are all devastated by this news, and very saddened by the loss of this exceptional ministry. But [James] has dedicated a significant portion of his life in the service of the Church. And so it's my prayer that the Church will stand by [James] and his family over the coming weeks and months, and that they will be given all the love and compassion they need.[276]

---

270. "Section 28 Row."

271. ACEA had planned to challenge the Prime Minister at Faith in the Future. Gledhill, "Black Churches," 15. That challenge never materialized.

272. Gledhill, "Black Churches," 15.

273. This is a pseudonym to protect the individual's identity.

274. ACUTE, *Homosexuality*, 31.

275. "Have We Become Christian Pharisees?," 11.

276. Reported in James, "Popular Bible Teacher."

Principles and practicalities in the interactions of 2000–2005   233

Ryan subsequently left his wife and three children, having stood down from his pastorate, going on to set up a website advocating that evangelicals adopt a more tolerant approach to homosexuality.

However, a more tolerant approach to homosexuality was not to the fore in African neo-Pentecostal thinking. Some African neo-Pentecostal leaders found it perplexing that the EA should "pursue an important EA member church," such as KICC over prosperity theology, when it hesitated to challenge Ryan "who left his wife to live with a man."[277] Wale Babatunde spoke for many when he contrasted biblical laws with national laws and spelled out his attitude to homosexuality. The ongoing push to repeal Section 28 and to lower the age of consent for homosexual activity following Labour's 2001 re-election both came in for his denunciation:

> It seems that in the last couple of decades there has been a determined and concerted effort by various governments not only to abolish restrictions on homosexual practice and propaganda, but . . . to present [it as] . . . an acceptable alternative lifestyle.
>
> That the issue of whether or not to lower the age of consent to 16 should come up for debate is itself a disgrace! For a Parliament that was once built on Christian teachings, this is something for which we should feel ashamed! As far as I am concerned the issue should not even in the first place be that of lowering the age of consent; it should be about banning it altogether and trying to find ways of helping those caught up in this sin . . . *because of such things God's wrath comes on those who are disobedient* (Eph 5:6).[278]

Babatunde was not alone in his conviction that homosexual practice could have dire consequences; fellow African neo-Pentecostal Don-Dawodu writing on deliverance ministry declared: "Sinful sexual life-style of fornications [sic], adultery, rape, incest, abortion, masturbation and perversities, like homosexuality, bestiality and sexual fantasies practices [sic] all provides [sic] a doorway for unclean spirits to attack a person."[279]

Yet not everyone in the African and Caribbean constituency appeared to share their opinions. A survey of BMC leaders on issues of sexuality in 2000 showed figures up to 30 percent below those obtained by the EA in its 1996 survey of members:

   277. Informal conversation after IGOC meeting, August 28, 2003.
   278. Babatunde, *Great Britain Has Fallen!*, 68, 71–72.
   279. Don-Dawodu, *War Theatre*, 72.

67% believed that homosexuality and heterosexuality are not morally equal, and the Government's fixation with homosexuality is damaging its relationship with the Black community.
84% believe that homophobic practice is not the same as racial prejudice, because homosexuality is about behaviour and race is about the identity, culture and ethnic background of your family and ancestors. No one equated homophobic prejudice with racial prejudice!
60% believe that Section 28, which prohibits the promotion of homosexuality in schools by local authorities, provides an adequate safeguard for children and should be retained.[280]

With 2003 seeing Civil Partnership Legislation proposed in July, the repeal of Section 28 succeed in the Local Government Act in September, the Gender Recognition Bill coming before Parliament in November, and the Anglican struggles over the proposed appointment of Canon Jeffrey John as Bishop of Reading from June onwards, African neo-Pentecostals began to think of ways of gaining a stronger, clearer voice to represent their views.[281] "Ministers Together," the Ministers' fellowship hosted by Ashimolowo in Hackney, offered one possibility but in 2003 the team leading it was still proceeding with care. However, African neo-Pentecostals were not the only group looking for a voice.

Incitement to Religious Hatred and freedom of expression

The first time many evangelicals heard of the Christian lobbying agency Christian Voice was when an email from its director Stephen Green was widely circulated following a speech entitled "Sideline the Extremists" given by Home Secretary David Blunkett on July 7, 2004. The email asked "Who did he mean?" and went on to say,

> The Rt Hon David Blunkett MP has announced an intention to bring in a religious hatred law. . . . In his speech, Mr Blunkett curiously included "far-Right evangelical Christians" with "extremists in the Islamic faith" as examples of people "who would take our lives because they reject our faith." Mr Blunkett actually

---

280. "What's On Their Minds?," 12.

281. See ACEA Senior African Church Leaders' Meeting Minutes, February 20, 2003. Note that the EA lobbied extensively on the Gender Recognition Bill. See Horrocks, "No Condemnation," 27, and Evangelical Alliance Policy Commission, "Transsexuality."

departed from his pre-published version to make the unscripted attack on "right-wing evangelicals."[282]

As plans for the law unfolded, Christian Voice stayed at the forefront of protests, being joined by a wide group of Christians and other interested parties as the debate turned into one about freedom of speech. Ironically before the Incitement to Religious Hatred debate came to public attention, Christian Voice was at the forefront of another free speech issue, this time concluding free speech had gone too far, with the BBC 2 broadcast on January 8, 2005 of "Jerry Springer: the Opera." Whilst the protest outside the BBC on the night of the broadcast only comprised some one-hundred-and-fifty protestors, "[a]t least 45,000 people contacted the BBC about the show, mainly to complain about swearing and religious themes."[283] Given the show's portrayal of Jesus, Green of Christian Voice protested that "If this show portrayed Mohammed or Vishnu as homosexual, ridiculous and ineffectual, it would never have seen the light of day."[284] The EA sent its head of theology to see the West End show ahead of the broadcast, so as to make informed comment. It then "lodged a formal complaint in writing with the BBC governors, OFCOM and The Department of Culture, Media and Sport."[285] As the protest against the Incitement to Religious Hatred Bill got underway, the earlier protest over the Springer show opened the lobbyists up to criticism:

> Many conservative Christians fear that [the Bill] may also restrict their evangelistic efforts and mean they are unable to legally criticise other religions. . . . However, the stand by the Christian groups some of whom also opposed the recent showing of "Jerry Springer: the Opera" on BBC Two, has opened them up to charges of double standards. Conservative Christians, it is suggested, appear happy to defend their right to criticise other faiths when it suits, but protest vigorously when anyone raises questions about their own beliefs.[286]

Such accusations notwithstanding, many did come together to object to the Incitement Bill, with rallies outside Parliament on July 12, and October 11, 2005.[287] Whilst the climax of this process lies outside the time frame

282. Email from Christian Voice to Church Leaders, July 24, 2004.
283. "Protests as BBC Screens Springer," para. 2.
284. "Protests as BBC Screens Springer," para. 12.
285. Email to EA members, January 14, 2005.
286. "Incitement to Religious Hatred." See https://www.old.ekklesia.co.uk/research.
287. "Your Voice," 4.

of this study, it is worthy of note that working alongside Christian Voice, the EA and ACEA in these protests was a coalition from London's BMCs coordinated by Ade Omooba of Christian Victory Group I Care Projects. The group had the backing of Dye and Ashimolowo and as the protests gained momentum, it sought to emphasize its unity and clarity by taking the name Cohesive and Coherent Voice. As 2005 closed, it began to broaden its remit and look at the problems KICC faced over the proposed compulsory purchase of its Hackney site in readiness for the 2012 Olympics.[288] With news that a "massive mosque that will hold 40,000 worshippers is being proposed beside the Olympic complex in London to be opened in time for the 2012 Games," the group was keen to ensure even-handedness in local authority planning departments.[289] For them, ensuring freedom of speech, and in this instance freedom of worship, had become an ongoing process.[290]

CONCLUSION

At the beginning of the period covered by this chapter, both evangelicals and African neo-Pentecostals (the latter operating within the context of BMCs) were a focus of electoral attention. However, the interest in Christian groups shown by the political parties in the lead-up to the 2001 General Election was not repeated in the campaigning for the 2005 General Election.

In the intervening period a number of issues also brought African neo-Pentecostal churches to the attention of the press. The issues ranged from accusations of child abuse, through charges of financial mismanagement to issues of governance. Evangelicals were in the main careful not to take sides in these debates but the press reports on African neo-Pentecostal church finances became entangled with the publication of the EA's report on prosperity teaching and this caused a souring of evangelical and African neo-Pentecostal relations. Meanwhile the evangelical constituency, having started the decade by launching *A Movement for Change*, came to public attention over its protests against homosexuality, transsexuality and incitement to religious hatred. If anything, African neo-Pentecostals felt even more strongly on these issues than evangelicals and began to create a corporate response from within their own constituency.

It was a period when principles were much in evidence. Sometimes it was the principles that seemed most likely to bring unity, which actually brought division. This was true for issues relating to public morality.

288. Charity Commission, "Report on The King's Ministries," para. 28.
289. Baird, "Giant Mosque," para. 1.
290. Dye, "London Churches Unite," 18–19.

Both parties had clear views but evangelicals were inclined to show more latitude in application. It was also a period when, in the face of African neo-Pentecostal difficulties with the Charity Commission and some local authorities, evangelicals seemed to prefer a degree of detachment to overt engagement, apparently in the hope of minimizing African neo-Pentecostal discomfort. Such detachment appears to have been particularly evident with the issues of deliverance and governance. With prosperity, however, it was the EA report that created tensions; tensions that were not even eased by evangelicals criticizing the overreactions of the press. It could be argued that more positive engagement by evangelicals with African neo-Pentecostals on the issues of prosperity, deliverance and governance might have eased discomfort, as the debates would have become more clearly defined. Many evangelicals' opinion on African neo-Pentecostals remained largely shaped by the national press.

Conclusion
Balancing principles and practicalities

FROM THE EARLIER HISTORY of British evangelicalism's inclusiveness, the interaction with African neo-Pentecostalism could have gone in any of three directions: prolonged consideration (as with the classical Pentecostals where decades of disenchantment eventually gave way to acceptance), immediate acceptance (as seemed to be the case with the Charismatic Movement) or some kind of parallelism (as with the Caribbean denominations). In some ways evangelicalism tried all three approaches. Given that classical Pentecostalism, the Charismatic Movement and the Caribbean denominations had presented evangelicalism with all the challenges it was about to face in African neo-Pentecostalism, immediate acceptance may have been anticipated. However, African neo-Pentecostalism had its own characteristics, confidently embraced and securely established from the 1970s onwards in Africa, and evangelicalism's openness was not openness at any price.

The interactions between British evangelicalism and African neo-Pentecostalism that took place from 1985 to 2005 illustrate three strong commitments: first, evangelicalism's commitment to inclusiveness; second, African neo-Pentecostalism's commitment to distinctiveness; third, evangelicalism's own commitment to distinctiveness. It is these three commitments that have led to the constant interplay between adherence to principles and adoption of practicalities throughout the twenty-year period. If any one of these three elements had been missing it would have made consideration of evangelical unity much simpler. A non-distinctive African neo-Pentecostalism could have united with a distinctive and inclusive British evangelicalism, just as a distinctive African neo-Pentecostalism could have united with a non-distinctive but inclusive evangelicalism. Even with both parties firmly holding to distinctiveness and shunning inclusiveness, the feasibility of their uniting could have been quickly determined. Given such practical challenges, the application of a pre-determined theoretical model has an appeal. At first reading, Stott's approach, outlined in the introduction, would seem to offer the basis for such a methodology. All that should be required is to first separate *adiaphora* from core beliefs on revelation (biblicism), redemption (crucicentrism) and transformation (conversionism and activism) and then to ensure that all core beliefs are compatible. Having examined the interaction between British evangelicalism and African neo-Pentecostalism over a twenty-year period, it is now possible to offer an explanation as to why such a methodological approach is so hard to adopt.

THE LIMITATIONS OF APPLYING A THEORETICAL METHODOLOGY

Four specific limitations of applying a theoretical methodology have become evident during the years of British evangelical and African neo-Pentecostal interaction. The indications are that more regard has to be given to momentum, flexibility, theological complexities and countering superficiality than rigorous application of a pre-determined theoretical structure would allow.

The challenge of momentum

The first is related to the momentum that builds up between and around groups as they interact. It is hard to carry out an accurate evaluation of such groups' evangelical orthodoxy and orthopraxis in a constantly changing situation. Accurate evaluation is best carried out in a static situation. The context in which British evangelicalism and African neo-Pentecostalism began to relate was anything but static. Initially there was the pressure of a large-scale mission where it was important to the organizers that the ethnic makeup of the participants should reflect the ethnic makeup of those likely to be attending. This was followed by a conviction on the part of some charismatic prayer leaders that building relationships with African neo-Pentecostals was a necessary part of identificationally repenting for colonialism. Cerullo's MTL then put pressure on the situation as conservative evangelicals critical of Cerullo struggled not to be seen as criticizing the African neo-Pentecostals in his congregations. By contrast, after the Cerullo event, came the upsurge in Christian broadcasting, where African neo-Pentecostal enthusiasm was needed to sustain the projects. In the new millennium, when government was courting BMCs, evangelicals could not stand apart, especially as African neo-Pentecostal ideas fitted so well with the new evangelical agenda for change. Furthermore, there was no way that evangelicals could remain totally impartial when their fellow Christians, African neo-Pentecostals, were facing criticism in the press over deliverance ministry, prosperity teaching, financial mismanagement and governance. Clearly pressures are always to hand that militate against calm, unbiased evaluation of theological and ecclesiological compatibility.

The benefits of flexibility

The second limitation is related to the benefits of flexibility. There are obviously advantages in not being too quick to announce a total compatibility. Conditional acceptance allows for flexibility making it possible to declare a greater or lesser degree of commitment as the socio-political climate demands. Whilst it is unlikely that such a policy of expedient flexibility was ever deliberately adopted, it is clear that evangelical endorsement of African neo-Pentecostalism, at least unofficially, moved between enthusiasm and caution. Sometimes what was not said registered more than what was said. African neo-Pentecostals definitely felt under-supported at times; left to fight their own battles when it would have been better to have others standing with them. This was particularly true over the prosperity teaching issue. When the *Times* targeted KICC in March 2003, a stronger evangelical explanation of the findings of the EA's prosperity report would have helped the African neo-Pentecostal constituency.[1] Ashimolowo was sufficiently concerned about this and about support levels in the midst of subsequent problems he went through, to withdraw KICC's membership of the EA.[2]

A theological complication

The third area of challenge is theological. It is not straightforward to distinguish core beliefs from *adiaphora* and to confirm the compatibility of different groups' core beliefs. Applying Stott's trinitarian framework of revelation, redemption and transformation to African neo-Pentecostal teaching, it is clear that there are differences between African neo-Pentecostal and "standard" evangelical theology even in such essentials.

---

1. Peek, "Prosperity," 4.
2. Whilst being interviewed by Cindy Kent on Premier Christian Radio in October 2005, he stated, "KICC and myself are not members of the Evangelical Alliance, neither are we members of ACEA. And on principle it is because I feel that these two organizations sit on the fence, particularly when individual members of local churches go through trying times, they are left to go through it alone."

Varying concepts of revelation

Stott's "the revelatory initiative of God the Father" aligns with Bebbington's biblicism. Early in his book Stott addressed biblicism by seeking to separate out evangelicalism from fundamentalism. He began with three disclaimers concerning evangelical faith: it is "not a recent innovation," it is "not a deviation from Christian orthodoxy," and it is "not a synonym for fundamentalism." He then explained that evangelicalism and fundamentalism have different histories and different connotations. Within this explanation he listed ten tendencies of fundamentalism in a Christian context.[3] In each case I give the first sentence of his descriptive paragraph (including his asides).[4] They were:

1. In relation to *human thought*, fundamentalists of the old school give the impression that they distrust scholarship, including the scientific disciplines; some tend towards a thoroughgoing anti-intellectualism, even obscurantism.

2. In relation to the *nature of the Bible*, fundamentalists are said by the dictionaries to believe that "every word of the Bible is literally true."

3. In relation to *biblical inspiration*, fundamentalists have tended to regard it as having been a somewhat mechanical process, in which the human authors were passive and played no active role.

4. In relation to *biblical interpretation*, fundamentalists seem to imply that they can apply the text directly to themselves as if it had been written primarily for them.

5. In relation to *the ecumenical movement*, fundamentalists tend to go beyond suspicion (for which there is ample justification) to a blanket, uncritical, even vociferous rejection.

6. In relation to *the church*, fundamentalists have tended to hold a separatist ecclesiology, and to withdraw from any community which does not agree in every particular with their own doctrinal position.

7. In relation to *the world*, fundamentalists have tended sometimes to assimilate its standards and values uncritically (e.g., the prosperity gospel) and at other times to stand aloof from it, fearing contamination.

8. In relation to *race*, fundamentalists have shown a tendency—especially in the United States and South Africa—to cling to the myth of white supremacy and to defend racial segregation, even in the church.

3. Stott, *Evangelical Truth*, 21–24.
4. Stott, *Evangelical Truth*, 21–24.

9. In relation to *the Christian mission*, fundamentalists have tended to insist that "mission" and "evangelism" are synonyms and that the vocation of the church is *tout court* to proclaim the gospel.

10. In relation to *the Christian hope*, fundamentalists tend to dogmatize about the future, although to be sure they hold no monopoly on dogmatism.

On the basis of this list, with the definite exception of point 8 and the probable exception of point 10, many African neo-Pentecostal churches at the start of the twenty-first century are more fundamentalist in their stance than evangelical. However, this would not seem to be a hindrance to evangelical unity. Stott quoted Beyerhaus's 1975 categorization of evangelicalism into six strands, acknowledging that a former General Director of the UK Evangelical Alliance seemed able to cope with twelve![5] At number two on Beyerhaus's list were the Strict Fundamentalists. They appeared immediately after the New Evangelicals and preceded the Confessing Evangelicals, the Pentecostals/Charismatics, the Radical Evangelicals and the Ecumenical Evangelicals.[6] Such a list would seem to suggest that African neo-Pentecostalism could be a subset of at least two categories. Perhaps it is this dual fundamentalist and Pentecostal identity that makes any fundamentalist tendencies within African neo-Pentecostalism less of a problem for evangelicalism as African neo-Pentecostalism does not present a crusading form of fundamentalism as its public face. At times, though, this is how it is read by the press in regard to matters such as deliverance and prosperity. Understandings of biblicism in the context of evangelical unity can clearly be wider than the hermeneutical preferences of conservative evangelicals.

Varying concepts of redemption

Stott's "the redemptive work of God the Son" aligns with Bebbington's crucicentrism. Many of today's African neo-Pentecostal churches have a doctrine of the cross that is inclined to center more on releasing believers from hindrances to their success than on removing from believers the guilt and separation caused by sin.[7] Forgiveness is still preached but freedom from

---

5. Calver and Warner, *Together We Stand*, 128–30.

6. Künneth and Beyerhaus, *Reich Gottes*, 307, 308. Quoted in Stott, *Evangelical Truth*, 25. Stott compares Fackre's six categories: fundamentalists, old evangelicals, new evangelicals, justice and peace evangelicals, charismatic evangelicals and ecumenical evangelicals. Fackre, *Ecumenical Faith*.

7. Gifford, *Ghana's New Christianity*, 109.

curses, demonic possession and oppression, poverty and sickness, tend to come to the fore. This would seem to be a significant deviation from the standard evangelical approach. It raises the possibility that it might take more than churches having a way of placing the cross central in their teaching to declare that unity has been achieved on this evangelical essential. However, this could be an example of *adiaphora* occurring within essential beliefs. If African neo-Pentecostals still have an underlying belief that the cross brings forgiveness of sin and restores oneness with God, then the strong emphasis on the crucifixion's role in dealing with poverty and sickness could be classed as *adiaphora*; a case of non-essentials within the essentials. This would seem to be how Stott views the matter. In his major work on the cross, he referred indirectly to the Word of Faith stand on the subject:

> The Christian conviction that Christ "has destroyed death" (2 Tim. 1:10) has led some believers to deduce that he has also destroyed disease, and that from the cross we should claim healing as well as forgiveness. A popular exposition of this topic is *Bodily Healing and the Atonement* (1930) by the Canadian author T. J. Macrossan, which has recently been re-edited and re-published by Kenneth E. Hagin of the pentecostal Rhema Church. McCrossan states his case in these terms: "All Christians should expect God to heal their bodies today, because Christ died to atone for our sickness as well as our sins."[8]

Stott subsequently argued that "[w]e should not therefore affirm that Christ died for our sickness as well as for our sins, that 'there is healing in the atonement,' or that health is just as readily available to everybody as forgiveness."[9] Nonetheless, in his treatise on evangelical unity he made no mention of healing in the atonement as a distraction from crucicentrism. He saved that criticism for an exponent of logical positivism for whom "vicarious atonement" was "intellectually contemptible and morally outrageous."[10] Such objections are a far cry from African neo-Pentecostalism's stance.

Varying concepts of transformation

Stott's "the transforming ministry of the Holy Spirit" broadly aligns with Bebbington's conversionism and activism. With conversionism the key issue

---

8. Stott, *Cross*, 244; McCrossan, *Bodily Healing*, 10.
9. Stott, *Cross*, 245.
10. Stott, *Evangelical Truth*, 100.

for evangelicals is the genuineness of repentance and faith. Repentance for sin has always figured large in evangelical thought and evangelicals have always been keen to make a distinction between "sin" as a condition and "sins" as an accumulation of misdeeds. The evangelical insistence has always been that repentance is for the former, the condition, and not just the latter, the accumulation. This is a nicety that does not always seem to be brought out in the African context, where people are encouraged to simply repent of what they have done rather than of who they are. Evangelicals adhere to a doctrine of basic human "fallenness" whereas Pentecostals, and not just African neo-Pentecostals, can appear in practice, if not in theory, to hold to a doctrine of basic human goodness. A notice board outside a South London AoG church that made a specialty of creating evangelistic comment out of television soap operas illustrates the point: "Fame Academy: Think you've got what it takes to be the next big thing? In God's eyes you are already a winner!"[11]

In its doctrine of conversion, evangelicalism is clear on the need for both repentance and faith and would question as spurious any conversion where repentance is marginalized. Legislating on such points is not possible, though, in doctrinal statements. If there is agreement on the need for a personal new birth through the ministry of the Holy Spirit, then unity can be reached on this particular evangelical essential.

As for activism, the only difficulty here is that for many African neo-Pentecostals coming to Britain the levels of evangelical activism are less than they were used to in Africa. African neo-Pentecostals coming to Britain are inclined to look for evidence of significant activism prior to any affiliation.

A counter to superficiality

The fourth area which highlights the limitation of applying a purely theoretical methodology to evangelical unity is that a protracted and apparently disorganized approach allows for any latent superficiality to be countered. When quick decisions are reached on evangelical compatibility or incompatibility there is a risk that a lack of significant exposure has led either to an over-judgmental attitude or to an over-sentimental response. With time, issues arise that confront such superficiality and force a reappraisal. At a

---

11. Outside Bromley Christian Centre, August 13, 2003.

number of points in the twenty-year period I have examined, there has been evidence of over-hasty judgement based on superficial understanding. Early on there was the assumption that African neo-Pentecostals would attend a breakfast meeting but when it was discovered that they preferred the occasional all-night event on a Friday, this was heralded as a prayer breakthrough presaging revival rather than acknowledged as essentially a cultural preference. When charismatic prayer leaders were repenting of colonialism it was all too easy to adopt a potentially patronizing attitude to African neo-Pentecostals, "our children have turned their hearts to us, their spiritual fathers."[12] When African immigration was seen to be improving church attendance figures for the 1998 church attendance survey, again it was all too easy to put African neo-Pentecostal churches on pedestals as congregations saving the nation from spiritual decline. When an African leader such as Babatunde spoke out on the state of the nation he was granted a more ready hearing as a "missionary from Africa" and his words were given added weight.[13] On the negative side, some have believed critical press coverage without examining the facts; only time will tell how such impressions will be corrected.

PREDICTING THE FUTURE

The Incitement to Religious Hatred Bill had yet to reach its finally approved form at the end of 2005 but protest on this particular issue had led to new relationships being forged. As 2005 ended there were signs that the African neo-Pentecostal churches involved might use their recently discovered unity to speak out on other things. If the umbrella group which was formed for the protest and became known as Cohesive and Coherent Voice should become a lobbying group in its own right, this would have interesting consequences for the relationship with British evangelicalism. The need to speak with a common voice has at times offered British evangelicalism its greatest opportunity for unity with African neo-Pentecostalism. ACEA seeks to speak on behalf of all BMCs and the EA seeks to speak for evangelicalism at its broadest. If the African neo-Pentecostal constituency secures its own representation, the relationship between British evangelicalism and African neo-Pentecostalism would enter a new phase, with each group standing alone and umbrella organization speaking to umbrella organization; ACEA and

---

12. Concept based on Mal 4:6; Babatunde, *Great Britain Has Fallen!*, 4; Rennie, "War Room."

13. Babatunde, *Great Britain Has Fallen!*, 11–15.

the EA to an African neo-Pentecostal grouping, an African neo-Pentecostal grouping to the EA and ACEA, and so forth.

British evangelicalism might have expected to embrace African neo-Pentecostalism with the same "assimilate now and resolve the issues later" approach that it adopted with the Charismatic Movement, but it seems that the protracted inclusion of classical Pentecostalism, or more likely the parallelism that has marked the integration of the Caribbean churches, will prove to be the more accurate model.

Appendix

Literature Reviews

ACADEMIC RESEARCH IS A collaborative process and each new piece of work takes its place within the framework of existing academic literature. The findings in this book sit in the context of the literature on similar themes published in or before its 1985-2005 time-frame. It is these writings that are considered in the two reviews that follow.

A REVIEW OF THE LITERATURE ON THE CARIBBEAN CHURCHES

This review provides an opportunity to consider how researchers have assessed the ongoing development of Caribbean Pentecostalism in Britain since the 1980s and how they have extended such study to include the African churches through the concept of Black Majority Church. In doing this I will be contending that the continuity assumed by some researchers, a continuity which implies that African and Caribbean church life in Britain are all of a piece, needs refinement. There are a number of reasons for challenging such an assumption. Not least among them are the strong tradition of denominationalism within Caribbean Christianity and the equally determined commitment to independence within much of African neo-Pentecostalism. A comparison of African neo-Pentecostalism and Caribbean Christianity is not a comparison of like with like. This disparity is emphasized when historical contexts are brought into consideration. The development of a Caribbean diaspora in the Britain of the 1960s is very different from the development of an African diaspora in the Britain of the 1990s. History does not necessarily repeat itself. With African neo-Pentecostalism, British evangelicalism is facing a fresh challenge. I assess the research on Caribbean Christianity with this in mind.

Studies of British Caribbean church life undertaken in the 1950s and 1960s by Clifford Hill and Malcolm Calley were essentially sociological and contrasted the Caribbean diaspora in Britain with its Caribbean roots.[1] Among other things both writers were interested in the change in church attendance patterns, attendance being far lower in the diaspora community than in the Caribbean.[2] Subsequent researchers, however, have acknowledged the role of the British Caribbean church in maintaining a sense of community within the Caribbean diaspora and this in itself has become a topic of study, as has the nature of the ecclesiology, theology, and praxis of the British Caribbean churches. Within these topics identity and liberation have been recurring themes as one would expect from a culture that may regard itself as historically African but which has been reconfigured through the pain of past dislocation and subjugation. For some, changing patterns of Caribbean church attendance could be simply symptomatic of a sense of further freedom in a new cultural setting. However, the situation was undoubtedly more complex for the Caribbean diaspora of the 1960s than for the African diaspora of the 1990s.

MacRobert's work on the Caribbean churches in Wolverhampton (a borough that attracted much attention in the late 1960s through the racially provocative views of Enoch Powell, its Member of Parliament) has for well over a decade provided a useful reference point when considering Caribbean ecclesiological identity.[3] Writing in 1989, he assumed no prior knowledge of Pentecostalism on the part of his readers and consequently described in detail every aspect of Caribbean church life.[4] He focused particularly on Jamaican immigration and identified two dominant migrational triggers: "the push of poverty" causing unsustainability in the Caribbean and "the pull of the Mother Country" drawing Commonwealth citizens towards, an often utopianized, Britain.[5] Whilst much African migration is economic and unrealistic expectations may persist, aspirations are generally tempered by the greater general global awareness of the 1990s. MacRobert's underlying thesis throughout was that, both in Britain and the Caribbean, the theology of the Caribbean church-goer (which he sees as having a residual

1. Hill, *Black and White*; Calley, *God's People*.

2. Calley, *God's People*, 119; Hill, *West Indian Migrants*, 6. Hill's figures were: for 1961 attendance in the Caribbean 69 percent, for 1963 attendance of West Indians in London 4 percent.

3. MacRobert, "Black Pentecostalism," 188–203.

4. Note his chapter entitled "Black Pentecostalism: Syncretistic and Christian?"

5. MacRobert, "Black Pentecostalism," 125–38.

West-African dimension) provided an empowerment for surviving and comprehending the complexities of life. He summarized his analysis of Caribbean Pentecostal identity as follows:

> Black settlers—primarily from rural Jamaica—arrived in urban England to face the racism and rejection, not only of the wider society but also of the white denominations. With them they brought types of Pentecostalism which are similar to, and in some ways quite different from, both the mainstream denominations and white indigenous Pentecostalism. Although black Pentecostalism has syncretised certain West African leitmotive [sic] and holds to a number of distinctive doctrines it nevertheless stands close to some of the worshipping communities of the New Testament.[6]

It is important not to confuse the West African *leitmotif* of African American and Caribbean Pentecostalism, which pre-dates African neo-Pentecostalism, with the later construct of African neo-Pentecostalism itself on which this study focuses.

In many ways Wilkinson's research, completed a year later, complemented that of MacRobert.[7] Wilkinson's interest lay with the Caribbean Christians within Anglicanism. However, he too saw personal empowerment through faith as a major feature for his focus group and made a plea for white Christians to contribute towards a localized liberation agenda for Caribbean believers worshipping in a shared context. For him, "[t]he meeting of white and Black in the church is an encounter of historic oppressor and victim."[8] He wrote, "the most important resource available for the struggle against racism and oppression is that which Black people find within themselves when they 'drink from their own wells,'" adding that "[a]t the heart of this observation is the deep Black Christian conviction that God created African people in his own image and revealed himself to them in African culture."[9] For Wilkinson there was an onus on white Christians to "create 'free space' in which Black identity can live within the Church," concluding that "[e]ven this role is only possible because, in the gathering around Sacrament and Word, they have found themselves converted by the Black Christ who meets them there."[10] In reading Wilkinson, one senses that further weight for his arguments must come from Caribbean advocates of

6. MacRobert, "Black Pentecostalism," Abstract.
7. Wilkinson, "Church."
8. Wilkinson, "Church," synopsis.
9. Wilkinson, "Church," 391.
10. Wilkinson, "Church," 392.

such constructs as "revealed . . . in African culture" and the "Black Christ." As the 1990s progressed, such advocates were readily forthcoming. However, they were less sympathetic towards his concept of white Christians creating "free space" in acknowledgement of an "encounter of historic oppressor and victim." This, therefore, does not commend itself as a dominant theme in considering African neo-Pentecostal and British evangelical interaction.

In the mid-1990s, Beckford, Nathan and Alexander were all working on aspects of liberation theology, and Beckford in particular was studying concepts related to the "Black Christ."[11] In her research, completed in 1996, Alexander acknowledged that "Beckford's analysis, like that of Nathan, makes an important contribution to the direction of Liberation Theology in Britain at the professional level. Both theologians engage in constructive critical reflection on the liberational praxis of the BLC [Black Led Church]."[12] Her own contribution was to raise the possibility of developing a more active radicalism within the churches she studied; "a conscious theological understanding of God's alignment with the struggles of the oppressed and the conviction, therefore, that the Church has both a divine calling and a social responsibility to speak out against oppression in the Church and in society."[13]

Both Nathan and Beckford have built on these concepts. Nathan has worked on an analysis of the pan-Africanism of Marcus Garvey.[14] Beckford's subsequent research has sought to establish a political theology for the Black church in Britain.[15] There are questions, however, as to the attainability of Beckford's goal. Whilst his particular "liberation and oppression" foundation does not by any means take his political theology beyond the realm of an African continental experience (there is more than an echo of oppression in colonialism), it does resonate more readily with a Caribbean experience of deportation and slave labor. Nonetheless, the issue for African and Caribbean British residents is not just the past but the present. One commentator has written, "[w]hilst the reality of oppression remains a part of the Black experience in Britain, it does not carry the overarching prevalence suggested by Beckford's analysis."[16] This highlights a limitation for any researcher choosing to look at African and Caribbean Church developments in Britain through a specifically liberation lens.

11. Beckford, *Jesus Is Dread*.
12. Alexander, "Breaking Every Fetter," 325.
13. Alexander, "Breaking Every Fetter," 251.
14. Nathan, "Pan-Africanism," 9–21.
15. Beckford, *Dread and Pentecostal*.
16. Aldred, *Respect*, 160.

Before moving on from the work of Alexander and Beckford it is worth noting that, despite the rise of African neo-Pentecostal churches throughout the 1990s the focus for Alexander and Beckford's research was essentially the churches of the British Caribbean diaspora. Alexander's study was based on five denominations each with well-documented ties to the Caribbean: The First United Church of Jesus Christ Apostolic, the New Testament Church of God, the Seventh Day Adventist Church, Shiloh Pentecostal Fellowship, and the Wesleyan Holiness Church. Beckford used two case studies, an East London branch of the New Testament Church of God and the independent Brixton-based congregation, Ruach Ministries.[17] Beckford's case studies made for an interesting comparison. The independence of Ruach Ministries as it broke away from Caribbean denominationalism has generated an approach to church life that has brought it much closer in its ecclesiology, theology and praxis to the independent African neo-Pentecostal churches that form the focus of my research. This is a point that I do not overlook in my study. A greater understanding of independence by Caribbean denominations (and a better comprehension of denominationalism by African independents) would pave the way for closer ties. However, the occurrence of independent Caribbean congregations is relatively rare so the opportunity for gaining such understanding is limited. Furthermore, African and Caribbean inter-church relations can only form a small part of a study examining the interaction between African neo-Pentecostalism and British evangelicalism in all its breadth.

By the late 1990s it was becoming clear that two strands of research were developing within Caribbean Pentecostal studies: one strand seeking to approach identity issues with a strong liberation emphasis and the other strand seeing liberation concepts as secondary whilst seeking to identify issues by other means. Having commented on the first strand I will now comment briefly on the other, aware that neither has a strong bearing on the principal players whose interaction is researched in this study.

In 1997 Toulis published her work on the role of Pentecostalism in mediating Jamaican ethnicity and gender in England. Once again identity was the focus and a branch of the New Testament Church of God, this time in Birmingham, provided the case study.[18] Toulis had as her specific focus first-generation Caribbean women and argued that the church provided a space in which they could make sense of their new environment with its tensions between familiar Caribbean experience and unfamiliar British experience. Beckford, however, has questioned whether Toulis uncovered the

---

17. Beckford, *Dread and Pentecostal*, 50–62.
18. Toulis, *Believing Identity*.

full story when she focused on a passive response to racism.[19] For Toulis, "the church offers a way of transcending the suffering engendered by such forces [as 'racism and disadvantage in Britain']."[20] Her overriding argument was that religious identity in the British Caribbean community transcends ethnic identity; "[b]y explicitly drawing the boundaries of identity around that which is religious rather than that which is ethnic, members assert their right to self-representation."[21] The implication here is that whether defining identity or asserting rights for self-representation, people in the British Caribbean community are responding (albeit passively) to disadvantage. The African community in Britain would find it hard to concede this point.

Aldred is a Bishop within the Church of God of Prophecy which is one of the strongest denominations in the Caribbean. His earlier research focused on governance within one British congregation of that denomination. He was concerned that the local church had "failed to respond adequately to changing generational perceptions, in terms of both mission and ministry, in deference to maintaining entrenched positions." He was keen to move the congregation's "perception of the Church from a 'top-down' model to a more collegial model [and] . . . to help the congregation move towards a greater sense of 'ownership' and local autonomy." It was significant research in that it signaled up a problem, at least within certain Caribbean denominations, of a staidness emanating from a failure to allow the views of younger members to carry sufficient weight (which surely is the meaning of Aldred's juxtaposition of "changing generational perceptions" and "maintaining entrenched positions"). Whilst this is something that the British African neo-Pentecostal churches will have to be aware of in time, it is currently of secondary importance. It merely serves to emphasize the contrast between two groups, separated by differences in developmental stages, interests and concerns yet frequently brought together under common terminology, such as Black, Black-Led or Black Majority. Of more potential importance for my study, given the evangelical unity context of my research, is Aldred's subsequent work on respect, which he not only pursued in a setting that was specifically "Caribbean British Christian" but which he named as such.[22]

Following a comprehensive review of all the Caribbean church groups and agencies operating in Britain, Aldred sought to link biblical reflection and an analysis of Caribbean church context so as to create a "new theological premise . . . a 'theology of respect.'" Aldred saw Caribbean British

---

19. Beckford, *Dread and Pentecostal*, 49.
20. Toulis, *Believing Identity*, 209.
21. Toulis, *Believing Identity*, 209.
22. Aldred, *Respect*.

Christians as a people deserving respect; "a people who are sure of their identity and strong in their faith; not a people preoccupied with a longing to be free, but a people already free to be themselves."[23] He believed that a theology of respect would "change the nature of Black/White relationship from one of victim/victor, oppressed/oppressor, to one of equality in humanity and faith."[24] Respect obviously plays a vital part in all relationship-building and clearly must exist in all intra-evangelical relationships. It is in effect the "charity" (mentioned in the maxim popularized by Baxter and quoted in the introduction to this study) that enables differences in doctrine and practice to be labelled as *adiaphora* in the context of evangelical unity theory. However, whilst Aldred's respect approach is designed to break down barriers, evangelical unity theory is designed to assess such barriers as may exist and to determine which ones should be left in place and which ones can be safely ignored. As my research focuses on the interaction between African neo-Pentecostals and British evangelicals, it is the evangelical unity theory outlined in the introduction that has to form the template for my assessments. That is not to say that my narrative of interaction could not be described in terms of varying levels of respect. Having expressed my approval of Aldred's ability to so clearly define his core group, I turn to Sturge's exploration of Black Christian faith in Britain which seeks to offer a more inclusive model.[25]

In this brief review of what is essentially the literature on the Caribbean church in Britain, Africa has been a recurring theme. From the 1950s to the late 1980s it was possible for researchers to speak of Black Pentecostalism's African influences in Pentecostal experience with the confidence that such influences would be understood to be coming to Britain via Africa and the Caribbean. From the late 1980s onwards, greater clarification has been required. However, it has not always been given, since, for those researching Caribbean church from a liberation perspective, Africa is more than an influence on Pentecostalism it is a key part of their identity. There are others, though, for whom too great a distinction between Caribbean churches and African churches would be unhelpful, namely for those who seek to speak on minority ethnic issues. For them a strong common identity for both African and Caribbean church is invaluable. The final piece of work in this literature review could be said to have "the value of common identity" as a subtext.

23. Aldred, *Respect*, 180.
24. Aldred, *Respect*, 180.
25. Sturge, *Look*.

In chapter 1 of this book I have referred to Sturge's work that built on Edward's analysis of Caribbean church growth in Britain.[26] This analysis is in fact part of a wider picture that Sturge, as General Director of the African and Caribbean Evangelical Alliance, sought to present as an explanation of the nature of Black Christian faith in Britain to what essentially, given his choice of publisher, would have been a white evangelical readership. Although it does highlight some of the differences between African and Caribbean Christians, unity was the major theme of his book. He wrote from a standpoint that African and Caribbean churches in general had been accepted within the evangelical fold, but had issues (in particular "Unitarianism," Sabbatarianism and Prosperity Theology) that needed to be addressed in order to preserve and strengthen this unity. In summary, his analysis offered an overview that encompassed in passing what my research covers in depth. The application of evangelical unity theory was not explicitly used as the basis of his analysis. In order to embrace the African diaspora churches into his overall sweep, Sturge has defined four more developmental phases beyond the six already listed in chapter 1. They are: "The diverse church (1980–1993)," "The revitalised apostolic church (1990–1996)," "The recognised church (1997–2003)," and "The maturing church" (undated).[27] His "diverse church" category covers the establishing of early African neo-Pentecostal congregations and his "revitalised apostolic church" category serves as an umbrella for their multiplication. In the "revitalised apostolic church category," however, he gives particular prominence to the relatively few independent Caribbean congregations that emerged in this period, saying: "[t]hese churches were not just from the African diaspora; integral to this move were congregations like Ruach Inspirational Church of God, Aka [sic] Ruach Ministries led by Bishop John Francis, Rhema Ministries led by Pastor Mark Goodridge, Victory Christian Centre (with a chequered history) led by Pastor Douglas Goodman, and Christian Life City led by Bishop Wayne Malcolm."[28] This is obviously an appropriate approach for Sturge's overview but a parallel move occurring at the fringes of the Caribbean denominations must not be allowed to mask the issues of African neo-Pentecostal church growth examined in this study, even if ultimately independence goes on to become a much more common feature of Caribbean church life and the distinctions between independent African neo-Pentecostal churches and independent Caribbean "apostolic" churches disappear as congregations mix and the commonality of their independent

26. See p. 27.
27. Sturge, Look, 98–107.
28. Sturge, Look, 102.

approach becomes mutually appreciated. This probability, though, lays way beyond the timescale of this review.

A REVIEW OF THE LITERATURE ON AFRICAN PENTECOSTALISM AND GLOBALIZATION

This review offers the opportunity to establish, for the purposes of further research, an alternative setting for the findings in this book. Undoubtedly, the evangelical unity theory articulated by Stott and described in the introduction to this study affords the most appropriate vehicle for any evaluation of intra-evangelical interaction, and as such is the context for my work. African Pentecostal research, however, particularly that which has analyzed developments as a Christian response to globalizing pressures throughout sub-Saharan Africa, could be used to create a context for examining the exportation of African neo-Pentecostalism to Britain as a possible extension of Pentecostalism's engagement with globalization. To facilitate this as a future area of study and to enhance the background information that my research provides, I will briefly review the literature on African Christianity with an emphasis on African Pentecostalism as a response to the globalizing factors dominant within the last quarter of the twentieth century.

When, in 1975, Hastings completed his survey of twenty-six years of African Christianity, globalization was not the dominant theme.[29] Leaders of African churches were particularly concerned about independency as were the leaders of their nations and Hastings reflected this in his writing.[30] African distinctiveness was already a dominant theme in religious studies, from Parrinder's *West African Religion* published in the late 1940s to Mbiti's *African Religions and Philosophy* and *Introduction to African Religion* published in the 1960s and 1970s.[31] From the same period Peel's work published in 1968, which provided academia with detailed insight into aspects of Aladura belief and practice in Nigeria, served to highlight differences between African Christianity and European Christianity.[32] A reasonable expectation for the 1980s and 1990s was that independency would increase the distinctiveness of African Christianity as Christian theological motifs continued to be reworked in Africa's increasingly African-conscious contexts. This expectation was not without foundation as research continued

29. Hastings, *History of African Christianity*.
30. Hastings, *History of African Christianity*, 67–85, 121–30, 175–83, 256–57.
31. Parrinder, *West African Religion*; Mbiti, *Religions and Philosophy*; Mbiti, *Introduction*.
32. Peel, *Aladura*. Also from this period, see Turner, *African Independent Church*.

into developments within African Christian Theology. Parratt's *Reinventing African Christianity* and Bediako's *Christianity in Africa* were both published in the 1990s, with Bediako's *Jesus in Africa* following in 2000.[33] None of these works, however, Afro-centric though they were, showed signs of an African-consciousness that was inward looking. Each writer emphasized the increasing relevance of the African church globally, as the weight of Christianity's numerical adherence shifted from the northern hemisphere to the southern.[34] Parratt analyzed the ideas of a wide range of African theologians who had written in the 1970s and 1980s and sought to systematize them into a distinctive African theological perspective. Bediako provided his own perspective for the twenty-first century which built on the work of some of his fellow theologians, many of whom Parratt had also assessed. Both writers left no doubt that a distinct African contribution should be welcomed by the worldwide church.[35]

However, by 1990 Gifford was already seeking to raise academic awareness of a different aspect of globalization affecting African Christianity. In his paper *Christianity: To Save or Enslave?* He examined how American prosperity teaching was impacting the African church.[36] In globalization terms, here was something being portrayed as having global reach, not so much because of its cultural flexibility but because of the opposite, the strength of its "one-size fits all" convictions and its ability to persuade people, in Gifford's opinion against all the evidence to the contrary, of its universal relevance.[37] These conclusions of Gifford came across more trenchantly in *Exporting the American Gospel*, where, with Brouwer and Rose, aspects of commodification were explored.[38] Nonetheless Coleman's criticism of Gifford's earlier work in this area, that "[o]ccasionally, the metaphor of a 'conduit' . . . or . . . that of a 'channel' is used to depict a relatively hypodermic-like diffusion of religious ideology to African countries," was interesting.[39] Coleman himself in his book *The Globalisation of Charismatic Christianity* demonstrated how

---

33. Parratt, *Reinventing Christianity*; Bediako, *Christianity in Africa*; Bediako, *Jesus in Africa*.

34. Parratt, *Reinventing Christianity*, 3; Bediako, *Christianity in Africa*, xiii.

35. Parratt, *Reinventing Christianity*, 1–2; Bediako, *Christianity in Africa*, viii.

36. Gifford, *Christianity*.

37. A form of homogenous globalization described subsequently by Ritzer. Ritzer, *MacDonaldization of Society*.

38. Brouwer et al., *Exporting the American Gospel*. Hackett published her observations on the newer churches in Nigeria at about this time. She was less trenchant than Brouwer et al. but recognized the American-style, born-again, Spirit-filled emphasis of these churches. Hackett, "Prosperity."

39. Coleman, "Faith Movement," 10.

Appendix

a high level of commodification enabled the *Livets Ord* church in Sweden to develop its form of the prosperity gospel into a homogenously transferable brand, where local cultural adjustment could be minimalized.[40] Gifford's own balance on cultural adjustment, however, was clearly evident in his paper: "The complex provenance of some elements of African Pentecostal theology," where he took a further look at the faith gospel alongside deliverance and Christian Zionism and spoke of the need to "take into consideration both the local and the external element."[41] Even so, he undoubtedly saw the external elements as particularly significant, as was clear from his arguments on extraversion in concluding his detailed analysis of the public role of Christianity in Ghana, Uganda, Zambia and Cameroon:

> Mechanics of the process of globalisation are evident here ... religious networks function in the same way as the new global industries like banking, law, health, sport, technology and science, or higher education. We have considered African Christianity as a means of plugging into such global religious networks, all the more important since Africa tends to be bypassed by many of the others.[42]

Gifford still had this point in mind in his subsequent in-depth work on Ghana published in 2004.[43]

From the 1990s onwards there was wide academic agreement as to the extent of prosperity teaching's impact on Christianity within sub-Saharan Africa. There was, however, as is clear from my review of Gifford's work, much debate as to the extent of cultural adjustment that such concepts had

---

40. Coleman, *Globalisation*. For discussion on cultural adjustment (the concepts of global flux and local fix), see Meyer and Geschiere, *Globalization*, 1–15.

41. Gifford, "Complex Provenance," 77. Similar points are made in Gifford, "Bible," 16–28.

42. Gifford, *African Christianity*, 320–21.

43. Gifford, *Ghana's New Christianity*, 198. Asamoah Gyadu covered much the same material, themes and timespan as Gifford, and they complemented each other rather than disagreed. Asamoah-Gyadu was more concerned to situate the newer developments in the tradition of "Spiritual Churches" (he uses the Ghanaian name *Sunsum sore*) and gave them their full importance. His work was also more theological, dealing with the new churches' contribution to transformation and empowerment, healing and deliverance, and prosperity. He ranged more widely in his data, not restricting himself to the "megachurches" that particularly interested Gifford, and, as might be expected of an insider, his treatment was slightly more sympathetic. Asamoah-Gyadu, *African Charismatics*.

experienced in their importation; not least the extent to which they echoed with more traditional African views. If the work of Marshall-Fratani, Meyer, Behrend, Maxwell, and Anderson is taken to provide something of a continental spread, the key aspects of the academic discussion become clear. A quote from the conclusion of Peel's 2000 work on the Yoruba can set the tone:

> when a leading born-again advocate of the fashionable "gospel of prosperity" defines it as a "state of well-being in your spirit and body . . . a life of plenty and fulfilment . . . life on a big scale," his idea of it hardly differs from the traditional notion of *alafia*. And their project for individual and national renewal continues to presume the existence of a plurality of spiritual powers, demonic as well as divine, a reminder that the missionaries, while they could require converts to hand in their idols for destruction, were less successful in persuading them that they represented nothing but their imaginings. When modernity is offered on these premises, old demands for inculturation lose much of their appeal. The pendulum of cultural change which for many decades has swung towards Africanization, now swings back to more transnational idioms such as Pentecostalism provides.[44]

Marshall-Fratani's work on the uptake of new global Pentecostal trends within Nigeria focused mainly on aspects of societal transformation and the impact of Pentecostal beliefs on the political attitudes of Pentecostalism's adherents.[45] Her work also extended to issues of personal identity and the reconciling of "local pasts" and "global modernities" in the Pentecostal context.[46] In all of her work there has been an awareness of the interplay between the local and the global so that the outworking of transnational trends have been examined in their acquired Nigerian setting. Still with a focus on Nigeria, Burgess's work on Eastern Nigerian neo-Pentecostalism has provided a useful Igbo-focused compliment to Marshall-Fratani's more Yoruba-centric studies. Burgess, like Marshall-Fratani, has been mindful of local-global interaction and has been alert to the commodification factors

---

44. Peel, *Religious Encounter*, 318.
45. Marshall, "Power"; Marshall, "God Is Not a Democrat."
46. Marshall-Fratani, "Global and Local." Ojo has made a similar point, writing of Nigeria's new Pentecostal churches that they "are increasingly responding to the needs and aspirations of Nigerians amid the uncertainties of their political life and the pain of their constant and unending economic adjustments." Ojo, "Church in the African State," 25. Ojo's earlier work on campus Christianity in western Nigeria is referred to earlier in this chapter. Ojo, "Campus Christianity." For analysis of an African Initiated Church see Omoyajowo, *Cherubim and Seraphim*.

highlighted by Coleman. Burgess has written of Igbo-founded neo-Pentecostal churches that

> the inherent flexibility of neo-Pentecostal spirituality has enabled them to adapt their message and methodology to suit local contexts and cater for consumer demands. Their emphasis on the Bible, innovative worship styles, community ethos, and proclamation of a holistic gospel have appealed to those with disintegrating social and economic relationships, and accustomed to a universe alive with spiritual forces.[47]

Meyer's work on African Pentecostalism has been based in Ghana and both prosperity teaching and deliverance have received her attention.[48] With prosperity teaching she has also focused on commodification.[49] Indeed, her work is characterized by a strong evaluation of the mediation between the local and the global and nowhere is this more evident than in her book *Translating the Devil*. Here Meyer sought to "understand African appropriations of Christianity through a focus on the occult" fully aware that this could "confirm existing stereotypes and exoticise Africans" but convinced, nonetheless, that "the image of the Devil and demons is a product of the encounter between Africans and Western missionaries, a hybrid form which helped to constitute the reality in which both parties came to terms with each other."[50] This approach via the occult had the advantage of enabling the researcher to direct her focus immediately on the inevitable negotiations between local beliefs and newly introduced external concepts. Her arguments demonstrated how there can be, on the one hand, a Pietistic rupture between a "traditional" past and a Christian future with, on the other, a more mediated response where past understanding of spirits becomes engrossed in a new understanding of the demonic.[51] For Meyer this is a possible explanation of Pentecostalism's growth in Africa: "Pentecostalism offers a new form, it can easily become localised and thus express a highly culturally specific version of Christianity."[52]

Before moving on to review literature on Pentecostalism's engagement in central, eastern and southern Africa, three other writers on Ghanaian Pentecostalism deserve mention. Gifford and Meyer's work is complemented in various ways by that of van Dijk, Larbi and Onyinah. I will comment

47. Burgess, "Civil War Revival," 373.
48. Meyer, *Translating the Devil*; Meyer, "Pentecostalism," 67–87.
49. Meyer, "Commodities," 151–76.
50. Meyer, "Commodities," xxiii.
51. Meyer, "Commodities," 213–15.
52. Meyer, "Commodities," 215.

briefly on Larbi and Onyinah's work now but in acknowledgement of van Dijk's recent emphasis on the Ghanaian diaspora in the Netherlands I will consider his emphasis separately towards the end of this section. The virtue of Larbi's *Pentecostalism* is that it provided a comprehensive history of the Pentecostal movement in Ghana.[53] Understandably much space was devoted to the Apostolic Church, the Christ Apostolic Church and the Church of Pentecost, Ghana's three largest Pentecostal denominations. Whilst his preliminary chapters covered some of the interaction between Christianity and what he described as the "traditional world view," the interplay between the local and the global became a theme once again towards the end of his work when he evaluated neo-Pentecostalism in Ghana and asked is it "indigenous or foreign?"[54] At this point he saw himself as taking an opposite view to Gifford in concluding that neo-Pentecostalism in Ghana was essentially indigenous, despite its American connections, and that the prosperity gospel preached by the neo-Pentecostal churches marked a step towards self-theologizing for the Ghanaian Church.[55]

Turning to Onyinah, occult themes were once again to the fore. His work focused on Akan witchcraft and the concept of exorcism in the Church of Pentecost, in which church he himself serves as an Apostle.[56] As deliverance ministry, amongst both evangelicals and African neo-Pentecostals, is a theme that I have addressed in chapter 5 of this study, it is pertinent to note some of Onyinah's conclusions here by way of relevant background. Onyinah expressed his conviction that, for Ghana and the Church of Pentecost, "the Pentecostal type of exorcism, though, performed under the guise of the Christian faith, was strongly based on the Akan cosmology" and that Akan cosmology provided the framework for "both the exorcists and their methods."[57] He also argued that "in the 1980s, through the influence of the global Charismatic renewal in Christianity, a distinct ministry," which he termed "witchdemonology," "developed in Ghanaian Christianity, particularly in COP [the Church of Pentecost]."[58] He described this "witchdemonology" as "the amalgamation of Akan traditional religion, preaching and the media materials and practices of some Western evangelists, and other Christian beliefs and practices."[59] This suggested a considerable de-

---

53. Larbi, *Pentecostalism*.
54. Larbi, *Pentecostalism*, 307.
55. Larbi, *Pentecostalism*, 307–15.
56. Onyinah, "Akan Witchcraft."
57. Onyinah, "Akan Witchcraft," 385–86.
58. Onyinah, "Akan Witchcraft," 389–90.
59. Onyinah, "Akan Witchcraft," 390.

gree of local cultural adjustment to what Onyinah himself was recognizing as a global movement; a global movement which, it must be remembered, others had seen as so dominantly global as to have entered African culture with such minimal cultural adjustment and to have stood out as a foreign import. In Onyinah's argument he drew on the tendency he had registered with those he interviewed to refer to certain demonic spirits as "witch spirits." As a caveat, it has to be said that many African neo-Pentecostals would want to make it clear that identifying demons as "witch spirits" and accepting such demonic forces as being released by those practicing witchcraft, is not an indication that those performing deliverance ministry are themselves engaged in any form of witchcraft. "Witchdemonology" may be something they recognize but do not see themselves as practicing. Part of the concern expressed by Onyinah in his thesis, however, was that the diagnosis of "witchdemonology" was fundamentally erroneous and that Pentecostalism was again exhibiting that characteristic which earlier researchers had defined as a recovery of "primal spirituality" with Charismatic healing and deliverance being centered on 'the sacred self.'"[60] In a subsequent paper Onyinah took this further. Having stated that "[t]he African Pentecostal churches attempt to appropriate the Pentecostal understanding of Christianity against a background of African spirituality," he rightly recorded that "[i]n many parts of Africa, there is still the strong belief that sufferings are mainly of supernatural origin." He then went on to demonstrate how readily a focus on witchcraft and sorcery can result in a situation where "most neurotic people are considered to be witches who are suffering from evil acts."[61] It is ironic that a Pentecostal deliverance ministry that is supposed to center on the "sacred self," so hastily labels individuals in a way that does little to enhance self-worth. The role of "self" in deliverance ministry cannot be seen as straightforward.

Onyinah's work on demonology provides a link to Behrend's work on spirit possession in Uganda.[62] Whilst Gifford in his work on African Christianity's public role provided an overview of Christianity in Uganda in the 1990s and Ward has furnished academia with further insights into the Church of Uganda's history, Behrend's work focused away from the denominational and neo-Pentecostal churches and concentrated on the very different Pentecostal manifestation of the Lord's Resistance Army in

60. Onyinah, "Akan Witchcraft," 392.
61. Onyinah, "God's Grace," 121.
62. Behrend, "Power to Heal." For a more general East African perspective: Spear and Kimambo, *East African*.

Northern Uganda.[63] Like Meyer and Onyinah she looked at issues of occult engagement, so local appropriations and adaptations were much to the fore. Although in many ways Behrend's work is tangential to a study on neo-Pentecostalism, it does provide the opportunity to comment on an issue that is relevant to this study; namely that of past British evangelical perceptions of African Christian identity. An attachment by British evangelicals, particularly from the 1950s onwards, to the news of the East African revival left a perception of African Christianity, and especially Ugandan Christianity, that has not moved on with time.[64] The complexities of the Lord's Resistance Army's spirituality and the rise of Ugandan neo-Pentecostalism have been slow to enter British evangelical consciousness. Even when British Christians have become aware of neo-Pentecostal developments, it has been hard to ensure a realistic focus. Meyer is quoted earlier in this review as not wanting to "confirm existing stereotypes and exoticise Africans," but exoticism readily occurs and such exoticism is of no assistance when African churches become diaspora churches, moving from where they once could be appreciated from afar to where they now have to be experienced in the neighborhood next door.[65]

Two other geographical areas should be brought into this literature review before concluding with a comment on van Dijk's research on African churches in diaspora. The first is central Africa where Maxwell's research into Pentecostalism, prosperity, and modernity in Zimbabwe has seemed to support Gifford's findings of "born-again Christians . . . vulnerable to the agendas of the American New Religious Right."[66] Indeed, Maxwell has concluded that "the specific forms of contemporary Pentecostalism (often known as the born-again movement) make it difficult to focus on just their economic or political aspect while ignoring the other," adding that "[t]he growing influence of what is known as the 'prosperity gospel' has implications for both the formation of capitalist attitudes and activities, and for shaping political activism."[67] However, Maxwell's views were not that a local national Christian community was being overwhelmed by a global Pentecostal force. He has also written of "[t]he African born-again movement as a local and global religion" and concluded his thoughts with a telling illustration of this duality:

63. Behrend, *Alice Lakwena*.
64. Price and Randall, *Transforming Keswick*, 122.
65. Meyer, *Translating the Devil*, xxiii.
66. Maxwell, "Delivered," 350. His reference to "southern African sources" for Zimbabwean Pentecostal prosperity teaching in this paper should not be seen as a denial of indirect American influence.
67. Maxwell, "Delivered," 350.

> The tension between the local and the global is most apparent in the role of African born-again leaders. . . . From the global perspective they participate in a network of high-flying religious executives who travel the convention circuits exchanging the latest Holy Spirit-inspired "teachings" and physical manifestations of the "gifts." . . . From the local perspective they look very different . . . they are heirs of the community and nationalist leaders of the 1950s.[68]

In Maxwell's analysis it is possible to see not only the homogenous impact of global Pentecostalism but also its heterogenous impact reinforcing the conclusion that Pentecostalism can be regarded as a globalizing agency both because of the uniformity it brings and the diversity it allows.

Having started this review with a focus on the more homogenous aspects of globalization within Pentecostalism and raised Coleman's criticism of presentations of appropriation that suggested "a relatively hypodermic-like diffusion of religious ideology to African countries," it is fitting to conclude with some of Anderson's thoughts on the local appropriation of global trends within Pentecostalism.[69] Anderson has intimate understanding of South African Pentecostalism in all its forms and has written of the considerable continuity in Pentecostalism's differing expressions.[70] He has recognized the African Initiated Churches and newer Pentecostal and Charismatic churches as having "much in common."[71] His work has shown a consistent commitment to a view of Pentecostal origins that has Pentecostalism's roots spreading beyond and before Azusa Street and his commitment to the eclectic nature of Pentecostalism's origins has been matched by his commitment to Pentecostalism's subsequent diversity of expressions (to the surprise of at least one evangelical reviewer).[72] There is throughout Anderson's work a strong emphasis on localization and this has been the case when he has written of the newer Pentecostal churches:

> There *are* connections between some of the NPCs [newer Pentecostal and Charismatic churches] and the American "health and wealth movement," and it is also true that some of the newer African churches reproduce and promote this teaching and literature. But identifying NPCs with the American "prosperity gospel" is a generalization that particularly fails to appreciate

68. Maxwell, "African Gifts," 168–69.
69. Coleman, "Faith Movement," 10.
70. Anderson, *African Reformation*.
71. Anderson, *African Reformation*, 183.
72. Anderson, *Introduction*; O'Callaghan, "Review," 103–4.

the reconstructions and innovations made by these new African movements in adapting to a radically different context, just as the older AICs did years before.[73]

Clearly the globalization debate will continue. The homogenists will continue to see a commodification of strands of Christianity to the point where it is globally transferable with minimal modification. For them, globalization will tend towards the production of a carefully tuned form of Christianity designed to be accepted, almost regardless of its relevance, not only because of its boasted universality and its accompanying added appeal but as a result of the degree of extraversion in the societies that are keen to appropriate it.[74] The heterogenists will continue to see diversity as the essence of globalization, believing that that which is most flexible is most likely to succeed in what they would be less likely to describe as the transnational religious market place.[75] If Gifford and Anderson do to some extent represent different ends of the homogenous/heterogenous globalization spectrum (and in my opinion that implies a level of over-labelling), the research on the African neo-Pentecostal churches in Britain in my study offers an opportunity to test, through observing the processes and results of importation, the extent to which local forces do actually mold these churches. Using African neo-Pentecostal interaction with an existing strand of British Christianity such as evangelicalism should facilitate this observation. This said, though, globalization does in fact bring yet another twist to the debate. Diaspora churches have reasons for not modifying to local conditions and resident entities such as evangelicalism have their reasons for wanting to change.

Research is ongoing into the churches of the African diaspora in Europe and two comments from van Dijk's observations on Ghanaian Pentecostalism in the Netherlands are helpful.[76] Firstly:

> As Pentecostalism appears to cut across national and cultural borders, it can best be studied within the context of an anthropology of transnationalism. This approach investigates how identities are formed in situations where, as a result of diasporic

---

73. Anderson, *African Reformation*, 183. See also Anderson's thorough-going contribution to the Pentecostal globalization debate prepared for Churches Together in Britain and Ireland. Anderson, "Globalization of Pentecostalism."

74. Coleman's work investigates this approach.

75. The work of Cox, Martin and Dempster, Klaus and Petersen are in this vein. Cox, *Fire*; Martin, *Pentecostalism*.

76. Van Dijk has written on Malawi and Ghana. The work of ter Haar and Hunt is referred to later in this study. The work of Jehu-Appiah has been referred to earlier. Jehu-Appiah, "Overview."

flows, communities arise that neither seem to have a firm "geographical" anchor nor the means to create the individual as a local, cultural subject.[77]

Secondly: "Ghanaian Pentecostalism is . . . neither fully global nor fully local. Instead, it appears to thrive on an active contestation of both."[78] The fact that van Dijk refers to "Ghanaian Pentecostalism" in his diasporic considerations demonstrates the degree to which localization that has occurred in Pentecostalism's appropriation in Africa. However, it is clear that there is no guarantee that Ghanaian Pentecostalism will become "Netherlands' Pentecostalism" or indeed "Netherlands' Ghanaian Pentecostalism." Global and local tensions may remain.

Having set this review of the literature on African Pentecostalism in the context of globalization, a brief final paragraph on British evangelicalism and globalization will reaffirm the interactive nature of this study. As stated above, it is reasonable to assume that, regardless of the flexibility or otherwise of diasporic African neo-Pentecostalism, evangelicalism may have had its reasons for wanting to change in the face of ongoing globalizing pressures. In chapter 4 of this study I relate British evangelicalism's engagement with postmodernism in the 1990s, where, despite its fragmentary nature, or because of it, postmodernism was being seen by many evangelicals as a globalizing force that must be responded to. Responses varied from Drane's anti-MacDonaldization stance to Hilborn's carefully balanced analysis of possible evangelical uptake of ongoing cultural trends.[79] The work to cause most ripples within evangelicalism was Tomlinson's proposal of a post-evangelicalism which advocated radically alternative models of church, which many evangelicals have since experimented with.[80] From a theological perspective, Hicks produced an epistemological response to postmodernity.[81] Between 1985 and 2005 African neo-Pentecostalism was not engaging with a static evangelicalism.

77. Van Dijk, "Time and Transcultural," 218.
78. Van Dijk, "Soul," 50.
79. Drane, *MacDonaldization of the Church*; Hilborn, *Picking Up*.
80. Tomlinson, *Post-Evangelical*. Literature abounds on what is called "The Emerging Church" within British evangelicalism.
81. Hicks, *Evangelicals and Truth*.

Bibliography

ACEA. Minutes of Church Leaders' Meeting, May 21, 2004.
———. Minutes of Senior African Church Leaders' Meeting, February 20, 2003.
———. Minutes of Senior African Church Leaders' Meeting, March 15, 2006.
———. "Response to Victoria Climbié Inquiry Discussion Paper, Seminar 1: Discovery and Inclusion." London: ACEA, n.d.
———. "Response to Victoria Climbié Inquiry Discussion Paper, Seminar 3: Determining Requirements." London: ACEA, n.d.
"ACEA to Lead Disclosure Campaign with New Membership Criteria." *Focus* (June–Aug 2002) 13.
ACUTE. *Faith, Hope and Homosexuality*. Carlisle, UK: Paternoster, 1998.
———. *The Nature of Hell*. Carlisle, UK: Paternoster, 2000.
———. *What Is an Evangelical? Setting the Scene for a Serious Debate*. London: The Evangelical Alliance, 1996.
Adamo, David T. "African Cultural Hermeneutics." In *Vernacular Hermeneutics*, edited by R. S. Sugirtharajab, 66–90. Sheffield, UK: Sheffield Academic, 1999.
Adegbola, Ade E. A. *Traditional Religion in West Africa*. Nairobi, Ken.: Uzima, 1983.
Adegboyega, S. G. *Short History of the Apostolic Church of Nigeria*. Ibadan, Nig.: Rosprint, 1978.
Adeyemo, Tokunboh. *Salvation in African Tradition*. 2nd ed. Nairobi, Ken.: Evangel, 1997.
"African Bishops Seize Initiative at Lambeth Conference." *Focus* (Sept–Nov 1998) 7.
"Africans and Caribbeans Do Belong Together—Conference Told." *Focus* (Sept–Nov 1998) 5.
Aguiar, Shirin. "Pastor in 'Cinema Assault.'" *The Voice* (June 2, 2003) 6.
———. "'Rape Pastor' Praying On: 'King of Hearts' Church Leader in Dock for Abusing Women and Position." *The Voice* (May 26, 2003) 4.
"Aiming for GOAL." *Focus* (Mar–May 2003) 13.
Akanle, Grace. *Satan-Proof Your Children: Red Alert Signal for Parents with Children in Schools*. London: Emmanuel House, 1999.
Akwahboah, Francis. *Bewitched*. Kumasi, Gha.: Christian Hope Ministry, n.d.
Aldred, J. D. *Respect: Understanding Caribbean British Christianity*. Peterborough, UK: Epworth, 2005.
Alec, Wendy. *Against All Odds: The Story of Europe's First Daily Christian Television Network—Now Impacting the Globe*. Sunderland, UK: Warboys Media, 2004.

Bibliography

Alexander, Valentina E. "'Breaking Every Fetter?' To What Extent has the Black Led Church in Britain Developed a Theology of Liberation?" PhD diss., University of Warwick, 1996.

Amaramiro, Alex. *Doctrinal Ideas of the Eternal Sacred Order of Cherubim and Seraphim.* Owerri, Nig.: Ihem Davis, 1989.

"An American Friend." Video. Channel 4, September 1992. Video copy available from Charis Communications, St Paul's House, Edison Road, Bromley, BR2 0EP, UK.

Anderson, Allan. *African Reformation: African Initiated Christianity in the 20th Century.* Trenton, NJ: Africa World, 2001.

———. "The Globalization of Pentecostalism." CTBI Churches' Commission on Mission, September 2002.

———. *Introduction to Pentecostalism.* Cambridge: Cambridge University Press, 2004.

———. "New African Initiated Pentecostalism and Charismatics in South Africa." *Journal of Religion in Africa* 35 (2005) 66–92.

Anderson, Allan H., and Walter J. Hollenweger, eds. *Pentecostals after a Century: Global Perspectives in a Movement in Transition.* Sheffield, UK: Sheffield Academic, 1999.

Anderson, R. M. *Vision of the Disinherited: The Making of American Pentecostalism.* New York: Oxford University Press, 1979.

Anderson, Robert. "'Spirit Manifestations' and 'The Gift of Tongues.'" *Evangelical Christendom* (Mar–Apr 1909) 48.

Anim, Emmanuel Kwesi. "A Paradigm Shift in the Theology of Salvation: An Examination of Cultural and Socio-Economic Effects on the Soteriology of the Church of Pentecost with Special Reference to the Elim Church of Pentecost in Britain." MA thesis, All Nations Christian College (Hertfordshire), 1999.

Anjorin, Femi. "Convention of Excellence." http://www.thenewsng.com/modules/zmagazine/print.php?atricleid=2753.

"Any Questions? Joel Gives Evangelical Answers." *Idea* (Mar–Apr 2001) 5.

Appiagyei, Kingsley. "The Growth of Ethnic Churches in the Capital." In *Mission in the New Millennium: A Fresh Challenge and Call to Christian Commitment in the Capital,* edited by Clive Doubleday, 60–63. London: London Baptist Association, 1998.

"Arbitron Audience Survey." Commissioned by Premier Christian Radio, Summer 2003. Premier Media Group, London SW1P 4XP.

Asamoah-Gyadu, J. Kwabena. *African Charismatics: Current Developments within Independent Indigenous Pentecostalism in Ghana.* Leiden, UK: Brill, 2005.

Ashimolowo, Matthew. *Keeping Your Dreams Alive: How to Fulfil Your God-Given Vision.* London: Mattyson Media, 1993.

———. *Take a Giant Leap: How to Motivate Yourself for a Successful Christian Life.* London: Mattyson Media, 1992.

———. *Warriors of Righteousness: Occupy Your Place for the Battle of the End Times.* London: Mattyson Media, 1992.

Ayisi, Eric O. *An Introduction to the Study of African Culture.* Nairobi, Ken.: East African Educational, 1992.

Babatunde, Wale. *Great Britain Has Fallen!—How to Restore Britain's Greatness as a Nation.* Chichester, UK: New Wine, 2002.

Baird, Tom. "Giant Mosque for 40,000 May Be Built at London Olympics." *Sunday Times* (Nov 27, 2005). https://web.archive.org/web/20051203151854/http://www.timesonline.co.uk/article/0,,2087-1892780,00.html.

Bakare, Tunde. "Prophetic Insight into Transitional Debacle." *Harvestime* 3 (1993) 4.
Barclay, Oliver. *Evangelicalism in Britain 1935–1995*. Leicester, UK: InterVarsity, 1997.
Bares, Alison, ed. *All African Lutheran Consultation on Christian Theology and Christian Education in the African Context*. Gaborone, Botsw.: Lutheran World Federation Department of Church Cooperation, 1978.
Barron, Bruce. *Heaven on Earth: The Social and Political Agendas of Dominion Theology*. Grand Rapids, MI: Zondervan, 1992.
Bartholomew, Craig, et al., eds. *The Futures of Evangelicalism: Issues and Prospects*. Leicester, UK: InterVarsity, 2003.
Bartleman, Frank. *Azusa Street*. Plainfield, NJ: Logos International, 1980.
Bebbington, D. W. *Evangelicalism in Modern Britain: A History from the 1730s to the 1980s*. London: Routledge, 1989.
Beckford, Robert. *Dread and Pentecostal: A Political Theology for the Black Church in Britain*. London: SPCK, 2000.
———. *Jesus Is Dread: Black Theology and Culture in Britain*. London: Darton, Longman & Todd, 1998.
Bediako, Kwame. *Christianity in Africa: The Renewal of a Non-Western Religion*. Edinburgh, UK: Edinburgh University Press, 1995.
———. *Jesus in Africa: The Christian Gospel in African History and Experience*. Carlisle, UK: Regnum Africa, 2000.
Behrend, Heike. *Alice Lakwena and the Holy Spirits*. Oxford: Currey, 1999.
Behrend, Heike, and Ute Luig, eds. *Spirit Possession, Modernity and Power in Africa*. Oxford: Currey, 1999.
Bernard, H. Russell. *Research Methods in Anthropology*. 2nd ed. Walnut Creek, CA: AltaMira, 1995.
"Black and Blessed." *Graduate V, The Independent* (Sept 18, 2004).
"Black Church Builds for Future." *Idea* (Jan–Mar 1996) 14.
Blair, Tony. "Speech to Faithworks." March 22, 2005. http://www.faithworks.info/Standard.asp?ID=4770.
Bolton, Frances Lawjua. *And We Beheld His Glory: A Personal Account of the Revival in Eastern Nigeria in 1970/'71*. Harlow, UK: Christ the King, 1992.
Bowder, Bill. "Change of Status Gives Hope in Kingsway Saga." *Church Times* (Jan 29, 2004). https://www.churchtimes.co.uk/articles/2004/30-january/news/uk/change-of-status-gives-hope-in-kingsway-saga.
Brady, Steve, and Harold Rowdon, eds. *For Such a Time as This*. Milton Keynes, UK: Scripture Union, 1996.
Brencher, John. *Martyn Lloyd-Jones (1899–1981) and Twentieth Century Evangelicalism*. Carlisle, UK: Paternoster, 2002.
Brierley, Peter. *Christian England: What the English Church Census Reveals*. London: MARC Europe, 1991.
———. *The Tide Is Running Out: What the English Church Attendance Survey Reveals*. London: Christian Research, 2000.
Briggs, John. "The Salvation Army." In *A Lion Handbook: The History of Christianity*, edited by Tim Dowley, 522–23. Oxford: Lion Publishing, 1977.
Broadbent, E. H. *The Pilgrim Church*. London: Pickering and Inglis, 1974.
Brouwer, Steve, et al. *Exporting the American Gospel: Global Christian Fundamentalism*. New York: Routledge, 1996.
Brown, Rebecca. *He Came to Set the Captives Free*. Springdale: Whitaker, 1992.

Bruce, Steve. *Fundamentalism*. Cambridge: Polity, 2000.
———. *Religion in Modern Britain*. Oxford: Oxford University Press, 1995.
Brumback, Carl. *Like a River: The Early Years of the Assemblies of God*. Springfield: Gospel Publishing House, 1977.
Bulle, Florence. *God Wants You Rich and Other Enticing Doctrines*. Minneapolis: Bethany, 1983.
Burgess, Richard H. "The Civil War Revival and Its Pentecostal Progeny: A Religious Movement among the Igbo People of Eastern Nigeria." PhD diss., Birmingham University, 2004.
Burnett, David. *Clash of Worlds*. Crowborough, UK: MARC, 1990.
Buthelezi, Manas. "Black Theology—A Quest for the Liberation of Christian Truth." In *All African Lutheran Consultation on Christian Theology and Christian Education in the African Context*, edited by Alison Bares, 52-59. Gaborone, Botsw.: Lutheran World Federation Department of Church Cooperation, 1978.
Byaruhanga-Akiiki, A. T. B., ed. *African World Religion: A Grassroot Perspective*. Kampala, Ug.: Makerere University Printery, n.d.
Calley, Malcolm J. *God's People: West Indian Pentecostal Sects in England*. London: Oxford University Press, 1965.
Calver, Clive. "The Rise and Fall of the Evangelical Alliance: 1835–1905." In *For Such a Time as This*, edited by Steve Brady and Harold Rowdon, 148–62. Milton Keynes, UK: Scripture Union, 1996.
Calver, Clive, and Rob Warner. *Together We Stand: Evangelical Convictions, Unity and Vision*. London: Hodder & Stoughton, 1996.
Calver, Clive, et al. *Who Do Evangelicals Think They Are?* London: The Evangelical Alliance, n.d.
Capon, John, and Derek Williams. *Billy Graham: The Man and His Mission*. Northwood, UK: Creative Publishing, 1984.
Carpenter, Joel A. *Revive Us Again: The Reawakening of American Fundamentalism*. Oxford: Oxford University Press, 1997.
Carrette, Jeremy, and Mary Keller. "Religions, Orientation and Critical Theory." *Theology and Sexuality* 11 (1999) 21–43.
Cartledge, Mark. "A Spur to Holistic Discipleship." In *'Toronto' in Perspective: Papers on the New Charismatic Wave of the Mid-1990s*, edited by David Hilborn, 64–74. Carlisle, UK: ACUTE, 2001.
Cartwright, Desmond. "From the Back Streets of Brixton to the Royal Albert Hall: British Pentecostalism 1907-1926." Conference paper, European Pentecostal Theological Association. Leuven, Belgium, December 28–29, 1981.
———. *The Great Evangelists: The Lives of George and Stephen Jeffreys*. Basingstoke, UK: Marshall Pickering, 1986.
———. *The Real Smith Wigglesworth: The Man, The Myth, The Message*. Tonbridge, UK: Sovereign World, 2000.
Cave, Dave. "Truth, Unity and the Future of Evangelicals," *Idea* (January–March 1997), 27.
Centre for Caribbean Studies. *A Handbook of Afro-Westindian Churches in Britain: 1984 Edition*. London: The Centre for Caribbean Studies, 1984.
Cerullo, Morris. *Son, Build Me an Army! My Life Story*. San Diego, CA: MCWE, 1999.
Charity Commission. "Appointment of Interim Manager at KICC." Press release, January 12, 2002.

Bibliography

———. "Minutes of Charity Commission Meeting." May 27, 2004.
———. "Register of Charities." http://www.charity-commission.gov.uk/registeredcharities/showcharity.asp?remchar=&chyno=1014084.
———. "Report of the Inquiry into Victory Christian Centre." September 7, 2004. http://www.charity-commission.gov.uk/investigations/inquiryreports/victory.asp.
———. "Report on The King's Ministries Trust." October 6, 2005. http://www.charity-commission.gov.uk/investigations/inquiryreports/kmt.asp.
Chevreau, Guy. *Catch the Fire: The Toronto Blessing: An Experience of Renewal and Revival.*
Chigbundu, Abraham. *I Believe in Deliverance: Deliverance Made Easy.* Benin City, Nig.: Voice of Freedom Publications, n.d.
"Christian TV Station Launched in Britain." *Idea* (Jan–Mar 1996) 14.
"Church Charity Cash Mismanaged." *BBC News World Edition* (Sept 7, 2004). http://news.bbc.co.uk/1/hi/england/northamptonshire/3635230.stm.
"Church Leaders Meet Metropolitan Police Commissioner." *Focus* (August–October 1999) 12.
"Churches Pose Threat to Children." *New Nation* (Jan 4, 2002).
Clough, Sue. "Churchgoers Pray for Jailed Preacher." *The Daily Telegraph* (May 8, 2004) https://www.telegraph.co.uk/news/uknews/1461283/Churchgoers-pray-for-jailed-preacher.html.
———. "Preacher Preyed on Young Women in His Adoring Flock." *The Daily Telegraph* (March 3, 2004) 6.
Coffey, John. "The State and Societal Transformation." In *Movement for Change: Evangelical Perspectives on Social Transformation*, edited by David Hilborn, 95–112. Carlisle, UK: Paternoster, 2004.
Coleman, Simon. "The Faith Movement: A Global Religious Culture?" *Culture and Religion* 3 (2002) 3–19.
———. *The Globalisation of Christianity: Spreading the Gospel of Prosperity.* Cambridge: Cambridge University Press, 2000.
Collier, Richard. *The General Next to God: The Story of William Booth and the Salvation Army.* London: Collins, 1965.
Combe, Victoria. "Richest Parish Invites All England to Bible Classes." *The Daily Telegraph* (Feb 11, 1998).
"Conferences Respond to the Macpherson Report." *Focus* (April–June 1999) 15.
Cooperman, Alan, and Thomas B. Edsall. "Evangelicals Say They Led Charge for the GOP." *The Washington Post* (Nov 11, 2004) A01.
Cooper, Simon, and Mike Farrant. *Fire in Our Hearts—The Story of the Jesus Fellowship.* Eastbourne, UK: Kingsway, 1991.
Corten, André, and Ruth Marshall-Fratani, eds. *Between Babel and Pentecost: Transnational Pentecostalism in Africa and Latin America.* Bloomington, IN: Indiana University Press, 2001.
Cotton, Ian. *The Hallelujah Revolution: The Rise of the New Christians.* London: Warner, 1995.
Cox, Harvey. *Fire from Heaven: The Rise of Pentecostal Spirituality and the Reshaping of Religion in the Twenty-First Century.* Cambridge, MA: Da Capo. 1995.
Cray, Graham, et al. *The Post-Evangelical Debate.* London: Triangle SPCK, 1997.

Cridge, Mary. "Church and Charity Commission Work Together." *Focus* (Jan–Mar 2005) 17.
———. "Church and Charity Commission Work Towards Common Goals." *Focus* (Sep–Nov 2003) 14–15.
Davie, Grace. *Religion in Britain since 1945—Believing without Belonging*. Oxford: Blackwell, 1994.
Davie, Martin. "A Real but Limited Renewal." In *'Toronto' in Perspective: Papers on the New Charismatic Wave of the Mid 1990s*, edited by David Hilborn, 35–44. Carlisle, UK: ACUTE, 2001.
Davies, Sîan. "EA Examines Prosperity Gospel." *Church of England Newspaper* (Mar 23, 2003).
Dawson, John. *Healing America's Wounds*. California: Regal, 1994.
———. *Taking Our Cities for God: How to Break Spiritual Strongholds*. Lake Mary, FL: Creation, 1989.
"Delegation Meets Home Office Minister." *Focus* (August–October 1999) 12.
Dempster, Murray W., et al., eds. *The Globalization of Pentecostalism: A Religion Made to Travel*. Carlisle, UK: Regnum, 1999.
Denver, David. "The Results: How Britain Voted (or Didn't)." In *Labour's Second Landslide: The General Election 2001*, edited by Andrew P. Geddes and Jonathan Tonge, 9–27. Manchester, UK: Manchester University Press, 2002.
Dixon, Marcia. "Cash, Bang, Wallop! Church Furious at *Times* Article on Prosperity Gospel." *The Voice* (Mar 3, 2001) 9.
———. "More Than Just a Gospel of Greed?" *The Voice* (Mar 3, 2003).
Dixon, Patrick. *Signs of Revival: Detailed Historical Research Throws Light on Today's Move of God's Spirit*. Eastbourne, UK: Kingsway, 1994.
Don-Dawodu, Ayo. *The Glorious People: With Power, Promise, Purpose and God's Perspective*. London: Don-Dawodu Foundation, 1995.
———. *War Theatre*. London: Dawodu Foundation, 1994.
Doubleday, Clive, ed. *Mission in the New Millennium: A Fresh Challenge and Call to Christian Commitment in the Capital*. London: London Baptist Association, 1998.
Dow, Graham. *Deliverance*. 2nd ed. Grand Rapids, MI: Chosen, 2003.
Dowley, Tim, ed. *A Lion Handbook: The History of Christianity*. Oxford: Lion Publishing, 1977.
Drane, John. *The MacDonaldization of the Church—Spirituality, Creativity and the Future of the Church*. London: Darton, Longman & Todd, 2000.
Dunn, James. "Pentecostalism and the Charismatic Movement." In *A Lion Handbook: The History of Christianity*, edited by Tim Dowley, 646–50. Oxford: Lion Publishing, 1977.
Duplantis, Jesse. *Heaven: Close Encounters of the God Kind*. Tulsa: Harrison, 1996.
Dye, Colin. *Building a City Church*. Eastbourne, UK: Kingsway, 1993.
———. *The Cry of the Lost*. London: Mission to London, 1998.
———. "London Churches Unite behind KICC." *Revival Times* 8 (Feb 2006), 18, 19.
———. "MTL School of Evangelism." *Mission to London Official Souvenir Programme* 1998.
Eden, Martyn, ed. *Britain on the Brink: Major Trends in Society Today*. Nottingham, UK: Crossway, 1993.
———. "Challenging the Gay Lobby." *Idea* (Sep–Oct 1997) 5.
Edwards, Joel. "All Change." *Idea* (Nov–Dec 2000) 15.

Bibliography

———. "The British Afro-Caribbean Community." In *Britain on the Brink: Major Trends in Society Today*, edited by Martyn Eden, 100-118. Nottingham, UK: Crossway, 1993.

———. "Foreword." In *'Toronto' in Perspective: Papers on the New Charismatic Wave of the Mid 1990s*, edited by David Hilborn, xiii-xiv. Carlisle, UK: ACUTE, 2001.

———, ed. *Let's Praise Him Again! An African-Caribbean Perspective on Worship*. Eastbourne, UK: Kingsway, 1992.

———. *The Jamaican Diaspora: A People of Pain and Purpose*. Kingston, Jam.: Morgan Ministries International, 1998.

———. "Letter Re: Charity Commission." Dec 20, 2002.

———. "Letter to EA Personal Members." Aug 23, 2002.

———. *Lord, Make Us One—But Not All the Same: Seeking Unity in Diversity*. London: Hodder & Stoughton, 1999.

Edwards, Richard. "Children Sacrificed in London Churches, Say Police." *The Evening Standard* (Jun 16, 2005) 1.

Emah, Ekong. "Transition in Nigeria: The Daniels Are Coming to Power." *Harvestime* (Lagos) 3 (Jul-Sep 1993) 14.

Emmanuel, Tokunbo. *The Charismatic Agenda: What in the World Are We Up to?* London: Emmanuel, 2000.

———. *Ultimate Destiny: Locating Our Present Mandate in the Lord's Final Agenda*. London: Emmanuel, 2001.

Encinas-Meade, Andrea. "Campaigning for Racial Justice—14 September." *Focus* (Sep-Oct 1997) 1.

Evangelical Alliance. *Assembly of Evangelical Christian Leaders 2001 Programme*. London: The Evangelical Alliance, 2001.

———. "'Euston' Statement." In *'Toronto' in Perspective: Papers on the New Charismatic Wave of the Mid 1990s*, edited by David Hilborn, 351-55. Carlisle, UK: ACUTE, 2001.

———. *The Evangelical Alliance Annual Review 2004-2005*. London: The Evangelical Alliance, 2006.

———. "Hope for London." Steering Group Minutes, Evangelical Alliance archive.

———. *London Leaders' Steering Group Minutes*, 1991-. Evangelical Alliance archive.

———. *Membership Information for Churches*. London: The Evangelical Alliance, n.d.

———. "Quotes on . . . Prosperity Theology." Jan 1996.

———. *Shaping the Future Together: The National Assembly of Evangelicals, 1996 Programme*. London: The Evangelical Alliance, 1996.

———. "Stop the World, I Want to Get On!" *Shaping the Future Together: The National Assembly of Evangelicals, 1996 Programme*, 4-5. London: The Evangelical Alliance, 1996.

Evangelical Alliance/Christian Impact. "The Prosperity Gospel: A Report on the Discussion of the Theological Commission of Christian Impact/Evangelical Alliance." N.d.

Evangelical Alliance Policy Commission. "Transsexuality: A Report." Carlisle, UK: Paternoster, 2000.

Evans, Eifion. *The Welsh Revival of 1904*. London: The Evangelical Press, 1969.

Fackre, Gabriel. *Ecumenical Faith in Evangelical Perspective*. Grand Rapids, MI: Eerdmans, 1993.

Faith City Church. "Is There Life after Death?" *YouTube*, June 8, 2022. https://www.youtube.com/watch?v=hzMYSry4yr4.
"'Faith in the Future' Features Best of Black British." *Idea* (June–Aug 2000) 8.
"Faith in the Future." *Focus* (Nov 1999–Jan 2000) 19.
Farah, Charles. *From the Pinnacle of the Temple*. Plainfield, NJ: Logos International, n.d.
Ferdinando, Keith. "Screwtape Revisited: Demonology Western African, and Biblical." In *The Unseen World*, edited by Anthony N. S. Lane, 103–32. Carlisle, UK: Paternoster, 1996.
Fola-Alade, Sola. *Discover Your Hidden Treasures: Making the Most of Life's Gifts and Opportunities*. London: Vision Media Communications, 2002.
Forbes, David. "From North Battleford to Toronto." In *Blessing the Church? A Review of the History and Direction of the Charismatic Movement*, edited by Clifford Hill et al., 62–102. Stoke-on-Trent, UK: Harvey Christian, 1995.
"Former ACEA General Secretary to Lead Evangelical Alliance UK into the New Millennium." *Focus* (Sept–Oct 1997) 2.
Forster, Roger. "Foreword." In *Let's Praise Him Again! An African-Caribbean Perspective on Worship*, edited by Joel Edwards, 6–8. Eastbourne, UK: Kingsway, 1992.
Fraser, Giles. "Evangelicals Have Become This Century's Witch Burners." *The Guardian* (Jul 14, 2003). https://www.theguardian.com/world/2003/jul/14/religion.uk.
Frodsham, Stanley Howard. *Smith Wigglesworth, Apostle of Faith*. Nottingham, UK: Assemblies of God Publishing, 1949.
Geddes, Andrew P., and Jonathan Tonge, eds. *Labour's Second Landslide: The General Election 2001*. Manchester, UK: Manchester University Press, 2002.
Gehman, Richard J. *Doing African Christian Theology: an Evangelical Perspective*. Nairobi, Ken.: Evangel, 1987.
Gerloff, Roswith. "An African Continuum in Variation: The African Christian Diaspora in Britain." *Black Theology in Britain* 4 (2000) 84–112.
———. "Pentecostals in the African Diaspora." In *Pentecostals after a Century: Global Perspectives in a Movement in Transition*, edited by Allan H. Anderson and Walter J. Hollenweger, 67–86. Sheffield, UK: Sheffield Academic Press, 1999.
Gibson, Alan F. *The Church and Its Unity*. Leicester, UK: InterVarsity, 1992.
Gifford, Paul. *African Christianity: Its Public Role*. London: Hurst, 1998.
———. "The Bible as a Political Document in Africa." In *Scriptural Politics: The Bible and Koran as Political Models in the Middle East and Africa*, edited by Niels Kastfelt, 16–28. London: Hurst, 2003.
———. *Christianity: To Slave or Enslave?* Ecumenical Documentation and Information Centre of Eastern and Southern Africa, 1990.
———. "The Complex Provenance of Some Elements of African Pentecostal Theology." In *Between Babel and Pentecost: Transnational Pentecostalism in Africa and Latin America*, edited by André Marshall-Fratani and Ruth Marshall-Fratani, 62–79. Bloomington, IN: Indiana University Press, 2001.
———, ed. *The Christian Churches and the Democratisation of Africa*. Leiden, UK: Brill, 1995.
———. *Ghana's New Christianity: Pentecostalism in a Globalising African Economy*. Bloomington, IN: Indiana University Press, 2004.
———. "Prosperity: A New and Foreign Element in African Christianity." *Religion* 20 (1990) 373–88.

Bibliography

Gill, Perdeep, and Mor Dioum. "Community Partnership Project 2004-2005: Final Report." Aditi Consultancy Services for the Metropolitan Police, May 20, 2005. Cited with Metropolitan Police permission.

Gledhill, Ruth. "Black Churches Challenge Section 28." *The Times* (Jul 6, 2000) 15.

———. "Charity Law to End Fraud in Black Churches." *The Times* (Oct 6, 2004) 3.

———. "Christians Send an Invitation to Everyone." *The Times* (Nov 2, 1998).

———. "Pastor to Repay £200,000 after Buying Florida Timeshare on Church Visa Card." *The Times* (Jul 10, 2005) 3.

———. "Poor Christians Are Deluded by 'Grab It' Gospel." *The Times* (Mar 17, 2003) 4.

———. "Praying for Votes: Inside Britain's Bible Belt." *Times 2 Supplement* (Apr 19, 2000) 3-4.

———. "The Sound of Pure Faith." *The Times* (Jul 22, 2000).

———. "Spread of Hysteria, Fad Worries Church." *The Times* (Jun 18, 1994) 12.

"GOAL Conference Gets Results." *Focus* (June-Aug 2003) 12.

Gordon, Bob. *Personally Speaking: The Principles and Power of Anointed Preaching and Teaching*. Tonbridge, UK: Sovereign World, 1995.

Green, Frank. "Identificational Repentance—Is It Necessary? Is It Biblical?" Paper presented at the C.Net Theological Forum, September 1999.

Griffin-Allwood, P. G. A. "Contemporary Evangelicalism: A Question of Continuity." *Faith Today* (February 1988).

Gumbel, Nicky. *Telling Others*. Eastbourne, UK: Kingsway, 1994.

Hackett, Rosalind. "The Gospel of Prosperity in West Africa." In *Religion and the Transformations of Capitalism*, edited by R. H. Roberts, 199-214. London: Routledge, 1995.

Hallesby, Ole. *Prayer*. London: Inter-Varsity Fellowship, 1948.

"Hall of Shame." *Idea* (Apr-May 1998) 26-28.

Hamilton, Malcolm B. *The Sociology of Religion: Theoretical and Comparative Perspectives*. London: Routledge, 1995.

Hammond, Frank, and Ida Mae Hammond. *Pigs in the Parlour: A Practical Guide to Deliverance*. Kirkwood, MO: Impact, n.d.

Hamon, Bill. *Apostles, Prophets and the Coming Moves of God: God's End-Time Plan for His Church and Planet Earth*. Shippensburg, PA: Destiny Image Publishers, 1997.

Hand, Chris. "The Alpha Course: Is the Popular Alpha Course Leading People Astray?" http://www.banner.org.uk/misc/alpha.html.

Hanegraaff, Hank. *Christianity in Crisis*. Eugene, OR: Harvest, 1993.

Harper, Michael. *Spiritual Warfare*. London: Hodder & Stoughton, 1970.

Harris, Harriet A. "Fundamentalism in a Protestant Context." In *Fundamentalism, Church and Society*, edited by Martyn Percy and Ian Jones, 7-24. London: SPCK, 2002.

———. "How Helpful Is the Term 'Fundamentalist'?" In *Fundamentalisms*, edited by Christopher H. Partridge, 3-18. Carlisle, UK: Paternoster, 2001.

Hastings, Adrian. *A History of African Christianity 1950-1975*. Cambridge: Cambridge University Press, 1979.

———. *A History of English Christianity 1920-2000*. London: SCM, 2001.

———, ed. *A World History of Christianity*. London: Cassell, 1999.

Hathaway, Malcolm R. "The Elim Pentecostal Church: Origins, Developments and Distinctives." In *Pentecostal Perspectives*, edited by Keith Warrington, 1-39. Carlisle, UK: Paternoster, 1998.

———. "The Role of William Oliver Hutchinson and the Apostolic Faith Church in the Formation of the British Pentecostal Churches." *Journal of the European Pentecostal Theological Association* 15 (1996) 40–57.

"Have We Become Christian Pharisees?" *Idea* (Nov–Dec 1998) 11.

Haynes, Jeff. *Religion and Politics in Africa*. London: Zed, 1996.

———. *Religion, Fundamentalism and Ethnicity: A Global Perspective*. Geneva: UN Research Institute for Social Development, 1995.

Hayter, Teresa. *Open Borders*. London: Pluto, 2000.

Heimann, Mary. "Christianity in Western Europe from the Enlightenment." In *A World History of Christianity*, 458–507. London: Cassell, 1999.

Hemry, Melanie. "Heir to the Throne." *Believer's Voice of Victory* (Feb 2001) 9.

Hepburn, Ian. "Let Us Prey: 'Father-Figure' Churchman Forced Sex on Girls from Adoring Flock, Court Told." *The Sun* (May 22, 2003) 11.

Hesse, Barnor, ed. *Un/settled Multiculturalisms, Diasporas, Entanglements, Transruptions*. London: Zed, 2000.

Hickin, Marlene. *Uncomfortable Reality: Abuse, the Bible and the Church*. Swanley, UK: The Churches Child Protection Advisory Service, 2004.

Hicks, Peter. *Evangelicals and Truth: A Creative Proposal for a Postmodern Age*. Leicester, UK: Apollos, 1998.

Hiebert, Paul G. *Anthropological Insights for Missionaries*. Grand Rapids, MI: Baker, 1985.

———. "The Flaw of the Excluded Middle." *Missiology* (Jan 1982) 35–47.

Hilborn, David. "Beyond Belief." *Idea* (June–Aug 1998) 12–13.

———. "Letter Re: Prosperity Report." February 3, 2003.

———. "Long Overdue Apology." *Idea* (Mar–Apr 2002) 13.

———, ed. *Movement for Change: Evangelicals and Societal Transformation*. Carlisle, UK: Paternoster, 2004.

———. *Picking Up the Pieces: Can Evangelicals Adapt to Contemporary Culture?* London: Hodder & Stoughton, 1997.

———, ed. *"Toronto" in Perspective: Papers on the New Charismatic Wave of the Mid-1990s*. Carlisle, UK: ACUTE, 2001.

Hill, Clifford S. H. *Black and White in Harmony: The Drama of West Indians in the Big City from a London Minister's Notebook*. London: Hodder & Stoughton, 1958.

———. *West Indian Migrants and the London Churches*. London: Oxford University Press for the Institute of Race Relations, 1963.

Hill, Clifford, et al. *Blessing the Church? A Review of the History and Direction of the Charismatic Movement*. Stoke-on-Trent, UK: Harvey Christian, 1995.

Hocken, Peter. *Streams of Renewal: The Origins and Early Developments of the Charismatic Movement in Great Britain*. Rev. ed. Carlisle, UK: Paternoster, 1997.

Hollenweger, Walter J. *Pentecostalism: Origins and Developments Worldwide*. Peabody, MA: Hendrickson, 1997.

Holloway, Lester. "What the Juju Is Going On?" *Black Information Link* (June 17, 2005).

Holmes, Nigel. *Losing Faith in the BBC*. Carlisle, UK: Paternoster, 2000.

Horrobin, Peter. *Healing through Deliverance*. Vol. 2, *The Practice of Deliverance Ministry*. Grand Rapids, MI: Chosen, 2003.

Horrocks, Don. "No Condemnation." *Idea* (May–June, 2001) 27. http://www.blink.org.uk/pdescription.asp?key=7701&grp=1.

Hunt, Dave. *Whatever Happened to Heaven?* Eugene, OR: Harvest, 1988.

Hunt, Stephen. *Anyone for Alpha? Evangelism in a Post-Christian Society*. London: Darton, Longman & Todd, 2001.

———. "The British Black Pentecostal 'Revival': Identity and Belief in the New Nigerian Churches." *Ethnic and Racial Studies* 24 (2001) 104–24.

———. "The Devil's Advocates: The Function of Demonology in the World View of Fundamentalist Christianity." In *Fundamentalism, Church and Society*, edited by Martyn Percy and Ian Jones, 66–91. London: SPCK, 2002.

———. "The 'New' Black Pentecostal Churches in Britain." Paper presented at CESNUR conference, Riga, Latvia, August 2000. http://www.cesnur.org/conferences/riga2000/hunt.htm.

Hunt, Stephen, and Nikki Lightly. "Growing a Church for All Nations." *Renewal* 287 (Apr 2000) 12–15.

Hunt, Stephen J. *Alternative Religions: A Sociological Introduction*. Aldershot, UK: Ashgate, 2003.

Hylson-Smith, Ken. "Roots of Pan-Evangelicalism: 1735–1835." In *For Such a Time as This*, edited by Steve Brady and Harold Rowdon, 137–47. Milton Keynes, UK: Scripture Union, 1996.

Hywel-Davies, Jack. *Baptised by Fire: the Life of Smith Wigglesworth,* London: Hodder & Stoughton, 1987.

———. *The Kensington Temple Story*. Crowborough, UK: Monarch, 1998.

"Incitement to Religious Hatred: Growing Disagreement between Christians." *Ekklesia* (January 18, 2005). http://www.ekklesia.co.uk/content/news_syndication/article _050118hatred.shtml.

Irvine, Doreen. *From Witchcraft to Christ*. London: Concordia, 1973.

Jackson, Robert. "Prosperity Theology and the Faith Movement." *Themelios* 15 (Oct 1989) 16–24.

James, Philip. "For God's Sake." *Guardian Unlimited* (Apr 23, 2004). http://www.guardian.co.uk/uselections2004/story/0,13918,1201933,00.html.

James, Rob. "Popular Bible Teacher Quits." *Christian Herald* (Jan 5, 2003). http://www.jmm.org.au/articles/8075.htm.

Jehu-Appiah, Jerisdan H. "An Overview of Indigenous African Churches in Britain: An Approach through the Historical Survey of African Pentecostalism." Paper presented at the Consultation between the World Council of Churches and African and African-Caribbean Church Leaders in Britain, Leeds, Nov 30–Dec 12, 1995. http://www.pctii.org/wcc/jehu95.html.

Jefferson, Bill, and Derek Williams. *Billy Graham Mission '89: From London to the World*. Minneapolis: Billy Graham Evangelistic Association, 1990.

Jenkins, Philip. *The Next Christendom: The Coming of Global Christianity*. Oxford: Oxford University Press, 2002.

John, Cindi. "Exorcisms Are Part of Our Culture." *BBC News*, June 3, 2005. http://news.bbc.co.uk/1/hi/uk/4596127.stm.

Johnson, Douglas. *Contending for the Faith: A History of the Evangelical Movement in the Universities and Colleges*. Leicester, UK: InterVarsity, 1979.

Kastfelt, Neils, ed. *Scriptural Politics: The Bible and the Koran as Political Models in the Middle East and Africa*. London: Hurst, 2003.

Kay, William. "Assemblies of God." In *Pentecostal Perspectives*, edited by Keith Warrington, 40–63. Carlisle, UK: Paternoster, 1998.

Kay, William K. *Pentecostals in Britain*. Carlisle, UK: Paternoster, 2000.

Kendall, R. T. *In Pursuit of His Glory*. London: Hodder & Stoughton, 2002.
Kennedy, John. *The Torch of the Testimony*. Bombay, IN: Gospel Literature Service, 1965.
KICC. "Birth of KICC." In *Winning Ways* (March 2002) 5.
———. *Friends of KICC* 1 (Feb 2006).
———. "London Calling." In *Winning Ways* (March 2002) 5.
———. "Prophecy for KICC." April 12, 2002.
Killingray, David, ed. *Africans in Britain*. Ilford, UK: Cass, 1994.
Küng, Hans, and Jürgen Moltmann, eds. *Fundamentalism as an Ecumenical Challenge*. London: SCM, 1992.
Künneth, Walter, and Peter Beyerhaus, eds. *Reich Gottes oder Weltgemeinschaft*. Bad Liebenzell, Germ.: Verlag der Liebenzeller Mission, 1975.
Lake, J. G. *The Astounding Diary of John G. Lake*. Dallas: Christ for the Nations, 1987.
Lamming, Lord. *The Victoria Climbié Inquiry: Summary and Recommendations*. Norwich, UK: HMSO 2003.
Lane, Anthony N. S. *The Unseen World*. Carlisle, UK: Paternoster, 1996.
Larbi, E. Kingsley. *Pentecostalism: The Eddies of Ghanaian Christianity*. Accra, Ghan.: Centre for Pentecostal and Charismatic Studies, 2001.
Lewis, C. S. *The Screwtape Letters*. New York: Macmillan, 1961.
Lewis, Peter. "Renewal, Recovery and Growth: 1966 Onwards." In *For Such a Time as This*, edited by Steve Brady and Harold Rowdon, 178–91. Milton Keynes, UK: Scripture Union, 1996.
Liardon, Roberts. *I Saw Heaven*. Tulsa: Harrison, 1983.
Little, Matthew. "Pay Scandals Provoke New Rules for Churches." *Third Sector* (Nov 16, 2005) 1.
Lloyd-Jones, D. M. *What Is an Evangelical?* Edinburgh, UK: Banner of Truth, 1992.
Lowe, Chuck. *Territorial Spirits and World Evangelisation?* Sevenoaks, UK: OMF, 1998.
MacPherson of Cluny. *The Inquiry into the Matters Arising from the Death of Stephen Lawrence*. February 15, 1999. http://www.archive.official-documents.co.uk/document/cm42/4262/sli-06.htm.
MacRobert, Iain. "Black Pentecostalism: Its Origins, Functions and Theology with Special Reference to a Midland Borough." PhD diss., University of Birmingham, 1989.
"The Man Who Saw Heaven." *Alive* (Dec 1999) 4.
Marshall-Fratani, Ruth. "Meeting the Global and Local in Nigerian Pentecostalism." In *Between Babel and Pentecost: Transnational Pentecostalism in Africa and Latin America*, edited by André Corten and Ruth Marshall-Fratani, 80–105. Bloomington, IN: Indiana University Press, 2001.
Marshall, Ruth. "'God Is Not a Democrat': Pentecostalism and Democratisation in Nigeria." In *The Christian Churches and the Democratisation of Africa*, edited by P. Gifford, 239–60. Leiden, UK: Brill, 1995.
———. "Mediating the Global and Local in Nigerian Pentecostalism." *Journal of Religion in Africa* 28 (1998), 278–315.
———. "Power in the Name of Jesus: Societal Transformation and Pentecostalism in Western Nigeria Revisited." In *Legitimacy and the State in Twentieth Century Africa*, edited by T. Ranger and O. Vaughan, 213–46. Oxford: Macmillan, 1993.
Martin, David. *Pentecostalism: The World Their Parish*. Oxford: Blackwell, 2002.

———. *Tongues of Fire: The Explosion of Protestantism in Latin America.* Oxford: Blackwell, 1990.
Martin, S. I. *Britain's Slave Trade.* London: Channel 4 Books, 1999.
Marty, Martin E. "What Is Fundamentalism? Theological Perspectives." In *Fundamentalism as an Ecumenical Challenge,* edited by Hans Küng and Jürgen Moltmann, 1–11. London: SCM, 1992.
Massey, Richard. *Another Springtime: The Life of Donald Gee, Pentecostal Leader and Teacher.* Guildford: Highland, 1992.
Masters, Peter. *The Healing Epidemic.* London: Wakeman Trust, 1988.
Maxwell, David. "African Gifts of the Spirit: Fundamentalism and the Rise of the Born-Again Movement in Africa." In *Fundamentalism, Church and Society,* edited by Martyn Percy and Ian Jones, 168–69. London: SPCK, 2002.
———. "Delivered from the Spirit of Poverty: Pentecostalism, Prosperity and Modernity in Zimbabwe." *Journal of Religion in Africa* 28 (1998) 350–73.
Mbiti, John S. *African Religions and Philosophy.* Nairobi, Ken.: East African Educational, 1969.
———. *Introduction to African Religion.* 2nd ed. Nairobi, Ken.: East African Educational, 1991.
McConnell, Dan. *The Promise of Health and Wealth: A Historical and Biblical Analysis of the Modern Faith Movement.* London: Hodder & Stoughton, 1990.
McCrossan, T. J. *Bodily Healing and the Atonement.* Tulsa, OK: Faith Library Publications, 1994.
McGrath, Alister. *Evangelicalism and the Future of Christianity.* London: Hodder & Stoughton, 1994.
"Media Spotlight on EA over Homosexual Sex." *Idea* (Jan–Mar 1997) 31.
"Meet Joel Edwards." *Idea* (Sept–Oct 1997) 22.
"Men Who Obeyed God: Benson Idahosa." *Miracle Healing Faith* 3 (Feb 2005) 33.
Meyer, Birgit. "Commodities and the Power of Prayer: Pentecostalist Attitudes Towards Consumption in Contemporary Ghana." In *Globalization and Identity: Dialectics of Flow and Closure,* edited by Birgit Meyer and Peter Geschiere, 151–76. Oxford: Blackwell, 1999.
———. "Pentecostalism, Prosperity and Popular Cinema in Ghana." *Culture and Religion: An Interdisciplinary Journal* 3 (May 2002) 67–87.
———. *Translating the Devil: Religion and Modernity among the Ewe in Ghana.* Edinburgh, UK: Edinburgh University Press, 1999.
Meyer, Birgit, and Peter Geschiere, eds. *Globalization and Identity: Dialectics of Flow and Closure.* Oxford: Blackwell, 1999.
Middlemiss, David. *Interpreting Charismatic Experience.* London: SCM, 1996.
"A Mighty Wind from Toronto." *HTB in Focus* (August 14, 1994) 10.
"Millennium Celebration—'Faith in the Future.'" *Focus* (Apr–June 1999) 13.
Miller, Donald E. *Reinventing American Protestantism; Christianity in the New Millennium.* Berkeley, CA: University of California Press, 1997.
Mills, Brian, and Roger Mitchell. *Sins of the Fathers.* Tonbridge, UK: Sovereign World, 1999.
Missed, Alfred. "Peace Prevails While Bombs Fall." *Joy Magazine* 107 (Aug 2003) 27–28.
Mission to London. "Mission to London 1992." *Mission to London Newsletter* 2 (June 1993) 6–7.
Mohabir, Philip. *Building Bridges.* London: Hodder & Stoughton, 1988.

Molyneux, Gordon K. *African Christian Theology: The Quest for Selfhood*. Lampeter, UK: Mellen University Press, 1993.

Montgomery, Jim. *Dawn 2000: 7 Million Churches to Go*. Crowborough, UK: Highland, 1990.

Moore, Natalie Y. "Black Republicans: A Turn in the Culture Wars." *Open Democracy* (Feb 10, 2006). https://www.opendemocracy.net/en/black_republicans_3256jsp/.

Morgan, Timothy C. "The Alpha-Brits Are Coming." *Christianity Today* (Feb 1998). https://www.christianitytoday.com/ct/1998/february9/8t2036.html.

Moynagh, Michael. *Changing Church: Changing World*. London: Monarch, 2001.

Mugambi, J. N. Kanyua. *African Christian Theology: An Introduction*. Nairobi, Ken.: East African Educational Publishers, 1989.

Murray, Iain H. *Evangelicalism Divided: A Record of Crucial Change in the Years 1950–2000*. Edinburgh, UK: Banner of Truth, 2000.

Mwangi, Sophia. "Brighton Rocks to Blair and Hague." *Focus* (Sep–Nov 2000) 9.

Nanjo, James Osborn. *The Dynamic of Moral Integrity*. London: Emmanuel, 2001.

Nathan, Ronald A. "Pan-Africanism: What of the Twenty-First Century? A British Program." *Black Theology in Britain* 4 (May 2000) 9–21.

Nazir-Ali, Michael, and Derek Pattinson, eds. *The Truth Shall Make You Free*. Anglican Consultative Council, 1988.

Neil Richardson. "The Toronto Blessing: A Different Gospel (Alan Morrison, 1994)." *YouTube*, February 7, 2012. https://www.youtube.com/watch?v=eYmSoAWgQ44.

Newbigin, Lesslie. *The Gospel in a Pluralist Society*. Grand Rapids, MI: Eerdmans, 1989.

Nicholls, C. S. *David Livingstone*. Stroud, UK: Sutton, 1998.

Noakes, David. "A Personal and Biblical Perspective on Renewal." In *Blessing the Church? A Review of the History and Direction of the Charismatic Movement*, edited by Clifford Hill et al., 146–50. Stoke-on-Trent, UK: Harvey Christian Publishers, 1995.

"No Apologies for IR Meeting." *Idea* (Sept–Oct 2001) 5.

Noble, John. *Forgive Us Our Denominations*. Private publication. 1973.

O'Callaghan, Sean. "Review of 'Introduction to Pentecostalism.'" *Themelios* 31 (Oct 2005) 103–4.

O'Donovan, Wilbur. *Biblical Christianity in Modern Africa*. Carlisle, UK: Paternoster, 2000.

———. *Introduction to Biblical Christianity from an African Perspective*. Ilorin, Nig.: Nigeria Evangelical Fellowship, 1992.

Ojo, Matthews A. "Campus Christianity in West Africa." PhD diss., London University, 1987.

———. "The Church in the African State: The Charismatic/Pentecostal Experience in Nigeria." *Journal of African Thought* 1 (1998) 25–32.

Oke, Francis Wale. *The Power That Works in Us*. London: Victory Literature Crusade, 1993.

Okonkwo, Mike. *Breakthrough on Your Knees*. Lagos, Nig.: Dunamis, 1995.

Olasky, Marvin. *Compassionate Conservatism*. New York: Free Press, 2000.

Omole, Charles. *Prosperity Unleashed: A Definitive Christian Guide to Biblical Economics*. London: Winning Faith Outreach Ministries, 2005.

Omoyajowo, J. Akinyele. *Cherubim and Seraphim: The History of an African Independent Church*. Lagos, Nig.: NOK, 1982.

Onyinah, Opoku. "Akan Witchcraft and the Concept of Exorcism in the Church of Pentecost." PhD diss., Birmingham University, 2002.
———. "God's Grace, Healing and Suffering." *International Review of Mission* 95 (Jan/Apr 2006) 117–27.
Osgood, Hugh. "Prosperity Teaching and Evangelical Unity." Unpublished paper for the ACUTE Consultation on Prosperity Teaching, June 2, 1998.
———. "Some Eschatological and Soteriological Aspects of Prosperity Teaching." Unpublished paper presented to the ACUTE Study Group on Prosperity Teaching, 1999.
———. "Survey of London Oversight Boundaries." Presentation to *Key London Leaders*, May 1997.
Oshun, Christopher O. "Aladura Evangelists in Britain: An Assessment of Spiritual Adventurism." *Journal of Black Theology in Britain* 3 (1999) 9–32.
———. "Christ Apostolic Church of Nigeria, 1918–1978." PhD diss., University of Exeter, 1981.
Owens, Richard. "The Azusa Street Revival: The Pentecostal Movement Begins in America." *The Century of the Holy Spirit: 100 years of Pentecostal and Charismatic Renewal*, edited by Vinson Synan, 39–68. Nashville: Nelson, 2001.
———. "Pope Asks for Forgiveness over Crusades." *The Times* (Mar 13, 2000) 5L.
Packer, J. I. *The Evangelical Anglican Identity Problem: An Analysis*. Oxford: Latimer, 1978.
Pain, Timothy, and Clive Manning. *Miracles Are Impossible: You Decide*. Robertsbridge, UK: Battle, 1993.
Pakenham, Thomas. *The Scramble for Africa*. London: Abacus, 1992.
Parker, Russ. *Healing Wounded History*. London: Darton, Longman & Todd, 2001.
Parratt, John. *Reinventing Christianity: African Theology Today*. Grand Rapids, MI: Eerdmans, 1995.
Parrinder, E. Geoffrey. *West African Religion: A Study of the Beliefs and Practices of Akan, Ewe, Yoruba, Ibo, and Kindred Peoples*. 2nd ed. London: Epworth, 1961.
Partridge, Christopher H., ed. *Fundamentalisms*. Carlisle, UK: Paternoster, 2001.
Pawson, David. "A Mixed Blessing." In *'Toronto' in Perspective: Papers on the New Charismatic Wave of the Mid 1990s*, edited by David Hilborn, 75–87. Carlisle, UK: ACUTE, 2001.
———. *Word and Spirit Together: Uniting Charismatics and Evangelicals*. 2nd ed. London: Hodder & Stoughton, 1998.
Peek, Laura. "Prosperity Is the Promise of God." *The Times* (Mar 17, 2003) 4.
Peel, J. D. Y. *Aladura: A Religious Movement amongst the Yoruba*. Oxford: Oxford University Press, 1968.
———. *Religious Encounter and the Making of the Yoruba*. Bloomington, IN: Indiana University Press, 2000.
Percy, Martyn. "'Join-the-Dots Christianity'—Assessing ALPHA." *Reviews in Religion and Theology* 4 (1997) 14–18.
Percy, Martyn, and Ian Jones, eds. *Fundamentalism, Church and Society*. London: SPCK, 2002.
Perriman, Andrew, ed. *Faith, Hope and Prosperity: A Report on 'Word of Faith' and 'Positive Confession' Theologies by The Evangelical Alliance (UK) Commission on Unity and Truth among Evangelicals*. Carlisle, UK: Paternoster, 2003.

Petre, Jonathan. "Church to Spend £2m on Sex and Lies Advert." *Sunday Telegraph* (Oct 21, 2001) 15.

Petre, Jonathan, and George Jones. "'Keep Election Religion-Free', Says Blair." *Daily Telegraph* (Mar 23, 2005) 8.

"Pilgrimage Home and Away." *Idea* (Jan–Mar 1997) 1–2.

"Pioneer Finds New Trail." *Focus* (Aug–Oct 1999) 13.

"Politicians Should Have the Courage of Their Faith." *Daily Telegraph* (March 3, 2005).

Pollock, John. *The Cambridge Seven*. London: InterVarsity, 1966.

Poloma, Margaret M. "The 'Toronto Blessing' in Postmodern Society: Manifestations, Metaphor and Myth." In *The Globalization of Pentecostalism: A Religion Made to Travel*, edited by Murray W. Dempster et al., 363–85. Carlisle, UK: Regnum, 1999.

———. "A Reconfiguration of Pentecostalism." In *"Toronto" in Perspective: Papers on the New Charismatic Wave of the Mid-1990s*, edited by David Hilborn, 99–127. Carlisle: ACUTE, 2001.

Poole-Conner, E. J. *Evangelicalism in England*. Worthing, UK: Walter, 1966.

Pope-Hennessy, James. *Sins of the Fathers: The Atlantic Slave Trade 1441–1807*. London: Phoenix, 2000.

Price, Charles, and Ian Randall. *Transforming Keswick: The Keswick Convention Past, Present and Future*. Carlisle, UK: OM Publishing, 2000.

Prince, Derek. *They Shall Expel Demons: What You Need to Know about Demons—Your Invisible Enemies*. Baldock, UK: Derek Prince Ministries, 1998.

"Protests as BBC Screens Springer." *BBC News* (Jan 10, 2005). http://news.bbc.co.uk/1/hi/entertainment/tv_and_radio/4154071.stm.

Quinn, James, dir. *God Is Black*. United Kingdom: Diverse Productions, 2004. https://www.imdb.com/title/tt1209327/.

Randall, Ian. "Old Time Power: Relationships between Pentecostalism and Evangelical Spirituality in England." *PNEUMA: The Journal of the Society for Pentecostal Studies* 19 (Spring 1997) 53–80.

———. "Schism and Unity: 1905–1966." In *For Such a Time as This*, edited by Steve Brady and Harold Rowdon, 163–77. Milton Keynes, UK: Scripture Union, 1996.

Randall, Ian, and David Hilborn. *One Body in Christ: The History and Significance of the Evangelical Alliance*. Carlisle, UK: Paternoster, 2001.

Ranger, Terence, and Olufemi Vaughan, eds. *Legitimacy and the State in Twentieth-Century Africa*. Oxford: Macmillan, 1993.

Ravenhill, Leonard. *Why Revival Tarries*. Minneapolis: Bethany Fellowship, 1979.

Reader, John. *Africa: A Biography of a Continent*. London: Penguin, 1998.

Reddie, Richard. "Christians Urged to Fight the Evils of Racism." *Focus* (Sept–Nov 1998) 1.

———. "Is the Charity Commission Undermining Leadership in the Church?" *Focus* (Mar–May 2003) 7.

———. "Stars in Their Eyes." *Focus* (Mar–May 2002) 6–7.

Reid, Gavin. *To Reach a Nation: The Challenge of Evangelism in a Mass-Media Age*. London: Hodder & Stoughton, 1987.

Reid, Michael S. B. *Strategic Level Spiritual Warfare: A Modern Mythology?* Fairfax, VA: Xulon, 2002.

Rennie, Simon. "The War Room." *M25 Prayernet* 2 (Feb 2000).

Renwick, A. M., and A. M. Harman. *The Story of the Church*. 3rd ed. Leicester, UK: InterVarsity, 1998.

Richards, Anne. "The Toronto Experience, an Exploration of the Issues." Board of Mission Occasional Paper no. 7, Church House Publishing, 1997.
Ritzer, George. *The MacDonaldization of Society.* Thousand Oaks, CA: Pine Forge Press, 1993.
———. *The MacDonaldization Thesis: Explorations and Extensions.* Thousand Oaks, CA: Pine Forge, 1998.
Roberts, R. H., ed. *Religion and the Transformations of Capitalism.* London: Routledge, 1995.
Robinson, Chidi, and Yinka Olaleye. "African Congress on Evangelism in Focus." *Power in the Word* (The Redeemed Evangelical Mission's Publication) 3 (Oct 1992) 8–10.
Rosman, Doreen. *The Evolution of the English Churches 1500–2000.* Cambridge: Cambridge University Press, 2003.
Sanneh, Lamin, and Joel A. Carpenter, eds. *The Changing Face of Christianity: Africa, the West, and the World.* Oxford: Oxford University Press, 2005.
"Saying Sorry." *Idea* (June–Aug 2000) 19–21.
Schaefer, Nancy A. "Morris Cerullo's London Revivals as 'Glocal' (Neo-)Pentecostal Movement Events." *Culture and Religion* 3 (May 2002) 103–23.
Scotland, Nigel. *Charismatics and the New Millennium.* 2nd ed. Guildford: Eagle, 2000.
"Section 28 Row Intensifies." *BBC News* (Jan 25, 2000). http://news.bbc.co.uk/1/hi/uk_politics/618034.stm.
Segun, Gbenga. "Robed in White: Syncretistic, Sects or Just Another Denomination?" *Focus* (Aug–Oct 1999) 10–11.
Sentamu, John. "The Damilola Taylor Murder Investigation Review." December 2002. https://image.guardian.co.uk/sys-files/Guardian/documents/2002/12/09/damilola.pdf.
Setiloane, Gabriel. "Where Are We in African Theology?" In *All African Lutheran Consultation on Christian Theology and Christian Education in the African Context,* edited by Alison Bares, 15–26. Gaborone, Botsw.: Lutheran World Federation Department of Church Cooperation, 1978.
Seyi-Ogedengbe, Paul. *The African Story: A Scriptural Perspective for the Stirring up and Transformation of Black People across the Earth.* Lagos, Nig.: The Lord Reigns Ministries, 2002.
Shaull, Richard, and Waldo Cesar. *Pentecostalism and the Future of the Christian Churches: Promises, Limitations, Challenges.* Grand Rapids, MI: Eerdmans, 2000.
Shaw, Adrian. "Women 'Lured by Sex Pest Pastor.'" *Daily Mirror* (May 22, 2003).
Sheppard, David. *Bias to the Poor.* London: Hodder & Stoughton, 1983.
Shifrin, Tash. "Church Victorious in Management Wrangle." *The Guardian* (Jan 21, 2004). https://www.theguardian.com/society/2004/jan/21/charitymanagement.uknews.
Sizer, Stephen. "A Sub-Christian Movement." In *'Toronto' in Perspective: Papers on the New Charismatic Wave of the Mid 1990s,* edited by David Hilborn, 45–63. Carlisle, UK: ACUTE, 2001.
Slater, Ross. "It's Easy to Set Up a Church." *New Nation* (Nov 4, 2002).
Spear, Thomas, and Isaria Kimambo, eds. *East African Expressions of Christianity.* Athens, OH: Ohio University Press, 1999.
Spurgeon, Charles H. *An All-Round Ministry.* London: Banner of Truth, 1960.

Bibliography

Staff Writers. "Evangelical Alliance Lays into Popular Black Theologian over C4 Documentary." *Ekklesia* (June 16, 2004). http://www.ekklesia.co.uk/content/news_syndication/article_040616black.shtml.

Stickler, Angus. "Church of Christ the Mission." *Today* (Jan 12, 2006).

"Stop the Racial and Religious Hatred Bill." *Christian Voice* (n.d.). https://web.archive.org/web/20051124155152/http://www.christianvoice.org.uk/hate.html.

Stormont, George. *Wigglesworth: A Man Who Walked with God*. Chichester, UK: Sovereign World, 1990.

Stott, John R. W. *The Baptism and Fullness of the Holy Spirit*. London: InterVarsity, 1964.

———. *Baptism and Fullness: The Work of the Holy Spirit Today*. Leicester, UK: InterVarsity, 1975.

———. *Calling Christian Leaders: Biblical Models of Church, Gospel and Ministry*. Leicester, UK: InterVarsity, 2002.

———. *The Cross of Christ*. Leicester, UK: InterVarsity, 1986.

———. *Evangelical Truth: A Personal Plea for Unity*. Leicester, UK: InterVarsity, 1999.

"Struggling for Unity." *Idea* (Jan–Mar 1997) 3.

Sturge, Mark. "BMCs Response to the Stephen Lawrence Murder." Draft paper circulated to ACEA Council members, March 1999.

———. "Churches under the Spotlight: Don't Let Satan Take Advantage." *Focus* (Mar–May 2003) 10.

———. *Look What the Lord Has Done! An Exploration of Black Christian Faith in Britain*. Bletchley, UK: Scripture Union, 2005.

———. "Lord, Have Mercy on Us All!" *Focus* (Jan–Mar 2001) 10–11.

———. "We're So Sorry!" *Focus* (Aug–Oct 2004) 10.

———. "Where Are the Apostles and Prophets? Why Is There So Little Accountability Among Leaders?" *Focus* (Sept–Dec 2002) 10–11.

———. "Why Is the Issue of Racism Such a Taboo in Our Churches?" *Focus* (Aug–Oct 1999) 6–7.

Sturge, Mark, and Joe Aldred, eds. *Black Majority Churches UK Directory 2003/4*. London: ACEA and CTBI, 2003.

Subritzky, Bill. *Demons Defeated*. Chichester, UK: Sovereign World, 1986.

Sugirtharajab, R. S., ed. *Vernacular Hermeneutics*. Sheffield, UK: Sheffield Academic Press, 1999.

"Summertime, and the Living Is Busy . . ." *Idea* (Sept–Oct 2001) 4.

Sundkler, Bengt G. M. *Bantu Prophets in South Africa*. London: Oxford University Press, 1961.

Sylvester, Rachel. "Hague's Latest Helper Believes Right Is Right." *Daily Telegraph* (June 24, 2000).

———. "Hague to Consider 'Christian Welfare.'" *Daily Telegraph* (June 20, 2000) 11.

Sylvester, Rachel, and Benedict Brogan. "Labour and Tories Put Faith in Wooing the 'Spiritual Vote.'" *Daily Telegraph* (June 22, 2000) 10.

Synan, Vinson. *The Century of the Holy Spirit: 100 Years of Pentecostal and Charismatic Renewal*. Nashville, TN: Nelson, 2001.

———. "Introduction." In *Azusa Street*, edited by Frank Bartleman, ix–xxv. Plainfield, NJ: Logos International, 1980.

Taylor, John V. *The Go-Between God: The Holy Spirit and the Christian Mission*. London: SCM, 1972.

Ter Haar, Gerrie. *Halfway to Paradise: African Christians in Europe*. Cardiff, UK: Cardiff Academic Press, 1998.

Thompson, Damian. *Waiting for Antichrist: Charisma and Apocalypse in a Pentecostal Church*. Oxford: Oxford University Press, 2005.

Thwaites, James. *The Church beyond the Congregation*. Carlisle, UK: Paternoster, 1999.

Tidball, Derek. *Who Are the Evangelicals?* London: Marshall Pickering, 1994.

Tomlinson, Dave. "Foreword." In *The Promise of Health and Wealth: A Historical and Biblical Analysis of the Modern Faith Movement*, edited by Dan McConnell, ix–xiii. London: Hodder & Stoughton, 1990.

———. *The Post-Evangelical*. London: Triangle SPCK, 1995.

"The Tory Party at Prayer." *Daily Telegraph* (June 24, 2000).

Toulis, Nicole Rodriguez. *Believing Identity: Pentecostalism and the Mediation of Jamaican Ethnicity and Gender in England*. Oxford: Berg, 1997.

Turner, Harold W. *African Independent Church*. Oxford: Clarendon, 1967.

———. *Religious Innovation in Africa*. Boston: Hall, 1979.

Ungar, Merrill. *Demons in the World Today: A Study of Occultism in the Light of God's Word*." Wheaton, IL: Tyndale, 1971.

Vallely, Paul. "The Believers." *The Independent* (July 18, 2005) 34.

Vamadeva, Charles, and Ian Thompson. *A Directory of London Church/Ministry Profiles 1993*. London: Jubilee, 1993.

Van Dijk, Rijk. "The Soul Is the Stranger: Ghanaian Pentecostalism and the Diasporic Contestation of 'Flow' and 'Individuality.'" *Culture and Religion* 3 (2002) 49–65.

———. "Time and Transcultural Technologies of the Self in the Ghanaian Pentecostal Diaspora." In *Between Babel and Pentecost: Transnational Pentecostalism in Africa and Latin America*, edited by André Corten and Ruth Marshall-Fratani, 216–34. Bloomington, IN: Indiana University Press, 2001.

Vanhoozer, Kevin J. "Evangelicalism and the Church: The Company of the Gospel." In *The Futures of Evangelicalism: Issues and Prospects*, edited by Craig Bartholomew, Robin Parry and Andrew West, 40–99. Leicester, UK: InterVarsity, 2003.

Vann, David. "Faith and the General Election." *Focus* (May–Aug 2005) 7.

Vasey, Michael. *Strangers and Friends*. London: Hodder & Stoughton, 1995.

Vaughan, I. J. *Nigeria: The Origins of Apostolic Church Pentecostalism 1931–52*. Ipswich, UK: Ipswich Book Company, 1991.

"Vote of Confidence." *Idea* (Mar–Apr 2001) 16–17.

Wagner, C. Peter, ed. *Territorial Spirits: Insights into Strategic-Level Spiritual Warfare and Intercession*. Chichester, UK: Sovereign World, 1991.

Wagner, C. P., and F. Douglas Pennoyer, eds. *Wrestling with Dark Angels*. Eastbourne, UK: Monarch, 1990.

Walker, Andrew. *Restoring the Kingdom: The Radical Christianity of the House Church Movement*. Rev. and exp. ed. Guildford, UK: Eagle, 1998.

———. "Foreword." In *Anyone for Alpha? Evangelism in a Post-Christian Society*, by Stephen Hunt, vii–xvi. London: Darton, Longman & Todd, 2001.

Ward, Kevin. "Africa." In *A World History of Christianity*, edited by Adrian Hastings, 192–237. London: Cassell, 1999.

Ward, Kevin, and Brian Stanley, eds. *The Church Mission Society and World Christianity, 1799–1999*. Grand Rapids, MI: Eerdmans, 2000.

Ward, Pete. *Liquid Church*. Carlisle, UK: Paternoster, 2002.

Warner, Rob. *21st Century Church: Preparing Your Church for the New Millennium*. Rev. and exp. ed. Eastbourne, UK: Kingsway, 1999.

———. *Prepare for Revival*. London: Hodder & Stoughton, 1995.

Warren, Rick. *The Purpose Driven Church; Growth without Compromising Your Message or Mission*. Grand Rapids, MI: Zondervan, 1995.

Warrington, Keith, ed. *Pentecostal Perspectives*. Carlisle, UK: Paternoster, 1998.

Watson, Bernard. *A Hundred Years' War: The Salvation Army*. London: Hodder & Stoughton, 1965.

Watson, David. *You Are My God*. London: Hodder & Stoughton, 1983.

Westhead, James. "Abuse Case Sparks New Fears." *BBC News* (June 3, 2005). http://news.bbc.co.uk/1/hi/uk/4602543.stm.

"What's On Their Minds?" *Focus* (Jan–Mar 2001) 12.

"When ACEA Speaks . . ." *Focus* (Feb–Apr 2000) 13.

"When Superman Slips." *Idea* (Jan–Mar 2000) 21–23.

Whittaker, J. "Black Spirituality as a Key Dimension of the Pentecostal Movement." Unpublished BA research submitted to ANCC, June 1997.

Wilkinson, John Lawrence. "Church in Black and White—The Black Christian Tradition in 'Mainstream' Churches in England: A White Response and Testimony." M.Litt. thesis, University of Birmingham, 1990.

Wimber, John. *Power Evangelism*. London: Hodder & Stoughton, 1985.

"Window of Opportunity." *Idea* (May–June 2001) 20–22.

Wither, James K. "British Bulldog or Bush's Poodle? Anglo-American Relations and the Iraq War." *Parameters* 33 (2003) 67.

"Without Prejudice? Exploring Ethnic Differences in London: Key Findings." http://www.blacklondon.org.uk/news/rptwoutprejudice.htm.

Wolffe, John. "Protestant Societies and Anti-Catholic Agitation in Great Britain, 1829–1860." PhD diss. Oxford, 1984.

Woodroffe, Noel. *The Ultimate Warrior: Avoiding Defilement*. Trinidad: EMI, 1994.

———. *Understanding God's Prophetic Move Today*. Trinidad: Elijah Ministries International, 1991.

Woodroffe, Noel, and Graham Taylor. *Spiritual Government*. Trinidad: EMI, 1994.

Yaqoob, Tahira. "Minister 'Groomed' Teenage Girls for Sexual Assaults." *Daily Mail* (May 22, 2003) 43.

"Your Voice in Parliament." *Idea* (Jan–Feb 2006) 4.

Index

abuse, caution and concern regarding
  of "Adam," 191–94
  of Child B, 189–94
  of Damilola Taylor, 187–89
  overview of, 185
  of Victoria Climbié, 185–87
Accra International Worship Center (Pentecostal International Worship Centre), 52
activism, defined, xxii
"Adam," 191–94
Adebayo, Clement, 141
Adeboye, Enoch Adejare, 48, 49, 73, 80, 117
Adegboye, George, 56, 63, 77
Adeyemi, Tayo, 227
Adeyemo, Tokunboh, 45
adiaphora, 243
Adu-Gyamfi, Mark, 60, 61–62
Advertising Standards Authority, 120
African and Caribbean Evangelical Alliance (ACEA)
  accountability and, 209
  approval from, 208
  conference of, 135–36
  delegation of, 139
  Faith in the Future conference of, 178
  investigation by, 212–14
  Making the Grade conference of, 180–81
  membership policy of, 143–44
  name change of, 29
  press release of, 217–18
  quote of, 229
  speaking out of, 245–46
  submissions of, 193–94
  unity plea of, 135–36
African identity, issues of
  British charismatic identificational repentance events and, 124–33
  changes in British public opinion and, 137–40
  Highway and, 133–37
  independence and, 140–44
African Independent Churches, 47
African Initiated Churches, 36, 50
African neo-Pentecostalism
  benefits of, 245
  Caribbean neo-Pentecostalism compared to, 141
  deliverance practice of, 200–201
  effect of initial evangelical input in, 31–34
  emergence of less culturally adjusted forms of Christianity in, 46–52
  importing of a globalized neo-Pentecostalism and, 52–57
  momentum of, 239–40
  overview of, 57–58
  Pentecostal missionary endeavor in, 35–46
  prayer style of, 115–16, 117
  review of literature of, 255–65
  See also specific churches
Africans, in Britain, conditions of, 141–42
Afro-Caribbean Evangelical Alliance, 83, 111

(Afro-Caribbean Evangelical Alliance continued). See also West Indian Evangelical Alliance (WIEA)
Afro West-Indian United Council of Churches (AWUCOC), 28
Ajah, Friday Thomas, 128
Akande, David, 178–79
Akindayomi, Josiah, 48–49, 80
Akinsowon, Abiodun, 36
Aldred, Joe, 223, 252–53
Alec, Rory and Wendy, 166, 167
Alexander, Valentina, 250–51
Alliance Commission on Unity and Truth among Evangelicals (ACUTE), xxvi, 122–23, 151–52, 153–54, 160–61, 174–75, 230–31
alliances, in evangelicalism, 4–5
Alpha course, 157–60
Amoako, Francis, 62
Anderson, Allan, 258, 263–64
Anderson, Sir Robert, 8
Angell James, John, 6
Anglicanism, 18, 21, 175, 190, 249
Anglin, Len, 113
Anglo-Catholicism, 8
Anim, Emmanuel Kwesi, 77–78, 79, 96
"Any Questions?," 172–73, 185
Apeagyei-Collins, Celia, 64
Apostolic and Prophetic reformation, 134
Apostolic Church of Wales, 10, 14, 35–36
Apostolic Faith Church, 10
Appiagyei, Kingsley, 61, 101n6
Ashimolowo, Matthew
  Alpha and, 158
  background of, 52
  as church planter, 65, 71, 81
  Evangelical Alliance (EA) and, 113
  IDTV and, 166
  intellectual property rights of, 219–20
  leadership of, 211–12, 234, 240
  memorial service attendance by, 187–88
  Nigerian Ministers' Fellowship and, 74
  overview of, 84–90
  prosperity gospel and, 226
  quote of, 127, 227–28
  Toronto Blessing and, 154
Assemblies of God (AoG), 10, 14, 41
Association for Charities, 218
Azusa Street Revival, 9–10, 35

Babalola, Joseph, 40–41, 42
Babatunde, Wale, 101n6, 233, 245
Badejo, Wilson, 48
Bakare, Tunde, 55, 77, 93, 106
Baker, Joel, 63
Banful, Kofi, 94, 98
Baptist Union, 22–23
Bassett, Michael, 91, 98
Baxter, Richard, xxii
BBC, 143, 167, 170, 189–90, 232, 235
Bebbington, David, 2, 21, 241, 242, 243–44
Beckford, Robert, 190–91, 207–8, 250–52
Bediako, Kwame, 256
Behrend, Heike, 258, 261–62
Bello, Ransom, 68
Bendalites, 50
Berlin Declaration of 1909, 8
Berra, Yogi, 88
Bethesda, 64–65
Biafran War, 47
biblicism, xxii, 241–42
Billy Graham Evangelistic Association, 112
Black and White Christian Partnership, 61
Black Christian Civic Forum, 139
Black community social concerns, 141
Black Entertainment Television (BET), 166–67
Black Led Church (BLC), 250
Black Majority Churches (BMC), 28, 139, 179–81
Black-on-Black crime, 188–89
Black Pentecostalism, 183
Blackson, Kwame, 77

Index

Blair, Tony, 180, 181, 194
Blunkett, David, 234–35
Boafo, Samson Kwaku, 60, 62–63
Boateng, Paul, 139, 188
Boddy, Alexander, 10, 35
Bolton, Frances, 47
Bonnke, Reinhard, 76
Brem-Wilson, Thomas, 59
Brethrenism, 7, 19
Brierley, Peter, 113
Britain
   called to plant phase in, 103–8
   constrained to plant phase in, 60–65
   demographics of, 141
   sent to plant phase in, 65–81
   trained to plant phase in, 90–103
   transferred to plant phase in, 81–90
British and Foreign Bible Society, 4
British Apostolic Church, 39–40, 41–42
British charismatic identificational repentance events, 124–33
British Charismatic Movement, 15–24, 27, 92–93
British Evangelical Council, 15
British evangelicalism, birth of, 2
. *See also* evangelicalism
British Pentecostalism, 7–14
British Youth for Christ, 20
broadcasting, Christian, approaches to, 163–71
Brooke, James, 35–36
Brotherhood of the Cross and Star, 47
Brouwer, Steve, 256
Brown, E. K., 63
Bruce, Steve, 182
Buchanan, Duncan, 229
Buckman, Charles, 113
Buganda, 32
Bulger, Jamie, 151, 188
Burgess, Richard H., 258–59
Burton, William P. F., 35
Bush, George W., 177, 181, 183–84
Buzz magazine, 20

Cain, Paul, 145

called to plant phase, 60, 103–8
Calley, Malcolm, 248
Calver, Clive, 3, 7, 21–22, 24, 156–57
Carey, George, 158
Caribbean churches
   decline of, 113–14
   evangelicalism and, 24–29
   identity of, 249
   prosperity gospel in, 222
   review of literature on, 247–55
. *See also specific churches*
Caribbean identity, issues of
   British charismatic identificational repentance events and, 124–33
   changes in British public opinion and, 137–40
   Highway and, 133–37
   independence and, 140–44
Caribbean neo-Pentecostalism, 141
Caribbeans, in Britain, conditions of, 141–42
Carter, Howard, 92
Cartwright, Desmond, 11
Catholic Global Network, 169
Catholicism, 5, 6, 8
Cave, Dave, 122–23, 221
Celestial Church, 47
Centre for International Christian Ministries, 101
Cerullo, Morris, 53, 55, 69, 85, 100, 118–24, 152, 166, 169, 222
charismatic concerns
   evangelicalism and postmodernism as, 160–63
   National Alpha Campaign as, 157–60
   nature of hell as, 150–52
   Toronto Blessing as, 153–57
   Word and Spirit as, 145–50
charismatic demonology, 194–202, 260–61
Charismatic Movement, 15–24, 27, 146
Charity Commission, 105, 203–4, 210–20
Cherubim and Seraphim, 36, 47
Cherubim and Seraphim Society, 36–37, 42

Chigbundu, Abraham, 201
Child B, 189–94
Child Protection Policy, 194
Christ Apostolic Church, 36, 38, 42
Christ Family Church, 82–84
Christian broadcasting, approaches to, 163–71
Christian Channel Europe, 87, 166, 168
Christian Impact, 221
Christian Life City, 254
Christian Media Trust, 164
Christian Voice, 235
Christian Zionism, 257
Christocentrism, 156
"Christ or Witchcraft?" campaign, 40
Christ's Chapel, 53
Chukwuma, Emmanuel, 229
Churches Child Protection Advisory Service, 186–87
Churches Together in England, xxvi
Churches Together in Britain and Ireland (CTBI), 28
Church Missionary Society (CMS), 32
Church of Christ in Nigeria (COCIN), 46
Church of God of Prophecy, 252
Church of Pentecost, 51, 52, 77, 80
Church of the French Christian Community Bethel, 189–90
church-planting
 called to plant phase in, 103–8
 constrained to plant phase in, 60–65
 ease of, 207–8
 sent to plant phase in, 65–81
 trained to plant phase in, 90–103
 transferred to plant phase in, 81–90
City Academies, 180
Civil Partnership Legislation, 234
Clapham Sect, 4
Clark, A., 38
Climbié, Victoria, 185–87
Coates, Gerald, 89, 124–25, 163
Coffey, John, 174–75
Cohesive and Coherent Voice, 245
Coker, Julius, 47
Coleman, Simon, 256–57, 263

colleges/universities, 48, 51–52
colonialism, identificational repentance (IR) for, 131–32, 245
Combat Spirituel, 189
commodification, 259
Conder, Howard, 166, 168
conditionalism, 150
Condon, Paul, 139
Congolese churches, 189–90
constrained to plant phase, 59, 60–65
conversionism, 243–44
Copeland, Kenneth, 52, 53, 91, 93, 166, 202, 203
Cornerstone Christian Centre, xxvi, 87, 166
Council of African and Afro-Caribbean Churches (CAACC), 28
Council of Reference (KICC), 89
coversionism, xxii
Cox, Harvey, 9
Cray, Graham, 161
Cridge, Mary, 214, 215–17
Criminal Records Bureau, 194
crucicentrism, xxii, 242
Crusade Reconciliation Walk, 130

Darnell, Wilmer and Jean, 71
Darragh, Robert E., 11
David, Titus, 65, 69–71, 74, 75, 81–84, 89–90, 106
Davidson, Pastor (pseudonym), 202–9
Davidson-Gotabed, Rosemarie, 135–36
Davie, Grace, 162
Dawson, John, 124–26
Daystar, 169
debt, 202–9
Deeper Christian Life Ministry, 51
Deeper Life Bible Church, 51, 65, 66–68, 69, 80
Deeper Life Campus Fellowship, 49–51
deliverance, caution and concern regarding
 of "Adam," 191–94
 in African Pentecostalism, 200–201

Index

charismatic demonology and, 194–202
of Child B, 189–94
of Damilola Taylor, 187–89
literature of, 260–61
overview of, 185, 242–43
of Victoria Climbié, 185–87
deliverance ministry, 45
demonology, charismatic, 194–202, 260–61
denominations, broadening of, 3
. *See also specific denominations*
devil/demonic activity, 43–44
discrimination, 181
Dixon, Marcia, 226–27
Doddridge, Philip, 4
Douglas, David, 106
Dove channel, 169
Dow, Graham, 196, 197, 199
Down Grade Controversy, 6–7
Drane, John, 162
Duncan-Williams, Nicholas, 93, 94
du Plessis, David, 14
Dye, Colin, 85–87, 99–103, 124, 146, 151

Eden, Martyn, 230
Edmonton Temple, 63
Edsor, Albert W., 11
education, debate on, 179–81
Edwards, Joel
  appointment of, 140–44
  Black Alliance viewpoint of, 25–28
  contributions of, 1
  investigation by, 212
  leadership of, 83, 89, 111, 112, 113
  media coverage of, 172–73, 185
  memorial service attendance by, 187–88
  quote of, 2, 25–29, 120, 123–24, 150, 152, 155, 158, 173–74, 175, 185, 191, 222, 226–27, 232
Efford, Clive, 138
electoral attention, focus of, 176–85
Elijah Ministries International, 134
Elim Churches, 10
Elim Church of Pentecost, 77, 101

Elim Evangelistic Band, 10
Elim Foursquare Gospel Alliance, 77
Elim Mission Board, 10
Elim Pentecostal Alliance, 10, 14
Elton, Sidney G., 47, 56
"Emerging Church" Movement, 163
emotionalism, 5
English Church Attendance Survey, 173–74
Eternal Word TV, 169
Ethiopian churches, 34
Euston Statement, 154
Evangelical Alliance (EA)
  birth of, 5–7
  Caribbean churches and, 24–29
  Catholicism approach of, 6, 8
  Christian TV support from, 167
  conference of, 160
  expansion of, xxv–xxvi
  Governance, Openness, Accountability and Leadership (GOAL) Conference of, 214
  Greater London Crusade and, 12
  homosexuality and, 229–30, 233
  investigation by, 212, 221
  media strategy of, 172–73
  membership growth in, xxiii, 14, 21, 144
  Mission '89 of, 112
  as "Movement for Change," 173
  MTL and, 121–23
  press coverage of, 142–44
  press release of, 217–18
  prosperity teaching and, 121–23
  recovery of, 16–17
  slogan of, 15
  Spring Harvest and, 21
  unity in diversity of, 21
  wounded history and identificational repentance (IR) and, 130, 132
Evangelical Awakening, 3
Evangelical Church of West Africa (ECWA), 46
evangelical concerns
  evangelicalism and postmodernism as, 160–63

National Alpha Campaign as, 157–60
nature of hell as, 150–52
Toronto Blessing as, 153–57
Word and Spirit as, 145–50
evangelicalism
  agenda of, 174
  alliance forming in, 4–5
  British Charismatic Movement and, 15–24
  British Pentecostalism and, 7–14
  Caribbean churches and, 24–29
  characteristics of, 2–3
  devil/demonic activity approach of, 44
  postmodernism and, 160–63
  Protestantism as compared to, 2
  tolerance in, 175–76
  as transdenominational, 3–4
  twelve tribes of, 21
  values of, 244
evangelical unity, xxiii, 253
evangelism, 109–24

Facevalues campaign, 182–83
Faith Christian Fellowship, 91
"Faith in the Future" conference (ACEA), 178
Faith Tabernacle (Nigeria), 38–42
Faith Tabernacle (Philadelphia), 38
Fefegha, Sunday, 74–75, 113
Ferdinando, Keith, 201
first-century church, patterns of, 1–2
First United Church of Jesus Christ Apostolic, 251
fivefold ministry in Nigerian Pentecostalism, 56
forgiveness, 242–43
Foursquare, 41, 65, 71, 80–81
Foursquare Bible College, 52
Francis, John, 86, 140, 254
Fraser, Giles, 176
Free Churches Group, xxvi
freedom of expression, 234–36
Freedom's Ark, 98
Full Gospel Business Men's Fellowship, 91
fundamentalism, 182

Garvey, Marcus, 250
Gathering of Champions, 86
Gee, Donald, 12
Gender Recognition Bill, 234
Gerloff, Roswith, 61
Ghana/Ghanians
  African neo-Pentecostalism in, 260
  in called to plant phase, 103–8
  Christianity movements in, 33
  in constrained to plant phase, 60–65
  deliverance ministry and, 45
  Pentecostal Christianity in, 51–52, 62
  in sent to plant phase, 65–81
  in trained to plant phase, 90–103
  in transferred to plant phase, 81–90
Ghana Student Fellowship Church (Universal Prayer Fellowship), 60–61
Ghanian Christian Fellowship, 60
Ghanian Church of Pentecost, 77–80
Ghanian Pentecostalism, 264–65
Gifford, Paul, 256, 257
Gledhill, Ruth, 179, 225–26
globalization, review of literature of, 255–65
Glory Bible Church (Green Pastures Ministries), 98
Glory House (Glory Bible Church), 103
Glory of God Fellowship, 48–49
GOD TV, 168, 169–70
Goodman, Douglas, 98–99, 254
Goodridge, Mark, 140, 254
gospel, Christian responsibility regarding, 174
Gospel Channel Europe, 169
governance, caution and confusion regarding, 202–9
Governance, Openness, Accountability and Leadership (GOAL) Conference, 214
government funding, to faith-based groups, 181–82

Index

government legislation, proximity and unanimity over, 228–36
Graham, Billy, 12, 15, 46–47, 109–18, 120
Greater London Crusade, 12
Green, Lynn, 125, 130
Green, Stephen, 234–35
Greenford Baptist Church, 138–39
Green Pastures Ministries (Glory Bible Church), 98
Greenwood, Harry, 221
The Guardian, 219
Gyasi, Alex, 62

Hagin, Kenneth, 52, 53, 91, 221
Hague, William, 176–77, 179, 180–81
Hammond, Frank, 198–99, 200
Hammond, Ida Mae, 198–99, 200
Hamon, Bill, 134
Hampel, Prince, 60, 64–65
Hampstead Bible School of Faith, 90, 91–99
Hargreaves, George, 63
Haringey Peace Alliance, 141
Harmony Christian Ministries, 63
Harper, Michael, 17–18
Harris, Harriet, 160, 182
Harris, William Wade, 33
Harrison, Buddy, 91
Harvest Bible College, 94
Harvest College, 94
Hastings, Adrian, 18, 255–56
Hathaway, Malcolm, 20–21
Haynes, Jeff, 182
healings/healing services, 43, 120–24
Heimann, Mary, 13
hell, nature of, 150–52
Hephzibah Christian Centre, 63
Heron, David, 164
Hicks, Peter, 162
Hiebert, Paul, 128
Highway, 133–37
Highway to Holiness, 62
Hilborn, David, 132–33, 223
Hill, Clifford, 248
Hinn, Benny, 221
Hinton, J. Howard, 5–6

HMS Windrush, 135–36
Hocken, Peter, 17
holiness, 67–68, 93
Holiness Movement, 10
Holiness Pentecostal Church of America, 101n7
Holmes, Nigel, 167
Holy Ghost Festivals of Life, 73–74
Holy Spirit, 9–10, 243–44
Holy Trinity, Brompton, 153, 157–60
homogeneous principle of church growth, 100–101
homosexuality, 229–34
Horrobin, Peter, 196, 199
Hoskins, Richard, 189
House Church Movement, 92–93
Howard-Browne, Rodney, 153, 154
Hunt, Dave, 174
Hunt, Stephen, 159–60
Hutchinson, W. O., 10
Hylson-Smith, Ken, 4

I Care Projects, 141
Ichthus Christian Fellowship, 153
Idahosa, Benson, 53, 57, 62, 66, 68, 93
Idea (magazine), 229–30, 231
identificational repentance (IR), 125, 126–27, 129–30, 131–33
Identity Channel (IDTV), 87, 166–67
Igbos, 50
Incitement to Religious Hatred Bill, 235–36, 245
Inland Revenue for Gift Aid, 105
Inspiration Network International, 169
International Bible Institute of London (IBIOL), 90, 99–103
International Church of the Foursquare Gospel, 71
International Convention of Faith Ministers, 91
International Gathering of Champions (IGOC), 86–87
International House, 72–73
International Ministerial Council of Great Britain (IMCGB), 28, 106
Iraq, invasion of, 183

Irende, Lola, 188
Irukwu, Agu, 72, 86
Isaac, Les, 113, 133–37
Ishmael and Isaac, 145–46
Islam, 50
Ivory Coast, 33

Jackson, Robert, 221
Jakes, T. D., 105–6
Jeffreys, George, 10, 11
Jehu-Appiah, Jerisdan, xxiii–xxiv
Jesus Fellowship, 22–23
Jesus House, 72
Jinadu, Paul, 70–71, 178
Joda, Tunde, 53–54, 77
John, Jeffrey, 234
Joshua, T. B., 190
Jubilee Year, 122
justice, 136–37

Kendall, R. T., 145–46, 148, 149–50
Kensington Temple (KT), 66, 68, 76–77, 85–86, 99–103, 119, 124
Kerridge, Peter, 87–88, 164–65
Kese, Laurence, 62
Keswick Convention, 20, 35
Kimbanguists, 34
King, Benny, 87
Kingsway International Christian Centre (King's Ministries (KICC)), 84–90, 210–28, 240
Kirby, Gilbert, 12, 22
Kirby, Katei, 192
Kirker, Richard, 229
Kontor, Henry, 113
Kouao, Marie-Therese, 185–87
Kumuyi, William Folorunso, 48, 49–51, 66

Lagos University, 48, 49, 55
Lake, John G., 35
Lambeth Conference, 229
Laming, Lord, 186
Larbi, Kingsley, 51–52
Larbie, Sam, 86

Latter Rain Assembly, 55, 56
Latter Rain movement, 56, 155
Lawrence, Neville, 138
Lawrence, Stephen, 137–38, 151, 188
legalism, 51, 52–53
Lesotho, 33
Lewis, Wynne, 76–77, 99
liberalism, 5, 8
liberation theology, 250
Light of the Word Ministries (New Life International Ministries), 61–62
Lillie, David, 17–18
litigation, 202–9
Livingstone, David, 32
Lloyd-Jones, Martyn, 15
Local Government Act, 234
London Bible College, 101, 101n6
London Christian Radio, 87, 164
London Leaders' prayer gathering, 114–15, 116, 117–18, 171
London Leaders' steering group, 116, 148–49
London Missionary Society (LMS), 32
"London overview" consultation, 114–15
Long, Eddie, 105
Lord's Resistance Army, 261–62
Lowe, Chuck, 129
Lukongo, Antoine, 190

Mackay, Alexander, 32
Macmillan, Harold, 16–17
Macpherson, Sir William, 137
MacRobert, Iain, 248–49
Major, John, 176
Making the Grade conference (ACEA), 180–81
Malcolm, Wayne, 227, 254
manifestation, demonic, 197–98
Manning, Carl John, 185
Marshall-Fratani, Ruth, 53–54, 258
Masters, Peter, 21–22, 147
materialism, 92, 93
Matitta, Walter, 33
Maxwell, David, 258, 262–63
Mbiti, John, 45

Index

McCann, Michael, 94–95
McCauley, Ray, 93, 100, 105, 206
McCormack, Ian, 151
McWhirter, James, 11
Meadows, Peter, 163–64
Methodism, 2, 3, 13
Meyer, Birgit, 45, 258, 259
Middlemiss, David, 194–96, 199
Millar, Sandy, 157–60
Mills, Brian, 130–31
miracles, 43, 118–24
Mission '89 (Billy Graham), 109–18
missionaries, in African neo-Pentecostalism, 35–46
Mission Ensemble pour Christ, 186
Mission to London (MTL), 85–87, 100, 107, 118–24, 151, 239
Mitchell, Roger, 130–31
model documents, structure of, 215
modernism, 7
Moffat, Robert, 32
Mohabir, Philip, 24, 25, 110, 111–12, 113, 139
money, 118–24
Montgomerie, Tim, 177
Moore, Philip, 101
Morgan, G. Campbell, 8
Morris Cerullo World Evangelism (MCWE), 121–23
Moses and Miriam, 138
Muchopa, Naboth, 136–37
Mulinde, John, 131
Muluyu, Modeste, 189–90
Munroe, Myles, 106

Nathan, Ronald A., 250
National Alpha Campaign, 157–60
National Assembly of Evangelicals, 161–62
National Evangelical Anglican Conference, 18
New Churches Movement, 24, 215
New Covenant Church, 65, 69–71, 80, 82
newer Pentecostal and Charismatic churches (NPC), 263–64
New Frontiers International, 153

New Life International Ministries (Light of the Word Ministries), 61–62
New Testament Church of God, 251
Nigeria/Nigerians
  Biafran War in, 47
  in called to plant phase, 103–8
  campus Christianity in, 46, 48, 51
  in constrained to plant phase, 60–65
  fivefold ministry (Nigerian Pentecostalism) in, 56
  Islam in, 50
  Latter Rain movement in, 56
  missionaries in, 41
  Pentecostal trends in, 258
  political climate of, 54–56
  prosperity teaching in, 53
  in sent to plant phase, 65–81
  in trained to plant phase, 90–103
  in transferred to plant phase, 81–90
Nigerian Ministers' Fellowship, 74, 75–76, 83
Nigerian Pentecostalism, 46–47, 56, 258
non-denominationalism, 51
Nottingham Evangelical Anglican Congress, 18–19
Nwator, Friday, 139

O'Brien, Mike, 140
Obunge, Nims, 97–98, 141
Odonko, J. M., 60–61
Odubanjo, David Ogunleye, 38–39, 42
Odulele, Albert, 98, 136, 178
Odulele, Vincent, 98
Ofaso, Frank, 61
Ofousuware, Shadrach, 63
Ogedengbe, Paul, 133–37
Ohene-Apraku, Sam, 61, 63
Oke, Francis Wale, 56–57, 106, 149
Okonkwo, Mike, 53, 77
Okorende, Ade, 71–74, 139
Okunade, David, 65, 71
Olaksy, Marvin, 177
Olatunji, Mark, 66, 111
Olulana, Adewale, 63

Omilana, Kunle, 168
Omooba, Ade, 141, 236
Onyinah, Opoku, 260–61
Oppong, Sampson, 33
Oritsejafor, Ayo, 53
Osborn, T. L., 46–47
Oshuntola, Abraham, 74, 75
Overseas Fellowship of Nigerian Christians (OFNC), 60
Ovia, Pre, 65, 66, 67, 74, 76
Oyedepo, David, 56

Packer, J. I., 221
Pain, Timothy, 120
Palau, Luis, 109–18, 120
Parker, Russ, 132–33
Parkyns, Edgar, 48
Parratt, John, 256
Parrinder, E. Geoffrey, 255
Partridge, Chris, 182
Patton, Linda, 166
Pawson, David, 147–48
Pearson, Carlton, 166
Pearson, David, 186, 187, 192
Peel, J. D. Y., 36, 42, 255
Pentecostal International Worship Centre (Accra International Worship Center), 52
Pentecostalism
  characteristics of, 14
  criticism of, 8
  denominational differences in, 84
  devil/demonic activity approach of, 44
  divisions within, 120–21
  in Ghana, 51–52, 62
  legalism in, 51
  Protestantism as compared to, 12
  revivals in, 9–10
  Word and Spirit theology in, 146–47
  . *See also* African neo-Pentecostalism; Nigerian Pentecostalism
Pentecostal Missionary Union, 10, 35
Percy, Cnon Martyn, 159
personal faith, public dimension of, 184

Phillips, Trevor, 139
Plymouth Brethren, 17
Polhill, Cecil, 10
politics, religion and, 181–84
Poloma, Margaret, 155–56, 157
Poole-Conner, E., 1
postmodernism, 160–63
Powell, Enoch, 248
Praise Chapel, 98
prayer, 37, 115–17
Premier Christian Radio, 87, 164–65, 167
press, caution and confusion regarding, 202–9
Price, Frederick K. C., 166
Prince, Derek, 196
prophet-healing, 34
"Prophetic and Apostolic Conference," 134
"Prophetic Prayer" event, 134
prosperity teaching, 53, 92–93, 121, 220–28, 257–65
Protestant Alliance, 6
Protestantism, 2, 12

Queen's Road Baptist Church, 153

racism, 137–38
Randall, Ian, 7–8, 12
Rapu, Tony, 72
Reconciliation Walk, 130
Redeemed Christian Church of God (RCCG), 48–49, 65, 71–74, 80, 117–18, 169
The Redeemed Evangelical Mission (TREM), 53
redemption, 242–43
Redemption Ministries, 74–75
Reformation, 18–19
reformed theology, 149–50
Reid, Gavin, 110
Reid, Michael, 128–29
religious hatred, incitement to, 234–36
respect, theology of, 252–53
Resurrection Power Ministries, 62

Revelation TV, 168–69
revivalism, 9–11, 35, 156
Rhema Ministries, 254
Rich, David, 210
Richards, Anne, 154
Riches of Grace (British Apostolic Church), 39
Roberts, Evan, 9
Roberts, Oral, 52
Rosman, Doreen, 16–17
Ruach Inspirational Church of God (Ruach Ministries), 254
Ryan, James (pseudonym), 232–33

Salvation Army, 7, 13
Savelle, Jerry, 93
Schaefer, Nancy, 85, 86
Scotland, Nigel, 16–17
Scripture Union (SU), 46, 47, 52
Section 28, 229–34
secular-dismissive approach to Christian broadcasting, 163–71
secular-sensitive approach to Christian broadcasting, 163–71
seeker-sensitive services, 164
Semple McPherson, Aimee, 71
Sentamu, John, 139, 189
sent to plant phase, 59, 65–81
Seventh Day Adventist Church, 251
sexuality, government legislation and, 229–34
Shaftesbury, Earl of, 7
Sheppard, David, 92
Shiloh Pentecostal Fellowship, 251
Sierra Leone, 32–33
Sinclair, Matthew, 35
Sizer, Stephen, 154
slave-holders, 5–6
slavery, identificational repentence (IR) for, 131–32
social concerns, Black community, 141
South London Temple, 63
spiritual warfare, 125–33
Spong, John, 229
Spring Harvest, 20, 21, 176
Spurgeon, Charles Haddon, 6–7

Stanton, Noel, 22
Sterling, Nezlin, 136
Stickler, Angus, 190
Stone, Richard, 139
Stott, John, xxii–xxiii, 15, 74–75, 240–42, 243–44
strategic level spiritual warfare (SLSW), 125, 127, 129
Student Christian Movement (SCM), 48
Sturge, Mark
  contributions of, 254
  integration and, 27
  investigation by, 212–14
  leadership of, 139–40, 178
  quote of, 28–29, 137, 138–39, 179–80, 188, 192–94, 207, 208–9, 227
Sunderland Conventions, 35
Sundkler, Bengt, 34
superficiality, counter to, 244–45
supernatural immanence, 195
supernaturalism, 43

Taylor, Damilola, 187–89
television, Christian, 166, 168
ter Haar, Gerrie, 78–79
territorial spirits, 125–26, 129
theological methodology, limitations of, 239–45
Timms, Stephen, 177
tolerance, 175, 233
Tomlinson, Dave, 161, 220–21
Toronto Blessing, 153–57
Toulis, Nicole Rodriguez, 251–52
trained to plant phase, 59–60, 90–103
transferred to plant phase, 59, 81–90
transformation, 243–44
Trinity Broadcasting Network (TBN), 169
True Teachings of Christ's Temple, 78–79
trustees, payments to, 215–16
Tukela, Dr., 190
Tunolase, Moses Orimolade, 36
UCB TV, 169
Uganda, 125–26, 262

United Christian Broadcasters, 169
Universal Church of the Kingdom of God, 186
Universal Prayer Fellowship (Ghana Student Fellowship Church), 60–61
Universal Prayer Group (UPG), 63–64
Urquhart, Colin, 82, 83

van Dijk, Rijk, 259–60, 262, 264–65
van Gundy, Mark, 94, 95, 98
Vasey, Michael, 230
Vatican Council II, 19
Vaughan, Idris, 39–41
Venn, Henry, 33
vicarious repentance, 130
Victory Christian Centre (VCC), 99, 202–9, 210, 254
Victory Church, 66, 68, 91–99
Vineyard Fellowship, 153

Wagner, C. Peter, 127–28, 129
Wallis, Arthur, 17–18
Warner, Timothy, 127
Warren, Rick, 164
Watson, David, 18–19
wealth, 92
Welsh Revival, 9, 11, 13, 35
Wembley Praise-Days, 24
Wesley, Charles, 2, 4
Wesley, John, 150
Wesleyan Holiness Church, 251

West African neo-Pentecostalism, 77
West Indian Evangelical Alliance (WIEA), 24, 29, 111
Wigglesworth, Smith, 11, 14, 147
Wilkinson, John Lawrence, 249–50
Williams, Doug, 222–23
Williams, D. P., 10
Wimber, John, 128, 145
witchcraft, 189–94, 201, 260–61
witchdemonology, 260–61
Woodroffe, Noel, 134–35
Word and Spirit, as evangelical and charismatic concerns, 145–50
Word and Spirit Conference, 145
Word of Faith teaching, 53, 92–93
Word of Faith Teaching Academy, 91
Word of Life Bible College, 63
World Council of Churches, 106
World Evangelical Fellowship, 221
World of Faith movement, 223–25
wounded history, 125, 126–27, 129, 130
Wycliffe, John, 1

Yoruba, 50, 258
Youth Service, 50
Youth With A Mission (YWAM), 125

Zambia, xxv, 257
Zimbabwe, 262
Zionist churches, 34

www.ingramcontent.com/pod-product-compliance
Lightning Source LLC
Chambersburg PA
CBHW061427300426
44114CB00014B/1575